CoNLL 2016 Shared Task: Multilingual Shallow Discourse Parsing

Held at ACL 2016

Berlin, Germany
7 - 12 August 2016

ISBN: 978-1-5108-8136-5

Printed by Curran Associates, Inc. (2019)

For permission requests, please contact the Association for Computational Linguistics
at the address below.

Association for Computational Linguistics
209 N. Eighth Street
Stroudsburg, Pennsylvania 18360

Phone: 1-570-476-8006
Fax: 1-570-476-0860

acl@aclweb.org

Additional copies of this publication are available from:

Curran Associates, Inc.
57 Morehouse Lane
Red Hook, NY 12571 USA
Phone: 845-758-0400
Fax: 845-758-2633
Email: curran@proceedings.com
Web: www.proceedings.com

ACL 2016

**The 54th Annual Meeting of the
Association for Computational Linguistics**

**Proceedings of the SIGNLL Conference on Computational
Natural Language Learning: Shared Task**

August 7-12, 2016
Berlin, Germany

Introduction

This volume contains papers describing the CoNLL-2016 Shared Task and the participating systems. The 2016 shared task is on multilingual Shallow Discourse Parsing (SDP), and is a follow-on to the 2015 shared task. The languages covered in this shared task are English and Chinese. The SDP task involves identifying individual discourse relations that are present in a natural language text. A discourse relation can be expressed explicitly or implicitly, and takes two arguments realized as sentences, clauses, or in some rare cases, phrases. Shallow Discourse Parsing is a fundamental NLP task and can potentially benefit a range of natural language applications such as Information Extraction, Text Summarization, Question Answering, Machine Translation, and Sentiment Analysis.

A total of 24 teams from three continents participated in this task, and 20 of them submitted system description papers. Many different approaches were adopted by the participants, and we hope that these approaches help to advance the state of the art in Shallow Discourse Parsing. The training, development, and test sets for English and Chinese were adapted from the Penn Discourse TreeBank (PDTB) and the Chinese Discourse TreeBank (CDTB) respectively. In addition, we also annotated a blind test set for each language following the PDTB and CDTB guidelines solely for the shared task. The results on the blind test sets were used to rank the participating systems. The evaluation scorer, also developed for this shared task, adopts an F1 based metric that takes into account the accuracy of identifying the senses and arguments of discourse relations as well as explicit discourse connectives. We hope that the data sets and the scorer, which are freely available upon the completion of the shared task, will be a useful resource for researchers interested in discourse parsing.

As with the 2015 CoNLL shared task on SDP, participants did not each run their systems locally on the test set. Instead, they were asked to deploy their systems on a remote virtual machine and use a web-based evaluation platform called TIRA to run their systems on the test set. This kept them from seeing the data set, thus preserving its integrity and ensuring its replicability.

We would like to thank all the participants of the 2016 Shared Task, as well as the program committee for helping us review the system description papers. Special thanks are due to the SIGNLL board members, Xavier Carreras and Julia Hockenmaier, for their support of the shared task over the last two years. We would also like to thank the PDTB team and CDTB team for providing annotated data for the shared task, and the Linguistic Data Consortium for their help with releasing the data to the participants. Special thanks go to Martin Potthast and the TIRA team, who provided their computing resources and more importantly their time in assisting teams to run their systems.

Nianwen Xue, Hwee Tou Ng, Sameer Pradhan, Attapol Rutherford, Bonnie Webber, Chuan Wang, and Hongmin Wang
Organizers of the CoNLL-2016 Shared Task
July 2016

Table of Contents

Conference Program

Friday, Aug. 12

14:15–15:45 **Oral Presentations**

CoNLL 2016 Shared Task on Multilingual Shallow Discourse Parsing
Nianwen Xue, Hwee Tou Ng, Sameer Pradhan, Attapol Rutherford, Bonnie Webber, Chuan Wang and Hongmin Wang

OPT: Oslo–Potsdam–Teesside. Pipelining Rules, Rankers, and Classifier Ensembles for Shallow Discourse Parsing
Stephan Oepen, Jonathon Read, Tatjana Scheffler, Uladzimir Sidarenka, Manfred Stede, Erik Velldal and Lilja Øvrelid

An End-to-End Chinese Discourse Parser with Adaptation to Explicit and Non-explicit Relation Recognition
Xiaomian Kang, Haoran Li, Long Zhou, Jiajun Zhang and Chengqing Zong

Two End-to-end Shallow Discourse Parsers for English and Chinese in CoNLL-2016 Shared Task
Jianxiang Wang and Man Lan

Do We Really Need All Those Rich Linguistic Features? A Neural Network-Based Approach to Implicit Sense Labeling
Niko Schenk, Christian Chiarcos, Kathrin Donandt, Samuel Rönnqvist, Evgeny Stepanov and Giuseppe Riccardi

Discourse Sense Classification from Scratch using Focused RNNs
Gregor Weiss and Marko Bajec

17:00–18:00 **Poster Presentations**

Robust Non-Explicit Neural Discourse Parser in English and Chinese
Attapol Rutherford and Nianwen Xue

A Constituent Syntactic Parse Tree Based Discourse Parser
Zhongyi Li, Hai Zhao, Chenxi Pang, Lili Wang and Huan Wang

SoNLP-DP System for ConLL-2016 English Shallow Discourse Parsing
Fang Kong, Sheng Li, Junhui Li, Muhua Zhu and Guodong Zhou

Shallow Discourse Parsing Using Convolutional Neural Network
Lianhui Qin, Zhisong Zhang and Hai Zhao

CoNLL 2016 Shared Task on Multilingual Shallow Discourse Parsing

Nianwen Xue, Brandeis University,
`xuen@brandeis.edu`

Hwee Tou Ng, National University of Singapore,
`nght@comp.nus.edu.sg`

Sameer Pradhan, `cemantix.org` and Boulder Learning, Inc.,
`pradhan@cemantix.org`

Attapol Rutherford, Brandeis University,
`tet@brandeis.edu`

Bonnie Webber, University of Edinburgh,
`bonnie@info.ed.ac.uk`

Chuan Wang, Brandeis University,
`cwang24@brandeis.edu`

Hongmin Wang, National University of Singapore,
`wanghm@comp.nus.edu.sg`

Abstract

The CoNLL-2016 Shared Task is the second edition of the CoNLL-2015 Shared Task, now on Multilingual Shallow discourse parsing. Similar to the 2015 task, the goal of the shared task is to identify individual discourse relations that are present in natural language text. Given a natural language text, participating teams are asked to locate the discourse connectives (explicit or implicit) and their arguments as well as predicting the sense of the discourse connectives. Based on the success of the previous year, we continued to ask participants to deploy their systems on TIRA, a web-based platform on which participants can run their systems on the test data for evaluation. This evaluation methodology preserves the integrity of the shared task. We have also made a few changes and additions in the 2016 shared task based on the feedback from 2015. The first is that teams could choose to carry out the task on Chinese texts, or English texts, or both. We have also allowed participants to focus on parts of the shared task (rather than the whole thing) as a typical system requires sub-stantial investment of effort. Finally, we have modified the scorer so that it can report results based on partial matches of the arguments. 23 teams participated in this year's shared task, using a wide variety of approaches. In this overview paper, we present the task definition, the training and test sets, and the evaluation protocol and metric used during this shared task. We also summarize the different approaches adopted by the participating teams, and present the evaluation results. The evaluation data sets and the scorer will serve as a benchmark for future research on shallow discourse parsing.

1 Introduction

The shared task for the Twentieth Conference on Computational Natural Language Learning (CoNLL-2016) is a follow-on to the CoNLL-2015 shared task, and it is on *Multilingual Shallow Discourse Parsing (SDP)*. While the 2015 task focused on newswire text data in English, this year we added a new language, Chinese. Given a natural language text as input, the goal of an SDP system is to detect and categorize discourse relations between discourse segments in the text. The conceptual framework of the Shallow Discourse Parsing

Proceedings of the 54th Annual Meeting of the Association for Computational Linguistics, pages 1–19,
Berlin, Germany, August 7-12, 2016. ©2016 Association for Computational Linguistics

task is that of the Penn Discourse TreeBank
(PDTB) (Prasad et al., 2008; Prasad et al.,
2014), where a discourse relation is viewed as
a predicate that takes two abstract objects as
arguments. The two arguments may be realized as clauses or sentences, or occasionally
phrases. It is "shallow" in that sense that
the system is not required to output a tree
or graph that covers the entire text, and the
discourse relations are not hierarchically organized. As such, it differs from analyses according to either Rhetorical Structure (Mann
and Thompson, 1988) or Segmented Discourse
Representation Theory (SDRT) (Asher and
Lascarides, 2003).

The rest of this overview paper is structured
as follows. In Section 2, we provide a concise
definition of the shared task. We describe how
the training and test data are prepared in Section 3. In Section 4, we present the evaluation
protocol, metric and scorer. The different approaches that participants took in the shared
task are summarized in Section 5. In Section
6, we present the ranking of participating systems and analyze the evaluation results. We
present our conclusions in Section 7.

2   Task Definition

The goal of the shared task on shallow discourse parsing is to detect and categorize individual discourse relations. Specifically, given
a newswire article as input, a participating
system is asked to return the set of discourse
relations it can identify in the text. A discourse relation is defined as a relation taking two abstract objects (events, states, facts,
or propositions) as arguments (Prasad et al.,
2008; Prasad et al., 2014). Discourse relations may be expressed with explicit connectives like *because, however, but*, or implicitly
inferred between two argument spans inter-
pretable as abstract objects. In the current
version of the PDTB, only adjacent spans are
considered. Each discourse relation is labeled
with a sense selected from a sense hierarchy.
Its argument spans may be sentences, clauses,
or in some rare cases, noun phrases. To detect a discourse relation, a participating system needs to:

1. Identify the text span of an explicit discourse connective, if present, or the po-

sition between adjacent sentences as the
proxy site of an implicit discourse relation;

2. Identify the two text spans that serve as
   arguments to the relation;

3. Label the arguments as *Arg1* or *Arg2*, as
   appropriate;

4. Predict the sense of the discourse relation
   (e.g., "Cause", "Condition", "Contrast").

A full system that outputs all four components of the discourse relations usually comprises a long pipeline, and it is hard for teams
that do not have a pre-existing system to
put together a competitive full system. This
year we therefore allowed participants to focus solely on predicting the sense of discourse
relations, given gold-standard connectives and
their arguments.

3   Data

3.1   Training and Development

The training and development sets for English remain exactly the same as those used
in the CoNLL-2015 shared task. Details regarding how the data was adapted from the
Penn Discourse TreeBank 2.0 (PDTB 2.0)
are provided in the overview paper of the
CoNLL 2015 shared task (Xue et al., 2015).
The Chinese training and development sets
are taken from the Chinese Discourse Tree-
Bank (CDTB) 0.5 (Zhou and Xue, 2012;
Zhou and Xue, 2015), available from the
LDC (http://ldc.upenn.edu), supplemented
with additional annotated data from the Chinese TreeBank (Xue et al., 2005).

The CDTB adopts the general annotation
strategy of the PDTB, associating discourse
relations with explicit or implicit discourse
connectives and the two spans that serve as
their arguments. In the case of explicit discourse relations (Example 1), there is an overt
discourse connective, which may be realized
syntactically as a subordinating or coordinating conjunction, or a discourse adverbial. Implicit discourse relations are cases where there
is not an overt discourse connective (Example
2). Like PDTB, CDTB also annotates Alternative Lexicalizations (AltLex) and Entity Relations (EntRel) when no explicit or implicit
discourse relations can be identified.

(1) [Conn 尽管　　　　] [Arg1 亚洲　一些
　　　even though　　　　Asia　some
国家　的　金融　动荡　会　使
country DE financial turmoil will make
这些　国家　的　经济　增长
these country DE economy growth
受到　　严重　影响]．[Conn 但]
experience serious impact　,　　　but
[Arg2 就 整　个 世界 经济　而言，
　　　to whole CL world economy　　,
其他　国家　的　强劲　增长　势头
other country DE strong growth momentum
会　弥补　　这　一　损失]　。
will compensate this one loss　　．

"Even though the financial turmoil in
some Asian countries will affect the economic growth of these countries, as far as
the economy of the whole world is concerned, the strong economic growth of
other countries will make up for this loss."

(2) 其中　　　　[Arg1 出口　为
among them　　　export be
一百七十八点三亿 美元　,　比
17.83 billion　　　dollar ,　compared with
去年　　同　期　　下降
last year same period decrease
百分之一点三]；[Arg2 进口
1.3 percent　　；　　　import
一百八十二点七亿 美元　,　增长
18.27 billion　　　dollar ,　increase
百分之三十四点一]　。
34.1 percent　　　．

"Among them, export is 17.83 billion dollars, an 1.3 percent increase over the same
period last year. Meanwhile, import is
18.27 billion dollars, which is a 34.1 percent increase."

The CDTB also differs somewhat in its annotation practices. The first difference is in
the way that implicit discourse relations are
identified. PDTB uses sentence-final punctuation (periods, question or exclamation marks)
to identify where implicit discourse relations
might occur. However, since the concept of
"sentence" is less formalized in Chinese, and
since a comma may serve as a sentence-final
marker (as well as sentence-internal punctuation), CDTB identifies implicit relations by ex-
amining commas in addition to periods, question and exclamation marks, and disambiguating them to identify those serving as sentence-
final markers. Teams that exploited these
language-specific characteristics did well on

the Chinese task (Section 6). Table 1 shows
that the distribution of explicit and implicit
discourse relations also differs between Chinese and English: while there are about equal
numbers of explicit and discourse relations
in English, implicit discourse relations out-
number explicit discourse relations in Chinese.
The second difference in annotation practices
is how the arguments are labeled. In the
PDTB, the argument that is introduced by a
discourse connective (e.g., a subordinate conjunction) is labeled *Arg1* while the other argument is labeled *Arg2*. Since there are much
fewer explicit discourse relations than implicit
discourse relations, the argument labels are defined "semantically", meaning they are defined
based on how arguments are interpreted. For
example, for a Causation relation, *Arg1* is the
cause while *Arg2* is the result. Since arguments
are defined semantically, there is less of a need
to have Level-3 subtypes as in the PDTB.
For example, *Contingency:Cause:Reason* and
Contingency:Cause:Result are essentially the
same relation, just with the arguments re-
versed. For this reason, CDTB adopts a flat
set of 10 relations (Table 2), which are used in
this shared task without any modification.

The above discussion shows that PDTB-
style discourse relations are substantially, but
not fully language-independent due to different lexicalizations (e.g., explicit vs implicit
discourse connectives) and grammaticaliza-
tions (the formalization of the concept of sentence). As we shall see in Section 5 where we
discuss different approaches, teams that exploited these language-specific properties did
well on the Chinese task. For example, the
way in which implicit discourse relations are
annotated impacts how the arguments for implicit discourse relations are identified. In addition, because the smaller number of explicit
discourse relations, it makes less sense to train
separate models for explicit relations alone because many of the discourse connectives in the
training data will not repeat in the test data.
In addition, the senses of discourse relations
are less evenly distributed in Chinese than in
English. For example, "Conjunction" is a very
common category, presumably because without explicit discourse connectives, a discourse
relation is harder to judge, leading annotators

	Train	Dev	Test
Implicit	6,706	251	281
Explicit	2,225	77	96
EntRel	1,098	50	71
AltLex	211	5	7
Total	10,240	328	455

Table 1: The distribution of discourse relation types in the Chinese data

to use "Conjunction" as a default category.

3.2 Test Data

We provide two test sets for each language: a test set from a publicly available annotated corpus, and a blind test set specifically prepared for this task. The official ranking of the systems is based on their performance on the *blind test set*. We reused the English test sets from the 2015 shared task, details of which can be found in (Xue et al., 2015). For Chinese, one test set is from the CDTB, and uses the same data source as the training data. The *blind test set* is from Chinese Wikinews.

3.2.1 Data Selection and Post-processing

For the blind test data, 29,892 words of Chinese newswire texts were selected from a dump of Chinese Wikinews[1] created on 23rd October 2015, and annotated in accordance with the CDTB-0.5 annotation guidelines.

The raw Wikinews data was pre-processed as follows:

- News articles were extracted from the Wikinews XML dump[2] using the publicly available WikiExtractor.py script.[3]

- Additional processing was done to remove any remaining XML annotations and produce a raw text version of each article (including its title and date).

- Articles written purely in simplified Chinese were identified using the Dragon Mapper[4] Python library, and segmented using the NUS Chinese word segmenter (Low et al., 2005).

- Sentences in each article were manually segmented such that adjacent sentences were separated by a carriage return, and one extra carriage return was added between two paragraphs to ease paragraph boundary identification.

- Each article was named according to its unique Wikinews ID, accessible online at `http://zh.wikinews.org/wiki?curid=ID`.

Since longer articles with many multi-sentence paragraphs are more consistent with the CDTB-0.5 texts, 64 articles were randomly selected among the articles with more than 400 characters. Word segmentation errors and some typos were manually corrected.

3.2.2 Annotations

The *blind test set* was annotated by two of the shared task organizers, one of whom (seventh author) was the main annotator (MA) while the other (first author) acted as the reviewing annotator (RA), reviewing each relation annotated by the MA and recording agreement or disagreement. Annotation involved marking the relation type (Explicit, Implicit, AltLex), sense (alternative, causation, conditional, conjunction, contrast, expansion, purpose, temporal, EntRel, NoRel), and arguments (Arg1 and Arg2), using the PDTB annotation tool.[5]

Before commencing official annotation, the MA was trained in CDTB-0.5 style annotation by the RA. After a review of the guidelines, the MA annotated some CDTB texts that were already annotated, and then compared his annotations with the standard annotations. Some differences were discussed between the MA and the RA to further strengthen MA's knowledge of the guidelines.

4 Evaluation

The scorer that computes all of the available evaluation metrics is open-source with some contribution from the participants during the task period[6].

4.1 Main evaluation metric: End-to-end discourse parsing

A shallow discourse parser (SDP) is evaluated based on the end-to-end F_1 score on a per-

---

[1] https://zh.wikinews.org/

[2] https://dumps.wikimedia.org/zhwikinews/20151020/zhwikinews-20151020-pages-meta-current.xml.bz2

[3] http://medialab.di.unipi.it/wiki/Wikipedia_Extractor

[4] http://dragonmapper.readthedocs.io/en/latest/index.html

[5] https://www.seas.upenn.edu/~pdtb/tools.shtml#annotator

[6] http://www.github.com/attapol/conll16st.

Sense	Definition
Alternative	Relation between two alternatives
Causation	Relation between cause and effect
Condition	Relation between a supposed condition and a supposed result
Conjunction	Relation between two equal-status statements serving a common communicative function
Contrast	Relation between two statements, co-occurrence of which seems contradictory, counter-intuitive, out-of-ordinary, etc.
Expansion	Relation in which one argument is an elaboration or restatement of another
Purpose	Relation between an action and the intention behind it
Temporal	Relation that is temporal in nature, expressing temporal precedence, etc.
Progression	Relation in which one argument represents a progression from the other, in extent, intensity, scale, etc.
EntRel	Relation between two statements that are connected only by the fact that they are about the same entity or entities.

Table 2: Definitions of relation senses in the Chinese data.

discourse relation basis for both languages. The input to an SDP consists of documents with gold-standard word tokens along with their automatic parses. We do not pre-identify discourse connectives or any other elements of the discourse annotation. The SDP must output a list of discourse relations comprising argument spans and their labels, explicit discourse connectives where applicable, and the senses. The F_1 score is computed based on the number of predicted relations that match a gold standard relation exactly. Like the 2015 edition of the task, a relation is correctly predicted if and only if the text spans of its two arguments are correctly predicted (Arg1 and Arg2), as is its sense. The results from this evaluation is shown in Table 5.

An argument is considered correctly identified if and only if it matches the corresponding gold standard argument span exactly, and is also correctly labeled (Arg1 or Arg2). In the main evaluation, partial matching is given no credit. Sense classification evaluation is less straightforward, since senses are sometimes annotated partially or annotated with two senses. To be considered correct, the predicted sense for a relation must match one of the two senses if there is more than one sense. If the gold standard is partially annotated, the sense must match with the partially annotated sense although the blind test set contains no partial annotation.

4.2 Supplementary Evaluation: Discourse relation sense classification

Although the submissions are ranked based on the end-to-end F_1 score, discourse relation sense classification subtask has gained much attention from the community within the past years including some participants from last year. We provide the data and evaluation setup for participants who are only interested in the discourse relation sense classification subtask and for those who want to evaluate their system without the error propagation from argument extraction.

In this supplementary evaluation, the input is gold-standard argument pairs and their corresponding explicit discourse connectives if applicable. The goal is to fill in the senses including EntRel. The results from this evaluation are shown in Table 9

4.3 Component-wise and partial evaluation

For analytical purposes, the scorer also provides component-wise evaluation with error propagation and a breakdown of the discourse parser performance for explicit and non-explicit discourse relations. The scorer computes the precision, recall, and F_1 for the following tasks:

- Explicit discourse connective identification.

- Arg1 identification.

- Arg2 identification.

- Arg1 and Arg2 identification.

- Sense classification with error propagation from discourse connective and argument identification.

For purposes of evaluation, an explicit discourse connective predicted by a parser is considered correct if and only if the predicted raw connective includes the gold raw connective head, while allowing for the tokens of the predicted connective to be a subset of the tokens in the gold raw connective. We provide a function that maps discourse connectives to their corresponding heads. The notion of discourse connective head is not the same as its syntactic head. Rather, it is thought of as the part of the connective conveying its core meaning. For example, the head of the discourse connective "At least not when" is "when", and the head of "five minutes before" is "before". The non-head part of the connective serves to semantically restrict the interpretation of the connective.

Although Implicit discourse relations are annotated with an implicit connective inserted between adjacent sentences, participants are not required to provide the inserted connective. They only need to output the sense of the discourse relation. Similarly, for AltLex relations, which are also annotated between adjacent sentences, participants are not required to output the text span of the AltLex expression, but only the sense. The EntRel relation is included as a sense in the shared task, and here, systems are required to correctly label the EntRel relation between adjacent sentence pairs.

We also provide partial evaluation to assess how well a system does when we relax the criteria. The official full evaluation metric produces low scores due to error propagation from argument extraction. Partial evaluation instead allows 'fuzzy matching' in arguments. The extracted Arg1 and Arg2 are correct if and only if the average of F_1 score of the extracted Arg1 and Arg2 is greater than 0.7. This allows us to evaluate the sense classification of that relation even if the argument extraction is not perfect. The evaluation is also done for both explicit and non-explicit relations separately (Table 8) and together (Table 6).

4.4 Closed and open tracks

In keeping with the CoNLL shared task tradition, participating systems were evaluated in two tracks, a *closed* track and an *open* track. A participating system in the closed track could only use the provided PDTB training set but was allowed to process the data using any publicly available (i.e., non-proprietary) natural language processing tools such as syntactic parsers and semantic role labelers. In contrast, in the open track, a participating system could not only use any publicly available NLP tools to process the data, but also any publicly available (i.e., non-proprietary) data for training. A participating team could choose to participate in the closed track or the open track, or both.

The motivation for having two tracks in CoNLL shared tasks was to isolate the contribution of algorithms and resources to a particular task. In the closed track, the resources are held constant so that the advantages of different algorithms and models can be more meaningfully compared. In the open track, the focus of the evaluation is on the overall performance and the use of all possible means to improve the performance of a task. This distinction was easier to maintain for early CoNLL tasks such as noun phrase chunking and named entity recognition, where competitive performance could be achieved without having to use resources other than the provided training set. However, this is no longer true for a high-level task like discourse parsing where external resources such as Brown clusters have proved to be useful (Rutherford and Xue, 2014). In addition, to be competitive in the discourse parsing task, one also has to process the data with syntactic and possibly semantic parsers, which may also be trained on data that is outside the training set. As a compromise, therefore, we allowed participants in the closed track to use the following linguistic resources, in addition to the training set:

For English,

- Brown clusters
- VerbNet
- Sentiment lexicon
- Word embeddings (word2vec)

For Chinese, the following resources are provided, both trained on Gigaword Simplified Chinese data:

- Brown clusters (implementation from (Liang, 2005))
- Word embeddings (word2vec)

To make the task more manageable for participants, we provided them with training and test data with the following layers of automatic linguistic annotation produced using state-of-the-art NLP tools:
For English,

- Phrase structure parses predicted using the Berkeley parser (Petrov and Klein, 2007);
- Dependency parses converted from phrase structure parses using the Stanford converter (Manning et al., 2014).

For Chinese,

- Phrase structure parses predicted with 10-fold cross validation on CTB8.0 using the transition-based Chinese parser (Wang and Xue, 2014);
- Dependency parses converted from phrase structure parses using the Penn2Malt converter.

4.5 Evaluation Platform: TIRA

We use a new web service called TIRA as the platform for system evaluation (Gollub et al., 2012; Potthast et al., 2014). Traditionally, participating teams have been asked to manually run their system on the blind test set without the gold standard labels, and submit the output for evaluation. Starting with the 2015 shared task, however, we shifted this evaluation paradigm, asking participants to deploy their systems on a remote virtual machine, and to use the TIRA web platform (tira.io) to run their systems on the test sets without actually seeing them. The organizers would then inspect the evaluation results, and verify that participating systems yielded acceptable output.

This evaluation protocol allowed us to maintain the integrity of the blind test set and reduce the organizational overhead. On TIRA, the blind test set can only be accessed in the evaluation environment, and the evaluation results are automatically collected. Participants cannot see any part of the test sets and hence cannot do iterative development based on the test set performance, which preserves the integrity of the evaluation. Most importantly, this evaluation platform promotes replicability, which is crucial for proper evaluation of scientific progress. Reproducing all of the results is just a matter of a button click on TIRA. All of the results presented in this paper, along with the trained models and the software, are archived and available for distribution upon request to the organizers and upon the permission of the participating team, who holds the copyrights to the software. Replicability also helps speed up the research and development in discourse parsing. Anyone wanting to extend or apply any of the approaches proposed by a shared task participant does not have to re-implement the model from scratch. They can request a clone of the virtual machine where the participating system is deployed, and then implement their extension based off the original source code. Any extension effort also benefits from the precise evaluation of the progress and improvement since the system is based off the exact same implementation.

5 Approaches

Teams could participate in either English or Chinese or both, and either submit an end-to-end system or just compete in the discourse relation sense prediction component. All end-to-end systems for English adopted some variation of the pipeline architecture proposed by Lin et al (2014) and perfected by Wang and Lan (2015), which has components for identifying discourse connectives and extracting their arguments, for determining the presence or absence of discourse relations in a particular context, and for predicting the senses of the discourse relations. Here we briefly summarize the approaches used in each subtask.

Connective identification The identification of discourse connectives is not a simple dictionary lookup as some discourse connective expressions are ambiguous and may function as discourse connectives in some context but not in others. Several approaches to this

ID	Institution	Learning methods	Resources used	Extra resources
steven	Aicyber.com	-	-	-
bit (Jian et al., 2016)	BIT	SVM (for English explicits, English and Chinese implicits), rule-based method for Chinese explicit	Word embeddings	General Inquirer lexicon, HowNet, Central News of Taiwan
ttr (Ruther-ford and Xue, 2016)	Brandeis University	Feedforword (implicit sense only, pooling before hidden layers)	word embeddings	no
clac (Laali et al., 2016)	Concordia	CRF, decision tree (C4.5), Convolutional Network (implicit discourse senses)	syntactic parses, word embeddings	no
devenshu (Jain and Majumder, 2016)	DA-IICT	Maxent (openNLP)	syntactic parses	no
ecnucs (Wang and Lan, 2016)	ECNU	Liblinear, convolutional network for implicit relation (for English implicit)	phrase structure parses	no
goethe (Schenk et al., 2016)	Goethe University Frankfurt	Feed-forward neural network, CRF (connective and argument extraction), SVM (explicit sense)	syntactic parses, Brown clusters	no
gtnlp	Georgia Tech	-	-	-
tbmihaylov (Mihaylov and Frank, 2016)	Heidelberg	Liblinear (scikit-learn) (for explicit sense), CNN (for implicit sense)	word embeddings	no
aarjay	IIT-Hyderabad	-	-	-
iitbhu (Kaur et al., 2016)	IITBHU	Naive Bayes, MaxEnt	syntactic parses, MPQA subjectivity, VerbNet, Word embeddings (word2vec)	no
cip2016 (Kang et al., 2016)	Institute of Automation, CAS	MaxEnt (Mallet)	syntactic parses, word embeddings	no

Table 3: Approaches of participating systems (Part I). Teams that have not submitted a system description paper are marked with *.

subtask are represented in this competition. One is to collect all candidate discourse connective by looking up a list of possible connectives compiled from the training data and train a classifier to disambiguate them. There are two variants in this approach: one strategy is to train a classifier for each individual discourse connective expression (Oepen et al., 2016), and the other is to train one classifier for all discourse connective expressions (Wang and Lan, 2016; Kong et al., 2015; Laali et al., 2016). Alternatively, connective identification is treated as a token-level sequence labeling task, solved with sequence labeling models like CRF (Stepanov and Riccardi, 2016).

Argument extraction Different strategies were used for extracting the arguments for explicit and for implicit discourse relations. Determining the arguments of implicit discourse relations is relatively straightforward. Most systems adopted a heuristics–based extraction strategy that parallels the PDTB annotation strategy for implicit discourse relations: for each pair of adjacent sentences that do not straddle a paragraph boundary, if an explicit discourse relation does not already exist, posit

ID	Institution	Learning methods	Resources used	Extra resources
nguyenlab (Nguyen, 2016)	JAIST	CRF (CRF++) for detecting connectives and arguments, SMO and Random Forest for classifying senses	phrase structure trees, MPQA Subjectivity lexicon, word embeddings	none
gw0 (Weiss and Bajec, 2016)	Univ. of Ljubljana	Focused RNN (sense only, for both explicit and implicit)	word embeddings	none
olslopots (Oepen et al., 2016)	Olso-Potsdam-Teesside	SVM (SVM^{light}), heuristic argument extraction	Brown clusters	none
purduenlp (Pacheco et al., 2016)	Purdue University	SVM (explicit sense), Feedforword (implicit sense)	word embeddings	Wikipedia (for training event embeddings)
stepanov (Stepanov and Riccardi, 2016)	University of Trento	CRF++, AdaBoost	Brown clusters, dependency/phrase structure parses, VerbNet, MPQA Lexicon	none
tao0920 (Qin et al., 2016)	SJTU	SVM (explicit sense), CNN (implicit word sense)	word embeddings (implicit word sense)	none
Rival2710 (Li et al., 2016b)	SJTU	Maxent (OpenNLP)	syntactic parses	none
lib16b (Kong et al., 2016; Li et al., 2016a)	Soochow University	Maxent (OpenNLP), SVM (for Chinese)	syntactic parses, Brown clusters	none
Soochow (Fan et al., 2016)	Soochow	Averaged perceptron (for both sequence labeling and sense)	syntactic parses, Brown clusters	none
ykido (Kido and Aizawa, 2016)	University of Tokyo	SVM and Maxent (Scikit-learn)	Word embeddings, parse trees, MPQA subjectivity lexicon	none
VTNLPS16 (Chandrasekar et al., 2016)	Virginia Polytechnic and State University	Maxent (NLTK), Averaged Perceptron	syntactic parses (phrase/dependency), Brown clusters	none
nikko	University of Washington	-	-	-

Table 4: Approaches of participating systems (Part II). Teams that have not submitted a system description paper are marked with ∗.

an implicit discourse relation. It is possible that no discourse relation exists, but such cases are rare and most systems choose to ignore such a possibility (Oepen et al., 2016; Laali et al., 2016; Chandrasekar et al., 2016).

The extraction of the arguments for explicit discourse relations is more involved as their distribution is more diverse. The two arguments of an explicit discourse relations can be in either the same or different sentence. Identifying the argument spans of explicit discourse relations thus resembles finding the text span for discourse connectives, and there are two general approaches. One is to treat it a sequence labeling task and solve it with sequence labeling models like CRF (Fan et al., 2016; Stepanov and Riccardi, 2016), and the other is to identify candidate argument spans and train a binary classifier to determine if the candidate argument span is a true (fragment of) argument span. The difference is that the arguments are typically clauses or sentences while discourse connectives are typically single words (e.g., "as") or multi-word expressions (e.g.,"as long as"). Candidate arguments are typically identified with the help of syntactic parse trees rather than dictionaries (Oepen et al., 2016; Wang and Lan, 2016; Kong et al., 2016). The argument spans do not align perfectly with constituents in a tree, and participating systems have adopted two strategies to cope with this. One is to first identify pieces of an argument and compose them (Wang and Lan, 2016; Kong et al., 2016), and the other is to identify whole arguments but then edit them based on linguistically motivated heuristics (Oepen et al., 2016) or the prediction of classifiers (Laali et al., 2016).

Relation sense classification All systems have separate classifiers for explicit and implicit discourse connectives. For explicit relations, the discourse connective itself is the best predictor of the discourse relation. Many discourse connectives are unambiguous, always mapping to one discourse relation sense. For ambiguous discourse connectives, discourse relation sense classification amounts to word sense disambiguation. For explicit discourse relation senses, participants have generally adopted "conventional" machine learning techniques such as SVM and MaxEnt models that rely on manually designed features. Explicit discourse relation senses can be predicted with high accuracy. The main challenge is predicting implicit discourse relation senses, which has received a considerable amount of attention in recent years (Pitler et al., 2009; Biran and McKeown, 2013; Rutherford and Xue, 2014). Determining implicit discourse relation senses relies on information from the two arguments of the relation. For this subtask, there is a good balance between "conventional" machine learning techniques such as Support Vector Machines and Maximum Entropy models that rely heavily on handcrafted features, and neural network based approaches. A wide variety of features have been used for this subtask, and they include features extracted from syntactic parses (Kang et al., 2016; Kong et al., 2016; Stepanov and Riccardi, 2016; Jain and Majumder, 2016; Wang and Lan, 2016; Fan et al., 2016), Brown clusters (Kong et al., 2016; Stepanov and Riccardi, 2016; Oepen et al., 2016; Laali et al., 2016; Chandrasekar et al., 2016; Pacheco et

al., 2016), VerbNet classes (Stepanov and Riccardi, 2016; Kaur et al., 2016), and the MPQA lexicon (Stepanov and Riccardi, 2016; Kaur et al., 2016). However, features extracted from the two arguments for "conventional" machine learning methods are generally weak predictors of relation sense. Neural network based learning methods that are capable of learning representations for classification purposes seem to be particularly appealing in this learning scenario and many teams trained neural network models for the subtask of predicting the sense of implicit discourse relations. A variety of neural network architectures are represented. (Schenk et al., 2016) used a feedforward neural network, with dependency structures used to re-weight the word embeddings used as input to the network. (Wang and Lan, 2016; Qin et al., 2016) achieved competitive performance using a Convolutional Neural Network architecture for this subtask. Finally, (Weiss and Bajec, 2016) produced competitive results with a focused RNN. Word embeddings were typically used as input to the neural network models and different pooling methods have been used to derive the vectors for arguments. Rutherford and Xue (2016) used simple summation pooling in a feedforward network and achieved competitive performance in classifying implicit discourse relation senses.

Language (in-)dependence of the task To achieve competitive results, teams that participated in the Chinese task made significant changes to their systems, based on the linguistic characteristic and style of annotation for the Chinese data (Kang et al., 2016; Wang and Lan, 2016). The majority of Chinese discourse connectives are paired or discontinuous. When identifying discourse connectives, a system has to allow the possibility that different parts of the same connective may be separated from each other. The ECNU team devised a strategy that allowed their system to identify candidate discourse connectives that are discontinuous (Wang and Lan, 2016). Also, because different parts of a paired connective are text-bound to different arguments, it is no longer possible to follow the PDTB practice of labelling an argument based on whether it is bound to a connective or not (i.e, Arg2 is argument bound to the connective, while Arg1 is the other argument). As a result, the argument labels in the CDTB are defined semantically. The CAS team made labeling the argument a separate task from identifying the text spans of the argument (Kang et al., 2016), and (Wang and Lan, 2016) use a combination of classifiers and rules to determine the argument labels. Finally, because implicit discourse relations in Chinese text are not restricted to adjacent sentences with unambiguous punctuation marks, competitive Chinese systems realized the importance of disambiguating mid-sentence punctuation marks as anchors for identifying the argument spans (Kang et al., 2016; Wang and Lan, 2016).

6 Results

We provide no separate rankings for the closed track and open track, even though there are a few teams that used external resources. Also, no overall ranking is provided based on both English and Chinese, due to imbalanced participation.

Table 5 shows the performance of end-to-end systems based on the strict match of argument spans. We present results on three data sets for each language. For English the three data sets are (1) the blind test set (official); (2) the standard WSJ test set; and (3) the standard WSJ development set. The three data for Chinese are (1) the blind test set; (2) the CDTB test set; and (3) the CDTB development set. The official rankings are based on the blind test sets annotated specifically for this shared task. The three data sets for English are exactly the same as those we used for the 2015 shared task (Xue et al., 2015) so we can measure progress from year to year. The top-ranked submission for English is by the Olso-Potsdam-Teesside team, and their overall score based on strict match is 27.77% F1 score, which represents an improvement of 3.77% over last year's winning system submitted by the East China Normal University (ECNU) (Wang and Lan, 2015). Four other teams also beat the score of last year's winning system. There is considerable fluctuation in the rankings across the three data sets, with the ECNU system receiving the highest score on both the WSJ development and test sets.

The top ranked Chinese system was submitted by the Institute of Automation, Chinese Academy of Sciences, although the difference between the top two teams is only 0.3%. However, the rankings are very stable across data sets. Since there are many more teams that participated in the English task than the Chinese task, we decided not to provide an overall ranking based on the results of both languages. (In such a putative ranking, the ECNU system would be ranked top.)

Table 6 provides the ranking based on partial match of argument spans. The ranking remains largely unchanged when the scorer setting is changed from strict match to partial match for English. For the Chinese evaluation, the ranking is also to a large extent consistent with that based on strict match. For both English, the overall parser scores based on F1 score are considerably higher when the scorer shifts from a strict match setting to a partial match setting, indicating that error propagation is a serious issue when there is a long pipeline. Tables 7 and 8 present the accuracy of individual components for explicit and implicit discourse relations based on strict and partial match respectively. For English, the parser accuracy for explicit discourse relations is generally higher than that for implicit discourse relations, although the argument span extraction accuracy is higher for implicit discourse relations than for explicit discourse relations.

The overall parser accuracy for implicit relations is dragged down by the lower accuracy in predicting discourse relation sense, as is shown is Table 9, which compares the accuracy of classifying explicit and implicit discourse relation sense. This pattern does not consistently hold for results on Chinese across the three data sets. On the blind test set, the parser accuracy for some of the teams is actually higher for implicit discourse relations than for explicit discourse relations. Our hypothesis is that this is caused by the fact that there are much more instances for implicit discourse relations than explicit discourse relations. In this situation, the difference in discourse relation sense accuracy between explicit and implicit discourse relations is much smaller in Chinese than in English, an observation that is largely born

Language	Participant	Parser			Connective			Argument		
	ID	P	R	F	P	R	F	P	R	F
				Blind Test						
English	oslopots	27.75	27.79	27.77	93.53	90.12	91.79	48.30	48.18	48.24
English	ecnucs	25.69	26.30	25.99	90.11	92.61	91.34	48.06	46.82	47.43
English	stepanov	26.22	24.07	25.10	84.89	92.55	88.56	48.55	52.84	50.60
English	tao0920	24.41	24.81	24.61	88.67	93.73	91.13	48.47	47.64	48.05
English	goethe	24.29	24.65	24.47	86.87	92.00	89.36	46.73	46.01	46.37
English	li16b	30.36	20.26	24.31	90.47	92.80	91.62	30.19	45.17	36.19
English	Soochow	24.49	18.94	21.36	89.57	92.57	91.04	33.66	43.34	37.90
English	clac	21.11	21.01	21.06	91.91	88.56	90.20	39.04	39.20	39.12
English	nguyenlab	20.31	20.43	20.37	79.50	91.51	85.08	39.04	38.78	38.91
English	VTNLPS16	19.51	21.09	20.27	88.13	90.41	89.25	39.45	36.47	37.90
English	rival2710	12.62	18.94	15.15	98.56	98.21	98.38	36.15	24.09	28.91
English	devanshu	12.69	9.18	10.65	77.70	93.71	84.96	14.89	20.55	17.27
English	nikko	7.35	10.34	8.59	67.27	87.38	76.02	17.45	12.40	14.50
English	iitbhu	4.60	6.87	5.51	86.87	91.30	89.03	24.98	16.74	20.05
				Standard WSJ Test (Section 23)						
English	ecnucs	30.26	31.16	30.70	93.50	94.42	93.96	48.48	47.12	47.79
English	tao0920	29.90	30.65	30.27	92.42	94.88	93.63	49.10	47.96	48.52
English	goethe	29.54	30.03	29.78	89.82	93.57	91.65	49.97	49.14	49.55
English	li16b	33.07	25.48	28.78	94.04	95.38	94.71	36.87	47.92	41.68
English	oslopots	27.47	28.89	28.16	96.42	92.52	94.43	50.18	47.77	48.94
English	stepanov	27.64	27.96	27.80	90.57	94.36	92.43	48.68	48.19	48.44
English	Soochow	27.47	25.84	26.63	94.69	94.79	94.74	42.75	45.50	44.08
English	nguyenlab	25.52	23.88	24.67	83.42	92.22	87.60	40.59	43.46	41.97
English	clac	23.94	24.91	24.42	93.61	88.52	91.00	42.55	40.94	41.73
English	VTNLPS16	20.80	25.84	23.05	89.92	91.51	90.71	42.24	34.04	37.70
English	rival2710	20.13	22.33	21.17	99.67	98.19	98.92	40.33	36.39	38.26
English	devanshu	13.19	10.23	11.53	67.06	94.36	78.40	14.96	19.31	16.86
English	nikko	7.08	10.03	8.30	48.00	88.96	62.35	17.69	12.51	14.66
English	iitbhu	5.66	9.20	7.01	92.09	93.92	93.00	29.09	17.91	22.17
				Standard WSJ Development (Section 22)						
English	ecnucs	39.90	40.98	40.43	95.29	95.15	95.22	57.24	56.46	56.85
English	goethe	39.87	40.55	40.21	92.79	94.32	93.55	57.66	57.26	57.46
English	tao0920	38.20	38.99	38.59	93.82	95.08	94.45	56.55	56.04	56.29
English	li16b	39.86	32.10	35.56	93.53	94.93	94.22	42.97	54.03	47.87
English	oslopots	34.13	35.30	34.71	96.32	92.25	94.24	55.43	54.26	54.84
English	clac	32.12	33.10	32.60	94.26	89.90	92.03	49.72	48.87	49.29
English	stepanov	32.46	32.46	32.46	91.47	95.25	93.32	54.39	55.04	54.71
English	Soochow	32.72	30.47	31.56	93.53	95.07	94.29	47.84	52.08	49.87
English	VTNLPS16	28.58	33.59	30.88	93.09	92.95	93.02	50.21	43.33	46.52
English	nguyenlab	30.59	28.76	29.65	85.00	91.60	88.18	45.82	49.25	47.47
English	rival2710	27.78	30.33	29.00	99.71	98.40	99.05	48.40	44.93	46.60
English	devanshu	17.74	13.85	15.56	69.71	94.05	80.07	18.18	23.60	20.54
English	nikko	10.68	15.41	12.62	56.91	90.21	69.79	24.44	17.25	20.22
English	iitbhu	5.76	9.23	7.10	91.47	95.25	93.32	31.96	20.31	24.84
				Blind Test						
Chinese	cip2016	29.13	24.99	26.90	48.76	66.51	56.27	38.93	45.07	41.78
Chinese	ecnucs	26.74	26.46	26.60	60.95	65.34	63.07	41.79	42.19	41.99
Chinese	li16b	23.31	23.61	23.46	63.07	65.99	64.50	38.55	38.03	38.29
Chinese	goethe	16.12	10.76	12.90	45.23	46.97	46.08	21.94	32.13	26.07
Chinese	nikko	3.70	2.43	2.93	36.75	68.42	47.82	3.05	4.64	3.68
				Standard Xinhua Test						
Chinese	cip2016	39.67	42.20	40.89	67.71	78.31	72.63	56.26	52.24	54.18
Chinese	ecnucs	37.60	43.30	40.25	65.63	80.77	72.41	54.73	47.43	50.82
Chinese	li16b	34.07	37.14	35.54	75.00	80.00	77.42	48.79	44.76	46.69
Chinese	goethe	30.16	20.22	24.21	66.67	74.42	70.33	30.11	44.05	35.77
Chinese	nikko	4.59	3.74	4.12	45.83	84.62	59.46	6.37	7.84	7.03
				Standard Xinhua Development						
Chinese	ecnucs	38.32	47.52	42.42	85.71	86.84	86.27	58.75	47.37	52.45
Chinese	cip2016	39.47	43.08	41.20	79.22	88.41	83.56	55.87	50.71	53.17
Chinese	li16b	33.86	39.16	36.32	79.22	83.56	81.33	52.74	45.60	48.91
Chinese	goethe	24.68	20.10	22.16	61.04	65.28	63.09	31.59	38.66	34.77
Chinese	nikko	5.47	5.48	5.48	64.94	84.75	73.53	6.27	6.25	6.26

Table 5: Scoreboard for the CoNLL-2016 shared task showing performance (**strict** scoring) across the subtasks and the three data partitions—blind test, standard test and development set for both English and Chinese.

out in the results shown in Table 9.

7 Conclusions

Twenty three teams from three continents participated in the CoNLL-2016 Shared Task on multilingual shallow discourse parsing.

Language	Participant	Parser			Argument		
	ID	P	R	F	P	R	F
Blind Test							
English	oslopots	44.14	44.25	44.20	80.41	80.64	80.53
English	ecnucs	40.13	41.19	40.65	77.57	79.94	78.74
English	stepanov	38.34	35.24	36.72	79.85	72.41	75.95
English	tao0920	39.51	40.20	39.85	77.66	79.22	78.43
English	goethe	39.66	40.28	39.97	76.64	78.02	77.32
English	li16b	49.01	32.75	39.27	75.93	48.32	59.06
English	Soochow	42.60	33.09	37.24	78.21	58.36	66.85
English	clac	37.29	37.14	37.22	77.55	77.19	77.37
English	nguyenlab	32.46	32.67	32.56	63.15	63.63	63.39
English	VTNLPS16	35.32	38.21	36.71	68.76	75.16	71.82
English	rival2710	22.60	33.91	27.13	51.30	80.80	62.75
English	devanshu	38.13	27.63	32.04	77.12	53.25	63.00
English	nikko	15.34	21.59	17.94	25.09	36.10	29.61
English	iitbhu	20.45	30.52	24.49	45.82	71.62	55.89
Standard WSJ Test (Section 23)							
English	ecnucs	46.91	48.27	47.58	80.35	82.99	81.65
English	tao0920	45.84	46.93	46.37	79.51	81.66	80.57
English	goethe	45.48	46.25	45.86	79.14	80.66	79.90
English	li16b	50.13	38.60	43.62	75.82	56.94	65.03
English	oslopots	43.04	45.22	44.10	77.25	81.67	79.40
English	stepanov	41.94	42.38	42.16	78.21	79.12	78.66
English	Soochow	45.74	43.00	44.33	79.46	74.07	76.67
English	nguyenlab	38.78	36.28	37.49	66.09	61.26	63.58
English	clac	39.81	41.40	40.59	76.46	79.88	78.14
English	VTNLPS16	34.85	43.26	38.60	60.77	77.27	68.03
English	rival2710	35.62	39.48	37.45	72.15	81.06	76.34
English	devanshu	38.76	30.03	33.84	76.64	57.61	65.78
English	nikko	14.20	20.10	16.64	22.62	32.62	26.71
English	iitbhu						
Standard WSJ Development (Section 22)							
English	ecnucs	54.12	55.04	54.58	83.29	84.63	83.96
English	goethe	53.09	53.62	53.36	82.21	82.87	82.54
English	tao0920	52.21	52.84	52.52	82.46	83.32	82.89
English	li16b	56.53	45.17	50.22	80.58	62.33	70.29
English	oslopots	48.02	49.22	48.61	81.41	83.41	82.40
English	clac	46.04	47.02	46.52	79.50	81.09	80.29
English	stepanov	45.77	45.38	45.58	81.05	79.95	80.50
English	Soochow	49.50	45.53	47.43	82.41	74.76	78.40
English	VTNLPS16	41.13	47.94	44.28	65.66	77.46	71.08
English	nguyenlab	42.40	39.63	40.97	69.67	64.30	66.88
English	rival2710	41.42	44.89	43.08	75.75	82.48	78.97
English	devanshu	44.63	34.52	38.93	80.12	59.80	68.49
English	nikko	18.02	25.92	21.26	27.12	39.17	32.05
English	iitbhu						
Blind Test							
Chinese	cip2016	46.67	40.31	43.26	72.48	61.52	66.55
Chinese	ecnucs	42.10	41.69	41.89	68.76	68.02	68.39
Chinese	li16b	41.64	42.22	41.93	65.35	66.38	65.86
Chinese	goethe	32.40	22.13	26.30	64.50	42.88	51.51
Chinese	nikko	9.06	5.95	7.18	9.77	6.34	7.69
Standard Xinhua Test							
Chinese	cip2016	51.43	55.38	53.33	71.05	76.96	73.89
Chinese	ecnucs	50.86	58.68	54.49	68.57	80.45	74.03
Chinese	li16b	53.02	57.80	55.31	69.54	76.46	72.83
Chinese	goethe	45.02	30.77	36.55	69.44	46.30	55.56
Chinese	nikko	11.08	9.01	9.94	14.36	11.63	12.86
Standard Xinhua Development							
Chinese	ecnucs	50.95	63.19	56.41	65.07	82.37	72.70
Chinese	cip2016	53.79	59.27	56.40	68.85	76.68	72.55
Chinese	li16b	50.34	58.22	54.00	66.26	77.65	71.50
Chinese	goethe	39.62	32.38	35.63	58.95	47.32	52.50
Chinese	nikko	11.72	11.75	11.73	10.47	10.50	10.48

Table 6: Scoreboard for the CoNLL-2016 shared task showing performance (**partial** scoring) across the subtasks and the three data partitions—blind test, standard test and development set for both English and Chinese.

The shared task required the development of an end-to-end system, and the best system achieved an F1 score of 27.77% on the blind test set for English, and 26.90% for Chinese, reflecting the serious error propagation problem in such a system. The shared task exposed the most challenging aspect of shallow discourse parsing as a research problem, help-

Language	Participant ID	Explicit					Implicit			
		Parser F	Connective F	A1 F	A2 F	A12 F	Parser F	A1 F	A2 F	A12 F
Blind Test										
English	oslopots	34.45	91.79	52.43	75.20	43.95	21.89	64.60	76.40	52.02
English	ecnucs	33.94	91.34	51.05	74.20	42.84	19.54	61.05	75.83	51.15
English	stepanov	31.74	88.56	50.28	72.05	41.84	19.46	66.83	79.11	58.05
English	tao0920	31.64	91.13	48.43	73.57	41.40	19.01	61.61	77.82	53.35
English	goethe	30.74	89.36	48.84	71.97	41.07	19.63	60.77	74.63	50.44
English	li16b	31.18	91.62	47.18	68.85	38.25	16.10	42.22	44.83	33.73
English	Soochow	27.47	91.04	41.86	69.84	33.46	15.06	51.80	59.96	42.50
English	clac	31.10	90.20	48.37	70.61	39.89	12.19	54.06	60.94	38.44
English	nguyenlab	30.83	85.08	52.17	70.07	41.39	12.55	42.97	55.08	37.06
English	VTNLPS16	29.33	89.25	46.08	67.94	38.62	13.56	49.47	59.06	37.35
English	rival2710	25.31	98.38	41.29	73.43	33.39	10.11	37.30	41.70	26.30
English	devanshu	20.67	84.96	37.17	51.13	28.52	1.12	17.23	25.09	6.55
English	nikko	20.93	76.02	35.16	48.37	26.63	2.28	17.65	14.43	8.31
English	iitbhu	7.93	89.03	28.94	25.81	9.03	4.15	37.03	41.49	26.24
Standard WSJ Test (Section 23)										
English	ecnucs	40.31	93.96	51.39	76.43	44.31	22.38	64.66	66.86	50.83
English	tao0920	40.53	93.63	50.38	76.73	44.90	21.36	65.18	67.84	51.67
English	goethe	40.44	91.65	50.41	75.95	45.22	20.60	67.17	68.32	53.28
English	li16b	36.57	94.71	47.14	71.14	40.81	19.82	51.56	51.56	42.68
English	oslopots	39.38	94.43	51.99	72.57	43.93	18.02	69.92	71.45	53.47
English	stepanov	39.60	92.43	49.64	76.51	44.56	17.56	65.58	67.78	51.80
English	Soochow	32.97	94.74	44.99	72.09	37.40	20.51	63.36	66.81	50.52
English	nguyenlab	39.39	87.60	53.81	71.79	45.28	11.67	46.59	50.90	39.06
English	clac	35.72	91.00	47.29	72.56	40.23	13.95	60.05	57.13	43.11
English	VTNLPS16	36.41	90.71	47.21	69.62	40.87	13.31	50.97	47.32	35.39
English	rival2710	32.51	98.92	42.15	75.48	36.24	11.70	56.28	53.14	39.95
English	devanshu	23.70	78.40	33.44	48.26	27.87	1.18	21.05	22.77	7.30
English	nikko	21.13	62.35	28.43	43.91	23.22	2.70	19.88	15.46	10.92
English	iitbhu	11.93	93.00	29.98	34.35	12.80	4.24	38.59	36.44	27.42
Standard WSJ Development (Section 22)										
English	ecnucs	51.13	95.22	62.01	81.26	55.11	31.10	68.84	73.81	58.39
English	goethe	50.87	93.55	61.97	78.87	54.41	30.99	70.45	74.10	60.14
English	tao0920	49.70	94.45	60.99	79.94	53.44	28.98	68.71	74.19	58.80
English	li16b	42.97	94.22	52.89	74.81	46.37	27.54	58.31	59.77	49.51
English	oslopots	46.44	94.24	60.72	75.83	51.37	24.09	71.25	77.46	58.03
English	clac	44.57	92.03	56.71	75.95	48.67	21.67	63.70	63.70	49.87
English	stepanov	45.89	93.32	55.66	79.07	49.36	20.89	69.51	74.51	59.40
English	Soochow	39.30	94.29	51.00	73.98	42.70	24.21	66.86	72.12	56.76
English	VTNLPS16	46.21	93.02	57.90	73.77	50.26	19.08	56.58	55.20	43.59
English	nguyenlab	46.68	88.18	60.72	72.31	52.33	14.61	49.14	56.40	43.12
English	rival2710	41.49	99.05	50.55	78.89	45.29	18.57	61.09	60.72	47.71
English	devanshu	31.31	80.07	41.89	54.39	34.97	2.07	20.47	23.27	7.81
English	nikko	30.36	69.79	40.76	52.30	32.82	4.42	21.59	19.81	14.31
English	iitbhu	10.69	93.32	31.21	27.91	11.70	5.10	41.22	40.96	32.25
Blind Test										
Chinese	cip2016	24.46	56.27	38.53	44.44	26.50	27.12	55.26	60.17	44.57
Chinese	ecnucs	28.88	63.07	41.13	47.53	31.81	24.74	54.21	54.99	42.36
Chinese	li16b	20.63	64.50	37.40	39.93	23.31	23.75	53.27	54.74	41.93
Chinese	goethe	18.56	46.08	32.76	34.92	20.70	10.80	40.91	35.88	27.55
Chinese	nikko	6.21	47.82	13.10	23.22	7.13	1.69	12.87	8.12	2.37
Standard Xinhua Test										
Chinese	cip2016	48.59	72.63	55.87	68.16	49.16	38.69	62.66	67.62	53.79
Chinese	ecnucs	45.09	72.41	59.77	62.07	47.13	38.21	59.55	65.26	50.12
Chinese	li16b	26.88	77.42	41.94	54.84	29.03	36.34	59.08	65.62	49.15
Chinese	goethe	28.73	70.33	39.56	57.14	28.57	22.26	42.81	45.55	36.30
Chinese	nikko	12.16	59.46	21.62	32.43	12.16	2.36	12.70	11.23	5.61
Standard Xinhua Development										
Chinese	ecnucs	53.59	86.27	67.97	70.59	56.21	39.43	59.86	65.25	50.50
Chinese	cip2016	45.21	83.56	54.79	68.49	45.21	39.82	62.82	67.98	53.41
Chinese	li16b	34.67	81.33	46.67	60.00	34.67	36.09	59.47	65.68	50.30
Chinese	goethe	17.45	63.09	40.27	44.30	20.13	22.67	45.70	45.34	36.93
Chinese	nikko	11.76	73.53	19.12	30.88	11.76	4.12	20.60	12.36	5.07

Table 7: F-score (**strict** scoring) of all subtasks separated by *Explicit* and *Implicit* discourse relations across the three data partitions—blind test, standard test and development set for both English and Chinese.

ing future research better calibrate their efforts. The evaluation data sets and the scorer we prepared for the shared task will be a useful benchmark for future research on shallow discourse parsing.

Language	Participant	Explicit				Implicit			
	ID	Parser F	A1 F	A2 F	A12 F	Parser F	A1 F	A2 F	A12 F
					Blind Test				
English	oslopots	56.66	71.96	81.73	71.74	33.23	84.47	88.98	86.31
English	ecnucs	57.25	70.19	79.67	71.69	26.90	79.53	84.11	82.73
English	stepanov	51.03	65.71	78.05	63.83	24.24	80.54	85.49	84.43
English	tao0920	55.82	70.67	80.04	70.73	26.68	79.59	84.01	82.59
English	goethe	54.02	68.12	78.26	68.11	28.32	79.79	84.37	82.23
English	li16b	54.46	69.67	79.78	67.37	21.11	49.40	52.67	49.47
English	Soochow	54.11	64.79	79.52	66.08	19.73	64.14	69.07	66.11
English	clac	52.43	67.54	78.38	65.23	23.59	82.34	87.03	84.78
English	nguyenlab	52.74	66.52	75.65	67.13	17.16	56.09	60.85	56.31
English	VTNLPS16	54.46	68.47	78.14	68.70	22.83	70.89	75.26	72.02
English	rival2710	45.24	63.64	85.10	59.71	15.30	57.20	60.76	56.00
English	devanshu	47.79	62.33	73.16	62.86	17.04	60.11	63.30	60.84
English	nikko	40.65	56.08	56.50	50.23	5.19	23.16	21.81	16.52
English	iitbhu	47.19	62.48	64.70	54.53	11.51	56.74	60.37	55.63
					Standard WSJ Test (Section 23)				
English	ecnucs	69.21	72.16	88.62	74.89	28.60	82.78	85.65	86.55
English	tao0920	67.80	71.38	88.25	73.29	27.77	82.30	85.16	86.15
English	goethe	66.41	69.37	86.35	70.92	28.05	83.63	85.44	86.88
English	li16b	62.37	66.67	87.94	67.28	22.08	62.45	62.45	62.20
English	oslopots	65.96	70.75	86.90	71.27	24.36	84.74	86.47	85.85
English	stepanov	63.31	68.11	86.24	68.76	23.72	82.53	85.02	86.22
English	Soochow	64.13	67.17	86.50	69.50	25.12	79.54	81.94	82.55
English	nguyenlab	61.81	69.71	82.48	68.60	15.39	56.02	58.53	56.66
English	clac	62.49	66.58	84.78	67.77	20.11	82.34	84.96	85.99
English	VTNLPS16	64.55	70.39	84.26	70.39	19.37	64.65	65.45	64.25
English	rival2710	56.51	63.32	91.29	61.35	20.52	77.83	79.71	80.39
English	devanshu	51.36	56.71	70.68	56.92	19.49	66.27	65.63	65.38
English	nikko	42.54	46.26	51.51	43.83	4.79	25.04	20.87	17.24
English	iitbhu								
					Standard WSJ Development (Section 22)				
English	ecnucs	75.04	77.29	87.74	79.80	36.63	80.60	86.22	86.47
English	goethe	72.52	76.32	85.40	76.88	36.84	81.15	85.71	86.47
English	tao0920	73.48	76.20	86.79	78.16	34.32	79.92	85.79	85.84
English	li16b	67.38	71.88	85.04	71.28	31.69	66.61	68.73	68.10
English	oslopots	69.97	77.04	85.61	76.31	29.22	82.75	88.30	86.92
English	clac	66.67	70.94	83.56	71.51	28.03	80.32	86.04	85.74
English	stepanov	68.26	71.48	85.82	72.14	26.11	80.42	86.07	86.46
English	Soochow	67.79	70.58	84.34	72.65	28.14	79.09	82.50	82.32
English	VTNLPS16	70.45	74.75	83.88	75.48	24.22	65.67	68.32	66.41
English	nguyenlab	66.61	73.55	82.23	73.60	17.96	57.08	62.29	59.23
English	rival2710	63.32	70.30	89.85	67.64	25.11	77.20	82.78	81.81
English	devanshu	57.76	65.74	71.45	62.41	22.73	64.36	67.75	65.58
English	nikko	50.74	57.46	58.07	52.50	6.98	26.25	24.39	20.07
English	iitbhu								
					Blind Test				
Chinese	cip2016	48.11	53.21	53.21	48.77	40.82	71.33	70.39	67.02
Chinese	ecnucs	49.36	55.39	55.76	51.02	36.66	67.54	66.56	62.38
Chinese	li16b	43.36	53.12	55.65	47.17	38.09	67.77	64.60	61.57
Chinese	goethe	43.02	53.29	54.37	48.17	18.56	53.62	52.21	48.17
Chinese	nikko	18.16	22.53	31.72	16.22	3.14	19.92	9.50	4.44
					Standard Xinhua Test				
Chinese	cip2016	64.80	64.80	73.74	63.47	49.87	74.15	75.46	73.39
Chinese	ecnucs	66.67	67.82	72.41	65.82	49.63	72.21	72.46	71.04
Chinese	li16b	63.44	65.59	65.59	61.90	50.46	71.11	73.46	69.79
Chinese	goethe	62.64	62.64	68.13	60.49	27.74	53.77	54.79	50.36
Chinese	nikko	35.14	40.54	39.19	33.33	3.84	18.61	11.82	7.77
					Standard Xinhua Development				
Chinese	ecnucs	78.43	73.20	79.74	79.39	49.93	76.02	71.57	68.09
Chinese	cip2016	75.34	64.38	71.23	72.41	50.68	77.78	73.88	70.94
Chinese	li16b	65.33	56.00	74.67	62.90	49.41	75.96	72.61	68.77
Chinese	goethe	57.72	59.06	65.77	56.91	27.06	61.71	54.92	47.58
Chinese	nikko	29.41	33.82	39.71	26.98	6.97	23.45	14.58	6.30

Table 8: F-score (**partial** scoring) of all subtasks separated by *Explicit* and *Implicit* discourse relations across the three data partitions—blind test, standard test and development set for both English and Chinese.

Acknowledgments

We would like to thank the Penn Discourse TreeBank team and the Chinese Discourse TreeBank Team, for allowing us to use the PDTB corpus and the CDTB corpus for the shared task. Thanks also go the LDC (Linguistic Data Consortium), who helped distribute

Language	Participant	All Senses			Explicit Senses			Implicit Senses		
	ID	P	R	F	P	R	F	P	R	F
				Blind Test						
English	aarjay	41.51	41.44	41.47	78.70	78.42	78.56	9.95	9.95	9.95
English	BIT	18.69	18.69	18.69	17.99	17.99	17.99	19.30	19.30	19.30
English	clac	50.04	49.96	50.00	76.35	76.08	76.22	27.72	27.72	27.72
English	ecnucs	54.10	54.01	54.06	77.48	77.34	77.41	34.20	34.15	34.18
English	goethe	52.36	52.27	52.32	76.53	76.26	76.40	31.85	31.85	31.85
English	gtnlp	54.35	54.26	54.30	75.09	74.82	74.95	36.75	36.75	36.75
English	gw0	52.48	52.44	52.46	75.32	75.18	75.25	33.08	33.08	33.08
English	gw0	19.93	19.93	19.93	18.35	18.35	18.35	21.29	21.29	21.29
English	nguyenlab	51.37	51.28	51.32	74.91	74.64	74.77	31.44	31.39	31.42
English	oslopots	53.60	53.52	53.56	77.74	76.62	77.17	33.84	33.84	33.84
English	PurdueNLP	23.82	23.82	23.82	22.02	17.63	19.58	29.10	29.10	29.10
English	steven	41.44	41.44	41.44	65.42	62.95	64.16	24.04	23.12	23.58
English	tao0920	53.94	53.85	53.89	75.95	75.54	75.74	35.38	35.38	35.38
English	tbmihaylov	54.69	54.51	54.60	78.34	78.06	78.20	34.56	34.46	34.51
English	ykido	51.90	51.86	51.88	76.05	74.82	75.43	32.31	32.31	32.31
English	ttr	-	-	-	-	-	-	37.67	37.67	37.67
			Standard WSJ Test (Section 23)							
English	aarjay	50.90	50.90	50.90	89.70	89.70	89.70	15.60	15.60	15.60
English	BIT	20.41	20.41	20.41	24.62	24.62	24.62	16.58	16.58	16.58
English	clac	57.36	57.36	57.36	89.48	89.48	89.48	28.13	28.13	28.13
English	ecnucs	64.34	64.34	64.34	90.13	90.13	90.13	40.95	40.87	40.91
English	goethe	62.64	62.64	62.64	90.13	90.13	90.13	37.61	37.61	37.61
English	gtnlp	60.93	60.93	60.93	89.48	89.48	89.48	34.95	34.95	34.95
English	gw0	58.45	58.45	58.45	89.48	89.48	89.48	30.21	30.21	30.21
English	gw0	17.11	17.11	17.11	15.51	15.51	15.51	18.56	18.56	18.56
English	nguyenlab	57.36	57.36	57.36	88.72	88.72	88.72	28.83	28.83	28.83
English	oslopots	60.62	60.62	60.62	90.13	90.13	90.13	33.76	33.76	33.76
English	PurdueNLP	59.95	59.95	59.95	87.96	87.96	87.96	34.45	34.45	34.45
English	steven	44.70	44.70	44.70	73.88	71.48	72.66	20.83	20.34	20.58
English	tao0920	62.69	62.69	62.69	89.59	89.59	89.59	38.20	38.20	38.20
English	tbmihaylov	63.31	63.31	63.31	89.80	89.80	89.80	39.19	39.19	39.19
English	ykido	54.73	54.73	54.73	90.41	90.02	90.22	22.61	22.61	22.61
English	ttr	-	-	-	-	-	-	36.13	36.13	36.13
			Standard WSJ Development (Section 22)							
English	aarjay	62.43	62.43	62.43	91.50	91.50	91.50	36.85	36.85	36.85
English	BIT	20.10	20.10	20.10	23.22	23.22	23.22	17.36	17.36	17.36
English	clac	62.22	62.22	62.22	90.74	90.74	90.74	37.12	37.12	37.12
English	ecnucs	67.97	67.97	67.97	92.56	92.56	92.56	46.51	46.33	46.42
English	goethe	66.90	66.90	66.90	91.35	91.35	91.35	45.45	45.39	45.42
English	gtnlp	63.92	63.92	63.92	90.29	90.29	90.29	40.72	40.72	40.72
English	gw0	61.36	61.36	61.36	91.81	91.81	91.81	34.58	34.58	34.58
English	gw0	60.65	60.65	60.65	89.68	89.68	89.68	35.11	35.11	35.11
English	nguyenlab	60.51	60.51	60.51	90.29	90.29	90.29	34.31	34.31	34.31
English	oslopots	65.70	65.70	65.70	91.35	91.35	91.35	43.12	43.12	43.12
English	PurdueNLP	62.22	62.22	62.22	89.68	89.68	89.68	38.05	38.05	38.05
English	steven	46.88	46.88	46.88	72.30	70.11	71.19	26.94	26.44	26.68
English	tao0920	67.83	67.83	67.83	92.26	92.26	92.26	46.33	46.33	46.33
English	tbmihaylov	64.13	64.13	64.13	91.20	91.20	91.20	40.32	40.32	40.32
English	ykido	57.74	57.74	57.74	90.29	90.29	90.29	29.11	29.11	29.11
English	ttr	-	-	-	-	-	-	40.32	40.32	40.32
				Blind Test						
Chinese	BIT	33.51	33.51	33.51	75.27	75.27	75.27	18.11	18.11	18.11
Chinese	ecnucs	64.73	64.73	64.73	77.24	76.15	76.69	60.52	60.52	60.52
Chinese	goethe	63.73	63.73	63.73	80.39	80.39	80.39	57.59	57.59	57.59
Chinese	gw0	72.92	72.92	72.92	78.98	78.98	78.98	70.68	70.68	70.68
Chinese	gw0	57.97	57.97	57.97	29.15	29.15	29.15	68.60	68.60	68.60
Chinese	tao0920	61.02	61.02	61.02	75.82	73.67	74.73	56.35	56.35	56.35
Chinese	ttr	-	-	-	-	-	-	63.38	63.38	63.38
			Standard Xinhua Test							
Chinese	BIT	37.00	36.92	36.96	94.74	93.75	94.24	21.73	21.73	21.73
Chinese	ecnucs	77.09	76.92	77.01	94.74	93.75	94.24	72.42	72.42	72.42
Chinese	goethe	77.09	76.92	77.01	96.84	95.83	96.34	71.87	71.87	71.87
Chinese	gw0	70.11	70.11	70.11	92.71	92.71	92.71	64.07	64.07	64.07
Chinese	gw0	50.77	50.77	50.77	3.13	3.13	3.13	63.51	63.51	63.51
Chinese	tao0920	72.91	72.75	72.83	93.68	92.71	93.19	67.41	67.41	67.41
Chinese	ttr	-	-	-	-	-	-	70.47	70.47	70.47
			Standard Xinhua Development							
Chinese	BIT	36.03	36.03	36.03	92.21	92.21	92.21	21.90	21.90	21.90
Chinese	ecnucs	78.07	78.07	78.07	96.10	96.10	96.10	73.53	73.53	73.53
Chinese	goethe	75.72	75.72	75.72	96.10	96.10	96.10	70.59	70.59	70.59
Chinese	gw0	72.06	72.06	72.06	93.51	93.51	93.51	66.67	66.67	66.67
Chinese	gw0	68.15	68.15	68.15	94.81	94.81	94.81	61.44	61.44	61.44
Chinese	tao0920	76.76	76.76	76.76	97.40	97.40	97.40	71.57	71.57	71.57
Chinese	ttr	-	-	-	-	-	-	63.38	63.38	63.38

Table 9: Discourse relation sense classification evaluation results (Supplementary evaluation). All participants are given gold standard discourse connectives and argument pairs.

the training and development data to participating teams. We are also very grateful to the TIRA team, who provided their evaluation platform, and especially to Martin Potthast for his technical assistance in using the TIRA platform and countless hours of troubleshooting.

This work was partially supported by the National Science Foundation via Grant Nos. 0910532 and IIS-1421067 and by the Singapore Ministry of Education Academic Research Fund Tier 2 grant MOE2013-T2-1-150.

References

Nicholas Asher and Alex Lascarides. 2003. *Logics of conversation*. Cambridge University Press.

Or Biran and Kathleen McKeown. 2013. Aggregated word pair features for implicit discourse relation disambiguation. In *Proceedings of the 51st Annual Meeting of the Association for Computational Linguistics*.

Prashant Chandrasekar, Xuan Zhang, Saurabh Chakravarty, Arijit Ray, John Krulick, and Alla Rozovskaya. 2016. The virginia tech system at conll-2016 shared task on shallow discourse parsing. In *Proceedings of the Twentieth Conference on Computational Natural Language Learning: Shared Task*, Berlin, Germany, August. Association for Computational Linguistics.

Ziwei Fan, Zhenghua Li, and Min Zhang. 2016. Finding arguments as sequence labeling in discourse parsing. In *Proceedings of the Twentieth Conference on Computational Natural Language Learning: Shared Task*, Berlin, Germany, August. Association for Computational Linguistics.

Tim Gollub, Benno Stein, and Steven Burrows. 2012. Ousting Ivory Tower Research: Towards a Web Framework for Providing Experiments as a Service. In Bill Hersh, Jamie Callan, Yoelle Maarek, and Mark Sanderson, editors, *35th International ACM Conference on Research and Development in Information Retrieval (SIGIR 12)*, pages 1125–1126. ACM, August.

Devanshu Jain and Prasenjit Majumder. 2016. Da-iict submission for pdtb-styled discourse parser. In *Proceedings of the Twentieth Conference on Computational Natural Language Learning: Shared Task*, Berlin, Germany, August. Association for Computational Linguistics.

Ping Jian, Xiaohan She, Chenwei Zhang, Pengcheng Zhang, and Jian Feng. 2016. Discourse relation sense classification systems for conll-2016 shared task. In *Proceedings of the Twentieth Conference on Computational Natural Language Learning: Shared Task*, Berlin,

Germany, August. Association for Computational Linguistics.

Xiaomian Kang, Haoran Li, Long Zhou, Jiajun Zhang, and Chengqing Zong. 2016. An end-to-end chinese discourse parser with adaptation to explicit and non-explicit relation recognition. In *Proceedings of the Twentieth Conference on Computational Natural Language Learning: Shared Task*, Berlin, Germany, August. Association for Computational Linguistics.

Manpreet Kaur, Nishu Kumari, Anil Kumar Singh, and Rajeev Sangal. 2016. lit (bhu) submission on the conll-2016 shared task: Shallow discourse parsing using semantic lexicons. In *Proceedings of the Twentieth Conference on Computational Natural Language Learning: Shared Task*, Berlin, Germany, August. Association for Computational Linguistics.

Yusuke Kido and Akiko Aizawa. 2016. Discourse relation sense classification with two-step classifiers. In *Proceedings of the Twentieth Conference on Computational Natural Language Learning: Shared Task*, Berlin, Germany, August. Association for Computational Linguistics.

Fang Kong, Sheng Li, and Guodong Zhou. 2015. The SoNLP-DP system in the CoNLL-2015 shared task. In *Proceedings of the Nineteenth Conference on Computational Natural Language Learning: Shared Task*.

Fang Kong, Sheng Li, Junhui Li, Muhua Zhu, and Guodong Zhou. 2016. Sonlp-dp system for conll-2016 english shallow discourse parsing. In *Proceedings of the Twentieth Conference on Computational Natural Language Learning: Shared Task*, Berlin, Germany, August. Association for Computational Linguistics.

Majid Laali, Andre Cianflone, and Leila Kosseim. 2016. The clac discourse parser at conll-2016. In *Proceedings of the Twentieth Conference on Computational Natural Language Learning: Shared Task*, Berlin, Germany, August. Association for Computational Linguistics.

Junhui Li, Fang Kong, Sheng Li, Muhua Zhu, and Guodong Zhou. 2016a. Sonlp-dp system for conll 2016 chinese shallow discourse parsing. In *Proceedings of the Twentieth Conference on Computational Natural Language Learning: Shared Task*, Berlin, Germany, August. Association for Computational Linguistics.

Zhongyi Li, Hai Zhao, Chenxi Pang, Lili Wang, and Huan Wang. 2016b. A constituent syntactic parse tree based discourse parser. In *Proceedings of the Twentieth Conference on Computational Natural Language Learning: Shared Task*, Berlin, Germany, August. Association for Computational Linguistics.

Percy Liang. 2005. *Semi-supervised learning for natural language*. Ph.D. thesis, Massachusetts Institute of Technology.

Ziheng Lin, Hwee Tou Ng, and Min-Yen Kan. 2014. A PDTB-styled end-to-end discourse parser. *Natural Language Engineering*, 20(2):151–184.

Jin Kiat Low, Hwee Tou Ng, and Wenyuan Guo. 2005. A maximum entropy approach to Chinese word segmentation. In *Proceedings of the Fourth SIGHAN Workshop on Chinese Language Processing*, pages 161–164.

William C Mann and Sandra A Thompson. 1988. Rhetorical Structure Theory: Toward a functional theory of text organization. *Text*, 8(3):243–281.

Christopher D. Manning, Mihai Surdeanu, John Bauer, Jenny Finkel, Steven J. Bethard, and David McClosky. 2014. The Stanford CoreNLP natural language processing toolkit. In *Proceedings of the 52nd Annual Meeting of the Association for Computational Linguistics*.

Todor Mihaylov and Annette Frank. 2016. Discourse relation sense classification using cross-argument semantic similarity based on word embeddings. In *Proceedings of the Twentieth Conference on Computational Natural Language Learning: Shared Task*, Berlin, Germany, August. Association for Computational Linguistics.

Minh Nguyen. 2016. Sdp-jaist: A shallow discourse parsing system conll 2016 shared task. In *Proceedings of the Twentieth Conference on Computational Natural Language Learning: Shared Task*, Berlin, Germany, August. Association for Computational Linguistics.

Stephan Oepen, Jonathon Read, Tatjana Scheffler, Uladzimir Sidarenka, Manfred Stede, Eric Velldal, and Lilja Ovrelid. 2016. Opt: Oslo-potsdam-teesside. pipelining rules, rankers, and classifier ensembles for shallow discourse parsing. In *Proceedings of the Twentieth Conference on Computational Natural Language Learning: Shared Task*, Berlin, Germany, August. Association for Computational Linguistics.

Maria Leonor Pacheco, I-Ta Lee Lee, Xiao Zhang, Abdullah Khan Zehady, Pranjal Daga, Di Jin, Ayush Parolia, and Dan Goldwasser. 2016. Adapting event embedding for implicit discourse relation recognition. In *Proceedings of the Twentieth Conference on Computational Natural Language Learning: Shared Task*, Berlin, Germany, August. Association for Computational Linguistics.

Slav Petrov and Dan Klein. 2007. Improved inferencing for unlexicalized parsing. In *Proceedings of the Human Language Technology/North American Chapter of the Association for Computational Linguistics*.

Emily Pitler, Annie Louis, and Ani Nenkova. 2009. Automatic sense prediction for implicit discourse relations in text. In *Proceedings of the Joint Conference of the 47th Annual Meeting of the ACL and the 4th International Joint Conference on Natural Language Processing of the AFNLP*.

Martin Potthast, Tim Gollub, Francisco Rangel, Paolo Rosso, Efstathios Stamatatos, and Benno Stein. 2014. Improving the Reproducibility of PAN's Shared Tasks: Plagiarism Detection, Author Identification, and Author Profiling. In Evangelos Kanoulas, Mihai Lupu, Paul Clough, Mark Sanderson, Mark Hall, Allan Hanbury, and Elaine Toms, editors, *Information Access Evaluation meets Multilinguality, Multimodality, and Visualization. 5th International Conference of the CLEF Initiative (CLEF 14)*, pages 268–299, Berlin Heidelberg New York, September. Springer.

Rashmi Prasad, Nikhil Dinesh, Alan Lee, Eleni Miltsakaki, Livio Robaldo, Aravind Joshi, and Bonnie Webber. 2008. The Penn Discourse Treebank 2.0. In *Proceedings of the 6th International Conference on Language Resources and Evaluation*.

Rashmi Prasad, Bonnie Webber, and Aravind Joshi. 2014. Reflections on the Penn Discourse Treebank, comparable corpora, and complementary annotation. *Computational Linguistics*, 40(4):921–950.

Lianhui Qin, Zhisong Zhang, and Hai Zhao. 2016. Shallow discourse parsing using convolutional neural network. In *Proceedings of the Twentieth Conference on Computational Natural Language Learning: Shared Task*, Berlin, Germany, August. Association for Computational Linguistics.

Attapol Rutherford and Nianwen Xue. 2014. Discovering implicit discourse relations through Brown cluster pair representation and coreference patterns. In *Proceedings of the 14th Conference of the European Chapter of the Association for Computational Linguistics*.

Attapol T. Rutherford and Nianwen Xue. 2016. Robust non-explicit neural discourse parser in english and chinese. In *Proceedings of the Twentieth Conference on Computational Natural Language Learning: Shared Task*, Berlin, Germany, August. Association for Computational Linguistics.

Niko Schenk, Christian Chiarcos, Kathrin Donandt, Samuel Samuel Rönnqvist, Evgeny Stepanov, and Giuseppe Riccardi. 2016. Do we really need all those rich linguistic features?

a neural network-based approach to implicit sense labeling. In *Proceedings of the Twentieth Conference on Computational Natural Language Learning: Shared Task*, Berlin, Germany, August. Association for Computational Linguistics.

Evgeny Stepanov and Giuseppe Riccardi. 2016. Unitn end-to-end discourse parser for conll 2016 shared task. In *Proceedings of the Twentieth Conference on Computational Natural Language Learning: Shared Task*, Berlin, Germany, August. Association for Computational Linguistics.

Jianxiang Wang and Man Lan. 2015. A refined end-to-end discourse parser. In *Proceedings of the Nineteenth Conference on Computational Natural Language Learning: Shared Task*.

Jianxiang Wang and Man Lan. 2016. Two end-to-end shallow discourse parsers for english and chinese in conll-2016 shared task. In *Proceedings of the Twentieth Conference on Computational Natural Language Learning: Shared Task*, Berlin, Germany, August. Association for Computational Linguistics.

Zhiguo Wang and Nianwen Xue. 2014. Joint pos tagging and transition-based constituent parsing in chinese with non-local features. In *ACL (1)*, pages 733–742.

Gregor Weiss and Marco Bajec. 2016. Discourse sense classification from scratch using focused rnns. In *Proceedings of the Twentieth Conference on Computational Natural Language Learning: Shared Task*, Berlin, Germany, August. Association for Computational Linguistics.

Naiwen Xue, Fei Xia, Fu-Dong Chiou, and Marta Palmer. 2005. The penn chinese treebank: Phrase structure annotation of a large corpus. *Natural language engineering*, 11(02):207–238.

Nianwen Xue, Hwee Tou Ng, Sameer Pradhan, Rashmi Prasad, Christopher Bryant, and Attapol Rutherford. 2015. The CoNLL-2015 shared task on shallow discourse parsing. In *Proceedings of the Nineteenth Conference on Computational Natural Language Learning: Shared Task*.

Yuping Zhou and Nianwen Xue. 2012. PDTB-style annotation of Chinese text. In *Proceedings of the 50th Annual Meeting of the Association for Computational Linguistics*.

Yuping Zhou and Nianwen Xue. 2015. The chinese discourse treebank: a chinese corpus annotated with discourse relations. *Language Resources and Evaluation*, 49(2):397–431.

OPT: Oslo–Potsdam–Teesside
Pipelining Rules, Rankers, and Classifier Ensembles
for Shallow Discourse Parsing

Stephan Oepen♣, Jonathon Read♠, Tatjana Scheffler♡, Uladzimir Sidarenka♡◇,
Manfred Stede♡, Erik Velldal♣. and Lilja Øvrelid♣

♣ University of Oslo, Department of Informatics
♠ Teesside University, School of Computing
♡ University of Potsdam, FSP Cognitive Science
◇ Retresco GmbH

Abstract

The OPT submission to the Shared Task of the 2016 Conference on Natural Language Learning (CoNLL) implements a 'classic' pipeline architecture, combining binary classification of (candidate) explicit connectives, heuristic rules for non-explicit discourse relations, ranking and 'editing' of syntactic constituents for argument identification, and an ensemble of classifiers to assign discourse senses. With an end-to-end performance of 27.77 F_1 on the English 'blind' test data, our system advances the previous state of the art (Wang & Lan, 2015) by close to four F_1 points, with particularly good results for the argument identification sub-tasks.

1 Introduction

Being able to recognize aspects of discourse structure has recently been shown to be relevant for tasks as diverse as machine translation, question-answering, text summarization, and sentiment analysis. For many of these applications, a 'shallow' approach as embodied in the PDTB can be effective. It is shallow in the sense of making only very few commitments to an overall account of discourse structure and of having annotation decisions concentrate on the individual instances of discourse relations, rather than on their interactions.

Previous work on this task has usually broken it down into a set of sub-problems, which are solved in a pipeline architecture (roughly: identify connectives, then arguments, then discourse senses; Lin et al., 2014). While adopting a similar pipeline approach, the OPT discourse parser also builds on and extends a method that has previously achieved state-of-the-art results for the detection of speculation and negation (Velldal et al., 2012; Read

et al., 2012). It is interesting to observe that an abstractly similar pipeline—disambiguating trigger expressions and then resolving their in-text 'scope'—yields strong performance across linguistically diverse tasks. At the same time, the original system has been substantially augmented for discourse parsing as outlined below. There is no closely corresponding sub-problem to assigning discourse senses in the analysis of negation and speculation; thus, our sense classifier described has been developed specifically for OPT.

2 System Architecture

Our system overview is shown in Figure 1. The individual modules interface through JSON files which resemble the desired output files of the Task. Each module adds the information specified for it. We will describe them here in thematic blocks, while the exact order of the modules can be seen in the figure. Relation identification (§3) includes the detection of explicit discourse connectives and the stipulation of non-explicit relations. Our argument identification module (§4) contains separate subclassifiers for a range of argument types and is invoked separately for explicit and non-explicit relations. Likewise, the sense classification module (§5) employs separate ensemble classifiers for explicit and non-explicit relations.

3 Relation Identification

Explicit Connectives Our classifier for detecting explicit discourse connectives extends the work by Velldal et al. (2012) for identifying expressions of speculation and negation. The approach treats the set of connectives observed in the training data as a closed class, and 'only' attempts to disambiguate occurrences of these token sequences in new data. Connectives can be single- or multi-token sequences (e.g. 'as' vs. 'as long as'). In cases

Proceedings of the 54th Annual Meeting of the Association for Computational Linguistics, pages 20–26,
Berlin, Germany, August 7-12, 2016. ©2016 Association for Computational Linguistics

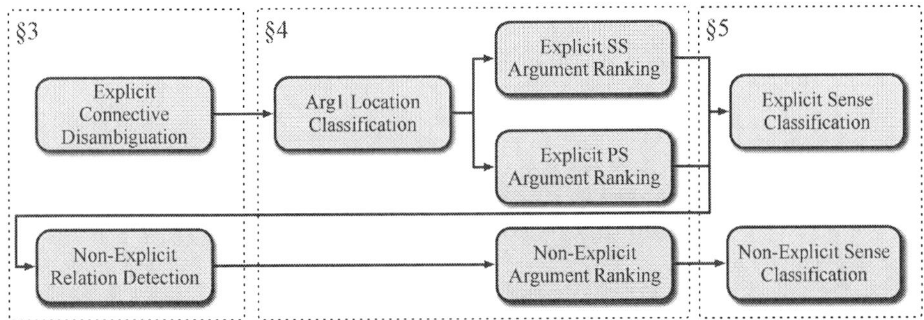

Figure 1: OPT system overview: Dotted boxes indicate sections that describe particular components.

of overlapping connective candidates, OPT deterministically chooses the longest sequence. The Shared Task defines a notion of *heads* in complex connectives, for example just the final token in 'shortly after'. As evaluation is in terms of matching connective heads only, these are the unit of disambiguation in OPT. Disambiguation is performed as point-wise ('per-connective') classification using the support vector machine implementation of the SVM^{light} toolkit (Joachims, 1999). Tuning of feature configurations and the error-to-margin cost parameter (C) was performed by ten-fold cross validation on the Task training set.

The connective classifier builds on two groups of feature templates: (a) the generic, surface-oriented ones defined by Velldal et al. (2012) and (b) the more targeted, discourse-specific features of Pitler & Nenkova (2009), Lin ct al. (2014), and Wang & Lan (2015). Of these, group (a) comprises n-grams of downcased surface forms and parts of speech for up to five token positions preceding and following the connective; and group (b) draws heavily on syntactic configurations extracted from the phrase structure parses provided with the Task data. During system development, a few thousand distinct combinations of features were evaluated, including variable levels of feature conjunction (called interaction features by Pitler & Nenkova, 2009) within each group. These experiments suggest that there is substantial overlap between the utility of the various feature templates, and n-gram window size can to a certain degree be traded off with richer syntactic features. Many distinct configurations yield near-identical performance in cross-validation on the training data, and we selected our final model by (a) giving preference to configurations with smaller numbers of features and lower variance across folds and (b) additionally evaluating a dozen

candidate configurations against the development data. The model used in the system submission includes n-grams of up to three preceding and following positions, full feature conjunction for the 'self' and 'parent' categories of Pitler & Nenkova (2009), but limited conjunctions involving their 'left' and 'right' sibling categories, and none of the 'connected context' features suggested by Wang & Lan (2015). This model has some 1.2 million feature types.

Non-Explicit Relations   According to the PDTB guidelines, non-explicit relations must be stipulated between each pair of sentences iff four conditions hold: two sentences (a) are adjacent; (b) are located in the same paragraph; and (c) are not yet 'connected' by an explicit connective; and (d) a coherence relation can be inferred or an entity-based relation holds between them. We proceed straightforwardly: We traverse the sentence bigrams, following condition (a). Paragraph boundaries are detected based on character offsets in the input text (b). We compute a list of already 'connected' first sentences in sentence bigrams, extracting all the previously detected explicit connectives whose Arg1 is located in the 'previous sentence' (PS; see §4). If the first sentence in a candidate bigram is not yet 'connected' (c), we posit a non-explicit relation for the bigram. Condition (d) is ignored, since NoRel annotations are extremely rare and EntRel vs. Implicit relations are disambiguated in the downstream sense module (§5). We currently do not attempt to recover the AltLex instances, because they are relatively infrequent and there is a high chance for false positives.

4   Argument Identification

Our approach to argument identification is rooted in previous work on resolving the scope of spec-

	Explicit		Non-Explicit	
	Arg1	**Arg2**	**Arg1**	**Arg2**
Ambiguity	3.4	4.6	3.1	3.2
Sentence spanning	.033	.070	.021	.015
Non-SS/PS Arg1	.116		.047	
Align. w/o edits	.483	.535	.870	.900
Align. with edits	.813	.840	.882	.900
Upper-bound	.692	.781	.822	.887

Table 1: Observations of arguments in the training data. Alignment rates are with respect to all arguments that do not span sentence boundaries and are located in SS or PS, while the upper-bound is with respect to all arguments.

	Exp. PS		Exp. SS		Non-Exp.	
	Arg1	**Arg2**	**Arg1**	**Arg2**	**Arg1**	**Arg2**
Connective Form			•			
Connective Category		•				
Connective Precedes				•		
Following Token				•		
Initial Token					•	
Path to Root		•	•		•	•
Path to Connective		•	•	•		
Path to Initial Token					•	•
Preceding Token		•	•		•	•
Production Rules	•	•			•	•
Size						•

Table 2: Feature types used to describe candidate constituents for argument ranking.

ulation and negation, in particular work by Read et al. (2012): We generate candidate arguments by selecting constituents from a sentence parse tree, apply an automatically-learned ranking function to discriminate between candidates, and use the predicted constituent's surface projection to determine the extent of an argument. Like for explicit connective identification, all classifiers trained for argument identification use the SVM^{light} toolkit and are tuned by ten-fold cross-validation against the training set.

Predicting Arg1 Location For non-explicit relations we make the simplifying assumption that Arg1 occurs in the sentence immediately preceding that of Arg2 (PS). However, the Arg1s of explicit relations frequently occur in the same sentence (SS), so, following Wang & Lan (2015), we attempt to learn a classification function to predict whether these are in SS or PS. Considering all features proposed by Wang & Lan, but under cross-validation on the training set, we found that the significantly informative features were limited to: the connective form, the syntactic path from connective to root, the connective position in sentence (tertiles), and a bigram of the connective and following token part-of-speech.

Candidate Generation and Ranking Candidates are limited to clausal constituents as these account for the majority of arguments, offering substantial coverage while restricting the ambiguity (i.e., the mean number of candidates per argument; see Table 1). Candidates whose projection corresponds to the true extent of the argument are labeled as correct; others are labeled as incorrect.

We experimented with various feature types to describe candidates, using the implementation of ordinal ranking in SVM^{light} (Joachims, 2002). These types comprise both the candidate's surface projection (including: bigrams of tokens in candidate, connective, connective category (Knott, 1996), connective part-of-speech, connective precedes the candidate, connective position in sentence, initial token of candidate, final token of candidate, size of candidate projection relative to the sentence, token immediately following the candidate, token immediately preceding the candidate, tokens in candidate, and verbs in candidate) and the candidate's position in the sentence's parse tree (including: path to connective, path to connective via root, path to initial token, path to root, path between initial and preceding tokens, path between final and following tokens, and production rules of the candidate subtree).

An exhaustive search of all permutations of the above feature types requires significant resources. Instead we iteratively build a pool of feature types, at each stage assessing the contribution of each feature type when added to the pool, and only add a feature type if its contribution is statistically significant (using a Wilcoxon signed-rank test, $p < .05$). The most informative feature types thus selected are syntactic in nature, with a small but significant contribution from surface features. Table 2 lists the specific feature types found to be optimal for each particular type of argument.

Constituent Editing Our approach to argument identification is based on the assumption that arguments correspond to syntactically meaningful units, more specifically we require arguments to be clausal constituents (S/SBAR/SQ). In order to test this assumption, we quantify the alignment of arguments with constituents in `en.train`, see Table 1. We find that the initial alignment (Align w/o edits) is rather low, in particular for Explicit arguments (.48 for `Arg1` and .54 for `Arg2`). We therefore formulate a set of *constituent editing* heuristics, designed to improve on this alignment by including or removing certain elements from the candidate constituent. We apply the following heuristics, with conditions by argument type (`Arg1` vs. `Arg2`), connective type (explicit vs. non-explicit) and position (SS vs. PS) in parentheses.

- add conjunction (CC) preceding constituent (`Arg1`)

- cut clause headed by connective (`Arg1`, explicit, SS)

- cut constituent-final CC (`Arg1`)

- cut constituent-final wh-determiner (`Arg1`)

- cut constituent-initial CC (`Arg2`, explicit)

- cut relative clause, i.e. SBAR initiated by WHNP/WHADVP

- cut connective

- cut initial and final punctuation

Following editing, the alignment of arguments with the edited constituents improves considerably for explicit `Arg1`s (.81) and `Arg2`s (.84), see Table 1.

Limitations The assumptions of our approach mean that the system upper-bound is limited in three respects. Firstly, some arguments span sentence boundaries (see Sent. Span in Table 1) meaning there can be no single aligned constituent. Secondly, not all arguments correspond with clausal constituents (approximately 1.7% of arguments in `en.train` align with a constituent of some other type). Finally, as reported in Table 1, several `Arg1`s occur in neither the same sentence nor the immediately preceding sentence. Table 1 provides system upper-bounds taking each of these limitations into account.

5 Relation Sense Classification

In order to assign senses to the predicted relations, we apply an ensemble-classification approach. In particular, we use two separate groups of classifiers: one group for predicting the senses of explicit relations and another one for analyzing the senses of non-explicit relations. Each of these groups comprises the same types of predictors (presented below) but uses different feature sets.

Majority Class Senser The first classifier included in both of our ensembles is a simplistic system which, given an input connective (`none` for non-explicit relations), returns a vector of conditional probabilities of its senses computed on the training data.

W&L$_{\text{LSVC}}$ Another prediction module is a reimplementation of the Wang & Lan (2015) system—the winner of the previous iteration of the ConNLL Shared Task on shallow discourse parsing. In contrast to the original version, however, which relies on the Maximum Entropy classifier for predicting the senses of explicit relations and utilizes the Naïve Bayes approach for classifying the senses of the non-explicit ones, both of our components (explicit and non-explicit) use the `LIBLINEAR` system (Fan et al., 2008)—a speed-optimized SVM (Boser et al., 1992) with linear kernel. In our derived classifier, we adopt all features[1] of the original implementation up to the Brown clusters, where instead of taking the differences and intersections of the clusters from both arguments, we use the Cartesian product (CP) of the Brown groups similarly to the token-CP features of the UniTN system from last year (Stepanov et al., 2015). Additionally, in order to reduce the number of possible CP attributes, we take the set of 1,000 clusters provided by the organizers of the Task instead of differentiating between 3,200 Brown groups as was done originally by Wang & Lan (2015).

Unlike the upstream modules in our pipeline, whose model parameters are tuned by 10-fold cross-validation on the training set, the hyper-parameters of the sense classifiers are tweaked towards the development set, while using the entire training data for computing the feature weights. This decision is motivated by the wish to harness the full range of the training set, since the number of the target classes to predict is much bigger than in the preceding sub-tasks and because some of the senses, e.g. Expansion.Exception, only appear a dozen of times in the provided dataset. For training the final system, we use the Crammer-Singer multi-class strategy (Crammer & Singer, 2001) with $L2$-loss,

---

[1]A detailed description of these features can be found in the original paper by Wang & Lan (2015) and their code posted on github: `https://github.com/lanmanok/conll2015_discourse`.

| | WSJ Test Set | | | | | Blind Test Set | | | | |
| | 2015 | 2016 | | OPT | | 2015 | 2016 | | OPT | |
	F_1	F_1	P	R	F_1	F_1	F_1	P	R	F_1
Explicit Connectives	94.8	**98.9**	96.4	92.5	94.4	91.9	**98.4**	93.5	90.1	91.8
Explicit Arg1 Extraction	50.7	**53.8**	53.1	50.9	52.0	49.7	52.4	53.4	51.5	**52.4**
Explicit Arg2 Extraction	**77.4**	76.7	74.1	71.1	72.6	74.3	75.2	76.6	73.8	**75.2**
Explicit Both Extraction	45.2	**45.3**	44.9	43.0	43.9	41.4	44.0	44.9	43.2	**44.0**
Explicit Sense Micro-Average			38.6	40.2	39.4			33.9	35.1	34.5
Non-Explicit Arg1 Extraction	67.2	69.9	72.0	68.0	**69.9**	60.9	**66.8**	63.7	65.5	64.6
Non-Explicit Arg2 Extraction	68.4	71.5	73.5	69.5	**71.5**	74.6	**79.1**	75.3	77.5	76.4
Non-Explicit Both Extraction	53.1	53.5	55.0	52.0	**53.5**	50.4	**58.1**	51.3	52.8	52.0
Non-Explicit Sense Micro-Average			17.5	18.6	18.0			22.0	21.6	21.9
All Both Extraction	49.4	**49.6**	50.2	47.8	48.9	46.4	**50.6**	48.3	48.1	48.2
Overall Parser Performance	29.7	**30.7**	27.5	28.9	28.2	24.0	27.8	27.8	27.8	**27.8**

Table 3: Per-component breakdown of system performance, compared to top performers in 2015/16.

optimizing the primal objective and setting the error penalty term C to 0.3.

W&L$_{\text{XGBoost}}$ Even though linear SVM systems achieve competitive results on many important classification tasks, these systems can still experience difficulties with discerning instances that are not separable by a hyperplane. In order to circumvent this problem, we use a third type of classifier in our ensembles—a forest of decision trees learned by gradient boosting (XGBoost; Friedman, 2000). For this part, we take the same set of features as in the previous component and optimize the hyperparameters of this module on the development set as described previously. In particular, we set the maximum tree depth to 3 and take 300 tree estimators for the complete forest.

Prediction Merging To compute the final predictions, we first obtain vectors of the estimated sense probabilities for each input instance from the three classifiers in the respective ensemble and then sum up these vectors, choosing the sense with the highest final score. More formally, we compute the prediction label $\hat{y}_i$ for the input instance x_i as $\hat{y}_i = \arg\max \sum_{j=1}^{n} \vec{v}_j$, where n is the number of classifiers in the ensemble (in our case three), and $\vec{v}_j$ denotes the output probability vector of the j-th predictor. Since the XGBoost implementation we use, however, can only return classifications without actual probability estimates, we obtain a probability vector for this component by assigning the score $1 - \epsilon$ to the predicted sense class (with the ϵ-term determined on the development and set to 0.1) and uniformly distributing the ϵ-weight among the remaining senses.

6   Experimental Results

Overall Results Table 3 summarizes OPT system performance in terms of the metrics computed by the official scorer for the Shared Task, against both the WSJ and 'blind' test sets. To compare against the previous state of the art, we include results for the top-performing systems from the 2015 and 2016 competitions (as reported by Xue et al., 2015, and Xue et al., 2016, respectively). Where applicable, best results (when comparing F_1) are highlighted for each sub-task and -metric. The highlighting makes it evident that the OPT system is competitive to the state of the art across the board, but particularly so on the argument identification sub-task and on the 'blind' test data: In terms of the WSJ test data, OPT would have ranked second in the 2015 competition, but on the 'blind' data it outperforms the previous state of the art on all but one metric for which contrastive results are provided by Xue et al.. Where earlier systems tend to drop by several F_1 points when evaluated on the non-WSJ data, this 'out-of-domain' effect is much smaller for OPT. For comparison, we also include the top scores for each submodule achieved by any system in the 2016 Shared Task.

Non-Explicit Relations In isolation, the stipulation of non-explicit relations achieves an F_1 of 93.2 on the WSJ test set ($P = 89.9$, $R = 96.8$). Since this sub-module does not specify full argument spans, we match gold and predicted relations based on the sentence identifiers of the arguments only. False positives include NoRel and missing relations. About half of the false negatives are relations within the same sentence (across a semicolon).

	WSJ Test Set			Blind Set		
	Arg1	Arg2	Both	Arg1	Arg2	Both
Explicit (SS)	.683	.817	.590	.647	.783	.519
Explicit (PS)	.623	.663	.462	.611	.832	.505
Explicit (All)	.572	.753	.474	.586	.782	.473
Non-explicit (All)	.744	.743	.593	.640	.758	.539
Overall	.668	.749	.536	.617	.769	.509

Table 4: Isolated argument extraction results (PS refers to the immediately preceding sentence only).

System	WSJ Test Set			Blind Set		
	Exp	Non-Exp	All	Exp	Non-Exp	All
2015	**90.79**	34.45	61.27	76.44	**36.29**	**54.76**
Majority	89.30	21.40	54.02	75.91	30.46	51.39
W&L$_{\mathrm{LSVC}}$	89.63	**37.18**	**62.29**	**77.86**	33.05	53.66
W&L$_{\mathrm{XGB}}$	89.41	34.12	60.64	76.27	34.42	53.62
OPT	89.95	33.53	60.64	76.81	33.66	53.54
LSTM*	89.90	33.76	60.78	77.63	33.69	53.29
OPT*	90.01	**41.12**	**64.70**	77.06	**37.20**	**55.55**

Table 5: Isolated results for sense classification (the bottom* model was not part of the submission).

Arguments Table 4 reports the isolated performance for argument identification. Most results are consistent across types of arguments, the two data sets, and the upper-bound estimates in Table 1, with Arg1 harder to identify than Arg2. However an anomaly is the extraction of Arg2 in explicit relations where the Arg1 is in the immediately preceding sentence, which is poor in the WSJ Test Set but better in the blind set. This may be due to variance in the number of PS Arg1s in the respective sets, but will be investigated further in future work on error analysis.

Sense Classification The results of the sense classification subtask without error propagation are shown in Table 5. As can be seen from the table, the LIBLINEAR reimplementation of the Wang & Lan system was the strongest component in our ensemble, outperforming the best results on the WSJ test set from the previous year by 0.89 F_1. The XGBoost variant of that module typically achieved the second best scores, being slightly better at predicting the sense of non-explicit relations on the blind test set. The majority class predictor is the least competitive part, which, however, is made up for by the simplicity of the model and its relative robustness to unseen data.

Finally, we report on a system variant that was not part of the official OPT submission, shown in the bottom rows of Table 5.

In this configuration, we added more features (types of modal verbs in the arguments, occurrence of negation, as well as the form and part-of-speech tag of the word immediately following the connective) to the W&L-based classifier of explicit relations, re-adjusting the hyper-parameters of this model afterwards; increased the ϵ-term of the XGBoost component from 0.1 to 0.5; and, finally, replaced the majority class predictor with a neural LSTM model (Hochreiter & Schmidhuber, 1997),

using the provided Word2Vec embeddings as input. This ongoing work shows clear promise for substantive improvements in sense classification.

7   Conclusion & Outlook

The most innovative aspect of this work, arguably, is our adaptation of constituent ranking and editing from negation and speculation analysis to the sub-task of argument identification in discourse parsing. Premium performance (relatively speaking, comparing to the previous state of the art) on this sub-problem is in no small part the reason for overall competitive performance of the OPT system, despite its relatively simplistic architecture. The constituent ranker (and to some degree also the 'targeted' features in connective disambiguation) embodies a strong commitment to syntactic analysis as a prerequisite to discourse parsing. This is an interesting observation, in that it (a) confirms tight interdependencies between intra- and inter-utterance analysis and (b) offers hope that higher-quality syntactic analysis should translate into improved discourse parsing. We plan to investigate these connections through in-depth error analysis and follow-up experimentation with additional syntactic parsers and types of representations. Another noteworthy property of our OPT system submission appears to be its relative resilience to minor differences in text type between the WSJ and 'blind' test data. We attribute this behavior at least in part to methodological choices made in parameter tuning, in particular cross-validation over the training data—yielding more reliable estimates of system performance than tuning against the much smaller development set—and selective, step-wise inclusion of features in model development.

Acknowledgments

We are indebted to Te Rutherford of Brandeis University for his effort in preparing data and infrastructure for the Task, as well as for shepherding our team and everyone else through its various stages. We are grateful to two anonymous reviewers for comments on an earlier version of this manuscript.

References

Boser, B. E., Guyon, I., & Vapnik, V. (1992). A training algorithm for optimal margin classifiers. In *Proceedings of the Fifth Annual ACM Conference on Computational Learning Theory* (p. 144–152). Pittsburgh, PA, USA.

Crammer, K., & Singer, Y. (2001). On the algorithmic implementation of multiclass kernel-based vector machines. *Journal of Machine Learning Research, 2*, 265–292.

Fan, R., Chang, K., Hsieh, C., Wang, X., & Lin, C. (2008). LIBLINEAR. A library for large linear classification. *Journal of Machine Learning Research, 9*, 1871–1874.

Friedman, J. H. (2000). Greedy function approximation. A gradient boosting machine. *Annals of Statistics, 29*, 1189–1232.

Hochreiter, S., & Schmidhuber, J. (1997). Long short-term memory. *Neural Computation, 9*(8), 1735–1780.

Joachims, T. (1999). Making large-scale SVM learning practical. In B. Schölkopf, C. Burges, & A. Smola (Eds.), *Advances in kernel methods. Support vector learning.* Cambridge, MA, USA: MIT Press.

Joachims, T. (2002). Optimizing search engines using clickthrough data. In *Proceedings of the 8th ACM SIGKDD International Conference on Knowledge Discovery and Data Mining* (p. 133–142). Edmonton, Canada.

Knott, A. (1996). *A data-driven methodology for motivating a set of coherence relations.* Unpublished doctoral dissertation, University of Edinburgh.

Lin, Z., Ng, H. T., & Kan, M.-Y. (2014). A PDTB-styled end-to-end discourse parser. *Natural Language Engineering, 20*(2), 151–184.

Pitler, E., & Nenkova, A. (2009). Using syntax to disambiguate explicit discourse connectives in text. In *Proceedings of the 47th Meeting of the Association for Computational Linguistics* (p. 13–16). Singapore.

Read, J., Velldal, E., Øvrelid, L., & Oepen, S. (2012). UiO1. Constituent-based discriminative ranking for negation resolution. In *Proceedings of the 1st Joint Conference on Lexical and Computational Semantics* (p. 310–318). Montréal, Canada.

Stepanov, E. A., Riccardi, G., & Bayer, A. O. (2015). The UniTN discourse parser in CoNLL 2015 Shared Task. Token-level sequence labeling with argument-specific models. In *Proceedings of the 19th Conference on Natural Language Learning* (p. 25–31). Bejing, China.

Velldal, E., Øvrelid, L., Read, J., & Oepen, S. (2012). Speculation and negation: Rules, rankers and the role of syntax. *Computational Linguistics, 38*(2), 369–410.

Wang, J., & Lan, M. (2015). A refined end-to-end discourse parser. In *Proceedings of the 19th Conference on Natural Language Learning* (p. 17–24). Bejing, China.

Xue, N., Ng, H. T., Pradhan, S., Prasad, R., Bryant, C., & Rutherford, A. (2015). The CoNLL-2015 shared task on shallow discourse parsing. In *Proceedings of the 19th Conference on Natural Language Learning: Shared task* (p. 1–16). Bejing, China.

Xue, N., Ng, H. T., Pradhan, S., Webber, B., Rutherford, A., Wang, C., & Wang, H. (2016). The CoNLL-2016 shared task on multilingual shallow discourse parsing. In *Proceedings of the 20th Conference on Natural Language Learning: Shared task.* Berlin, Germany.

An End-to-End Chinese Discourse Parser
with Adaptation to Explicit and Non-explicit Relation Recognition

Xiaomian Kang[1,2]**, Haoran Li**[1,2]**, Long Zhou**[1,2]**, Jiajun Zhang**[1,2]**, Chengqing Zong**[1,2,3]
[1]National Laboratory of Pattern Recognition,
Institute of Automation, Chinese Academy of Sciences
[2]The University of Chinese Academy of Sciences, Beijing, China
[3]CAS Center for Excellence in Brain Science and Intelligence Technology
`{xiaomian.kang,haoran.li,jjzhang,cqzong}@nlpr.ia.ac.cn`

Abstract

This paper describes our end-to-end discourse parser in the CoNLL-2016 Shared Task on Chinese Shallow Discourse Parsing. To adapt to the characteristics of Chinese, we implement a uniform framework for both explicit and non-explicit relation parsing. In this framework, we are the first to utilize a seed-expansion approach for the argument extraction subtask. In the official evaluation, our system achieves an F1 score of 26.90% in overall performance on the blind test set.

1 Introduction

Discourse parser analyzes the relations underlying text units to uncover abstractive structure information, which has a wide usage in different tasks in natural language processing, such as text summarization, question answering, information extraction and machine translation.

Since the release of the Penn Discourse Tree-Bank (PDTB) (Prasad et al., 2008), discourse parsing has drawn more and more attention. The PDTB-style parser puts emphasis on shallow discourse parsing, which annotates a piece of text with a set of discourse relations. The relations are divided into two types, explicit or non-explicit, depending on whether connectives exist or not. A complete discourse relation contains two discourse units called Argument1 (Arg1) and Argument2 (Arg2). An end-to-end parser usually consists of some components, such as discourse connective identification, argument extraction, explicit sense classification and implicit sense classification.

Pitler and Nenkova (2009) used syntactic features to disambiguate explicit discourse connectives. For argument extraction, Lin et al. (2014) used a tree subtraction algorithm to extract arguments and Kong et al. (2014) proposed a constituent-based approach to solve it. Recent researches mainly focus on the implicit sense classification. In this subtask, Lin et al. (2009) and Rutherford and Xue (2014) explored rich features such as word-pairs, dependency rules, production rules and Brown cluster pairs. Some studies (Rutherford and Xue, 2015) paid attention to the data expansion. Neural network approaches (Ji and Eisenstein, 2015; Zhang et al., 2015) were also applied to improve the classification performance. Lin et al. (2014) implemented a full end-to-end PDTB parser and Wang and Lan (2015) built a more refined system in the CoNLL-2015 Shared Task.

In contrast to English, there are limited studies on Chinese discourse parsing (Huang and Chen, 2011; Zong, 2013; Tu et al., 2014). One of the main reasons is the shortage of Chinese discourse corpus. Zhou and Xue (2012) annotated a PDTB-style Chinese Discourse TreeBank (CDTB), which is the data for Chinese shallow discourse parsing.

In this paper, we describe our approaches to implement the Chinese shallow discourse parser which is participated in the CoNLL-2016 Shared Task (Xue et al., 2016). In view of some typical characteristics in CDTB (Section 2), we adopt and extend the state-of-the-art English parser in CoNLL-2015 (Wang and Lan, 2015). A unified framework for both explicit and non-explicit parsing is built and a seed-expansion approach is utilized for argument extraction. Some useful features are selected to train classifiers (Section 3). Our system achieves 40.89% and 26.90% in F1-measure on the test and blind data set respectively (Section 4).

We make the following main contributions in this work:

- We implement a complete end-to-end PDTB-style discourse parser for Chinese.

- We design a uniform framework to recog-

27

Proceedings of the 54th Annual Meeting of the Association for Computational Linguistics, pages 27–32,
Berlin, Germany, August 7-12, 2016. ©2016 Association for Computational Linguistics

nize both explicit and non-explicit relations together.

- We utilize an effective seed-expansion approach to determine the exact span boundaries in the argument extraction subtask.

2 Corpus and Resources

In addition to the PDTB-style annotation, there are many special phenomena in CDTB. We enumerate several characteristics in (Zhou and Xue, 2015) and phenomena from the training data set.

- In contrast to the 54.53% in PDTB, the proportion of non-explicit relations is 78.27% in CDTB training set. PDTB's three-level sense hierarchy structure is replaced by 11 flat semantic types.

- Discourse connectives are flexible and the phenomenon of parallel connectives is obvious in Chinese. In our experiment, we extract 385 connectives from the training set as a connective dictionary.

- The span of an argument ranges from several words to sentences even to paragraphs. But in general, the span is in one sentence and the clauses split by punctuations can be regarded as the minimum constituent units.

- As shown in (Yang and Xue, 2012), punctuation marks play a significant role in Chinese discourse. Fortunately, CDTB has annotated those punctuations that may indicate discourse relations.

Inspired by the above phenomena, we design our system by fully considering these Chinese characteristics.

Besides the training data, we simply use skip-gram neural word embeddings provided by the CoNLL-2016 organizers to replace words in some features.

3 System Architecture

Zhou and Xue (2015) pointed out that discourse connectives and punctuation marks in Chinese can serve as anchors, which are clues of discourse relations. This opinion encourages us to treat explicit and non-explicit relations similarly. Therefore, the explicit and non-explicit parsers share the same

framework shown in figure 1. We divide the shallow discourse parsing into four subtasks: anchor identification, argument extraction, sense classification and argument relabeling

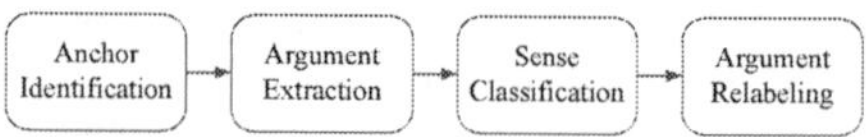

Figure 1: discourse parser framework

Anchor Identification. It is to recognize the anchors from candidates. For explicit parser, the connectives are important relation indicators. And the punctuations play the similar role in non-explicit parser.

Argument Extraction. It is to extract argument pair according to the anchor. We use a seed-expansion approach, transforming this subtask into argument boundary identification.

Sense Classification. It is to predict the type of relation sense between Arg1 and Arg2.

Argument Relabeling. It is to re-label the labels of two arguments. Although Arg1 is in front of Arg2 in most cases, the "Arg1" and "Arg2" labels for the argument pair are defined based on the semantics in CDTB (Zhou and Xue, 2012).

3.1 Anchor Identification

A full text is scanned to pick out the anchor candidate set. Then, a binary classifier is designed to check whether each candidate is anchor or not. The explicit connective candidate set is generated by matching the text with our connective dictionary. The non-explicit punctuation candidate set consists of all punctuations except for quotes, parentheses, and pause marks.

3.1.1 Connective Identification

A classifier is trained to recognize connectives. The features are chosen by referring to the best system in CoNLL-2015 (Wang and Lan, 2015). Zhou and Xue (2012) found that a discourse connective is almost always accompanied by punctuations, which help us to design the features.

The features we used are as follows:

- Lexical features: candidate itself, number of the candidate words, POS of the candidate, POS of the previous word, embeddings of the next three words, the previous word combined with the next word, location of the candidate in the sentence (start, middle, end), the previous/next punctuation, whether the previous or next character is punctuation.

- Syntactic features: the parent of candidate's node (the lowest node in the syntax tree that completely covers the candidate words), the left and right siblings of candidate's node, the production rules of candidate, the path from the candidate's node to root, whether the left sub-tree or right sub-tree contains VP or IP.

3.1.2 Punctuation Identification

According to their locations in sentences, punctuations are divided into two cases: MOS (middle of sentence) and EOS (end of sentence). In the 56.18% of non-explicit relations in the training data, Arg1 and Arg2 are in the same sentence. The anchor punctuation must be in the middle of the sentence in this case and we extract features from its left and right clauses. In another case that Arg1 and Arg2 is in different sentences, the anchor must be in the end of the sentence and we extract features from its left and right sentences. Since we cannot get the syntactic features from two different syntactic trees, the two classifiers' features are designed respectively.

MOS Punctuation Classification. By referring to (Yang and Xue, 2012; Xu et al., 2012), we extract features from the context clauses:

- Lexical features: embeddings of the first and last word in the context clauses, POS of the first and last word in the context clauses, punctuation itself.

- Syntactic features: the parent, left and right siblings of the punctuation's node, the left and right clause's node, the path from the punctuation's node to the right clause's node, whether the left sub-tree or the right sub-tree contains VP or IP, whether the leftmost sibling of punctuation's parent node is PP, the number of IP in siblings of the punctuation's parent node, whether the right sub-tree contains AD or CS if the leftmost sibling is IP.

EOS Punctuation Classification. We only use lexical features from the context sentences: punctuation itself, embeddings of the first and last three words in the context sentences, POS of the first and last three words in the context sentences.

3.2 Argument Extraction

Our approach is based on the following observations. It should be noted that "Arg1" and "Arg2" are defined by semantics rather than location. But for convenient expression, we temporarily name the front argument as "Arg1" and the following argument as "Arg2" before Argument Relabeling [1].

- *Observation* 1: In most cases, Arg1 and Arg2 are in the same sentence or two adjacent sentences respectively.

- *Observation* 2: An argument consists of one or several consecutive clauses.

- *Observation* 3: Explicit Arg2 is located in the same sentence as its connective anchor.

- *Observation* 4: The span of Arg1 and the span of Arg2 are adjacent. There is no clause between them.

The anchor can provide useful location information to determine the span of the argument especially in non-explicit relations. So after considering the special characteristics of argument pairs in CDTB, we utilize a seed-expansion approach to extract Arg1 and Arg2 based on the anchor. According to *Observation* 2, we regard the clauses as the minimum argument units. A seed is a clause which contains or adjoins the anchor. We think the seed must be in the argument and provides a good starting point for argument extraction.

The approach contains three steps: sentence scope determination, seed pair generation and seed expansion. Figure 2 shows the detailed process in explicit argument extraction to vividly explain the approach.

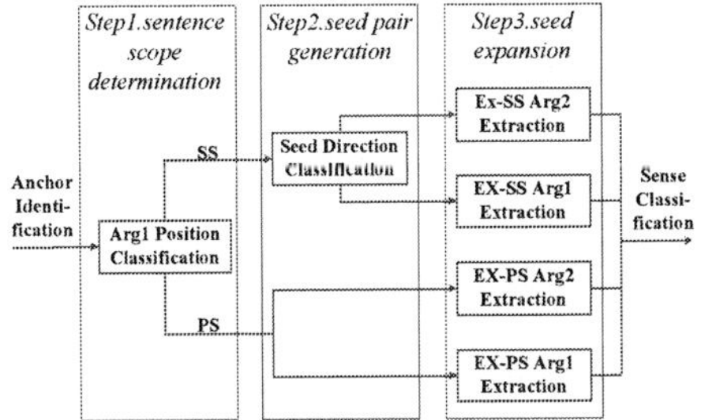

Figure 2: the explicit argument extraction process

---

[1] In Section 3.3, for convenience, we still temporarily name the "Arg1" and "Arg2" following the sequence order.

First, according to *Observation* 1, we determine the rough sentence-level scope of argument. Then according to *Observation* 4, we obtain a pair of adjacent clauses as the seed pair based on the anchor. Finally, we expand the seed clause-by-clause to obtain the argument pair.

3.2.1 Sentence Scope Determination

We determine the sentence scope of the argument in this step.

Explicit: *Observation* 3 has given the sentence scope of Arg2 in explicit relation. So we discuss the scope of Arg1. We divide the Arg1 into two cases: SS (Arg1 is in the same sentence as its connective anchor) and PS (Arg1 is in the previous sentence of the connective anchor). A classifier is trained to determine which case an Arg1 is.

For the Arg1 Position Classification, the features are about connective: connective itself, POS of the connective, the number of connective words, location of the connective in the sentence, whether the connective is in the first clause of the sentence, previous/next punctuation, the path from connective's parent node to root.

Non-Explicit: In Section 3.1.2, the punctuation anchors have been divided into MOS and EOS, respectively correspond to SS (Arg1 is in the same sentence as Arg2) and PS (Arg1 is in the previous sentence of the Arg2 sentence). So there is no need to take into account the sentence-level scope of non-explicit argument.

3.2.2 Seed Pair Generation

The seed pair is a pair of two adjacent clauses, which must be in Arg1 and Arg2 respectively.

Explicit: For SS case (Arg1 is in the same sentence as the connective), the current clause (clause contains the connective [2]) is a seed. Anther seed is the clause adjacent to the current. But when the current clause is in the middle of sentence, a question comes up: is anther seed the previous or the next clause? The Seed Direction Classification helps us to answer it.

The features are as follows: connective itself, POS of the connective, whether there are co-occurrence of nouns, verbs and quantifiers between current clause and previous/next clause, the

---

[2] If the connective is a parallel connective that spans clause boundaries, we regard these clauses as a whole current clause.

parent of previous/next clause's node, the punctuation between previous/next clause and current clause, the relationship of previous and current clause's node (left, right, middle, contain, none).

For PS case (Arg1 is in the previous sentence of the connective), there is no need to judge the seed direction. We directly take the last clause of the previous sentence as the front seed and the clause contains the connective as the following seed.

Non-Explicit: No matter where the location of the punctuation anchor, we treat the nearest left and right clauses of the punctuation as the seed pair.

3.2.3 Seed Expansion

After obtaining the seed pair, we expand the seed to grow into argument. The front seed expands forward and the following seed expands backward. We expand the span of argument clause-by-clause, from the seed clause, toward a fixed direction (forward or backward) in the sentence scope to generate candidate sets. So each candidate contains the seed clause. The current candidate has one clause more than the previous one. The classifiers decide whether the current candidate span is beyond of the argument boundary. We select the longest candidate predicted OK as the argument.

There are four cases totally: explicit SS, explicit PS, non-explicit SS and non-explicit PS. So we train eight classifiers for each case to extract Arg1 and Arg2 respectively. Each classifier uses the same feature template while Arg1 and Arg2 extraction have the opposite expansion direction. The features are as follows, and some are borrowed from (Lin et al., 2014; Wang and Lan, 2015).

- Lexical features are from the previous candidate and the current clause: embeddings of the first/last three words of them, POS of the first/last word of them, punctuations between them, whether there are co-occurrence of nouns/verbs between them, anchor itself.

- Syntactic features: the parent of anchor's node, the current clause's node and its left and right siblings, the current candidate's node and its parent, the path from previous candidate's node/seed clause's node to current clause's node, the relationship of current clause and the seed clause/previous candidate (left, right, middle, contain, none).

- Others: whether the current clause is the start/end of sentence, the relative length of current clause and seed clause/previous candidate (short, middle, long).

Through the above method, we can get the clause boundary of the argument pair. Finally, the post-processing is done: connectives and punctuations appear at the start or end of span are deleted.

3.3 Sense Classification

The sense of relation is decided after the anchor identification and argument extraction by a multi-class classifier.

Explicit: The huge contribution of discourse connectives to the explicit sense classification makes it possible that a small amount of features about connectives will produce good enough results.

- Lexical features: connective itself, POS of the connective, embedding of the connective, the previous and next punctuation of the connective.

- Syntactic features: the parent, left and right siblings of connective's node, the Arg1's node and Arg2's node, the parent of Arg1's node and Arg2's node, the relationship of Arg1's node and Arg2's node.

Non-Explicit: In this work, we decided to only use the production rules of Arg1, Arg2 and co-occurrence after trying other features in our experiments. We choose from all the production rules whose frequency is over 5 and finally select the 100 ones by calculating the information gain.

3.4 Argument Relabeling

This component is to re-label the argument labels. The features are listed as follows:

- Lexical features: anchor itself, POS of previous and next word of the anchor, location of the anchor in the sentence, whether there are co-occurrence of nouns, verbs and quantifiers between Arg1 and Arg2.

- Syntactic features are the same as the syntactic features in explicit sense classification (Section 3.3).

- Others: the relative length of Arg1 and Arg2, the relation sense.

4 Experiments and Results

Our end-to-end parser consists of 4 subtasks and 17 classifiers, trained on the corpora provided in the CoNLL-2016 Shared Task. All of the models are trained using the maximum entropy algorithm implemented in MALLET toolkit [3]. The system was evaluated on the TIRA evaluation platform (Potthast et al., 2014) on 3 data sets offered by CoNLL-2016: development set, test set and blind test set. Table 1 reported the official results of our parser.

	Task	Dev	Test	Blind
Explicit	*Conn*	0.8356	0.7263	0.5627
	Arg1	0.5479	0.5587	0.3853
	Arg2	0.6849	0.6816	0.4444
	Both	0.4521	0.4916	0.2650
	Sense	0.7534	0.6480	0.4811
	Parser	0.4521	0.4859	0.2446
Non-Explicit	*Conn*	–	–	–
	Arg1	0.6282	0.6266	0.5526
	Arg2	0.6798	0.6762	0.6017
	Both	0.5341	0.5379	0.4457
	Sense	0.5068	0.4987	0.4082
	Parser	0.3982	0.3869	0.2712
All	*Conn*	0.8356	0.7263	0.5627
	Arg1	0.6261	0.6328	0.5439
	Arg2	0.6932	0.6921	0.5843
	Both	0.5317	0.5418	0.4178
	Sense	0.5640	0.5333	0.4326
	Parser	**0.4120**	**0.4089**	**0.2690**

Table 1: The official subtasks and overall F1-measures of the parser on the development, test and blind test sets for explicit, non-explicit and all relations.

We provide some analysis from the results:

- More than 20% sharp decrease of F1 in explicit parser on the blind set is mainly due to the error propagation of connective identification. The error is mainly from two aspects. One is the flexible parallel connectives. Another is the ambiguous definition of connectives, especially in the middle of the sentence.

- The seed-expansion method can get acceptable results for argument extraction. It is hard to determine whether a clause is in the span of argument when it plays a role of supplement or conjunction to the basic semantic.

---

[3] http://mallet.cs.umass.edu/

This causes the main error. So more features about the span cohesion should be tried in future. The F1 of Arg1 and Arg2 individually is about 10% higher than jointly. Besides, the assumption that the span of argument is in one sentence is too strong.

5 Conclusion

We have built a PDTB-style end-to-end Chinese shallow discourse parser for the CoNLL-2016 Shared Task. Our system is adapted to the Chinese characteristics. A seed-expansion approach is proposed to extract the arguments correctly. On the official blind test set, we achieve the 26.90% in F1-measure.

Acknowledgments

The research work has been partially funded by the Natural Science Foundation of China under Grant No. 61333018 and No. 61303181 and supported by the Strategic Priority Research Program of the CAS (Grant XDB02070007).

References

Hen-Hsen Huang and Hsin-Hsi Chen. 2011. Chinese discourse relation recognition. In *IJCNLP*, pages 1442–1446.

Yangfeng Ji and Jacob Eisenstein. 2015. One vector is not enough: Entity-augmented distributed semantics for discourse relations. *Transactions of the Association for Computational Linguistics*, 3:329–344.

Fang Kong, Hwee Tou Ng, and Guodong Zhou. 2014. A constituent-based approach to argument labeling with joint inference in discourse parsing. In *EMNLP*, pages 68–77.

Ziheng Lin, Min-Yen Kan, and Hwee Tou Ng. 2009. Recognizing implicit discourse relations in the Penn Discourse Treebank. In *Proceedings of the EMNLP 2009*, pages 343–351.

Ziheng Lin, Hwee Tou Ng, and Min-Yen Kan. 2014. A PDTB-styled end-to-end discourse parser. *Natural Language Engineering*, 20(02):151–184.

Emily Pitler and Ani Nenkova. 2009. Using syntax to disambiguate explicit discourse connectives in text. In *Proceedings of the ACL-IJCNLP 2009 Conference Short Papers*, pages 13–16.

Martin Potthast, Tim Gollub, Francisco Rangel, Paolo Rosso, Efstathios Stamatatos, and Benno Stein. 2014. Improving the Reproducibility of PAN's Shared Tasks: Plagiarism Detection, Author Identification, and Author Profiling. In Evangelos Kanoulas, Mihai Lupu, Paul Clough, Mark Sanderson, Mark Hall, Allan Hanbury, and Elaine Toms, editors, *Information Access Evaluation meets Multilinguality, Multimodality, and Visualization. 5th International Conference of the CLEF Initiative (CLEF 14)*, pages 268–299, Berlin Heidelberg New York, September. Springer.

Rashmi Prasad, Nikhil Dinesh, Alan Lee, Eleni Miltsakaki, Livio Robaldo, Aravind K Joshi, and Bonnie L Webber. 2008. The Penn Discourse TreeBank 2.0. In *LREC*. Citeseer.

Attapol Rutherford and Nianwen Xue. 2014. Discovering implicit discourse relations through brown cluster pair representation and coreference patterns. In *EACL*, volume 645, page 2014.

Attapol Rutherford and Nianwen Xue. 2015. Improving the inference of implicit discourse relations via classifying explicit discourse connectives. In *Proceedings of the NAACL-HLT*.

Mei Tu, Yu Zhou, and Chengqing Zong. 2014. Automatically parsing Chinese discourse based on maximum entropy. *Acta Scientiarum Naturalium Universitatis Pekinensis*, 50(1):125–132.

Jianxiang Wang and Man Lan. 2015. A refined end-to-end discourse parser. *CoNLL 2015*, page 17.

Shengqin Xu, Fang Kong, Peifeng Li, and Qiaoming Zhu. 2012. A Chinese sentence segmentation approach based on comma. In *Chinese Lexical Semantics*, pages 809–817. Springer.

Nianwen Xue, Hwee Tou Ng, Sameer Pradhan, Bonnie Webber, Attapol Rutherford, Chuan Wang, and Hongmin Wang. 2016. The CoNLL-2016 Shared Task on multilingual shallow discourse parsing. In *Proceedings of the Twentieth Conference on Computational Natural Language Learning - Shared Task*, Berlin, Germany, August. Association for Computational Linguistics.

Yaqin Yang and Nianwen Xue. 2012. Chinese comma disambiguation for discourse analysis. In *Proceedings of the ACL 2012*, pages 786–794.

Biao Zhang, Jinsong Su, Deyi Xiong, Yaojie Lu, Hong Duan, and Junfeng Yao. 2015. Shallow convolutional neural network for implicit discourse relation recognition. In *Proceedings of the EMNLP 2015*, pages 2230–2235.

Yuping Zhou and Nianwen Xue. 2012. PDTB-style discourse annotation of Chinese text. In *Proceedings of the ACL 2012: Long Papers-Volume 1*, pages 69–77.

Yuping Zhou and Nianwen Xue. 2015. The Chinese Discourse TreeBank: A Chinese corpus annotated with discourse relations. *Language Resources and Evaluation*, 49(2):397–431.

Chengqing Zong. 2013. *Statistical Natural Language Processing*. Tsinghua University Press.

Two End-to-end Shallow Discourse Parsers for English and Chinese in CoNLL-2016 Shared Task

Jianxiang Wang,   Man Lan*
Shanghai Key Laboratory of Multidimensional Information Processing
Department of Computer Science and Technology,
East China Normal University, Shanghai 200241, P. R. China
51141201062@ecnu.cn, mlan@cs.ecnu.edu.cn*

Abstract

This paper describes our two discourse parsers (i.e., English discourse parser and Chinese discourse parser) for submission to CoNLL-2016 shared task on Shallow Discourse Parsing. For English discourse parser, we build two separate argument extractors for single sentence (SS) case, and adopt a convolutional neural network for Non-Explicit sense classification based on (Wang and Lan, 2015b)'s work. As for Chinese discourse parser, we build a pipeline system following the annotation procedure of Chinese Discourse Treebank in (Zhou and Xue, 2015). Our English discourse parser achieves better performance than the best system of CoNLL-2015 and the Chinese discourse parser achieves encouraging results. Our two parsers both rank second on the blind datasets.

1 Introduction

A discourse relation between two segments of textual units expresses how they are logically connected to one another (*cause* or *contrast*), which is considered a crucial step for the ability to properly interpret or produce discourse. It can be of great benefit to many downstream natural language processing (NLP) applications and has attracted lots of research (Pitler and Nenkova, 2009; Lin et al., 2009; Pitler et al., 2009; Lan et al., 2013; Rutherford and Xue, 2014; Lin et al., 2014; Kong et al., 2014; Ji and Eisenstein, 2015; Fisher and Simmons, 2015; Braud and Denis, 2015; Zhang et al., 2015).

Following the first edition in CoNLL-2015 (Xue et al., 2015), CoNLL-2016 (Xue et al., 2016) is the 2nd edition of the CoNLL Shared Task on Shallow Discourse Parsing, which contains following tasks: discourse parsing task and supplementary task (sense classification using gold standard argument pairs) in English and Chinese.

To build an English parser, we follow (Wang and Lan, 2015b)'s work except for several modifications described later in section 2. In consideration of distinct linguistic and syntactic difference between English and Chinese, for Chinese parser, we design a new pipeline system which simulates the annotation procedure of Chinese Discourse Treebank in (Zhou and Xue, 2015). And for both English and Chinese sense classification (i.e., supplementary task), we just regard them as parts of the whole parser.

2 English Discourse Parser

2.1 System Overview

The English discourse parser shown in Figure 1 is a pipeline system, which is quite similar with that in (Wang and Lan, 2015b) except for several differences in: (1) build two separate argument extractors for single sentence (SS) case; (2) adopt a convolutional neural network for Non-Explicit Sense Classification; (3) add or remove several features for each component based on hill-climbing strategy.

Therefore, we only describe the differences above-mentioned in details in this paper.

2.2 Separate SS Arguments Extractor

Unlike the work in (Kong et al., 2014; Wang and Lan, 2015b) which built global argument extractor for the SS case in Explicit parser, we build two different argument extractors for

Proceedings of the 54th Annual Meeting of the Association for Computational Linguistics, pages 33–40,
Berlin, Germany, August 7-12, 2016. ©2016 Association for Computational Linguistics

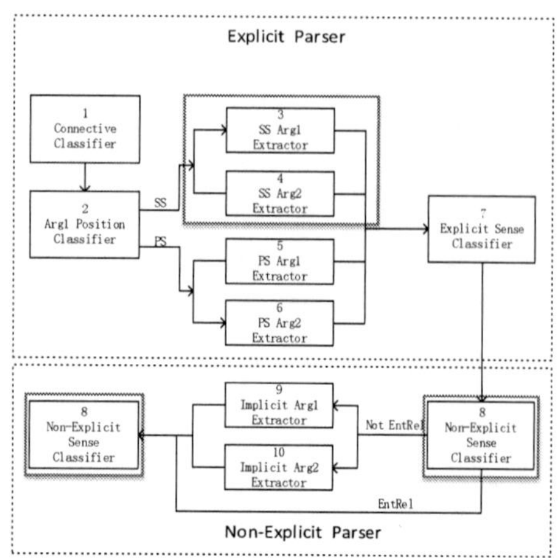

Figure 1: System pipeline for the English discourse parser

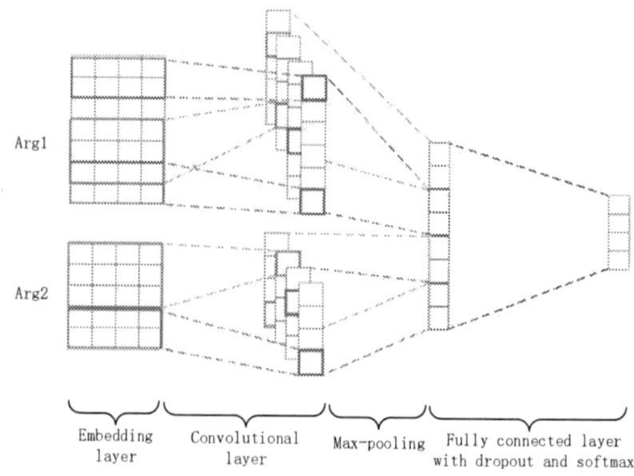

Figure 2: Convolutional neural network for Non-Explicit sense classification

Arg1 and Arg2 separately. Our consideration is that these two arguments have different syntactic and discourse properties and a unified model with the same feature set used for both cases may not have enough discriminating power (Wang and Lan, 2015a).

Specifically, we follow the constituent-based approach in (Kong et al., 2014) which consists of three steps: (1) collecting argument candidates (i.e., constituents) from the parse tree of the sentence containing the connective C; (2) deciding each constituent whether it belongs to Arg1, Arg2 or NULL; (3) merging all the constituents for Arg1 and Arg2 to obtain the Arg1 and Arg2 text spans respectively.

In the second step, however, different from (Kong et al., 2014), we view it as a binary classification. That is, we use two argument extractors to determine each constituent whether it belongs to the argument (Arg1 or Arg2) or not. And in the third step, we merge the constituents for Arg1 and Arg2 from **SS Arg1 Extractor** and **SS Arg2 Extractor** to obtain the Arg1 and Arg2 text spans, respectively.

2.3 Convolutional Neural Network for Non-Explicit Sense Classification

Instead of using lots of handcrafted features, we adopt a convolutional neural network (CNN) to perform Non-Explicit sense classification as shown in Figure 2.

The inputs are two tokenized sentences (i.e., Arg1 and Arg2). For each token, the 300-dimensional word vector representation is obtained from pre-trained word2vec model which was trained on 100 billion words from Google News using the skip-gram architecture (Mikolov et al., 2013) and then we convert each of them into a sentence matrix. We denote the sentence matrix by $\mathbf{A} \in \mathbb{R}^{s \times d}$ (s is the length of sentence and d is the dimensionality of the word vector), and use $\mathbf{A}[i : j]$ to represent the sub-matrix of $\mathbf{A}$ from row i to row j. A convolution operation involves a *filter* $\mathbf{w} \in \mathbb{R}^{h \times d}$ (h is the height of filter, window size of the filter). The output sequence $\mathbf{o} \in \mathbb{R}^{s-h+1}$ of the convolution operator is obtained by repeatedly applying the filter on sub-matrices of $\mathbf{A}$:

$$o_i = \mathbf{w} \cdot \mathbf{A}[i : i + h - 1] \qquad (1)$$

where $i = 1 \ldots s - h + 1$, $\cdot$ is the dot product between the sub-matrix and the filter (a sum over element-wise multiplications). A bias term $b \in \mathbb{R}$ and an activation function f are added to each o_i to compute the *feature map* $\mathbf{c} \in \mathbb{R}^{s-h+1}$ for this filter:

$$c_i = f(o_i + b) \qquad (2)$$

The *max pooling* operation is applied over each feature map to take the maximum value $\hat{c} = max\{\mathbf{c}\}$, and then the outputs generated from each feature map can be concatenated into a fixed-length feature vector (i.e., the representation of the input sentence). We apply convolution and *max pooling* over Arg1 and Arg2 sentence matrix to obtain the Arg1 and

Arg2 representation respectively, then concatenate them to obtain the representation of discourse relation (penultimate layer in CNN) which will be passed to a fully connected softmax layer. Moreover, we apply dropout (Hinton et al., 2012) to penultimate layer. We choose cross-entropy loss as our training objective and use AdaGrad (Duchi et al., 2011) with a learning rate of 0.01 and a minibatch size of 50 to train the model. Table 1 shows the configuration of our model.

Description	Values
input word vectors	Google word2vec
filter window size	(4, 6, 13)
feature maps	100
activation function	Tanh
pooling	max pooling
dropout rate	0.5

Table 1: Configuration of our CNN model

2.4 Feature Engineering

Following (Wang and Lan, 2015b) and (Wang and Lan, 2015a)' work, we tune the features for each component according to hill-climbing strategy. Table 2 lists the specific features for each component in English discourse parser.

Note that for a node in the parse tree, we use the POS combinations of the node, its parent, its right sibling and left sibling to represent the *node context*, and use the POS combinations of the node, its parent, its children to represent the *linked context*. And we use *level distance* to represent the distance between the heights of two nodes in the parse tree. For the Connective Classifier, $prev_1$ and $next_1$ indicate the first previous word and the first next word of connective C. For SS Arg1&2 extractors, we use NT to indicate the constituent. For PS Arg1&2 Extractor and Implicit Arg1&2 Extractor, *prev*, *curr*, *next* refer to previous, current, next clause in the sentence respectively.

For the detail explanation of the features, please refer to (Wang and Lan, 2015b) and (Wang and Lan, 2015a).

3 Chinese Discourse Parser

Due to the distinct differences between English and Chinese language, the discourse annotation procedure of Chinese is quite different from that of English. There are three main differences between English and Chinese parsers.

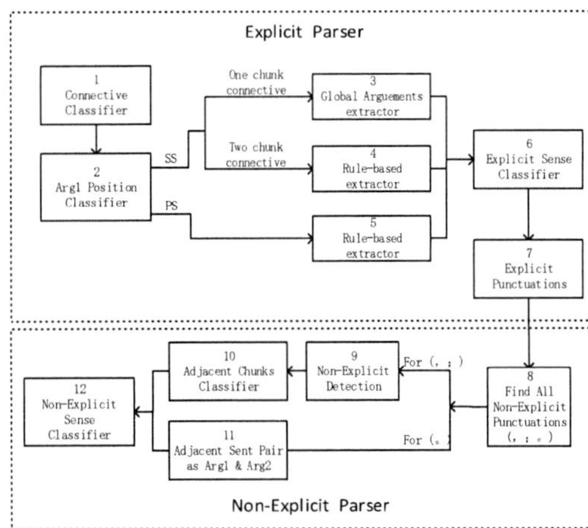

Figure 3: System pipeline for the Chinese discourse parser

Firstly, there are many punctuations in one Chinese sentence, which indicate discourse relations between text spans, therefor it is important to use them as potential indicators to indicate discourse relations. Secondly, in the case of Explicit connectives, Arg2 in English parser is always the argument to which the connective is syntactically bound, while in Chinese parser the relative positions of Arg1 and Arg2 in Explicit relation are dependent on the relation sense rather than the position of explicit connective. Thirdly, most English discourse connectives are single words while most Chinese discourse connectives come in pairs (e.g., in train set, 62.46% of the connectives are in pairs).

Following the annotation procedure of the Chinese discourse, we design the pipeline system for Chinese discourse parser as shown in Figure 4. Although the Chinese discourse parser is divided into Explicit parser and Non-Explicit parser, which is similar with English discourse parser, most components in Chinese parser perform quite differently as described in following section.

3.1 Explicit Parser

3.1.1 Connective Classifier

First, we use three punctuations (i.e., comma, semi-colon and colon) to split all sentences into *chunks*. Then, we only identify the connectives which span no more than two *chunks*. That is, we do not consider the connectives ranging

35

Component	Features
Connective Classifier	lowercased C string, C category, C POS, $C + next_1$, $prev_1 + C$, $prev_1$ POS + C POS, path of C's parent $\rightarrow$ root, the POS tags of nodes from C's parent $\rightarrow$ root, *self category*, *right sibling category*, *left sibling category*, *self category* + *right category*, C + *node context* of *right sibling category*, C + *linked context* of *right sibling category*, C + *node context* of *parent category*, C + *linked context* of *parent category*
SS Arg1 Extractor	C category, C iLSib, *self category*, *left sibling category*, path of C's parent $\rightarrow$ root, the *node context* of the *parent category*, *node context* of NT, path of $NT \rightarrow$ root, NT iRSib, *node context* of NT's parent, path from current $NT \rightarrow$ next NT, *level distance* between current and previous NT, path of $NT \rightarrow C$, C NT position , whether C and NT are in the same clause, whether previous and current NT are in the same clause, whether current and next NT are in the same clause
SS Arg2 Extractor	C category, C iLSib, *self category*, *right sibling category*, the POS tags of nodes from C's parent $\rightarrow$ root, *node context* of NT, *node context* of NT's parent, path of $NT \rightarrow$ root, path from previous $NT \rightarrow$ current NT, path from current $NT \rightarrow$ next NT, path of $NT \rightarrow C$, C NT position, *level distance* between C and NT, whether previous and current NT are in the same clause
PS Arg1 Extractor	*curr* first + *next* first, *curr* last + *next* first, *curr* last + *curr* last, path from *curr* first to *prev* last in parse tree
PS Arg2 Extractor	C string, lowercased C string, C category, path of C's parent $\rightarrow$ root, compressed path of C's parent $\rightarrow$ root, *next* first, *prev* first, *prev* last + *curr* last, production rule of *curr*, *curr* + the first lemma verb of *curr*.
Explicit Sense Classifier	C + *prev*, C POS, *self category*, *parent category*, *left sibling category*, *right sibling category*, Syn-Syn, C + *left sibling category*, C + *right sibling category*, C + the *node context* of *left sibling category*, *node context* of C, *linked context* of C, previous connective and its POS of as and previous connective and its POS of when.
Implicit Arg1 Extractor	immediately preceding punctuations of *curr*, first lowercased verb in *curr*, *curr* first + first lemma verb in *curr*, *curr* first + *curr* last, path from *curr* first to *prev* last in the parse tree, *prev* first, *prev* first + *curr* first, *prev* last + *curr* last, *prev* last + *curr* first.
Implicit Arg2 Extractor	*curr* first punctuation, *curr* first + first lemma verb in *curr*, *curr* first punctuation + *curr* last punctuation, *prev* first, *prev* last + *curr* first, *prev* first + *curr* first, *prev* last + *curr* last,

Table 2: Features for the components in English discourse parser

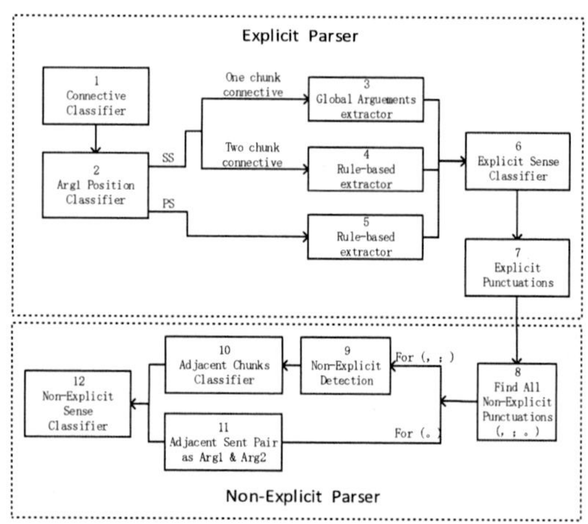

Figure 4: System pipeline for the Chinese discourse parser

across three or more chunks since their frequency is quite low in our preliminary statistics. Here we refer *one chunk* connective to the connectives ranging across only one chunk, and *two chunk* connective to the connectives cross two chunks. For example, "并" and "在

$\cdots$ 情况下" are *one chunk* connectives in Example 1 and 2, whereas "除 $\cdots$ 外 $\cdots$ 还" is *two chunk* connective in Example 3.

(1) 德波尔大名鼎鼎，[今年入选荷兰队]$_{Arg1}$，并 [在法国世界杯赛上打入半决赛]$_{Arg2}$ 。

(2) 分析表明，在 [机遇良多、国际形势十分有利]$_{Arg1}$ 的情况下 ，[中国今年经济发展仍面临严竣挑战]$_{Arg2}$ 。

(3) 他们指出，除 [比索汇率过高]$_{Arg1}$ 外，[墨出口今年 还 将面临一些新的不利因素]$_{Arg2}$ 。

For each identified connective, we build a connective classifier to decide whether they function as discourse connective or not. The features we used in connective classifier are as follows: C + *node context* of C, $prev_1 + C$, $prev_1$ POS, $prev_1$ POS + C POS, *left sibling category* + *right sibling category*, path of C's parent $\rightarrow$ root, compressed path of C's parent $\rightarrow$ root, the POS tags of nodes from C's parent $\rightarrow$ root. Note that $prev_1$ indicate the first previous word of C. The *self category*, *parent category, left sibling category, right sibling category* features are borrowed from (Pitler and Nenkova, 2009).

3.1.2 Arg1 Position Classifier

The Arg1 Position Classifier is to identify the relative position of Arg1 as whether it is located within the same sentence as the connective (SS) or in some previous sentences of the connective (PS).

The features consist of the following: C string, path of $C \rightarrow$ root, $prev_1$, $prev_1 + C$, $prev_1$ POS $+ C$ POS, $prev_2$, $prev_2 + C$, $next_1$, $next_1 + C$, $next_1$ POS, $next_1$ POS $+ C$ POS, $next_2 + C$, $next_2$ POS, $next_2$ POS $+ C$ POS. Note that $prev_2$ and $next_2$ indicate the second previous word and the second next word of connective C, respectively.

3.1.3 SS Arguments Extractor

Unlike English discourse, even in SS case, most Chinese discourse connectives come in pairs, for example, "在 ⋯ 的情况下", "虽然 ⋯ 但是" etc, which makes it hard to label arguments for these connectives.

In the case that a connective is *one chunk* connective, we build a global extractor to label Arg1 and Arg2. In the case of *two chunk* connective, we then adopt a rule-based method to extract Arg1 and Arg2.

***One chunk* connective**: For the *chunks* in the sentence containing *one chunk* connective, we build a classifier to decide each *chunk* whether it belongs to Arg1, Arg2 or NULL, then merge all the *chunks* for Arg1 and Arg2 to obtain the Arg1 and Arg2 text spans respectively. Note that if the chunk contains the connective, we remove the connective from this chunk.

The features of this extractor consist of the following: *curr last, curr first*, the verbs in *curr, next first, next last*, the punctuations in the tail of the *curr, curr last + next last, curr last + next first, prev last + curr last, C ,C* + whether C in the *curr*, the relative position of C to *curr* (C before, after or in *curr*), the number of chunks from *curr* to C. Note that *curr* and *next* indicate the current and next following *chunk* respectively, and *first* and *last* mean the first and last word in the *chunk*.

***Two chunk* connective**: If the connectives are *two chunk* connectives, we then use a simple rule-based extractor to extract Arg1 and Arg2. We view the text spans from the first *chunk* to second chunk as Arg1, and the text span in the second *chunk* as Arg2.

3.1.4 PS Arguments Extraction

For the PS cases, we also use a rule-based extractor to extract the arguments. We label the previous sentence of the connective as Arg1, and the text span between the connective and the beginning of the next sentence as Arg2.

3.1.5 Explicit Sense Classifier

To build the Explicit sense classifier, we extract features from the connective C, its context and the parse tree of its sentence, which are listed in the following: C string, $C +$ previous word of C, $C +$ *self category*, $C +$ *left sibling category*, $C +$ *right sibling category*, C + the *node context* of *parent category*.

3.1.6 Explicit Punctuations

According to (Zhou and Xue, 2012), the general annotation procedure for Chinese parser is to scan the text for finding punctuations, and to judge whether there is a discourse relation when a punctuation is encountered. If yes, annotators then characterize the relation and if not, they keep on scanning, whereas they identify Explicit connective firstly. Inspired by this annotation, we present this component to obtain the Explicit punctuation for each Explicit relation according to the connective and its two arguments using the following strategy:

(1) If the two arguments are not embedded into each other, we use the punctuation between two arguments as Explicit punctuation, and if more than one punctuation between two arguments, choose the closest one to Arg1.

(2) If the two arguments are embedded into each other, choose the closest punctuation following Arg1.

3.2 Non-Explicit Parser

3.2.1 Find All Non-Explicit Punctuations

After the above-mentioned Explicit punctuations procedure, we denote all remaining (i.e., not identified as Explicit punctuations) three punctuations (i.e., 。, ，, ；) from the texts as Non-Explicit candidate punctuations.

3.2.2 For , ; punctuations

However, not each of the Non-Explicit candidate punctuations contains a Non-Explicit relation, for example, the first punctuation (,) in Example 2. Therefore, we use Non-Explicit Detection component to judge each of , ; punctuations whether or not, and if there is, an Adjacent Chunk Classifier is adopted to obtain its Arg1 and Arg2.

Non-Explicit Detection: The features for this component contain the following: *prev last*, first verb of *prev*, length of *prev*, *prev last + prev first*, unigram of *prev*, the punctuation token. *prev* denotes the previous *chunk* of the punctuation.

Adjacent Chunk Classifier: If there is a Non-Explicit relation in , or ; punctuation, we use an Adjacent Chunk Classifier to judge whether the previous one chunk or two chunks of the punctuation is labelled as Arg1 and whether the next one chunk or two chunks of the punctuation is labelled as Arg2.

We use the following features to build the classifier: unigram of *first*, length of *first*, first word of *first*, last word of *first*, first word of *first* + last word of *first*, unigram of *second*, length of *second*, first word of *second*, last word of *second*, first word of *second* + last word of *second*, the connectives in two chunks. Note that *first* and *second* refer to the first and second *chunk*, respectively.

3.2.3 For 。 punctuation

For all 。 punctuations, we assume each of them contains a Non-Explicit relation, and then extract Arg1 and Arg2 by labeling the previous sentence of the connective as Arg1, and the text span between the connective and the beginning of the next sentence as Arg2.

3.2.4 Non-Explicit Sense Classifier

From the previous components, we have obtained the two arguments of the Non-Explicit relations. To perform the Non-Explicit sense classification, we extract features from the arguments pair: *production rules*, word pairs in the first *chunk* of each argument, verb pairs in the argument pair, first verb pair in the argument pair, Arg1 *last*, Arg1 *first3*, Arg1 *first*, Arg1 *first* + Arg2 *last*, Arg1 *last* + Arg2 *last*, Arg2 *first3*.

4 Experiments

All classifiers in the two parsers are trained using logistic regression with the default parameters (i.e., c=1) implemented in LIBLINEAR toolkit [1]. We adopt the same Explicit Sense Classifier and Non-Explicit Sense Classifier used in the discourse parser for both English and Chinese supplementary tasks which are sense classification using gold standard argument pairs.

From Table 3, compared with the best system in CoNLL-2015 (Wang and Lan, 2015b) on blind dataset, our system achieves better performances on Explicit arguments extraction and Non-Explicit arguments extraction and beat them on the overall performance. From table 4, we see that the performance of Explicit sense classification is better on dev and blind test set, which is slight lower on the test set than the performance of (Wang and Lan, 2015b). As for the Non-Explicit sense classification in supplementary task, we achieve much better performance than (Wang and Lan, 2015b) on dev and test set when using CNN instead of handcrafted features. However, our CNN model achieve a worse performance on blind test set, the possible reason might be that the blind test set has a different sense distribution compared with dev and test sets. Note that the dev and test set are both from PDTB dataset, whereas the blind test set is annotated from English Wikinews [2].

For Chinese discourse parser, from table 3, we see the performance of the Explicit connective identification on Chinese is much lower than that in English and reduced a lot from dev to test and blind test, the possible reason might be that there are lots of connectives come in pairs and much more unseen connectives in the Chinese test than in English which makes it hard to detect and classify them from the texts. From Table 4, the performance of Non-Explicit sense classification in Chinese is much higher than in English, due to the high performance of the baseline system (labelling the sense of all the Non-Explicit relations as "Conjunction" can achieve the 64.61% accuracy on train set). Due to the variety distri-

---

[1] https://www.csie.ntu.edu.tw/ cjlin/libsvmtools/multicore-liblinear/

[2] https://en.wikinews.org/

	English				Chinese		
	dev	test	blind	(Wang and Lan, 2015b)'s blind	dev	test	blind
Explicit connective	95.22	93.96	91.34	91.86	86.27	72.41	63.07
Explicit Arg1 extraction	62.01	51.39	**51.05**	48.31	67.97	59.77	41.13
Explicit Arg2 extraction	81.26	76.43	74.20	74.29	70.59	62.07	47.53
Explicit Both extraction	55.11	44.31	**42.84**	41.35	56.21	47.13	31.81
Non-Explicit Arg1 extraction	68.84	64.66	**61.05**	60.87	59.86	59.55	54.21
Non-Explicit Arg2 extraction	73.81	66.86	**75.83**	74.58	65.25	65.26	54.99
Non-Explicit Both extraction	58.39	50.83	**51.15**	50.41	50.50	50.12	42.10
All Arg1 extraction	66.39	59.18	**57.22**	55.84	63.17	61.63	56.19
All Arg2 extraction	77.32	71.38	**75.10**	74.45	67.60	67.35	57.20
All Both extraction	56.85	47.79	**47.43**	46.37	52.45	50.82	41.99
Overall parser	40.43	30.70	**25.99**	24.00	42.42	40.25	26.60

Table 3: Results of our English and Chinese discourse parsers on dev, test and blind test datasets

	English			Chinese		
	dev	test	blind	dev	test	blind
Explicit	92.56 (90.00)	90.13 (90.79)	77.41 (76.44)	96.10	94.24	76.69
Non-Explicit	**46.51** (42.72)	**40.91** (34.45)	34.20 (36.29)	73.53	72.42	60.52
ALL	**67.97** (65.11)	**64.34** (61.27)	54.06 (54.76)	78.07	77.01	64.73

Table 4: Results of the supplementary tasks on both English and Chinese discourses, which are sense classification using gold standard argument pairs. The corresponding performance of (Wang and Lan, 2015b)'s system is shown within parentheses.

bution of the arguments, the arguments extraction is more challenging than other components, and achieve low performance on test set.

5 Conclusion

In this work, we improve the English discourse parser on previous best system (Wang and Lan, 2015b) in three aspects: (1) build two separate argument extractors for the SS case; (2) adopt convolutional neural network to do Non-Explicit Sense Classification; (3) add or remove some features for each component based on the hill-climbing strategy. And we build a Chinese discourse parser following the annotation procedure of Chinese Discourse Treebank. Our English discourse parser achieves a better performance than the best system in CoNLL-2015, and we have obtained encouraging results of the Chinese discourse parser.

Acknowledgements

This research is supported by grants from Science and Technology Commission of Shanghai Municipality under research grant no. (14DZ2260800 and 15ZR1410700) and Shanghai Collaborative Innovation Center of Trustworthy Software for Internet of Things (ZF1213).

References

Chloé Braud and Pascal Denis. 2015. Comparing word representations for implicit discourse relation classification. In *Proceedings of the 2015 Conference on Empirical Methods in Natural Language Processing*, pages 2201–2211, Lisbon, Portugal, September. Association for Computational Linguistics.

John Duchi, Elad Hazan, and Yoram Singer. 2011. Adaptive subgradient methods for online learning and stochastic optimization. *The Journal of Machine Learning Research*, 12:2121–2159.

Robert Fisher and Reid Simmons. 2015. Spectral semi-supervised discourse relation classification. In *Proceedings of the 53rd Annual Meeting of the Association for Computational Linguistics and the 7th International Joint Conference on Natural Language Processing (Volume 2: Short Papers)*, pages 89–93, Beijing, China, July. Association for Computational Linguistics.

Geoffrey E Hinton, Nitish Srivastava, Alex Krizhevsky, Ilya Sutskever, and Ruslan R Salakhutdinov. 2012. Improving neural networks by preventing co-adaptation of feature detectors. *arXiv preprint arXiv:1207.0580*.

Yangfeng Ji and Jacob Eisenstein. 2015. One vector is not enough: Entity-augmented distributed semantics for discourse relations. *Transactions of the Association for Computational Linguistics*, 3:329–344.

Fang Kong, Hwee Tou Ng, and Guodong Zhou. 2014. A constituent-based approach to argument labeling with joint inference in discourse parsing. In *Proceedings of the 2014 Conference on Empirical Methods in Natural Language Processing (EMNLP)*, pages 68–77, Doha, Qatar, October. Association for Computational Linguistics.

Man Lan, Yu Xu, Zheng-Yu Niu, et al. 2013. Leveraging synthetic discourse data via multi-task learning for implicit discourse relation recognition. In *ACL (1)*, pages 476–485. Citeseer.

Ziheng Lin, Min-Yen Kan, and Hwee Tou Ng. 2009. Recognizing implicit discourse relations in the Penn Discourse Treebank. In *Proceedings of the 2009 Conference on Empirical Methods in Natural Language Processing: Volume 1-Volume 1*, pages 343–351. Association for Computational Linguistics.

Ziheng Lin, Hwee Tou Ng, and Min-Yen Kan. 2014. A PDTB-styled end-to-end discourse parser. *Natural Language Engineering*, pages 1–34.

Tomas Mikolov, Kai Chen, Greg Corrado, and Jeffrey Dean. 2013. Efficient estimation of word representations in vector space. *arXiv preprint arXiv:1301.3781*.

Emily Pitler and Ani Nenkova. 2009. Using syntax to disambiguate explicit discourse connectives in text. In *Proceedings of the ACL-IJCNLP 2009 Conference Short Papers*, pages 13–16. Association for Computational Linguistics.

Emily Pitler, Annie Louis, and Ani Nenkova. 2009. Automatic sense prediction for implicit discourse relations in text. In *Proceedings of the Joint Conference of the 47th Annual Meeting of the ACL and the 4th International Joint Conference on Natural Language Processing of the AFNLP: Volume 2-Volume 2*, pages 683–691. Association for Computational Linguistics.

Attapol T Rutherford and Nianwen Xue. 2014. Discovering implicit discourse relations through brown cluster pair representation and coreference patterns. *EACL 2014*, page 645.

Jianxiang Wang and Man Lan. 2015a. Building a high performance end-to-end explicit discourse parser for practical application. In *Knowledge Science, Engineering and Management*, pages 324–335. Springer.

Jianxiang Wang and Man Lan. 2015b. A refined end-to-end discourse parser. In *Proceedings of the Nineteenth Conference on Computational Natural Language Learning - Shared Task*, pages 17–24, Beijing, China, July. Association for Computational Linguistics.

Nianwen Xue, Hwee Tou Ng, Sameer Pradhan, Rashmi Prasad, Christopher Bryant, and Attapol Rutherford. 2015. The CoNLL-2015 Shared Task on Shallow Discourse Parsing. In *Proceedings of the Nineteenth Conference on Computational Natural Language Learning: Shared Task*, Beijing, China.

Nianwen Xue, Hwee Tou Ng, Sameer Pradhan, Bonnie Webber, Attapol Rutherford, Chuan Wang, and Hongmin Wang. 2016. The conll-2016 shared task on multilingual shallow discourse parsing. In *Proceedings of the Twentieth Conference on Computational Natural Language Learning - Shared Task*, Berlin, Germany, August. Association for Computational Linguistics.

Biao Zhang, Jinsong Su, Deyi Xiong, Yaojie Lu, Hong Duan, and Junfeng Yao. 2015. Shallow convolutional neural network for implicit discourse relation recognition. In *Proceedings of the 2015 Conference on Empirical Methods in Natural Language Processing*, pages 2230–2235, Lisbon, Portugal, September. Association for Computational Linguistics.

Yuping Zhou and Nianwen Xue. 2012. Pdtb-style discourse annotation of chinese text. In *Proceedings of the 50th Annual Meeting of the Association for Computational Linguistics: Long Papers-Volume 1*, pages 69–77. Association for Computational Linguistics.

Yuping Zhou and Nianwen Xue. 2015. The chinese discourse treebank: A chinese corpus annotated with discourse relations. *Language Resources and Evaluation*, 49(2):397–431.

Do We Really Need All Those Rich Linguistic Features?
A Neural Network-Based Approach to Implicit Sense Labeling

Niko Schenk[*], **Christian Chiarcos**[*], **Kathrin Donandt**[*],
Samuel Rönnqvist[*,†], **Evgeny A. Stepanov**[‡] and **Giuseppe Riccardi**[‡]

[*]Applied Computational Linguistics Lab, Goethe University, Frankfurt am Main, Germany
[†]Turku Centre for Computer Science, TUCS, Åbo Akademi University, Turku, Finland
[‡]Signals and Interactive Systems Lab, DISI, University of Trento, Italy
`{schenk,chiarcos,donandt}@informatik.uni-frankfurt.de,`
`sronnqvi@abo.fi,{evgeny.stepanov,giuseppe.riccardi}@unitn.it`

Abstract

We describe our contribution to the CoNLL 2016 Shared Task on shallow discourse parsing.[1] Our system extends the two best parsers from previous year's competition by integration of a novel *implicit* sense labeling component. It is grounded on a highly generic, language-independent feedforward neural network architecture incorporating weighted word embeddings for argument spans which obviates the need for (traditional) hand-crafted features. Despite its simplicity, our system overall outperforms all results from 2015 on 5 out of 6 evaluation sets for English and achieves an absolute improvement in F_1-score of 3.2% on the PDTB test section for non-explicit sense classification.

1 Introduction

Text comprehension is an essential part of Natural Language Understanding and requires capabilities beyond capturing the lexical semantics of individual words or phrases. In order to understand how meaning is established, altered and transferred across words and sentences, a model is needed to account for contextual information as a semantically coherent representation of the logical *discourse structure* of a text. Different formalisms and frameworks have been proposed to realize this assumption (Mann and Thompson, 1988; Lascarides and Asher, 1993; Webber, 2004).

In a more applied NLP context, *shallow discourse parsing* (SDP) aims at automatically detecting relevant discourse units and to label the relations that hold between them. Unlike *deep discourse parsing*, a stringent logical formalization or the establishment of a global data structure, for instance, a tree, is not required.

With the release of the Penn Discourse Treebank (Prasad et al., 2008, PDTB) and the Chinese Discourse Treebank (Zhou and Xue, 2012, CDTB), annotated training data for SDP has become available and, as a consequence, the field has considerably attracted researchers from the NLP and IR community. Informally, the PDTB annotation scheme describes a discourse unit as a syntactically motivated character span in the text, augmented with relations pointing from the second argument (*Arg2*, prototypically, a discourse unit associated with an explicit discourse marker) to its antecedent, i.e., the discourse unit *Arg1*. Relations are labeled with a relation type (its *sense*) and the associated discourse marker (either as found in the text or as inferred by the annotator). PDTB distinguishes *explicit* and *implicit* relations depending on whether such a connector or cue phrase (e.g., *because*) is present, or not.[2] As an illustrative example without such a marker, consider the following two adjacent sentences from the PDTB:

Arg1: *The real culprits are computer makers such as IBM that have jumped the gun to unveil 486-based products.*
Arg2: *The reason this is getting so much visibility is that some started shipping and announced early availability.*

In this *implicit* relation, *Arg1* and *Arg2* are directly related. The discourse relation type is *Expansion.Restatement*—one out of roughly twenty finegrained tags marking the sense relation

---

[1]`http://www.cs.brandeis.edu/~clp/conll16st`
Our parser code is available at: `https://github.com/acoli-repo/shallow-discourse-parser`

[2]The set of relation types is completed by alternative lexicalization (*AltLex*, discourse marker rephrased), entity relation (*EntRel*, i.e., anaphoric coherence), resp. the absence of any relation (*NoRel*).

Proceedings of the 54th Annual Meeting of the Association for Computational Linguistics, pages 41–49,
Berlin, Germany, August 7-12, 2016. ©2016 Association for Computational Linguistics

between any given argument pair in the PDTB.

Our Contribution: We participate in the CoNLL 2016 Shared Task on SDP (Xue et al., 2016; Potthast et al., 2014) and propose a novel, neural network-based approach for implicit sense labeling. Its system architecture is modular, highly generic and mostly language-independent, by leveraging the full power of pre-trained word embeddings for the SDP sense classification task. Our parser performs well on both English and Chinese data and is highly competitive with the state-of-the-art, though does not require manual feature engineering as employed in most prior works on implicit SDP, but rather relies extensively on features learned from data.

2   Related Work

Most of the literature on automated discourse parsing has focused on specialized subtasks such as:

1. **Argument identification**
   (Ghosh et al., 2012; Kong et al., 2014)

2. **Explicit sense classification**
   (Pitler and Nenkova, 2009)

3. **Implicit sense classification**
   (Marcu and Echihabi, 2002; Pitler et al., 2009; Lin et al., 2009; Zhou et al., 2010; Park and Cardie, 2012; Biran and McKeown, 2013; Rutherford and Xue, 2014)

A minimal requirement for any full-fledged end-to-end discourse parser is to integrate at least these three processes into a sequential pipeline. However, until recently, only a handful of such parsers have existed (Lin et al., 2014; Biran and McKeown, 2015; duVerle and Prendinger, 2009; Feng and Hirst, 2012). It has been enormously difficult to evaluate the performance of these systems among themselves, and also to compare the efficiency of their individual components with other competing methods, as i.) those systems rely on different theories of discourse, e.g., PDTB or RST; and ii) different (sub)modules involve custom settings, feature- and tool-specific parameters, (esp. for the most challenging task of *implicit sense labeling*). Furthermore, iii) most previous works are not directly comparable in terms of overall accuracies as their underlying evaluation data suffers from inconsistent label sizes among studies (e.g., full sense inventory vs. simplified 1- or 2-level classes, cf. Huang and Chen (2011)).

Fortunately, with the first edition of the shared task on SDP, Xue et al. (2015) had established a *unified framework* and had made an independent evaluation possible. The best performing participating systems – most notably those by Wang and Lan (2015) and Stepanov et al. (2015) – have re-implemented the well-established techniques, for example the one by Lin et al. (2014).

2.1   Deep Learning Approaches to SDP

In last year's shared task, first implementations on *deep learning* have seen a surge of interest: Wang et al. (2015) and Okita et al. (2015) proposed a recurrent neural network for argument identification and a paragraph vector model for sense classification. Distributed representations for both arguments were obtained by vector concatenation of embeddings.

An earlier attempt in a similar direction of *representation learning* (Bengio et al., 2013) has been made by Ji and Eisenstein (2014). The authors demonstrated successfully how to discriminatively learn a latent, low-dimensional feature representation for RST-style discourse parsing, which has the benefit of capturing the underlying meaning of elementary discourse units without suffering from data sparsity of the originally high dimensional input data.

Closely related, Li et al. (2014) introduced a recursive neural network for discourse parsing which jointly models distributed representations for sentences based on words and syntactic information. The approach is motivated by Socher et al. (2013) and models the discourse unit's root embedding to represent the whole discourse unit which is being obtained from its parts by an iterative process. Their system is made up of a binary structure classifier and a multi-class relation classifier and achieves similar performance compared to Ji and Eisenstein (2014).

Very recently, Liu et al. (2016) and Zhang et al. (2015) have successfully applied convolutional neural networks to model implicit relations within the PDTB-framework. Along these lines and inspired by the work in Weiss (2015), we also see great potential in the use of neural network-based techniques to SDP. Similarly, our approach trains a modular component for shallow discourse parsing which incorporates distributed word representations for argument spans by abstraction from surface-level (token) information. Crucially, our approach substitutes the traditional sparse and hand-crafted features from the literature to account for a minimalist, but at the same time, general (latent) representation of the discourse units. In the next sections, we elaborate on our novel neural network-based approach for implicit sense labeling and how it is fit into the overall system architecture of the parser.

3 A Neural Sense Labeler for Implicit and Entity Relations

We construct a neural network-based module for the classification of senses for both implicit and entity (*EntRel*) relations.[3] As a very general and highly data-driven approach to modeling discourse relations, our classifier incorporates *only* word embeddings and basic syntactic dependency information. Also, in order to keep the setup easily adaptable to new data and other languages, we avoid the use of very specific and costly hand-crafted features (such as sentiment polarities, word-pair features, cue phrases, modality, production rules, highly specific semantic information from external ontologies such as VerbNet, etc.), which has been the main focus in traditional approaches to SDP (Huang and Chen, 2011; Park and Cardie, 2012; Feng and Hirst, 2012). Instead, we substitute (sparse) tokens in the argument spans, with dense, distributed representations, i.e. word embeddings, as the main source of information for the sense classification component. Closely related, Zhang et al. (2015) have explored a similar approach of constructing argument vectors by applying a set of aggregation functions on their token vectors, however, without the use of additional (syntactic) information, while embedding their vectors into a single-layer neural network only.

In our experiments, we used the pre-trained *GoogleNews* vectors (for English) and the *Giga-word*-induced vectors (for Chinese) provided by the shared task as a starting point.[4] We further trained the word vectors on the raw Wall Street Journal texts, thus tuning the embeddings toward the data at hand, with the goal of considerably improving their predictive power in the sense classification task. Specifically, the pre-trained vectors of size 300 were updated by the skip-gram method (Mikolov et al., 2013)[5] in multiple passes over the Newswire texts with decreasing learning rate. This procedure is supposed to improve the quality of the embeddings and also their coverage.

Our new word vector model provides general vector representations for each token in the two argument spans[6], which forms the basis for producing compositional vectors to represent the two spans. Compositional vectors that introduce a fixed-length representation of a variable-length span of tokens are practical features for feedforward neural networks. Thus, we may combine the token vectors of each span by simply averaging vectors, or – following Mitchell and Lapata (2008) – by calculating an aggregated argument vector $\vec{v'}$:

$$\vec{v'}(j) = \frac{1}{k(j)} \sum_{i=1}^{k(j)} V(j)_i + \prod_{i=1}^{k(j)} V(j)_i \quad (1)$$

for arguments $j \in \{1, 2\}$, where $k(j) = |t(j)|$ defines their lengths in the number of tokens and $\prod$ applies the pointwise product $\odot$ over the token vectors in $V(j)$.

Both procedures produce rather simple argument representations that do not account for word order variation or any other sentence structure information, yet they serve as decent features for discourse parsing and other related tasks. By introducing pointwise multiplication of the token vectors, the elements that represent assumed independent, latent semantic dimensions are not merely lumped together across vectors, but are allowed to scale according to their mutual relevance.[7]

Improving upon the compositional representation produced by Equation 1, we incorporate additional syntactic dependency information: for each token in an argument span, we calculate the depth d from the corresponding sentence's root node and weight the token vector by $\frac{1}{2^d}$ before applying the

---

[3]The reason to combine both relation types has been a design decision as *EntRels* are very similar to implicit relations and are also missing a connective. *AltLex* relations seemed too few to have any statistical impact on the performance of our experiments and have been ignored altogether.

[4]http://www.cs.brandeis.edu/~clp/conll16st/dataset.html

[5]We found window size of 8 and min term count $= 3$ to be optimal. Neural networks were trained using the *gensim* package: http://radimrehurek.com/gensim/.

[6]We ignore unknown tokens for which no vectors exist.

[7] In our experiments, Equation 1 outperformed simpler strategies of either average or multiplication alone. This also indicates that it is beneficial to not completely suppress dimensions with near-zero values for single tokens.

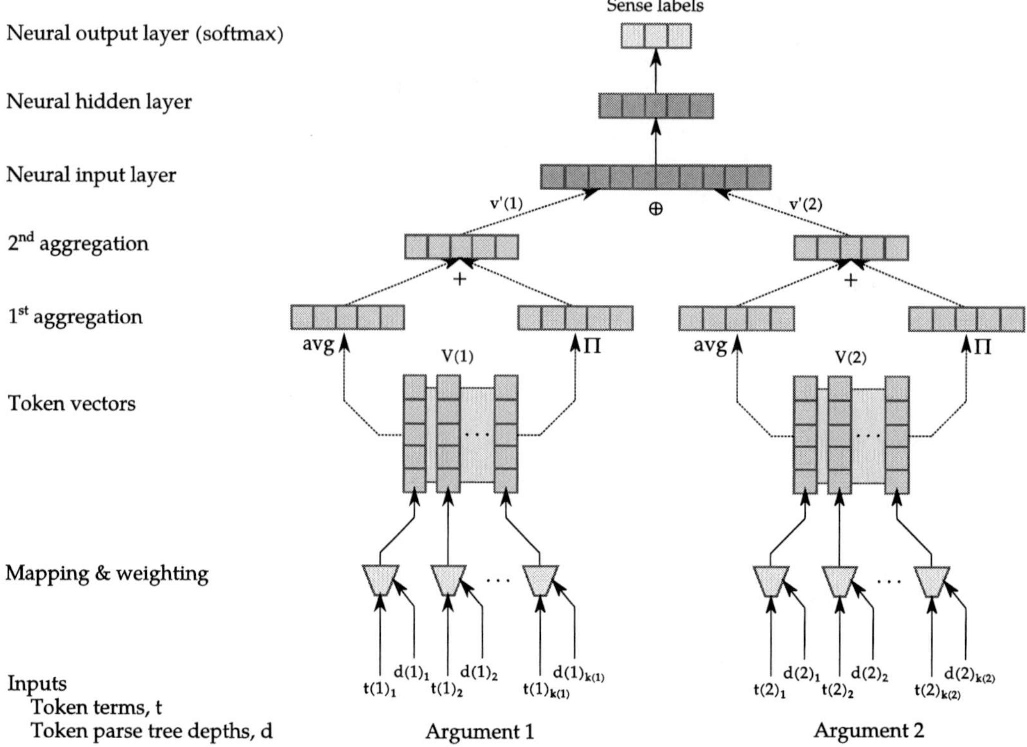

Figure 1: The feature construction process from argument spans (light blue) and neural architecture (dark blue) for implicit sense classification (incl. *EntRel*) . Dotted lines represent pointwise vector operations.

aggregating operators.[8]

The bottom of Figure 1 illustrates the first step of the process, i.e. mapping tokens to their corresponding vectors based on the updated word vector model, as well as the token depth weighting. Secondly, the aggregation operators are applied, i.e., the sum ($+$) of the pointwise product ($\prod/\odot$) and average (*avg*) of the vectors. Finally, the compositional vectors for each of the arguments are concatenated ($\oplus$) and serve as input to a feedforward neural network.

Given the composed argument vectors, we set up a network with one hidden layer and a softmax output layer to classify among 20 implicit senses for English and 9 for Chinese, plus an additional *EntRel* label. Other relations, such as *AltLex*, are not modeled. We train the network using Nesterov's Accelerated Gradient (Nesterov, 1983) and optimized all hyper-parameters on the development set. Best results were achieved with *rectified linear activation with learnable leak rate and gain*

(lgrelu), 40-60 hidden nodes and weight decay and hidden node regularization of 0.0001.[9]

4 The Competition Tasks & Pipelines

We participate in the *closed track* of the shared task, specifically in both *full* and *supplementary tasks (sense-only)* on English and Chinese texts. Full tasks require a participant's system to identify argument pairs and to label the sense relation that holds between them. In each supplementary task, gold arguments are provided so that the performance of sense labeling does not suffer from error propagation due to incorrectly detected argument spans.

We combine different *existent* modules to address the specific settings and classification needs of both full and supplementary tasks for both lan-

---

[8]Tokens that are missing in the parse tree, such as punctuation symbols, are weighted by 0.25, in our optimal setting.

[9]The learning rate was set to 0.0001. Momentum of 0.35-0.6 and 60 hidden nodes performed well for the English tasks, and momentum of 0.85 and 40 hidden nodes for Chinese (with fewer output nodes). Good results were also obtained by *Parametric Rectified Linear Unit (prelu)* activation, as well as the combination of larger hidden layer and stronger regularization (e.g., L1 regularization of 0.1 on 100 nodes).

guages. The modules and their combination with our implicit neural sense classifier will be outlined in the following sections.

4.1 English Full Task Pipeline (EFTP)

For the full task, we exploit the high-quality argument extraction modules of the two best-performing systems by Wang and Lan (2015, W&L) and Stepanov et al. (2015) from last year's competition (re-using their original implementations): Specifically, we initially run both systems for all *explicit* relations only, and keep those predicted arguments and sense labels – from either of the two systems – which maximize F_1-score on the development set. With this simple heuristic, we hope to improve upon the best results from W&L, as, for instance, Stepanov et al. (2015) perform particularly well on all temporal relations, while W&L's tool handles the majority of other senses well.

For all implicit and *EntRel* relations, we keep the exact argument spans obtained from the W&L system and reject all sense labels. In a second step, we *re-classify* all these implicit relations by our neural net-based architecture described in Section 3 given only the tokens and their dependencies in both argument spans. Finally, we merge all combined explicit and re-classified implicit relations into the final set for evaluation.

4.2 English Supplementary Task Pipeline (ESTP)

We make use of the system by Stepanov et al. (2015) to label all *explicit* relation senses, and classify all other relations with an empty token list for connectors (i.e., implicit and *EntRels*) by our neural network architecture from Section 3.

4.3 Chinese Full Task Pipeline (CFTP)

Since for the Chinese full task no reusable argument extraction tools were available, we have set up a minimalist (baseline) implementation whose individual steps we sketch briefly:

1. **Connective detection** is realized by means of a sequence labeling/CRF model.[10] Features are unigram and bigram information from the tokens, their parts-of-speech, dependency head, dependency chain, whether the token is found as a connector in the training set, and its relative position within the sentence.

2. **Argument extraction** is based on the output of predicted connectives for both inter- and intra-sentence relations. As an additional feature, we found the IOB chain for the syntactic path of a token to be useful.[11]

3. We heuristically **post-process** the CRF-labeled argument tokens in order to assign connectors to same-sentence or separate-sentence *Arg1* and *Arg2* spans.

4. The so-obtained **explicit argument pairs** are sense labeled by a (linear-kernel) SVM classifier[12] with the connector word as the only feature, following the minimalist setting in Chiarcos and Schenk (2015).

5. As **implicit relations** we consider *all intersentential relations* which are not already part of an explicit relation. Same-sentence relations are ignored altogether.

4.4 Chinese Supplementary Task Pipeline (CSTP)

For the provided argument pairs, we label *explicit* relations (i.e. those containing a non-empty connector) by the SVM classifier which has been trained using only a single feature – the connector token. For all other relations, we again employ our neural network-based strategy described in Section 3. The overall architecture is exactly the same as for the English subtask; only the (hyper)parameters have been updated in accordance with the Chinese training data.

5 Evaluation

5.1 English Full Task

Table 1 shows the performance of our full-task pipeline (EFTP) which integrates our novel feed-forward neural network architecture for implicit sense labeling. The figures suggest that our minimalist approach is highly competitive and can even outperform the best results from last year's competition in terms of F_1-scores on two out of three evaluation sets (cf. last *implicit* column).

Overall, with the integration of the combined systems by W&L and Stepanov et al. (2015), we can improve upon the state-of-the-art by an absolute increase in F_1-score of 0.5% on the blind test

---

[10]https://taku910.github.io/crfpp/

[11]This information was generated using the script from http://ilk.uvt.nl/team/sabine/chunklink/ chunklink_2-2-2000_for_conll.pl

[12]https://www.csie.ntu.edu.tw/~cjlin/ libsvm/

set– which is marginal but only due to the fruitful re-classification of the already-provided (and therefore fixed) argument spans.

Measured on the development set, we found that the *dependency depth weighting* contributes to an absolute improvement in accuracy of 1.5% for non-explicit relations.

set	system	overall	explicit	*implicit*
dev	W&L	37.84	48.16	28.70
	EFTP	**40.21**	**50.87**	**30.99**
test	W&L	29.69	39.96	**20.74**
	EFTP	**29.78**	**40.44**	20.60
blind	W&L	24.00	30.38	18.78
	EFTP	**24.47**	**30.74**	**19.63**

Table 1: English full task F_1-scores.

5.2 English Supplementary Task

Without error propagation from argument identification, and with the gold arguments provided in the evaluation sets, the performance of our implicit sense labeling component is even better; cf. Table 2: on both PDTB evaluation sets F_1-scores increase by 2.7% and 3.16% (absolute) and by 6.32% and up to **9.17%** (relative) on the development and test section, respectively.

Strikingly, however, the prediction quality on the blind test set is worse than expected. We assume that this is partly due to the (slightly) heterogeneous content of the annotated *Wikinews*, as opposed to the original Penn Discourse Treebank data on which our system performs extraordinarily well.

set	system	overall	explicit	*implicit*
dev	W&L	65.11	90.00	42.72
	ESTP	**66.90**	**91.35**	**45.42**
test	W&L	61.27	**90.79**	34.45
	ESTP	**62.64**	90.13	**37.61**
blind	W&L	**54.76**	**76.44**	**36.29**
	ESTP	52.32	76.40	31.85

Table 2: English sense-only task F_1-scores.

5.3 Chinese Full Task

This year's edition of the shared task has been the first to address shallow discourse parsing for Chinese Newswire texts. Given no prior (directly comparable) results on Chinese SDP so far, we simply report the performance of our system on all evaluation sets in Table 3.

set	system	overall	explicit	*implicit*
dev	**CFTP**	22.16	17.45	**22.67**
test	**CFTP**	**24.21**	**28.73**	22.26
blind	**CFTP**	12.90	18.56	10.80

Table 3: Chinese full task F_1-scores.

5.4 Chinese Supplementary Task

A final evaluation has been concerned with the sense-only labeling of gold-provided arguments for Chinese. We want to point out that the neural network architecture for implicit relations (with 70.59% F_1-score on the dev set, cf. Table 4) has beaten all our other experiments: In particular, we have conducted an SVM setup in which we employed the traditional word-pair features substituted by Brown clusters 3200 (65.12%), and special additive Arg1/Arg2 combinations of word embeddings – yielding only 62.8% which equals the majority class baseline indicating no predictive power for any given kernel type.

set	system	overall	explicit	*implicit*
dev	**CSTP**	75.72	96.10	70.59
test	**CSTP**	**77.01**	**96.34**	**71.87**
blind	**CSTP**	63.73	80.39	57.59

Table 4: Chinese sense-only task F_1-scores.

6 Conclusion

In the context of the CoNLL 2016 Shared Task on shallow discourse parsing, we have described our participating system and its architecture. Specifically, we introduced a novel feedforward neural network-based component for implicit sense labeling whose only source of information are pretrained word embeddings and syntactic dependencies. Its highly generic and extremely simple design is the main advantage of this module. It has proven to be language-independent, easy to tune and optimize and does not require the use of handcrafted – rich – linguistic features.

Still its performance is highly competitive with the state-of-the-art on implicit sense labeling and builds a solid groundwork for future extensions.

References

Yoshua Bengio, Aaron Courville, and Pascal Vincent. 2013. Representation Learning: A Review and New Perspectives. *IEEE Trans. Pattern Anal. Mach. Intell.*, 35(8):1798–1828, August.

Or Biran and Kathleen McKeown. 2013. Aggregated Word Pair Features for Implicit Discourse Relation Disambiguation. In *Proceedings of the 51st Annual Meeting of the Association for Computational Linguistics, ACL 2013, 4-9 August 2013, Sofia, Bulgaria, Volume 2: Short Papers*, pages 69–73.

Or Biran and Kathleen McKeown. 2015. PDTB Discourse Parsing as a Tagging Task: The Two Taggers Approach. In *Proceedings of the 16th Annual Meeting of the Special Interest Group on Discourse and Dialogue*, pages 96–104, Prague, Czech Republic, September. Association for Computational Linguistics.

Christian Chiarcos and Niko Schenk. 2015. A Minimalist Approach to Shallow Discourse Parsing and Implicit Relation Recognition. In *Proceedings of the 19th Conference on Computational Natural Language Learning: Shared Task, CoNLL 2015, Beijing, China, July 30-31, 2015*, pages 42–49.

David A. duVerle and Helmut Prendinger. 2009. A Novel Discourse Parser Based on Support Vector Machine Classification. In *Proceedings of the Joint Conference of the 47th Annual Meeting of the ACL and the 4th International Joint Conference on Natural Language Processing of the AFNLP: Volume 2 - Volume 2*, ACL '09, pages 665–673, Stroudsburg, PA, USA. Association for Computational Linguistics.

Vanessa Wei Feng and Graeme Hirst. 2012. Text-level Discourse Parsing with Rich Linguistic Features. In *Proceedings of the 50th Annual Meeting of the Association for Computational Linguistics: Long Papers - Volume 1*, ACL '12, pages 60–68, Stroudsburg, PA, USA. Association for Computational Linguistics.

Sucheta Ghosh, Giuseppe Riccardi, and Richard Johansson. 2012. Global Features for Shallow Discourse Parsing. In *Proceedings of the 13th Annual Meeting of the Special Interest Group on Discourse and Dialogue (SIGDIAL)*, pages 150–159.

Hen-Hsen Huang and Hsin-Hsi Chen. 2011. Chinese Discourse Relation Recognition. In *Proceedings of 5th International Joint Conference on Natural Language Processing*, pages 1442–1446, Chiang Mai, Thailand, November. Asian Federation of Natural Language Processing.

Yangfeng Ji and Jacob Eisenstein. 2014. Representation Learning for Text-level Discourse Parsing. In *Proceedings of the 52nd Annual Meeting of the Association for Computational Linguistics (Volume 1: Long Papers)*, pages 13–24, Baltimore, Maryland, June. Association for Computational Linguistics.

Fang Kong, Tou Hwee Ng, and Guodong Zhou. 2014. A Constituent-Based Approach to Argument Labeling with Joint Inference in Discourse Parsing. In *Proceedings of the 2014 Conference on Empirical Methods in Natural Language Processing (EMNLP)*, pages 68–77. Association for Computational Linguistics.

Alex Lascarides and Nicholas Asher. 1993. Temporal Interpretation, Discourse Relations and Commonsense entailment. *Linguistics and Philosophy*, 16(5):437–493.

Jiwei Li, Rumeng Li, and Eduard Hovy. 2014. Recursive Deep Models for Discourse Parsing. In *Proceedings of the 2014 Conference on Empirical Methods in Natural Language Processing (EMNLP)*, pages 2061–2069, Doha, Qatar, October. Association for Computational Linguistics.

Ziheng Lin, Min-Yen Kan, and Hwee Tou Ng. 2009. Recognizing Implicit Discourse Relations in the Penn Discourse Treebank. In *Proceedings of the 2009 Conference on Empirical Methods in Natural Language Processing: Volume 1 - Volume 1*, EMNLP '09, pages 343–351, Stroudsburg, PA, USA. Association for Computational Linguistics.

Ziheng Lin, Hwee Tou Ng, and Min-Yen Kan. 2014. A PDTB-styled end-to-end discourse parser. *Natural Language Engineering*, 20:151–184, 4.

Yang Liu, Sujian Li, Xiaodong Zhang, and Zhifang Sui. 2016. Implicit Discourse Relation Classification via Multi-Task Neural Networks. *CoRR*, abs/1603.02776.

William C. Mann and Sandra A. Thompson. 1988. Rhetorical structure theory: Toward a functional theory of text organization. *Text*, 8(3):243–281.

Daniel Marcu and Abdessamad Echihabi. 2002. An Unsupervised Approach to Recognizing Discourse Relations. In *Proceedings of the 40th Annual Meeting on Association for Computational Linguistics*, ACL '02, pages 368–375, Stroudsburg, PA, USA. Association for Computational Linguistics.

Tomas Mikolov, Kai Chen, Greg Corrado, and Jeffrey Dean. 2013. Efficient Estimation of Word Representations in Vector Space. In *Proceedings of Workshop at International Conference on Learning Representations*.

Jeff Mitchell and Mirella Lapata. 2008. Vector-based Models of Semantic Composition. In *Proceedings of Association for Computational Linguistics*, pages 236–244.

Yurii Nesterov. 1983. A method of solving a convex programming problem with convergence rate O (1/k2). In *Soviet Mathematics Doklady*, volume 27, pages 372–376.

Tsuyoshi Okita, Longyue Wang, and Qun Liu. 2015. The DCU Discourse Parser: A Sense Classification Task. In *Proceedings of the Nineteenth Conference on Computational Natural Language Learning - Shared Task*, pages 71–77, Beijing, China, July. Association for Computational Linguistics.

Joonsuk Park and Claire Cardie. 2012. Improving Implicit Discourse Relation Recognition Through Feature Set Optimization. In *Proceedings of the 13th Annual Meeting of the Special Interest Group on Discourse and Dialogue*, page 108–112, Seoul, South Korea, July. Association for Computational Linguistics, Association for Computational Linguistics.

Emily Pitler and Ani Nenkova. 2009. Using Syntax to Disambiguate Explicit Discourse Connectives in Text. In *ACL 2009, Proceedings of the 47th Annual Meeting of the Association for Computational Linguistics and the 4th International Joint Conference on Natural Language Processing of the AFNLP, 2-7 August 2009, Singapore, Short Papers*, pages 13–16.

Emily Pitler, Annie Louis, and Ani Nenkova. 2009. Automatic Sense Prediction for Implicit Discourse Relations in Text. In *Proceedings of the Joint Conference of the 47th Annual Meeting of the ACL and the 4th International Joint Conference on Natural Language Processing of the AFNLP: Volume 2 - Volume 2*, ACL '09, pages 683–691, Stroudsburg, PA, USA. Association for Computational Linguistics.

Martin Potthast, Tim Gollub, Francisco Rangel, Paolo Rosso, Efstathios Stamatatos, and Benno Stein. 2014. Improving the Reproducibility of PAN's Shared Tasks: Plagiarism Detection, Author Identification, and Author Profiling. In Evangelos Kanoulas, Mihai Lupu, Paul Clough, Mark Sanderson, Mark Hall, Allan Hanbury, and Elaine Toms, editors, *Information Access Evaluation meets Multilinguality, Multimodality, and Visualization. 5th International Conference of the CLEF Initiative (CLEF 14)*, pages 268–299, Berlin Heidelberg New York, September. Springer.

Rashmi Prasad, Nikhil Dinesh, Alan Lee, Eleni Miltsakaki, Livio Robaldo, Aravind Joshi, and Bonnie Webber. 2008. The Penn Discourse TreeBank 2.0. In *In Proceedings of LREC*.

Attapol Rutherford and Nianwen Xue. 2014. Discovering Implicit Discourse Relations Through Brown Cluster Pair Representation and Coreference Patterns. In *Proceedings of the 14th Conference of the European Chapter of the Association for Computational Linguistics*, pages 645–654. Association for Computational Linguistics.

Richard Socher, Alex Perelygin, Jean Wu, Jason Chuang, Christopher D. Manning, Andrew Y. Ng, and Christopher Potts. 2013. Recursive Deep Models for Semantic Compositionality Over a Sentiment Treebank. In *Proceedings of the 2013 Conference on Empirical Methods in Natural Language Processing*, pages 1631–1642, Stroudsburg, PA, October. Association for Computational Linguistics.

Evgeny Stepanov, Giuseppe Riccardi, and Orkan Ali Bayer. 2015. The UniTN Discourse Parser in CoNLL 2015 Shared Task: Token-level Sequence Labeling with Argument-specific Models. In *Proceedings of the Nineteenth Conference on Computational Natural Language Learning - Shared Task*, pages 25–31. Association for Computational Linguistics.

Jianxiang Wang and Man Lan. 2015. A Refined End-to-End Discourse Parser. In *Proceedings of the Nineteenth Conference on Computational Natural Language Learning - Shared Task*, pages 17–24. Association for Computational Linguistics.

Longyue Wang, Chris Hokamp, Tsuyoshi Okita, Xiaojun Zhang, and Qun Liu. 2015. The DCU Discourse Parser for Connective, Argument Identification and Explicit Sense Classification. In *Proceedings of the Nineteenth Conference on Computational Natural Language Learning - Shared Task*, pages 89–94. Association for Computational Linguistics.

Bonnie L. Webber. 2004. D-LTAG: extending lexicalized TAG to discourse. *Cognitive Science*, 28(5):751–779.

Gregor Weiss. 2015. Learning Representations for Text-level Discourse Parsing. In *Proceedings of the ACL-IJCNLP 2015 Student Research Workshop*, pages 16–21, Beijing, China, July. Association for Computational Linguistics.

Nianwen Xue, Hwee Tou Ng, Sameer Pradhan, Rashmi Prasad, Christopher Bryant, and Attapol Rutherford. 2015. The CoNLL-2015 Shared Task on Shallow Discourse Parsing. In *Proceedings of the Nineteenth Conference on Computational Natural Language Learning: Shared Task*, Beijing, China.

Nianwen Xue, Hwee Tou Ng, Sameer Pradhan, Bonnie Webber, Attapol Rutherford, Chuan Wang, and Hongmin Wang. 2016. The CoNLL-2016 Shared Task on Shallow Discourse Parsing. In *Proceedings of the Twentieth Conference on Computational Natural Language Learning - Shared Task*, Berlin, Germany, August. Association for Computational Linguistics.

Biao Zhang, Jinsong Su, Deyi Xiong, Yaojie Lu, Hong Duan, and Junfeng Yao. 2015. Shallow Convolutional Neural Network for Implicit Discourse Relation Recognition. In *Proceedings of the 2015 Conference on Empirical Methods in Natural Language Processing, EMNLP 2015, Lisbon, Portugal, September 17-21, 2015*, pages 2230–2235.

Yuping Zhou and Nianwen Xue. 2012. PDTB-style Discourse Annotation of Chinese Text. In *Proceedings of the 50th Annual Meeting of the Association for Computational Linguistics (Volume 1: Long Papers)*, pages 69–77, Jeju Island, Korea, July. Association for Computational Linguistics.

Zhi-Min Zhou, Yu Xu, Zheng-Yu Niu, Man Lan, Jian Su, and Chew Lim Tan. 2010. Predicting Discourse Connectives for Implicit Discourse Relation Recognition. In *Proceedings of the 23rd International Conference on Computational Linguistics: Posters*, COLING '10, pages 1507–1514, Stroudsburg, PA, USA. Association for Computational Linguistics.

Discourse Sense Classification from Scratch using Focused RNNs

Gregor Weiss, Marko Bajec
University of Ljubljana
Faculty of Computer and Information Science
Večna pot 113, Ljubljana, Slovenia
gregor.weiss@student.uni-lj.si
marko.bajec@fri.uni-lj.si

Abstract

The subtask of CoNLL 2016 Shared Task focuses on sense classification of multilingual shallow discourse relations. Existing systems rely heavily on external resources, hand-engineered features, patterns, and complex pipelines fine-tuned for the English language. In this paper we describe a different approach and system inspired by end-to-end training of deep neural networks. Its input consists of only sequences of tokens, which are processed by our novel focused RNNs layer, and followed by a dense neural network for classification. Neural networks implicitly learn latent features useful for discourse relation sense classification, make the approach almost language-agnostic and independent of prior linguistic knowledge. In the closed-track sense classification task our system achieved overall 0.5246 F_1-measure on English blind dataset and achieved the new state-of-the-art of 0.7292 F_1-measure on Chinese blind dataset.

1 Introduction

Shallow discourse parsing is a challenging natural language processing task and sense classification is its most difficult subtask (Lin et al., 2014; Xue et al., 2015). Given text spans for argument 1 and 2, connective, and punctuation, the goal is to predict the sense of the discourse relation that holds between them. These text spans can appear in various orders, are not necessarily continuous, can spread across multiple sentences, and sometimes connectives and punctuation are not even present. The CoNLL 2016 Shared Task (Xue et al., 2016) focuses on multilingual shallow discourse parsing based on the English Penn Discourse TreeBank (PDTB) (Prasad et al., 2008) and Chinese Discourse TreeBank (CDTB) (Zhou and Xue, 2012). Evaluation is performed on separate test and blind datasets on the remote TIRA evaluation system (Potthast et al., 2014).

Existing systems for discourse parsing rely heavily on existing resources, hand-engineered features, patterns, and complex pipelines fine-tuned for the English language (Xue et al., 2015; Wang and Lan, 2015; Stepanov et al., 2015). Such features include word lists, part-of-speech tags, chunking tags, syntactic features extracted from constituent parse trees, path features built around connectives or specific words, production rules, dependency rules, Brown cluster pairs, features that disambiguate problematic connectives, and similar. Similar to our system, these pipelines separately process explicit and non-explicit discourse relation types.

In this paper we describe a different approach and system inspired by end-to-end training of deep neural networks. Instead of engineering features and incorporating linguistic knowledge into them, its input consists of only sequences of tokens. They are processed by a neural network model that utilizes our novel focused recurrent neural networks (RNNs). It automatically learns latent features and how to allocate focus for our task. This way the system is independent of any prior knowledge, existing parsers, or external resources, what makes it almost language-agnostic. By only changing a few hyper-parameters, we successfully applied the same system to the English and Chinese datasets and achieved new state-of-the-art results on the Chinese blind dataset. Our system[1] was developed in Python using the Keras library (Chollet, 2015) that enables it to run on either CPU or GPU.

---

[1] http://github.com/gw0/conll16st-v34-focused-rnns/

50

Proceedings of the 54th Annual Meeting of the Association for Computational Linguistics, pages 50–54,
Berlin, Germany, August 7-12, 2016. ©2016 Association for Computational Linguistics

The system architecture is described in Section 2, followed by details of layers in our neural network and their training. Section 3 presents official evaluation results on English and Chinese datasets. Section 4 draws conclusions and directions for future work.

2 System Overview

Our system for discourse sense classification of the CoNLL 2016 Shared Task consists of two similar neural network models build from three types of layers (see Figure 1). In the spirit of end-to-end training its input consists of only tokenized text spans that are mapped to vocabulary ids, which are processed by our neural network to classify each discourse relation into a sense category.

Important steps of our system are:

- **Two models** for separately handling present and absent connectives in discourse relations.

- **Input** consists of four sequences of tokens mapped to vocabulary ids (for argument 1 and 2, connectives, and punctuations).

- **Word Embeddings** layer maps each token into a low-dimensional vector space using a lookup table.

- **Focused RNNs** layer focuses multiple RNNs onto different aspects of these sequences.

- **Classification** is performed with a dense neural network and logistic regression on top.

We used the same system on the English and Chinese datasets and each one uses two separate neural network models with only a few differences in its 18 parameters. Because of these differences, individual models are trained and applied completely separately, although parts could be shared. Total number of trainable weights for both neural network models is 1355661/1185006 for English and 369972/1276761 for Chinese.

2.1 Two models

According to suggestions from related work we separately handle discourse relations with and without given connectives. For each case we train a separate neural network model with the same architecture, but different hyper-parameters. Throughout the paper we present those differences in parameters with a/b, where a presents a value

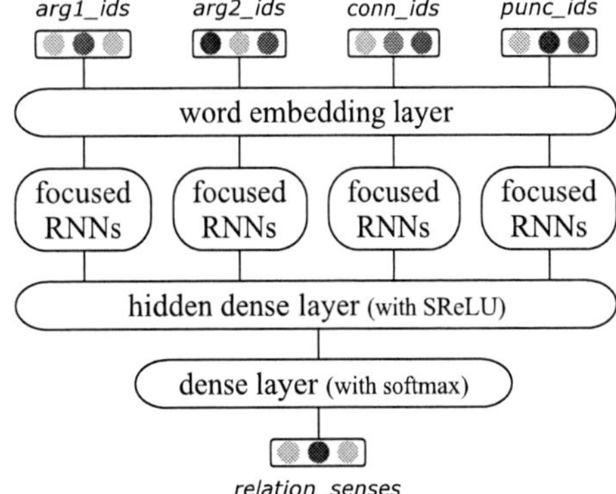

Figure 1: Our neural network model for end-to-end training of sense classification. Two such models are separately trained for each language.

used for Explicit and AltLex relation types (where connectives are present) and b for Implicit and EntRel relation types (where connectives are absent).

2.2 Input

Initially a vocabulary of all words or tokens in the training dataset is prepared mapping each one to a unique token id. Four text spans representing individual shallow discourse relations are tokenized and mapped into four sequences of vocabulary ids. Depending on the language these input sequences are cropped to different maximal lengths, see Table 1. Out-of-vocabulary words that are not present during training are mapped to a special id.

Relation part	English	Chinese
Argument 1	100	500
Argument 2	100	500
Connective	10	10
Punctuation	2	2

Table 1: Maximal lengths of input sequences in our system for English and Chinese datasets.

2.3 Word embeddings

A shared word embedding layer turns previous sequences of positive integers (token ids) into dense vectors of fixed size using a lookup table. These vector representations are automatically learned with the rest of the model using backpropagation. All four input sequences are mapped into the same low-dimensional vector space with 30/20 dimensions for English and 20/70 for Chinese. For regularization purposes we randomly drop embeddings during training with probability 0.1.

Although the closed-track allowed the use of pre-trained skip-gram neural word embeddings (Mikolov et al., 2013), we decided to learn them from scratch for each model separately.

2.4 Focused RNNs

These embeddings are processed by our novel focused RNNs layer. Any recurrent neural network (RNN) can be used as its building block, but we decided to use the GRU layer (Chung et al., 2014). First a special focus RNN with 4/6 dimensions for English and 4/5 for Chinese is used to assign multidimensional focus weights to the input sequence. For each focus dimension a separate RNN is applied to the input sequence multiplied with corresponding focus weights. This way different RNNs can focus on different aspects of input sequences— in our case on different words and senses. Final outputs of these RNNs are concatenated and used in the classification layers. Our system uses separate RNNs with 10/50 dimensions for English and 20/30 for Chinese. For regularization purposes we randomly drop 0.33 input gates of focus and separate RNNs, 0.66 recurrent connections of the focus RNN, and 0.33 of separate RNNs.

Note that our focused RNNs layer differs a lot from other attention mechanisms found in literature. They are designed to only work with question-answering systems, use a weighted combination of all input states, and can focus on only one aspect of the input sequence.

2.5 Classification

Classification into discourse sense categories is performed using a dense neural network. Merged outputs of all focused RNNs are first processed by a dense layer with 90/40 dimensions for English and 100/90 for Chinese, followed by the SReLU activation function (Jin et al., 2015). The S-shaped rectified linear activation unit (SReLU) consists of piecewise linear functions and can learn both convex and non-convex functions. Finally logistic regression, i.e. a dense layer followed by the softmax activation function, is applied to get classification probabilities. For regularization purposes we randomly drop connections before the second dense layers with probability 0.5.

2.6 Training

Loss function suitable for our classification task is the categorical cross-entropy. Training is achieved with backpropagation and any gradient descent optimization, such as Adam optimizer. To parallelize and speed up the learning process we train in batches of 64 training samples. During training we monitor the loss function on the validation dataset and stop if it does not increase in the last 20 epochs. For regularization purposes we also introduce 32 random noise samples for each discourse relation during training. Weights used by the resulting system are those with the best encountered validation loss.

3 Evaluation

Datasets used by the CoNLL 2016 Shared Task consist of PDTB for English, CDTB for Chinese, and two unknown blind test datasets from Wikinews. For each language there is a train dataset for training models, validation dataset for monitoring the learning process, and test and blind test datasets for evaluating its performance.

Metric used for this subtask of CoNLL 2016 Shared Task is the F_1-measure. It is computed based on the number of predicted discourse relation senses that match a gold standard relation.

3.1 Results for English

The training dataset from PDTB for English consists of 1756 documents with 15246 discourse relations that can be categorized into 15 different discourse relation senses.

Overall our system performs pretty well on all English datasets (see Table 2) despite not using any external resources or hand-engineered features. As expected it performs best on the validation dataset, achieves slightly lower scores (0.5845) on the test dataset, and performs the worst on the blind dataset (0.5246) that contains a different writing style than PDTB. For only explicit relations our system performs much better, close to inter-annotator agreement (91%) on development and test datasets, but without using any word lists or patterns like other systems. On the other hand non-explicit relations seem to be a much harder problem and the relatively small size of the training dataset does not contain enough information.

Detailed per-sense analysis on all discourse relations is shown in Table 3. We see

Type	Dev	Test	Blind
Our only explicit	0.9181	0.8948	0.7525
Our only non-explicit	0.3458	0.3021	0.3308
Our all senses	0.6136	0.5845	0.5246
Best only explicit	0.9256	0.9022	0.7856
Best only non-explicit	0.4642	0.4091	0.3767
Best all senses	0.6797	0.6434	0.546

Table 2: Overall F_1-measures of discourse relation sense classification evaluated on different relation types on English datasets from our and best competing system of CoNLL 2016 Shared Task (Xue et al., 2016).

that our system performs consistently well on Contingency.Condition, Temporal.Async.Precedence, and Temporal.Async.Succession, but fails on Comparison.Concession, Expansion.Instantiation, and Expansion.Restatement.

Sense	Dev	Test	Blind
Comparison.Concession	0.2000	0.2105	0.0370
Comparison.Contrast	0.7696	0.7690	0.3077
Contingency.Cause.Reason	0.4087	0.5155	0.3556
Contingency.Cause.Result	0.4490	0.4216	0.4110
Contingency.Condition	0.9318	0.8966	0.9811
EntRel	0.5458	0.4523	0.5228
Expansion.Alt	0.9231	0.9091	0.5455
Expansion.Alt.Chosen alt.	0.7692	0.2000	-
Expansion.Conjunction	0.7015	0.6938	0.7432
Expansion.Instantiation	0.2899	0.4496	0.2041
Expansion.Restatement	0.2748	0.2584	0.2378
Temporal.Async.Precedence	0.7812	0.8706	0.8409
Temporal.Async.Succession	0.8211	0.7611	0.8468
Temporal.Synchrony	0.7931	0.6889	0.6034
Overall (micro-average)	0.6136	0.5845	0.5246

Table 3: Per-sense F_1-measures of discourse relation sense classification evaluated on all relations on English datasets.

3.2 Results for Chinese

The training dataset from CDTB for Chinese consists of 455 documents with 2445 discourse relations that can be categorized into 10 different discourse relation senses.

Overall our system performs pretty well on all Chinese datasets (see Table 4) despite not using any external resources or hand-engineered features. Its overall performance is almost consistent across the validation, test (0.7011), and blind

(0.7292) datasets, although the last one probably contains a different writing style than CDTB. For only explicit relations our system performs much better on development and test datasets. For non-explicit relations the situation seems to be the opposite. This inconsistencies indicate that the relatively small size of the training dataset does not contain enough information.

Type	Dev	Test	Blind
Our only explicit	0.9351	0.9271	0.7898
Our only non-explicit	0.6667	0.6407	0.7068
Our all senses	0.7206	0.7011	0.7292
Best only explicit	0.9610	0.9634	0.8039
Best only non-explicit	0.7353	0.7242	0.6338
Best all senses	0.7807	0.7701	0.6473

Table 4: Overall F_1-measures of discourse relation sense classification evaluated on different relation types on Chinese datasets from our and best competing system of CoNLL 2016 Shared Task (Xue et al., 2016).

Detailed per-sense analysis on all discourse relations is shown in Table 5. We see that our system performs consistently well on Conjunction, Conditional, and Temporal, but does not perform at all on Alternative, EntRel, and Progression, because of insufficient number of samples.

Sense	Dev	Test	Blind
Alternative	-	-	0.0000
Causation	0.6857	0.4545	0.6748
Conditional	1.0000	0.7500	0.7455
Conjunction	0.8175	0.8228	0.8145
Contrast	0.6957	0.8571	0.6612
EntRel	0.0000	0.0000	0.0000
Expansion	0.5641	0.4628	0.5436
Progression	0.0000	0.0000	0.0000
Purpose	0.8000	0.7857	0.5172
Temporal	1.0000	0.8649	0.7979
Overall (micro-average)	0.7206	0.7011	0.7292

Table 5: Per-sense F_1-measures of discourse relation sense classification evaluated on all relations on Chinese datasets.

4 Conclusion

We have shown that it is possible to implement a shallow discourse relation sense classifier that does not depend on any external sources, hand-engineered features, patterns, and complex fine-tuned pipelines. Our system consists of two neural network models built from three types of layers and is trained end-to-end. As a consequence it is almost language-agnostic and we have evaluated its performance on the English and Chinese datasets.

References

François Chollet. 2015. Keras. `https://github.com/fchollet/keras`.

Junyoung Chung, Caglar Gulcehre, Kyunghyun Cho, and Yoshua Bengio. 2014. Empirical Evaluation of Gated Recurrent Neural Networks on Sequence Modeling. *arXiv*, pages 1–9.

Xiaojie Jin, Chunyan Xu, Jiashi Feng, Yunchao Wei, Junjun Xiong, and Shuicheng Yan. 2015. Deep Learning with S-shaped Rectified Linear Activation Units.

Ziheng Lin, Hwee Tou Ng, and Min-Yen Kan. 2014. A PDTB-Styled End-to-End Discourse Parser. *Nat. Lang. Eng.*, 20(2):151–184.

Tomas Mikolov, Kai Chen, Greg Corrado, and Jeffrey Dean. 2013. Distributed Representations of Words and Phrases and their Compositionality. *Nips*, pages 1–9.

Martin Potthast, Tim Gollub, Francisco Rangel, Paolo Rosso, Efstathios Stamatatos, and Benno Stein. 2014. Improving the Reproducibility of PAN's Shared Tasks: Plagiarism Detection, Author Identification, and Author Profiling. In Evangelos Kanoulas, Mihai Lupu, Paul Clough, Mark Sanderson, Mark Hall, Allan Hanbury, and Elaine Toms, editors, *Inf. Access Eval. meets Multilinguality, Multimodality, Vis. 5th Int. Conf. CLEF Initiat. (CLEF 14)*, pages 268–299, Berlin Heidelberg New York, sep. Springer.

Rashmi Prasad, Nikhil Dinesh, Alan Lee, Eleni Miltsakaki, Livio Robaldo, Aravind Joshi, and Bonnie Webber. 2008. The Penn Discourse TreeBank 2.0. *Proc. Sixth Int. Conf. Lang. Resour. Eval.*, pages 2961–2968.

Evgeny Stepanov, Giuseppe Riccardi, and Ali Orkan Bayer. 2015. The UniTN Discourse Parser in CoNLL 2015 Shared Task: Token-level Sequence Labeling with Argument-specific Models. *Proc. Ninet. Conf. Comput. Nat. Lang. Learn. - Shar. Task*, (Dcd):25–31.

Jianxiang Wang and Man Lan. 2015. A refined end-to-end discourse parser. In *Proc. Ninet. Conf. Comput. Nat. Lang. Learn. Shar. Task*, pages 17–24.

Nianwen Xue, Hwee Tou Ng, Sameer Pradhan, Rashmi Prasad, Christopher Bryant, and Attapol T. Rutherford. 2015. The CoNLL-2015 Shared Task on Shallow Discourse Parsing. In *Proc. Ninet. Conf. Comput. Nat. Lang. Learn. Shar. Task*, pages 1–16.

Nianwen Xue, Hwee Tou Ng, Sameer Pradhan, Bonnie Webber, Attapol Rutherford, Chuan Wang, and Hongmin Wang. 2016. The CoNLL-2016 Shared Task on Multilingual Shallow Discourse Parsing. In *Proc. Twent. Conf. Comput. Nat. Lang. Learn. - Shar. Task*, Berlin, Germany, aug. Association for Computational Linguistics.

Yuping Zhou and Nianwen Xue. 2012. PDTB-style Discourse Annotation of Chinese Text. *Proc. 50th Annu. Meet. Assoc. Comput. Linguist. (Volume 1 Long Pap.*, (July):69–77.

Robust Non-Explicit Neural Discourse Parser in English and Chinese

Attapol T. Rutherford[*]
Yelp
San Francisco, CA, USA
teruth@yelp.com

Nianwen Xue
Brandeis University
Waltham, MA, USA
xuen@brandeis.edu

Abstract

Neural discourse models proposed so far are very sophisticated and tuned specifically to certain label sets. These are effective, but unwieldy to deploy or re-purpose for different label sets or languages. Here, we propose a robust neural classifier for non-explicit discourse relations for both English and Chinese in CoNLL 2016 Shared Task datasets. Our model only requires word vectors and simple feed-forward training procedure, which we have previously shown to work better than some of the more sophisticated neural architecture such as long-short term memory model. Our Chinese model outperforms feature-based model and performs competitively against other teams. Our model obtains the state-of-the-art results on the English blind test set, which is used as the main criteria in this competition.

1 Introduction

In the context of CoNLL 2016 Shared Task, we participate partially in the English and Chinese supplementary evaluation, which is discourse relation sense classification (Xue et al., 2016). We focus on identifying the sense of non-explicit discourse relations in both English and Chinese. Previous studies including the results from CoNLL 2015 Shared Task have shown that classifying the senses of implicit discourse relations is the most difficult part of the task of discourse parsing (Xue et al., 2015). Therefore, we focus exclusively on this particular challenging subtask.

We want our system to be robust such that the system can be easily trained to handle different la-

bel sets and different languages. Neural network is attractive in this regard as we do not need hand-crafted linguistic resources, which are not readily available in all languages. The past neural network models for this task focus on top-level senses (Ji et al., 2016) or require parses (Ji and Eisenstein, 2015), redundant surface features (Rutherford and Xue, 2014), or extensive semantic lexicon (Pitler et al., 2009). The results from these systems are not likely to extend to languages that do not have as much linguistic resources as English. Therefore, we come up with a neural network model that requires no parses and specific model tuning. The only extra ingredient is word vectors, which are easily obtained through large amount of unannotated data.

Our past studies have indicated that feedforward neural networks outperform more complicated models such as long-short term memory models and perform comparably with systems with traditional surface features in this task (Rutherford et al., 2016). But we want to test our results further. We wonder whether our best feedforward architecture can be adopted to deal with a totally different language and a different label set put forth specifically for this shared task. We also want to know whether our model is robust against the slightly out-of-domain blind datasets.

The performance numbers from the experiments alone hardly provide us with insight into implicit discourse relations. We compare and contrast the two approaches in more detail to learn what we gain and lose by using each approach. The fundamental difference between our approach and the baseline is that our approach does not use surface features or semantic lexicons. We want to know the advantage one gains from shifting the paradigm from discrete surface features to continuous features. Are the errors made by two types of systems complementary?

---

[*]Work performed while being a student at Brandeis

55

Proceedings of the 54th Annual Meeting of the Association for Computational Linguistics, pages 55–59,
Berlin, Germany, August 7-12, 2016. ©2016 Association for Computational Linguistics

Our system is ranked the first on the English dataset and the third on the Chinese dataset. The accuracy on the English blind test set is 0.3767, and the accuracy on the Chinese blind test set is 0.6338. The performance on the test sets even exceeds the one on the development sets, which suggest the robustness of our model.

2   Model description

The Arg1 vector a^1 and Arg2 vector a^2 are computed by applying element-wise pooling function f on all of the N_1 word vectors in Arg1 $w^1_{1:N_1}$ and all of the N_2 word vectors in Arg2 $w^2_{1:N_2}$ respectively:

$$a^1_i = \sum_{j=1}^{N} w^1_{j,i}$$

$$a^2_i = \sum_{j=1}^{N} w^2_{j,i}$$

Inter-argument interaction is modeled directly by the hidden layers that take argument vectors as features. Discourse relations cannot be determined based on the two arguments individually. Instead, the sense of the relation can only be determined when the arguments in a discourse relation are analyzed jointly. The first hidden layer h_1 is the non-linear transformation of the weighted linear combination of the argument vectors:

$$h_1 = \tanh(W_1 \cdot a^1 + W_2 \cdot a^2 + b_{h_1})$$

where W_1 and W_2 are $d \times k$ weight matrices and b_{h_1} is a d-dimensional bias vector. Further hidden layers h_t and the output layer o follow the standard feedforward neural network model.

$$h_t = \tanh(W_{h_t} \cdot h_{t-1} + b_{h_t})$$
$$o = \mathrm{softmax}(W_o \cdot h_T + b_o)$$

where W_{h_t} is a $d \times d$ weight matrix, b_{h_t} is a d-dimensional bias vector, and T is the number of hidden layers in the network.

We think that this model architecture should be effective because we have run extensive studies and experiments on many configuration and architectures (Rutherford et al., 2016). We have experimented and tuned most components: pooling functions for the argument vectors, the type of word vectors, and the model architectures themselves. We found the model variant with two hidden layers and 300 hidden units to work well across many settings. The model has the total of around 270k parameters.

3   Experiments

Word vectors English word vectors are taken from 300-dimensional Skip-gram word vectors trained on Google News data, provided by the shared task organizers (Mikolov et al., 2013; Xue et al., 2015). We trained our own 250-dimensional Chinese word vectors on Gigaword corpus, which is the same corpus used by the 300-dimensional Chinese word vectors provided by the shared task organizers (Graff and Chen, 2005). We found the 250-dimensional version to work better despite fewer parameters.

Training Weight initialization is uniform random, following the formula recommended by Bengio (2012). Word vectors are fixed during training. The cost function is the standard cross-entropy loss function, and we use Adagrad as the optimization algorithm of choice. We monitor the accuracy on the development set to determine convergence.

Implementation All of the models are implemented in Theano (Bergstra et al., 2010; Bastien et al., 2012). The gradient computation is done with symbolic differentiation, a functionality provided by Theano. The models are trained on CPUs on Intel Xeon X5690 3.47GHz, using only a single core per model. The models converge in minutes. The implementation, the training script, and the trained model are already made available [1] .

Baseline The winning system from last year's task serves as a strong baseline for English. We choose this system because it represents one of the strongest systems that utilizes exclusively surface features and extensive semantic lexicon (Wang and Lan, 2015). This approach uses a MaxEnt model loaded with millions of features.

We use Brown cluster pair features as the baseline for Chinese as there is no previous system for Chinese. We use 3,200 clusters to create features and perform feature selection on the development set based on the information gain criteria (Rutherford and Xue, 2014). We end up with 10,000 features total.

4   Results and Discussion

The English results are summarized in Table 1. The English baseline we use is from the winning system from last year's task (Wang and Lan, 2015). Our system is more accurate than the baseline on the two test sets but not on the develop-

---

[1] https://github.com/attapol/nn_discourse_parser

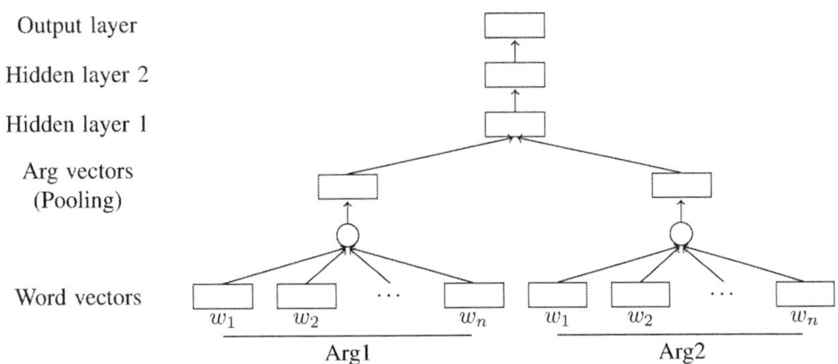

Figure 1: Model architecture

Sense	Development set		Test set		Blind test set	
	Baseline	Ours	Baseline	Ours	Baseline	Ours
Comparison.Concession	0	0	0	0	0	0
Comparison.Contrast	0.098	0.1296	0.1733	0.1067	0	0
Contingency.Cause.Reason	0.4398	0.3514	0.3621	0.4	0.2878	0.3103
Contingency.Cause.Result	0.2597	0.1951	0.1549	0.1722	0.2254	0.1818
EntRel	0.6247	0.5613	0.5265	0.4892	0.5471	0.5516
Expansion.Alternative.Chosen alternative	0	0	0	0	0	0
Expansion.Conjunction	**0.4591**	0.3874	**0.3068**	0.2468	**0.3154**	0.2644
Expansion.Instantiation	0.2105	**0.4051**	0.3261	**0.4962**	0.1633	**0.25**
Expansion.Restatement	0.3482	0.3454	0.2923	0.3483	0.3232	0.2991
Temporal.Asynchronous.Precedence	0	0.0714	0	0	0	0.125
Temporal.Asynchronous.Succession	0	0	0	0	0	0
Temporal.Synchrony	0	0	0	0	0	0
Accuracy	0.4331	0.4032	0.3455	0.3613	0.3629	0.3767
Most-frequent-tag Acc.	0.2320		0.2844		0.2136	

Table 1: F_1 scores for English non-explicit discourse relation. The bold-faced numbers highlight the senses where the classification of our model and the baseline model might be complementary.

ment set. Both systems only learn the top six or seven senses because the other senses constitute only around 5% of the training set, which might not be enough when compared to the complexity of the task.

Our system outperforms the most frequent tag baseline and Brown cluster pair baseline by 7% and by 3% (absolute) respectively in the CDTB datasets (Table 2). Our system only learns to distinguish between EntRel, Conjunction, and Expansion, which are the top three most frequent senses in the training set. The fourth most frequent class, Causation, constitute only around 200 instances in the training set, which is too small for machine learning approaches.

Generally, we would expect the performance on the in-domain test set to be worse than the performance on the in-domain development set. However, we do not observe this trend in the Chinese evaluation. This suggests that our model shows

some robustness. Similarly, we would expect the performance on the slightly-out-of-domain test set to be worse than the performance on the in-domain test set. This is also not the case for the English data, which suggests robustness of the model.

What is the trade-off in terms of the performance? The results suggests that the two approaches are partially complementary at least for English. For example, our system does significantly better on Expansion.Instantiation, but the surface feature system does significantly better on Expansion.Conjunction (Table 1). This suggests that surface feature approach still holds some advantage over the neural network approach that we propose here. In the next section, we compare the errors each of the systems more quantitatively.

5 Error Analysis

Comparing confusion matrices from the two approaches help us understand further what neural

	Development set		Test set		Blind test set	
Sense	Baseline	Ours	Baseline	Ours	Baseline	Ours
Alternative	0	0	0	0	0	0
Causation	0	0	0	0	0	0
Conditional	0	0	0	0	0	0
Conjunction	0.7830	0.7928	0.7911	0.8055	0.7875	0.7655
Contrast	0	0	0	0	0	0
EntRel	0.4176	0.4615	0.5175	0.5426	0.0233	0.0395
Expansion	0.4615	0.4167	0.2333	0.4333	0.2574	0.5104
Purpose	0	0	0	0	0	0
Temporal	0	0	0	0	0	0
Accuracy	0.6634	0.683	0.6657	0.7047	0.6437	0.6338
Most-frequent-tag Acc.	0.6176		0.6351		0.7914	

Table 2: F_1 scores for Chinese non-explicit discourse relation.

, confused as ... by ...	Instantiation	Contrast	Result	Precedence	Synchrony
Conjunction		+		#+	#+
Restatement	+				
Result		#			#
Reason			+		

The true sense is ...

Table 3: Confusion pairs made by our neural network (#) and the baseline surface features (+) in English.

networks have achieved. We approximate Bayes Factors with uniform prior for each sense pair (c_i, c_j) for gold standard g and system p:

$$\frac{P(p = c_i, g = c_j)}{P(p = c_i)P(g = c_j)}$$

We tabulate all significant confusion pairs (i.e. Bayes Factor greater than a cut-off) made by each of the systems (Table 3). This is done on the development set only.

The distribution of the confusion pairs suggest that neural network and surface feature systems complement each other in some way. We see that the two systems only share two confusion pairs in common.

Temporal.Asynchronous senses are confused with Conjunction by both systems. Temporal senses are difficult to classify in implicit discourse relations since the annotation itself can be quite ambiguous. Expansion.Instantiation relations are misclassified as Expansion.Restatement by surface feature systems. Neural network system performs better on Expansion.Instantiation than surface feature systems probably because neural network system can tease apart Expansion.Instantiation and Expansion.Restatement.

6 Conclusions

We present a robust neural network model, which is easy to deploy, retrain, and adapt to other languages and label sets. The model only needs word vectors trained on large corpora, which are available in most major languages. Our approach performs competitively if not better than traditional systems with surface features and MaxEnt model despite having one or two orders of magnitude fewer parameters. Our results suggest that simple feedforward architecture can be more powerful than more sophisticated neural architectures undertaken by other systems in this shared task.

References

Frédéric Bastien, Pascal Lamblin, Razvan Pascanu, James Bergstra, Ian J. Goodfellow, Arnaud Bergeron, Nicolas Bouchard, and Yoshua Bengio. 2012. Theano: new features and speed improvements. Deep Learning and Unsupervised Feature Learning NIPS 2012 Workshop.

Yoshua Bengio. 2012. Practical recommendations for gradient-based training of deep architectures. In *Neural Networks: Tricks of the Trade*, pages 437–478. Springer.

James Bergstra, Olivier Breuleux, Frédéric Bastien, Pascal Lamblin, Razvan Pascanu, Guillaume Desjardins, Joseph Turian, David Warde-Farley, and Yoshua Bengio. 2010. Theano: a CPU and GPU math expression compiler. In *Proceedings of the Python for Scientific Computing Conference (SciPy)*, June. Oral Presentation.

David Graff and Ke Chen. 2005. Chinese gigaword. *LDC Catalog No.: LDC2003T09, ISBN*, 1:58563–58230.

Yangfeng Ji and Jacob Eisenstein. 2015. One vector is not enough: Entity-augmented distributed semantics for discourse relations. *Transactions of the Association for Computational Linguistics*, 3:329–344.

Yangfeng Ji, Gholamreza Haffari, and Jacob Eisenstein. 2016. A latent variable recurrent neural network for discourse relation language models. In *Proceedings of the 2016 Conference of the North American Chapter of the Association for Computational Linguistics: Human Language Technologies*.

Tomas Mikolov, Kai Chen, Greg Corrado, and Jeffrey Dean. 2013. Efficient estimation of word representations in vector space. *CoRR*, abs/1301.3781.

Emily Pitler, Annie Louis, and Ani Nenkova. 2009. Automatic sense prediction for implicit discourse relations in text. In *Proceedings of the Joint Conference of the 47th Annual Meeting of the ACL and the 4th International Joint Conference on Natural Language Processing of the AFNLP: Volume 2-Volume 2*, pages 683–691. Association for Computational Linguistics.

Attapol T. Rutherford and Nianwen Xue. 2014. Discovering implicit discourse relations through brown cluster pair representation and coreference patterns. In *Proceedings of the 14th Conference of the European Chapter of the Association for Computational Linguistics (EACL 2014)*, Gothenburg, Sweden, April.

A. T. Rutherford, V. Demberg, and N. Xue. 2016. Neural Network Models for Implicit Discourse Relation Classification in English and Chinese without Surface Features. *ArXiv e-prints*, June.

Jianxiang Wang and Man Lan. 2015. A refined end-to-end discourse parser. In *Proceedings of the Nineteenth Conference on Computational Natural Language Learning - Shared Task*, pages 17–24, Beijing, China, July. Association for Computational Linguistics.

Nianwen Xue, Hwee Tou Ng, Sameer Pradhan, Rashmi Prasad, Christopher Bryant, and Attapol Rutherford. 2015. The conll-2015 shared task on shallow discourse parsing. In *Proceedings of the Nineteenth Conference on Computational Natural Language Learning - Shared Task*, pages 1–16, Beijing, China, July. Association for Computational Linguistics.

Nianwen Xue, Hwee Tou Ng, Sameer Pradhan, Bonnie Webber, Attapol Rutherford, Chuan Wang, and Hongmin Wang. 2016. The conll-2016 shared task on multilingual shallow discourse parsing. In *Proceedings of the Twentieth Conference on Computational Natural Language Learning - Shared Task*, Berlin, Germany, August. Association for Computational Linguistics.

A Constituent Syntactic Parse Tree Based Discourse Parser

Zhongyi Li[1,2], **Hai Zhao**[1,2,*],**Chenxi Pang**[1,2],**Lili Wang**[1,2],**Huan Wang**[3]
[1]Department of Computer Science and Engineering,
Shanghai Jiao Tong University, Shanghai, 200240, China
[2]Key Laboratory of Shanghai Education Commission for Intelligent Interaction
and Cognitive Engineering, Shanghai Jiao Tong University, Shanghai, 200240, China
[3]Omron Institute of Sensing & Control Technology(Shanghai)
{rival2710,wang_lili}@sjtu.edu.cn, zhaohai@cs.sjtu.edu.cn
pcx0558@163.com,hwang8@gc.omron.com

Abstract

This paper describes our system in the CoNLL-2016 shared task. Our system takes a piece of newswire text as input and returns the discourse relations. In our system we use a pipeline to conduct each subtask. Our system is evaluated on the CoNLL-2016 Shared Task closed track and obtains 0.1515 in F1 measurement, especially the part of detecting connectives, which achieves 0.9838 on blind test set.

1 Introduction

An end-to-end discourse parser is a system using natural language text as input and the discourse relation in labeled text as output. It has been widely used in the field of natural language processing, such as text classification, question answering system. In these discourse relations, two argument spans are marked as targets looked for by discourse relations, while conjunctions (connective) play an important role to confirm the relationship between the two argument spans. According to whether the conjunctions clearly appear in the text, discourse relations can be divided into two categories: explicit and non-explicit.

Penn Discourse Treebank (PDTB) has become the most important corpus in the field of discourse parsing. Previous work (Lin et al., 2014) integrated the entire training process together to form

*Corresponding author. This paper was partially supported by Cai Yuanpei Program (CSC No. 201304490199 and No. 201304490171), National Natural Science Foundation of China (No. 61170114 and No. 61272248), National Basic Research Program of China (No. 2013CB329401), Major Basic Research Program of Shanghai Science and Technology Committee (No. 15JC1400103), Art and Science Interdisciplinary Funds of Shanghai Jiao Tong University (No. 14JCRZ04), and Key Project of National Society Science Foundation of China (No. 15-ZDA041).

a complete discourse parser. There were five major components in the system, including Connective classifier, Argument labeler, Explicit classifier, Non-Explicit classifier, Attribution span labeler, with a part of PDTB as the training, which has achieved good prediction performance.

2 System Overview

We design our discourse parser as a sequential pipeline, shown in Figure 1. The whole system can be divided into two main parts: explicit and non-explicit.

The Explicit part contains:

(1) **Connective Classifier** Detects the discourse connectives. Note that not all commonly used conjunctions have the effect of connective, so we first identify the ones function as discourse connective.

(2) **Explicit Argument Labeler** Locates the relative positions and extracts spans of Arg1 and Arg2. We use an efficient method to extract for integrating Arg1 and Arg2 together.

(3) **Explicit Sense Classifier** Determines the discourse function of the detected connectives.

For the explicit part and non-explicit part, there is:

(4) **Filter** Gets rid of obviously incorrect parts, such as the ones that have already been marked as explicit relationship, with the remainder as the input part of non-explicit.

The non-explicit part contains:

(5) **Non-explicit Argument Labeler** marks the location and range of Arg1 and Arg2 in the case that lacks of connective.

(6) **Non-explicit Sense Classifier** Determines the discourse relations according to the semantic context of Arg1 and Arg2.

Proceedings of the 54th Annual Meeting of the Association for Computational Linguistics, pages 60–64,
Berlin, Germany, August 7-12, 2016. ©2016 Association for Computational Linguistics

3 System Components

Our system consists of six parts, and the general workflow refers to the shallow discourse parser based on the constituent parse tree (Chen et al., 2015). Feature extraction for training follows previous works (Kong et al., 2014; Lin et al., 2014; Pitler et al., 2009; Pitler and Nenkova, 2009).

We deduce each sentence into a constituent parse tree. Relative information is extracted from these constituent parse trees to train models and predict discourse relations.

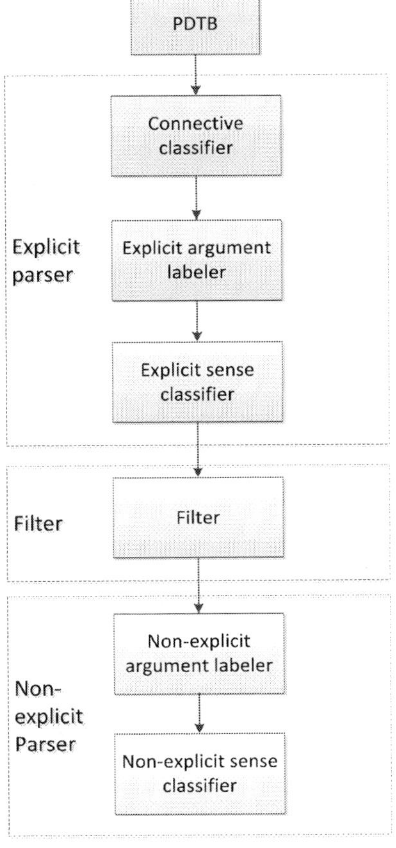

Figure 1: System overview

3.1 Explicit parser

3.1.1 Connective Classifier

In PDTB, there are 100 species of discourse connective, but not all conjunctions in the form of these 100 kinds of connective in the text are necessarily discourse relation. Thus, at first, we find out all connectives appearing in the text by scanning each constituent parse tree, then use the connective classifier to determine whether each connective functions as discourse connective.

The features in connective classifier are as follows.

(1) **ConnPos** The category of the tree node which covers the whole connective.

(2) **PrevConn** The previous word of the connective and the connective itself.

(3) **PrevPos** The category of the previous word of the connective.

(4) **PrevPosConnPos** The category of previous word and category of the connective.

(5) **ConnNext** The connective itself and the next word of the connective.

(6) **NextPos** The category of the next word of the connective.

(7) **ConnPosNextPos** The category of the connective itself and category of the next word.

After extracting the mentioned feature for each connective, we annotate it as 1 or 0 according to whether this word in PDTB functions as discourse connective. (Jia et al., 2013; Zhao and Kit, 2008) showed maximum entropy classifier performed well in relative tasks, so we apply it to our classification problem*. According to official evaluation, F1 score of this part in our system is 0.9905 on the dev set and 0.9838 on the blind test set, comparing to 0.9514 and 0.9186, the best result of CoNLL-2015. The detailed results are shown in Table 1.

set	P	R	F
dev	0.9971	0.9840	0.9905
test	0.9967	0.9819	0.9892
blind	0.9856	0.9821	0.9838

Table 1: Official scores of connective classifier

From the comparison, we can learn that

(1)From the constituent parse tree we build, we can extract connective features precisely.

(2)We use a straightforward way build our classifier. Comparing to previous works, our features and model are much more intuitively, and finally get even better result.

(3)There are different ways to process text, and our work shows that using constituent parse tree is a proper method in this task or similar ones.

---

*MaxEnt classifier of OpenNLP, an open-source toolkit. See http://opennlp.apache.org/

3.1.2 Argument labeler

In this part, we use interval mapping based on constituent parse tree and the extracting method proposed by (Kong et al., 2014). When training, in constituent parse tree, we start with the node of connective, and ended with the root node. Along the path, left and right sibling of each node have become the candidate member of the Argument. Given that some part of the explicit discourse relation used previous sentence (PS) as Arg1, we use the a efficient method (Kong et al., 2014), which is to treat the sentence previous to the one contained discourse connective as the candidate of Arg1. Later, we compare these candidates with PDTB, and label them as Arg1 and Arg2 or null, according to their uses in PDTB, of which null means that the candidate doesn't have the function of Arg1 or Arg2. By this means, we obtain satisfying effect of argument labeling.

The features were as follows:

(1) **ConStr** Prototype of connective in the text.

(2) **ConLStr** Lowercase of connective.

(3) **ConCat** Part of speech of connective.

(4) **ConLSib** Left sibling number of connective.

(5) **ConLSib** Right sibling number of connective.

(6) **CandiCtx** Candidate's category, category of parent node, category of left sibling, and category of right sibling.

(7) **ConCandiPath** Category of each node from the Candi to root node along the tree.

(8) **ConCandiPosition** The relative position between Candi and connective (left or right).

(9) **ConCandiPathLSib** Whether the left sibling number of the Candi is bigger than one.

3.1.3 Explicit Sense Classifier

In this part, we combine the feature of Lin's experiment with the feature of Pilter's, particularly as follows, (1) C prototype (2) C POS (3) prev+C (4) category of parent (5) category of left sibling (6) category of right sibling.

set	P	R	F
dev	0.4082	0.4219	0.4149
test	0.3226	0.3275	0.3251
blind	0.2527	0.2536	0.2531

Table 2: Official scores of explicit sense classifier

The detailed results are shown in Table 2. The results are also better than the best ones of CoNLL-2015, which were 0.3861 on the dev set and 0.2394 on the blind test set.

3.2 Filter

After identifying all explicit discourse relation connectives, and before non-explicit parser, we need to filter the training set. There are two cases for this filtering. (1) If one sentence, is labelled as Arg1 of some explicit discourse in previous step, then the related two sentences will not be considered by the following non-explicit parser. (2) In the original text, if two adjacent sentences are located between the last sentence of the previous paragraph and the first sentence of the next paragraph respectively, then these two sentences will not be considered, either.

3.3 Non-Explicit Parser

After explicit parser and filtering above, we take the rest part as input into non-explicit parser, for finding all the non-explicit discourse relations. In PDTB, there are three kinds of non-explicit discourse relations, which are Implicit, AltLex and EntRel. We notice that there is only 2.94% of AltLex. Besides, according to official evaluation criteria, we need to detect only 15 senses of the part of implicit. According to (Chen et al., 2015), we integrate EntRel together with implicit as a special sense for training and predicting.

3.3.1 Non-explicit Argument Labeler

In this part, we simply take the rest adjacent sentences which have been filtered as the argument span of non-explicit.

3.3.2 Non-explicit Sense Classifier

We perform sentence classification as mentioned above, practicing EntRel as a special sense of implicit, and ignored the senses which have few frequency of occurrences in PDTB. According to the previous works, the lost connective plays an important role in senses. Generally, connective appears at the beginning of the second sentence. According to this assumption, we use the following features.

(1) **Arg1Last** The last word of Arg1.

(2) **Arg1First** The first word of Arg1.

(3) **Arg2Last** The last word of Arg2.

(4) **Arg2Last** The first word of Arg2.

(5) **FirstS** The first word of Arg1 and Arg2.

(6) **LastS** The last word of Arg1 and Arg2.

(7) **Arg1First3** The first three words of Arg1.

(8) **Arg1First3** The first three words of Arg2.

(9) **Arg1Last3** The last three words of Arg1.

4 Results of Experiments

Our system is trained on the training set and evaluated on test set provided in the CoNLL-2016 Shared Task. We train our model of detecting connectives, extracting arguments of explicit part, predicting sense of connectives and predicting sense of non-explicit part, respectively.

The results of the official evaluation are shown in the Table 3, 4 and 5. From the result, we can learn that

(1) The part of connective detection and classification achieve great performances.

(2) The results of the sampled part are good, while there is still some gap between our system and the best one on the explicit and non-explicit part.

	P	R	F
Explicit Connective	0.9971	0.9840	0.9905
Extract Arg1	0.6128	0.5688	0.5900
Extract Arg2	0.7173	0.6658	0.6906
Extract Arg1&Arg2	0.4840	0.4493	0.4660
Parser	0.2778	0.3033	0.2900

Table 3: Official scores on dev set

	P	R	F
Explicit Connective	0.9967	0.9819	0.9892
Extract Arg1	0.5529	0.4988	0.5245
Extract Arg2	0.6674	0.6021	0.6331
Extract Arg1&Arg2	0.4033	0.3639	0.3826
Parser	0.2013	0.2233	0.2117

Table 4: Official scores on test set

	P	R	F
Explicit Connective	0.9856	0.9821	0.9838
Extract Arg1	0.5252	0.3501	0.4201
Extract Arg2	0.6675	0.4449	0.5339
Extract Arg1&Arg2	0.3615	0.2409	0.2891
Parser	0.1262	0.1894	0.1515

Table 5: Official scores on blind test set

5 Conclusion

In this paper, we present a complete discourse parser. Based on these previous works and through continuous improvement, our system has achieved good results. According to the official evaluation of CoNLL-2016 Shared Task closed track, our system gets 0.9905 in F1-measure on explicit connective classifier, and finally achieves 0.1515 in F1-measure on the official blind test.

References

Changge Chen, Peilu Wang, and Hai Zhao. 2015. Shallow discourse parsing using constituent parsing tree. In *Proceedings of the Nineteenth Conference on Computational Natural Language Learning - Shared Task*, pages 37–41, Beijing, China, July. Association for Computational Linguistics.

Zhongye Jia, Peilu Wang, and Hai Zhao. 2013. Grammatical error correction as multiclass classification with single model. In *Seventeenth Conference on Computational Natural Language Learning: Shared Task*, pages 74–81, Sofia, Bulgaria, August.

Fang Kong, Hwee Tou Ng, and Guodong Zhou. 2014. A constituent-based approach to argument labeling with joint inference in discourse parsing. In *Proceedings of the 2014 Conference on Empirical Methods in Natural Language rocessing*, pages 68–77, Doha, Qatar, October.

Fang Kong, Sheng Li, and Guodong Zhou. 2015. The sonlp-dp system in the conll-2015 shared task. In *Proceedings of the Nineteenth Conference on Computational Natural Language Learning - Shared Task*, pages 32–36, Beijing, China, July. Association for Computational Linguistics.

Ziheng Lin, Hwee Tou Ng, and Min-Yen Kan. 2014. A pdtb-styled end-to-end discourse parser. *Natural Language Engineering*, pages 151–184, April.

Emily Pitler and Ani Nenkova. 2009. Using syntax to disambiguate explicit discourse connectives in text. *Proceedings of the Joint Conference of the 47th Annual Meeting of the ACL and the 4th International Joint Conference on Natural Language Processing of the AFNLP*, pages 13–16, August.

Emily Pitler, Annie Louis, and Ani Nenkova. 2009. Automatic sense prediction for implicit discourse relations in text. *Proceedings of the Joint Conference of the 47th Annual Meeting of the ACL and the 4th International Joint Conference on Natural Language Processing of the AFNLP*, pages 683–691, August.

Rashmi Prasad, Dinesh Nikhil, Alan Lee, Eleni Miltsakaki, Livio Robaldo, Aravind K Joshi, and Bonnie L Webber. 2008. The penn discourse treebank 2.0. *The International Conference on Language Resources and Evaluation*, May.

Lianhui Qin, Zhisong Zhang, and Hai Zhao. 2016. Shallow discourse parsing using convolutional neural network. In *Proceedings of the Twentieth Conference on Computational Natural Language Learning - Shared Task*, Berlin, Germany, Augest. Association for Computational Linguistics.

Jianxiang Wang and Man Lan. 2015. A refined end-to-end discourse parser. In *Proceedings of the Nineteenth Conference on Computational Natural Language Learning - Shared Task*, pages 17–24, Beijing, China, July. Association for Computational Linguistics.

Rui Wang, Masao Utiyama, Isao Goto, Eiichiro Sumita, Hai Zhao, and Bao-Liang Lu. 2013. Converting continuous-space language models into n-gram language models for statistical machine translation. In *EMNLP*, pages 845–850.

Peilu Wang, Zhongye Jia, and Hai Zhao. 2014a. Grammatical error detection and correction using a single maximum entropy model. In *Proceedings of the Eighteenth Conference on Computational Natural Language Learning: Shared Task*, pages 74–82, Baltimore, Maryland, June. Association for Computational Linguistics.

Peilu Wang, Yao Qian, Frank K Soong, Lei He, and Hai Zhao. 2014b. Learning distributed word representations for bidirectional lstm recurrent neural network. In *Proceedings of NAACL*.

Rui Wang, Hai Zhao, Bao-Liang Lu, Masao Utiyama, and Eiichiro Sumita. 2014c. Neural network based bilingual language model growing for statistical machine translation. In *EMNLP*, pages 189–195.

Nianwen Xue, Hwee Tou Ng, Sameer Pradhan, Attapol T. Rutherford, Bonnie Webber, Chuan Wang, and Hongmin Wang. 2016. The conll-2016 shared task on multilingual shallow discourse parsing. In *In Proceedings of the Twentieth Conference on Computational Natural Language Learning: Shared Task*, Berlin, Germany.

Hai Zhao and Chunyu Kit. 2008. Parsing syntactic and semantic dependencies with two single-stage maximum entropy models. *Proceedings of the Twelfth Conference on Computational Natural Language Learning*, pages 203–207, August.

Hai Zhao, Wenliang Chen, and Chunyu Kit. 2009a. Semantic dependency parsing of nombank and propbank: An efficient integrated approach via a large-scale feature selection. In *Proceedings of the 2009 Conference on Empirical Methods in Natural Language Processing: Volume 1-Volume 1*, pages 30–39. Association for Computational Linguistics.

Hai Zhao, Wenliang Chen, Chunyu Kit, and Guodong Zhou. 2009b. Multilingual dependency learning: A huge feature engineering method to semantic dependency parsing. In *Proceedings of the Thirteenth Conference on Computational Natural Language Learning: Shared Task*, pages 55–60. Association for Computational Linguistics.

Hai Zhao, Yan Song, Chunyu Kit, and Guodong Zhou. 2009c. Cross language dependency parsing using a bilingual lexicon. In *Proceedings of the Joint Conference of the 47th Annual Meeting of the ACL and the 4th International Joint Conference on Natural Language Processing of the AFNLP: Volume 1-Volume 1*, pages 55–63. Association for Computational Linguistics.

Hai Zhao, Xiaotian Zhang, and Chunyu Kit. 2013. Integrative semantic dependency parsing via efficient large-scale feature selection. *Journal of Artificial Intelligence Research*.

Hai Zhao. 2009. Character-level dependencies in chinese: usefulness and learning. In *Proceedings of the 12th Conference of the European Chapter of the Association for Computational Linguistics*, pages 879–887. Association for Computational Linguistics.

SoNLP-DP System for ConLL-2016 English Shallow Discourse Parsing

Fang Kong[1]   **Sheng Li**[2]   **Junhui Li**[1]   **Muhua Zhu**[2]   **Guodong Zhou**[1]

[1]Natural Language Processing Lab, Soochow University, China
{kongfang, lijunhui, gdzhou}@suda.edu.cn
[2] Alibaba Inc., Hangzhou, China
{lisheng.ls, muhua.zmh}@alibaba-inc.com

Abstract

This paper describes the submitted English shallow discourse parsing system from the natural language processing (NLP) group of Soochow university (SoNLP-DP) to the CoNLL-2016 shared task. Our System classifies discourse relations into explicit and non-explicit relations and uses a pipeline platform to conduct every subtask to form an end-to-end shallow discourse parser in the Penn Discourse Treebank (PDTB). Our system is evaluated on the CoNLL-2016 Shared Task closed track and achieves the 24.31% and 28.78% in F1-measure on the official blind test set and test set, respectively.

1 Introduction

Discourse parsing determines the internal structure of a text via identifying the discourse relations between its text units and plays an important role in natural language understanding that benefits a wide range of downstream natural language applications, such as coherence modeling (Barzilay and Lapata, 2005; Lin et al., 2011), text summarization (Lin et al., 2012), and statistical machine translation (Meyer and Webber, 2013).

As the largest discourse corpus, the Penn Discourse TreeBank (PDTB) corpus (Prasad et al., 2008) adds a layer of discourse annotations on the top of the Penn TreeBank (PTB) corpus (Marcus et al., 1993) and has been attracting more and more attention recently (Elwell and Baldridge, 2008; Pitler and Nenkova, 2009; Prasad et al., 2010; Ghosh et al., 2011; Kong et al., 2014; Lin et al., 2014). Different from another famous discourse corpus, the Rhetorical Structure Theory(RST) Treebank corpus(Carlson et al., 2001), the PDTB focuses on shallow discourse relations either lexically grounded in explicit discourse connectives or associated with sentential adjacency. This theory-neutral way makes no commitment to any kind of higher-level discourse structure and can work jointly with high-level topic and functional structuring (Webber et al., 2012) or hierarchial structuring (Asher and Lascarides, 2003).

Although much research work has been conducted for certain subtasks since the release of the PDTB corpus, there is still little work on constructing an end-to-end shallow discourse parser. The CoNLL 2016 shared task evaluates end-to-end shallow discourse parsing systems for determining and classifying both explicit and non-explicit discourse relations. A participant system needs to (1)locate all explicit (e.g., "because", "however", "and".) discourse connectives in the text, (2)identify the spans of text that serve as the two arguments for each discourse connective, and (3) predict the sense of the discourse relations (e.g., "Cause", "Condition", "Contrast").

In this paper, we describe the system submission from the NLP group of Soochow university (SoNLP-DP). Our shallow discourse parser consists of multiple components in a pipeline architecture, including a connective classifier, argument labeler, explicit classifier, non-explicit classifier. Our system is evaluated on the CoNLL-2016 Shared Task closed track and achieves the 24.31% and 28.78% in F1-measure on the official blind test set and test set, respectively.

The remainder of this paper is organized as follows. Section 2 presents our shallow discourse parsing system. The experimental results are described in Section 3. Section 4 concludes the paper.

Proceedings of the 54th Annual Meeting of the Association for Computational Linguistics, pages 65–69,
Berlin, Germany, August 7-12, 2016. ©2016 Association for Computational Linguistics

2 System Architecture

In this section, after a quick overview of our system, we describe the details involved in implementing the end-to-end shallow discourse parser.

2.1 System Overview

A typical text consists of sentences glued together in a systematic way to form a coherent discourse. Referring to the PDTB, shallow discourse parsing focus on shallow discourse relations either lexically grounded in explicit discourse connectives or associated with sentential adjacency. Different from full discourse parsing, shallow discourse parsing transforms a piece of text into a set of discourse relations between two adjacent or non-adjacent discourse units, instead of connecting the relations hierarchically to one another to form a connected structure in the form of tree or graph.

Specifically, given a piece of text, the end-to-end shallow discourse parser returns a set of discourse relations in the form of a discourse connective (explicit or implicit) taking two arguments (clauses or sentences) with a discourse sense. That is, a complete end-to-end shallow discourse parser includes:

- connective identification, which identifies all connective candidates and labels them as whether they function as discourse connectives or not,

- argument labeling, which identifies the spans of text that serve as the two arguments for each discourse connective,

- explicit sense classification, which predicts the sense of the explicit discourse relations after achieving the connective and its arguments,

- non-explicit sense classification, for all adjacent sentence pairs within each paragraph without explicit discourse relations, which classify the given pair into EntRel, NoRel, or one of the Implicit/AltLex relation senses.

Figure 1 shows the components and the relations among them. Different from traditional approach (i.e., Lin et al. (2014)), considering the interaction between argument labeler and explicit sense classifier, co-occurrence relation between explicit and non-explicit discourse relations in a text, our system does not employ complete sequential pipeline framework.

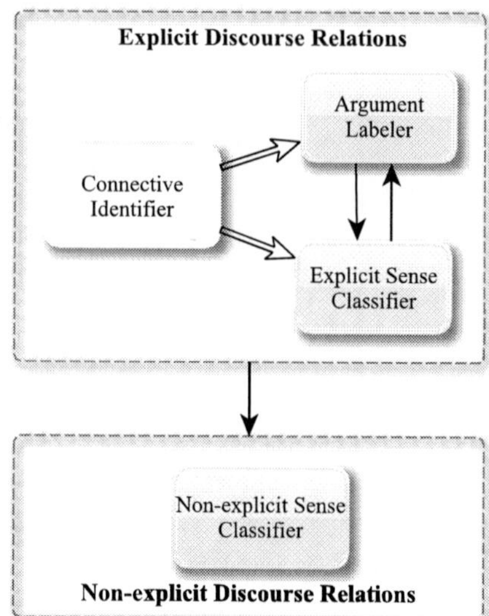

Figure 1: Framework of our end-to-end shallow discourse parser

2.2 Connective Identification

Our connective identifier works in two steps. First, the connective candidates are extracted from the given text referring to the PDTB. There are 100 types of discourse connectives defined in the PDTB. Then every connective candidate is checked whether it functions as a discourse connective.

Pitler and Nenkova (2009) showed that syntactic features extracted from constituent parse trees are very useful in disambiguating discourse connectives. Followed their work, Lin et al. (2014) found that a connective's context and part-of-speech (POS) are also helpful. Motivated by their work, we get a set of effective features, includes:

- Lexical: connective itself, POS of the connective, connective with its previous word, connective with its next word, the location of the connective in the sentence, i.e., start, middle and end of the sentence.

- Syntactic: the highest node in the parse tree that covers only the connective words (dominate node), the context of the dominate node [1], whether the right sibling contains a VP, the path from the parent node of the connective to the root of the parse tree.

---

[1] We use POS combination of the parent, left sibling and right sibling of the dominate node to represent the context. When no parent or siblings, it is marked NULL.

2.3 Argument Labeling

Argument labeler need to label the Arg1 and Arg2 spans for every connective determined by connective identifier. Following the work of Kong et al. (2014), we employ the constituent-based approach to argument labeling by first extracting the constituents from a parse tree are casted as argument candidates, then determining the role of every constituent as part of Arg1, Arg2, or NULL, and finally, merging all the constituents for Arg1 and Arg2 to obtain the Arg1 and Arg2 text spans respectively. Note that, we do not use ILP approach to do joint inference.

After extracting the argument candidates, a multi-category classifier is employed to determine the role of every argument candidate (i.e., Arg1, Arg2, or NULL) with features reflecting the properties of the connective, the candidate constituent and relationship between them. Features include,

- Connective related features: connective itself, its syntactic category, its sense class[2]

- Number of left/right siblings of the connective.

- The context of the constituent. We use POS combination of the constituent, its parent, left sibling and right sibling to represent the context. When there is no parent or siblings, it is marked NULL.

- The path from the parent node of the connective to the node of the constituent.

- The position of the constituent relative to the connective: left, right, or previous.

2.4 Explicit sense classification

After a discourse connective and its two arguments are identified, the sense classifier is proved to decide the sense that the relation conveys.

Although the same connective may carry different semantics under different contexts, only a few connectives are ambiguous (Pitler and Nenkova, 2009). Following the work of Lin et al. (2014), we introduce four features to train a sense classifier: the connective itself, its lower format, its POS and the combination of the previous word and the connective.

2.5 Non-explicit sense Classification

Referring to the PDTB, the non-explicit relations[3] are annotated for all adjacent sentence pairs within paragraphs. So non-explicit sense classification only considers the sense of every adjacent sentence pair within a paragraph without explicit discourse relations.

Our non-explicit sense classifier includes five traditional features:

Production rules: According to Lin et al. (2009), the syntactic structure of one argument may constrain the relation type and the syntactic structure of the other argument. Three features are introduced to denote the presence of syntactic productions in Arg1, Arg2 or both. Here, these production rules are extracted from the training data and the rules with frequency less than 5 are ignored.

Dependency rules: Similar with Production rules, three features denoting the presence of dependency productions in Arg1, Arg2 or both are also introduced in our system.

Fisrt/Last and First 3 words: This set of features include the first and last words of Arg1, the first and last words of Arg2, the pair of the first words of Arg1 and Arg2, the pair of the last words as features, and the first three words of each argument.

Word pairs: We include the Cartesian product of words in Arg1 and Arg2. We apply MI (Mutual Information) method to select top 500 word pairs.

Brown cluster pairs: We include the Cartesian product of the Brown cluster values of the words in Arg1 and Arg2. In our system, we take 3200 Brown clusters provided by CoNLL shared task.

Besides, we notice that not all adjacent sentences contain relation between them. Therfore, we view these adjacent sentences as NoRel relations like the PDTB.

3 Experimentation

We train our system on the corpora provided in the CoNLL-2016 Shared Task and evaluate our system on the CoNLL-2016 Shared Task closed track. All our classifiers are trained using the OpenNLP maximum entropy package[4] with the default pa-

---

[2]In training stage, we extract the gold sense class from the annotated corpus. And in testing stage, the sense classification will be employed to get the automatic sense.

[3]The PDTB provides annotation for Implicit relations, AltLex relations, entity transition (EntRel), and otherwise no relation (NoRel), which are lumped together as Non-Explicit relations.

[4]http://maxent.sourceforge.net/

rameters (i.e. without smoothing and with 100 iterations). We firstly report the official score on the CoNLL-2016 shared task on development, test and blind test sets. Then, the supplementary results provided by the shared task organizes are reported.

	Arg1&2	Conn	Parser
Dev	47.87	94.22	35.56
Test	41.68	94.71	28.78
Blind	36.19	91.62	**24.31**
Blind (Wang and Lan, 2015)	46.37	91.86	24.00

Table 1: the official F1 score of our system.

In Table 1, we present the official results of our system performances on the CoNLL-2016 development, test and blind test sets, respectively. In the blind test, our parser achieve a better result than the best system of last year (Wang and Lan, 2015).

		Arg1&2	Conn	Parser
Dev	Exp	46.37	94.22	42.97
	Non-Exp	49.51	-	27.54
Test	Exp	40.81	94.71	36.57
	Non-Exp	42.68	-	19.82
Blind	Exp	38.25	91.62	31.18
	Non-Exp	33.73	-	16.10

Table 2: the supplementary F1 score of our system.

In Table 2, we reported the supplementary results provided by the shared task organizes on the development, test and blind test sets. These additional experiments investigate the performance of our shallow discourse parsing for explicit and non-explicit relations separately. From the results, we can find that the sense classification for both explicit and non-explicit discourse relations are the biggest obstacles to the overall performance of discourse parsing.

Further, we reports all the official performance in Table 3 on the development, test and blind test set in detail. From the table, we observe:

- For argument recognition of explicit discourse relations, the performance of Arg2 is much better than that of Arg1 on all the three datasets. So the performance of *Arg1 & Arg2* recognition mainly depends on the performance of Arg1 recognition. With respect to non-explicit discourse relations, the performance gap of argument recognition on Arg1 and Arg2 is very small.

- With respect to explicit discourse relations, the sense classification works almost perfectly on development data. It also works well on the test and blind test sets. With respect to non-explicit discourse relations, the sense classification works much worse than that of explicit sense classification. The performance gap caused by non-explicit sense classification reaches 15% 16%.

4 Conclusion

We have presented the SoNLP-DP system from the NLP group of Soochow university that participated in the CoNLL-2016 shared task. Our system is evaluated on the CoNLL-2016 Shared Task closed track and achieves the 24.31% and 28.78% in F1-measure on the official blind test set and test set, respectively.

Acknowledgements

This research is supported by Key project 61333018 and 61331011 under the National Natural Science Foundation of China, Project 61472264, 61401295, 61305088 and 61402314 under the National Natural Science Foundation of China.

References

Nicholas Asher and Alex Lascarides. 2003. *Logics of Conversation*. Cambridge Unversity Press.

Regina Barzilay and Mirella Lapata. 2005. Modeling local coherence: An entity-based approach. In *Proceedings of the 43rd Annual Meeting of the Association for Computational Linguistics*.

Lynn Carlson, Daniel Marcu, and Mary Ellen Okurowski. 2001. Building a discourse-tagged corpus in the framework of rhetorical structure theory. In *Proceedings of Second SIGdial Workshop on Discourse and Dialogue*.

Robert Elwell and Jason Baldridge. 2008. Discourse connective argument identification with connective specific rankers. In *Second IEEE International Conference on Semantic Computing*.

Sucheta Ghosh, Richard Johansson, Giuseppe Riccardi, and Sara Tonelli. 2011. Shallow discourse parsing with conditional random fields. In *Proceedings of the 5th International Joint Conference on Natural Language Processing*.

Fang Kong, Hwee Tou Ng, and Guodong Zhou. 2014. A constituent-based approach to argument labeling

		Dev			Test			Blind test		
		P	R	F1	P	R	F1	P	R	F1
Explicit	Connective	93.53	94.93	94.22	94.04	95.38	94.71	90.47	92.80	91.62
	Arg1	52.50	53.28	52.89	46.80	47.47	47.14	46.58	47.79	47.18
	Arg2	74.26	75.37	74.81	70.64	71.65	71.14	67.99	69.74	68.85
	Arg1 & Arg2	46.03	46.72	46.37	40.52	41.10	40.81	37.77	38.75	38.25
	Overall	42.84	43.10	42.97	36.81	36.33	36.57	31.61	30.76	31.18
Non-Explicit	Connective	-	-	-	-	-	-	-	-	-
	Arg1	47.35	75.85	58.31	40.55	70.79	51.56	29.71	72.93	42.22
	Arg2	48.54	77.75	59.77	40.55	70.79	51.56	31.55	77.44	44.83
	Arg1 & Arg2	40.21	64.41	49.51	33.56	58.59	42.68	23.74	58.27	33.73
	Overall	35.67	22.43	27.54	27.19	15.60	19.82	27.82	11.33	16.10
All	Connective	93.53	94.93	94.22	94.04	95.38	94.71	90.47	92.80	91.62
	Arg1	50.35	63.31	56.09	43.89	57.04	49.61	37.55	56.19	45.02
	Arg2	60.72	76.36	67.65	54.87	71.31	62.02	48.30	72.28	57.91
	Arg1 & Arg2	42.97	54.03	47.87	36.87	47.92	41.68	30.19	45.17	36.19
	Overall	39.86	32.10	35.56	33.07	25.48	28.78	30.36	20.26	24.31

Table 3: Official results (%) of our parser on development, test and blind test sets. Group *Explicit* indicates the performance with respect to explicit discourse relations; group *Non-Explicit* indicates the performance with respect to non-explicit discourse relations, and group *all* indicates the performance with respect to all discourse relations, including both explicit and non-explicit ones.

with joint inference in discourse parsing. In *Proceedings of the 2014 Conference on Empirical Methods in Natural Language Processing*.

Ziheng Lin, Min-Yen Kan, and Hwee Tou Ng. 2009. Recognizing implicit discourse relations in the Penn Discourse Treebank. In *Proceedings of the 2009 Conference on Empirical Methods in Natural Language Processing*.

Ziheng Lin, Hwee Tou Ng, and Min-Yen Kan. 2011. Automatically evaluating text coherence using discourse relations. In *Proceedings of the 49th Annual Meeting of the Association for Computational Linguistics*.

Ziheng Lin, Chang Liu, Hwee Tou Ng, and Min-Yen Kan. 2012. Combining coherence models and machine translation evaluation metrics for summarization evaluation. In *Proceedings of the 50th Annual Meeting of the Association for Computational Linguistics*.

Ziheng Lin, Hwee Tou Ng, and Min-Yen Kan. 2014. A PDTB-styled end-to-end discourse parser. *Natural Language Engineering*, 20(2):151–184.

Mitchell P. Marcus, Beatrice Santorini, and Mary Ann Marcinkiewicz. 1993. Building a large annotated corpus of English: The Penn Treebank. *Computational Linguistics*, 19(2):313–330.

Thomas Meyer and Bonnie Webber. 2013. Implicitation of discourse connectives in (machine) translation. In *Proceedings of the Workshop on Discourse in Machine Translation*.

Emily Pitler and Ani Nenkova. 2009. Using syntax to disambiguate explicit discourse connectives in text. In *Proceedings of the ACL-IJCNLP 2009 Conference Short Papers*.

Rashmi Prasad, Nikhil Dinesh, Alan Lee, Eleni Miltsakaki, Livio Robaldo, Aravind Joshi, and Bonnie Webber. 2008. The Penn Discourse TreeBank 2.0. In *Proceedings of the LREC 2008 Conference*.

Rashmi Prasad, Aravind Joshi, and Bonnie Webber. 2010. Exploiting scope for shallow discourse parsing. In *Proceedings of the Seventh International Conference on Language Resources and Evaluation*.

Jianxiang Wang and Man Lan. 2015. A refined end-to-end discourse parser. In *Proceedings of the Nineteenth Conference on Computational Natural Language Learning - Shared Task*, pages 17–24, Beijing, China, July. Association for Computational Linguistics.

Bonnie Webber, Marcus Egg, and Valia Kordoni. 2012. Discourse structure and language technology. *Natural Language Engineering*, 18(4):437–490, 10.

Shallow Discourse Parsing Using Convolutional Neural Network

Lianhui Qin[1,2], **Zhisong Zhang**[1,2], **Hai Zhao**[1,2,*]
[1]Department of Computer Science and Engineering,
Shanghai Jiao Tong University, Shanghai, 200240, China
[2]Key Laboratory of Shanghai Education Commission for Intelligent Interaction
and Cognitive Engineering, Shanghai Jiao Tong University, Shanghai, 200240, China
`{qinlianhui, zzs2011}@sjtu.edu.cn,zhaohai@cs.sjtu.edu.cn`

Abstract

This paper describes a discourse parsing system for our participation in the CoNLL 2016 Shared Task. We focus on the supplementary task: Sense Classification, especially the Non-Explicit one which is the bottleneck of discourse parsing system. To improve Non-Explicit sense classification, we propose a Convolutional Neural Network (CNN) model to determine the senses for both English and Chinese tasks. We also explore a traditional linear model with novel dependency features for Explicit sense classification. Compared with the best system in CoNLL-2015, our system achieves competitive performances. Moreover, as shown in the results, our system has higher F1 score on Non-Explicit sense classification.

1 Introduction

This paper presents the Shanghai Jiao Tong University discourse parsing system for the CoNLL 2016 Shared Task (Xue et al., 2016) on Shallow Discourse Parsing and the supplementary tasks of sense classification for English and Chinese.

As shown by the results of the same task in CoNLL 2015 (Xue et al., 2015), sense classification has been found more difficult than other subtasks, especially determining Non-Explicit senses which is the bottleneck of the end-to-end discourse

parsing system. Without the discourse connectives which provide strong indications, the Non-Explicit relations between adjacent sentences are difficult to figure out. Therefore, our primary work is to improve sense classification components, especially on Non-Explicit relations. For other components such as connectives detection and arguments extraction, we just follow the top ranked system (Wang and Lan, 2015) in CoNLL-2015, which is as the baseline system in this paper.

In CoNLL-2015, various approaches were explored to conquer the sense classification problem, which is a straightforward multi-category classification task (Okita et al., 2015; Wang and Lan, 2015; Chiarcos and Schenk, 2015; Song et al., 2015; Stepanov et al., 2015; Yoshida et al., 2015; Sun et al., 2015; Nguyen et al., 2015; Laali et al., 2015). Typical data-driven machine learning methods, like Maximum Entropy and Support Vector Machine, were adopted. Some of them selected lexical and syntactic features over the arguments, including linguistically motivated word groupings such as Levin verb classes and polarity tags. Brown cluster features, surface features and entity semantics were also effective to enhance sense classification. Additionally, paragraph embeddings were also used to determine the senses (Okita et al., 2015). In other previous work of implicit sense classification, Chen et al (2015) used word-pair features for predicting missing connectives, Zhou et al. (2010) attempted to insert discourse connectives between arguments with the use of a language model, Lin et al. (2009) applied various feature selection methods. Although traditional methods have performed well on semantic tasks through feature engineering (Zhao et al., 2009a; Zhao et al., 2009b; Zhao et al., 2013), they still suffer from data sparsity problems.

Recently, Neural Network (NN) methods have shown competitive or even better performance

*Corresponding author. This paper was partially supported by Cai Yuanpei Program (CSC No. 201304490199 and No. 201304490171), National Natural Science Foundation of China (No. 61170114 and No. 61272248), National Basic Research Program of China (No. 2013CB329401), Major Basic Research Program of Shanghai Science and Technology Committee (No. 15JC1400103), Art and Science Interdisciplinary Funds of Shanghai Jiao Tong University (No. 14JCRZ04), and Key Project of National Society Science Foundation of China (No. 15-ZDA041).

Proceedings of the 54th Annual Meeting of the Association for Computational Linguistics, pages 70–77,
Berlin, Germany, August 7-12, 2016. ©2016 Association for Computational Linguistics

than traditional linear models with hand-crafted sparse features for some Nature Language Process (NLP) tasks (Wang et al., 2013; Wang et al., 2014; Cai and Zhao, 2016; Wang et al., 2016; Zhang and Zhao, 2016), such as sentence modeling (Kalchbrenner et al., 2014; Kim, 2014). In Non-Explicit sense classification, due to the absence of discourse connectives, the task is exactly to classify a sentence pair, where CNN could be utilized.

For Explicit sense classification which has strong discourse relation information provided by the connectives, we will use traditional linear methods with novel dependency features.

The rest of the paper is organized as follows: Section 2 briefly describes our system, Section 3 introduces the CNN model for modeling sentence pairs, Section 4 discusses our main works including Explicit sense classification and Non-Explicit sense classification, Section 5 shows our experiments on sense classification and Section 6 reports our results on the final official evaluation. Section 7 concludes this paper.

2   System Overview

Our parsing system uses the sequential pipeline following by (Lin et al., 2014; Wang and Lan, 2015). Figure 1 shows the system pipeline. The system can be roughly split into two parts: the Explicit parser and the Non-Explicit parser. We will give a brief introduction for every components. The overall parser starts from detecting discourse connectives for the Explicit Parser. Then the types of relative location of Argument1 (Arg1) and Argument2 (Arg2) are identified: Arg1 located in the exact previous sentence of Arg2 (noted as PS) or both arguments are within the same sentence (noted as SS). For the last part of Explicit parser, the tuples (Arg1, Connective, Arg2) are classified into one of the Explicit relation senses. For the Non-Explicit parser, it classifies the senses of Non-Explicit with original arguments and then extracts the arguments of the argument pairs. Finally, the senses of Non-Explicit argument pairs are again decided with refined arguments. Among all subtasks, we will focus on sense classification the other parts have been done relatively well in previous work.

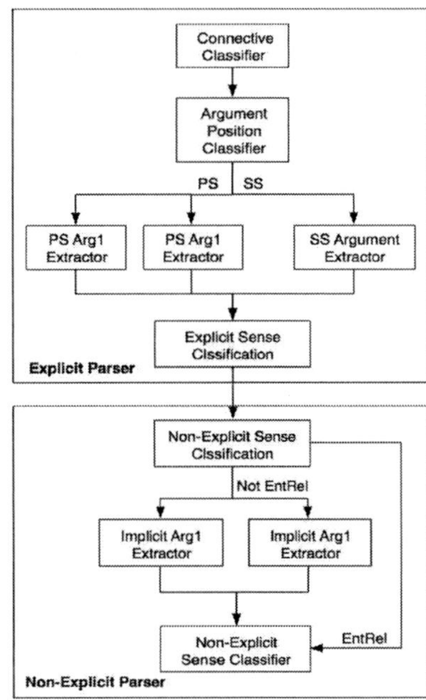

Figure 1: System pipeline for the discourse parser

3   Convolutional Neural Network

Each sentence could obtain a sentence vector through CNN and the final classification is based on the transformations of the sentence vectors. Although both Explicit and Non-Explicit tasks could utilize the neural model, CNN might be more apposite for the Non-Explicit one because of lacking indicating connectives.

The architecture of our CNN model, is illustrated in Figure 2. Firstly, a look-up table is utilized to fetch the embeddings of words and part-of-speech (POS) tags, forming two sentence embeddings which will be the input of the convolutional layer. Through the convolution and max pooling operations, two sentence vectors are obtained. Finally, these vectors will be sent to the final softmax layer after concatenated.

Embedding   For a sentence $\mathbf{S} = \mathbf{w}_1 \mathbf{w}_2 \ldots \mathbf{w}_n$ and POS sequence $\mathbf{P} = \mathbf{p}_1 \mathbf{p}_2 \ldots \mathbf{p}_n$, the sentence embedding M is formed through projection and concatenating. Following the jargons in the task, the input sentences will be called "Arguments" and the two arguments are represented as follows:

$$\mathbf{M}^1 = [\mathbf{w}_1^1 \oplus \mathbf{p}_1^1; \mathbf{w}_2^1 \oplus \mathbf{p}_2^1; \ldots; \mathbf{w}_n^1 \oplus \mathbf{p}_n^1]$$
$$\mathbf{M}^2 = [\mathbf{w}_1^2 \oplus \mathbf{p}_1^2; \mathbf{w}_2^2 \oplus \mathbf{p}_2^2; \ldots; \mathbf{w}_n^2 \oplus \mathbf{p}_n^2]$$

Here $\mathbf{w}_i^j \in \mathbb{R}^{d_w}$ is the word vector corresponding to the i-th word in the j-th argument, and $\mathbf{p}_i^j \in \mathbb{R}^{d_p}$ is the POS vector for $\mathbf{w}_i^j$, where d_w and d_p respectively stand for the dimensions of word and POS vectors. $\oplus$ and ; are the concatenation operators on different dimensions. Considering the efficiency, we specialize a max sentence length for both arguments, and apply truncating or zero-padding when needed.

Convolutional layer Filter matrices $[\mathbf{W}_1, \mathbf{W}_2, \ldots, \mathbf{W}_k]$ with several variable sizes $[l_1, l_2, \ldots, l_k]$ are utilized to perform the convolution operations for the sentence embeddings. Via parameter sharing, this feature extraction procedure become same for both arguments. For the sake of simplicity, ignoring the superscripts, we will explain the procedure for only one argument. The sentence embedding will be transformed to sequences $\mathbf{C}_j (j \in [1, k])$:

$$\mathbf{C}_j = [\ldots; \tanh(\mathbf{W}_j \cdot \mathbf{M}_{[i:i+l_j-1]} + \mathbf{b}_j); \ldots]$$

Here, $[i : i + l_j - 1]$ indexes the convolution window. Additionally, We apply wide convolution operation between embedding layer and filter matrices, because it ensures that all weights in the filters reach the entire sentence, including the words at the margins.

Max Pooling A one-max-pooling operation is adopted after convolution and the sentence vector s is obtained through concatenating all the mappings for those **k** filters.

$$\mathbf{s} = [\mathbf{s}_1 \oplus \cdots \oplus \mathbf{s}_j \oplus \cdots \oplus \mathbf{s}_k]$$
$$\mathbf{s}_j = \mathbf{max}(\mathbf{C}_j)$$

In this way, the model can capture the most important features in the sentence with different filters.

Concatenating and Softmax Now adding the superscripts and considering the two arguments ($\mathbf{s}^1$, $\mathbf{s}^2$), they are concatenated to form the argument-pair representation vector $\mathbf{v}$ as below:

$$\mathbf{v} = \mathbf{s}^1 \oplus \mathbf{s}^2$$

For the final labeling decision, a softmax layer will be applied using the argument-pair vector $\mathbf{v}$.

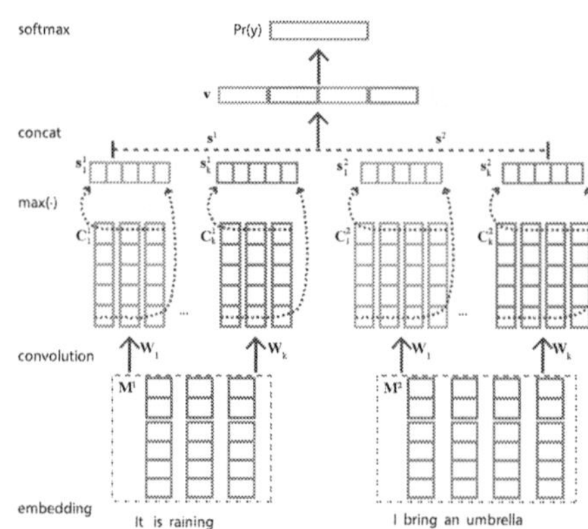

Figure 2: Our neural model for sentence classification.

Training The training object J will be the cross-entropy error E with $L2$ regularization:

$$E(\hat{y}, y) = -\sum_j^l y_j \times \log(Pr(\hat{y}_j))$$
$$J(\theta) = \frac{1}{m} \sum_k^m E(\hat{y}^{(k)}, y^{(k)}) + \frac{\lambda}{2} \|\theta\|^2$$

where y_j is the gold label and $\hat{y}_j$ is the predicted one. For the optimization process, we apply the diagonal variant of AdaGrad (Duchi et al., 2011) with mini-batches.

4 Sense Classification

Now we will discuss about the sense classification task. Both the Explicit and Non-Explicit labeling are typical classification tasks with the argument-pair as the input and the CNN model could be applied to both of them. However, the Explicit task provides the connectives which are the crucial indicators and we find that CNN performs slightly poorly on this task even if embeddings for indicators are concatenated. Thus, for the Explicit task, we will adopt the traditional linear model considering only the features related with the indicators and CNN model will be applied to the more difficult Non-Explicit task.

4.1 Explicit Sense Classification

For the Explicit classification task, connectives provide the crucial and decisive information. The connective itself has been found to be a very good

data set	baseline	C+C POS	add C-HP
English	90.14	91.35	92.11
Chinese	-	96.15	97.43

Table 1: Explicit Sense Classification on English and Chinese development sets without error propagation.

data set	baseline	CNN model
English	42.92	45.50
Chinese	-	71.57

Table 2: Non-Explicit Sense Classification on English and Chinese development sets without error propagation.

feature, as connectives are ambiguous as pointed out in Pitler et al. (2008), and the majority of the ambiguous connectives is highly skewed toward certain senses (Lin et al., 2014). Thus, the task is in fact to disambiguate the connective under different contexts.

Although the provided context contains the two whole arguments, the most crucial indicators are still the words that near the connectives or the ones that have close syntactic dependency relations with the connectives. This might explain why plain CNN model performs poorly on this task without these key features.

Thus, for the Explicit task, we will adopt the traditional method, using Support Vector Machines (SVM) with linear kernel and manually selected features. We consider only three features which are all related to Connective C: (1) C string (2) C POS (3) C string combined with POS of C's parent node in dependency tree (noted as C-HP).

We will use an example in the Chinese task to explain the influence of the third feature which utilizes the dependency tree.

(1) 男选手的成绩是近１０年来最差的一次，说明水平在下降[Arg1] 而 [Connective] 罗莉、乔娅和莫惠兰３名女选手都是第一次参加世界大赛，均表现不错。[Arg2]

(Contrast - CHTB_0310)

In Chinese, '而' is a connective with ambiguity relations of 'Contrast' and 'Conjunction'. Because 'Conjunction' accounts for a large part of these instances, the classifier will tend to predict '而' as 'Conjunction' if just using connective features. Like in this example, the sense of the in-

filter-size	on original Args
(2,3,3)	38.45
(2,4,5)	38.86
(2,6,12)	38.45
(3,3,3)	39.40
(4,8,12)	40.08
(6,8,18)	38.99

Table 3: F_1 scores (%) with different CNN filter sizes for Non-Explicit on **original** arguments on development set.

filter-size	on refined Args
(1,2,3)	45.11
(2,3,4)	44.18
(2,5,10)	44.97
(2,8,16)	43.25
(3,3,3)	45.50
(3,5,9)	43.92

Table 4: F_1 scores (%) with different CNN filter sizes for Explicit on **refined** arguments on development set.

stance is 'Contrast' but is predicted as 'Conjunction' if considering only the connective itself. But if we add the third feature, which means the combination feature '而-VC' will be added (C is '而' and POS of C's parent node is 'VC'), the classifier will correctly decide the right sense.

4.2 Non-Explicit Sense Classification

The situations for the Non-Explicit task are quite different. Without the information of connectives, we have to extract the discourse relations through the two arguments, which might need semantic comprehensions sometimes. This might be hard for traditional methods because it is not easy to extract hand-craft features. The neural models which can automatically extract features may be another solution.

We apply the CNN model described in Section 3 for this task. To simplify model building and parameter tuning, and also due to the similar architectures, the model structures for sense classification components in English and Chinese are identical.

5 Experiments

Our system is trained on the PDTB 2.0 corpus. Sections 02-21 are used as training set, and Section 22 as the development set. There are two tests

| Components | WSJ Test | | | | | |
| | baseline | | | our parser | | |
	P	R	F	P	R	F
ALL Explicit connective	94.83	93.49	94.16	92.42	94.88	93.63
Explicit Arg1 extraction	51.05	50.33	50.68	49.73	51.06	50.38
Explicit Arg2 extraction	77.89	76.79	77.33	75.73	77.75	76.73
Explicit Both extraction	45.54	44.90	45.22	44.31	45.49	44.90
Explicit only Parser	-	-	39.96	41.05	40.02	40.53
Non-Explicit Arg1 extraction	64.83	69.50	67.08	67.42	63.08	65.18
Non-Explicit Arg2 extraction	66.02	70.78	68.32	70.18	65.65	67.84
Non-Explicit Both extraction	51.20	54.89	52.98	53.44	50.00	51.67
Non-Explicit only Parser	-	-	20.74	20.66	22.11	21.36
All Arg1 extraction	59.20	61.03	60.10	59.67	58.29	58.97
All Arg2 extraction	71.43	73.64	72.52	72.82	71.13	71.97
All Both extration	48.62	50.13	49.36	49.10	47.96	48.52
All Parser	29.27	30.08	29.72	29.90	30.65	30.27

Table 5: Results of the Shallow Discourse Parsing task on English WSJ test set.

| Components | Blind Test | | | | | |
| | baseline | | | our parser | | |
	P	R	F	P	R	F
ALL Explicit connective	93.48	90.29	91.86	88.67	93.73	91.13
Explicit Arg1 extraction	49.16	47.48	48.31	47.12	49.81	48.43
Explicit Arg2 extraction	75.61	73.02	74.29	71.58	75.56	73.57
Explicit Both extraction	42.09	40.65	41.35	40.29	42.59	41.40
Explicit only Parser	-	-	30.38	32.57	30.76	31.64
Non-Explicit Arg1 extraction	58.66	63.25	60.87	64.01	59.38	61.61
Non-Explicit Arg2 extraction	71.88	77.49	74.58	80.86	75.00	77.82
Non-Explicit Both extraction	48.58	52.37	50.41	55.44	51.42	53.35
Non-Explicit only Parser	-	-	18.87	18.32	19.75	19.01
All Arg1 extraction	55.12	56.58	55.84	56.91	55.93	56.42
All Arg2 extraction	73.49	75.43	74.45	76.59	75.28	75.93
All Both extration	45.77	46.98	46.37	48.47	47.64	48.05
All Parser	23.69	24.32	24.00	24.41	24.81	24.61

Table 6: Results of the Shallow Discourse Parsing task on English Blind test set.

sets for the shared task: Section 23 of the PDTB, and a blind test prepared especially for this task. We participate in the closed track, so only two resources (Brown Clusters and MPQA Subjectivity Lexicon) are used. test platform of CoNLL-2016 still adopts still the TIRA evaluation platform (Potthast et al., 2014).

Non-Explicit relations contains three types: *Implicit, EntRel* and *AltLex*. Originally *EntRel* is not treated as discourse relation in Penn Discourse TreeBank (PDTB) (Prasad et al., 2008), but this category has been included in this task and we also count it as one sense. Some instances are annotated with two senses, so the predicted sense for a relation must match one of the two senses if there is more than one sense. We compare with the best system in the competition of CoNLL 2015 (Wang and Lan, 2015), which is regarded as the baseline.

5.1 Explicit Sense Classification

Table 1 reports our results of the Explicit sense classifier on both English and Chinese develop-ment sets. Compared with the baseline, our methods obtain progress and the overall F1 score of Explicit Sense classification increases by 1.97% for English task.

For both English and Chinese sense classification, the C string and C POS features can classify most of the relations correctly. Moreover, the new combination feature based on dependency relations helps effectively disambiguate senses.

5.2 Non-Explicit Sense Classification

For the Non-Explicit task, we utilize the CNN model to model the argument pairs. Following (Wang and Lan, 2015), in the final discourse parsing pipeline, we utilize the sense classifier twice, once for original arguments (adjacent sentence pairs) and once for redefined arguments (after argument extraction). Because the two classifiers expect different inputs, we train different CNN models for these two tasks and also with slightly different hyper-parameters.

components	WSJ Test			En Blind Test			CTB Test			CH Blind Test		
	P	R	F	P	R	F	P	R	F	P	R	F
Explicit Sense Classification	89.59	89.59	89.59	75.95	75.54	75.74	93.68	92.71	93.19	75.82	73.67	74.73
Non-Explicit Sense Classification	38.20	38.20	38.20	35.38	35.38	35.38	67.41	67.41	67.41	56.35	56.35	56.35
All Parser	62.69	62.69	62.69	53.94	53.85	53.89	72.91	72.75	72.83	61.02	61.02	61.02

Table 7: Results of the supplementary task on English and Chinese.

On Original Arguments The input for this classifier will be two adjacent sentences without Explicit discourse relations. The maximum input length for both sentences is set to 80, the dimensions for word embeddings and POS embeddings are 300 and 50 respectively. The word embeddings are initialized with pre-trained word vectors using *word2vec*[1] (Mikolov et al., 2013) and other parameters are randomly initialized including POS embeddings. We employ three categories of CNN filters, and choose 512 as the number of feature maps. About the filter region sizes, Zhang and Wallace (2015) have concluded that each dataset has its own optimal range. We set the three filter sizes to 4,8,12 separately according to the empirical results in Table 3.

On Refined Arguments This module is similar to the above one but with some differences. The input will be the refined arguments and correspondingly, golden argument pairs are utilized for training. Thus, we adopt slightly different hyperparameters. The number of feature maps for each filter categories is set to 1024, and the final filter region sizes are 3,3,3 accordingly to the empirical results in Table 4. For the choice of filter region sizes, we have attempted a lot of combinations, but only the best ones are shown.

Results of classification The trained model on refined arguments could be directly utilized for part of Non-Explicit sense classification in the supplementary task and Table 2 reports the results on English and Chinese development sets. Compared to the Explicit task, the Non-Explicit task is indeed much more difficult. Using CNN, we achieve an improvement of 2.58% compared to the baseline. This result fully illustrates that CNN model is suitable to determine the Non-Explicit relations.

6 Results

We report our official results and comparisons on Shallow Discourse Parsing task on English and the supplementary tasks of sense classification on English and Chinese.

Table 5 and 6 show the performance on two test sets for English: i) (Official) Blind test set; ii) Standard WSJ test set. Our parsers give higher F1 scores than baselines: 0.55% higher on WSJ test set and 0.61% on Blind Test set, though our Explicit connective detection F1 is less than theirs at the beginning of the pipeline, which might introduce more error propagations. This might suggest that our sense classifiers play key roles in the system.

To see the performances of the sense classifiers, Table 7 shows the results for English and Chinese supplementary tasks (sense classifications on golden argument pairs without errors propagation). For Explicit sense classification, the features we proposed are proved to be effective. For Non-Explicit sense classification, our CNN model also works well on the test sets. Compared to the performance of discourse parsing sense classification components (with error propagation), the subtask results are higher. The reasons include: i) Connective detection serves as the first component of the pipeline and plays an important role, because it has a major influence on Explicit sense classification which relies heavily on discourse connectives. ii) Arguments extraction also have important effects on the classifications for both Explicit and Non-Explicit relations.

7 Conclusions

This paper describes our discourse parsing system for the CoNLL 2016 shared Task and reports our results on test data and blind test data. Despite of the errors propagation in the beginning of discourse parsing pipeline, we still obtain improvements against baseline, and perform well on the supplementary tasks. Especially, the CNN model for Non-Explicit sense classification gives competitive performances. Actually, Non-Explicit sense classification performance can be furthermore improved in the future.

---

[1]http://www.code.google.com/p/word2vec

References

Deng Cai and Hai Zhao. 2016. Neural word segmentation learning for Chinese. In *Proceedings of ACL*, Berlin, Germany, August.

Changge Chen, Peilu Wang, and Hai Zhao. 2015. Shallow discourse parsing using constituent parsing tree. In *Proceedings of the Nineteenth Conference on Computational Natural Language Learning - Shared Task*, pages 37–41, Beijing, China, July. Association for Computational Linguistics.

Christian Chiarcos and Niko Schenk. 2015. A minimalist approach to shallow discourse parsing and implicit relation recognition. In *Proceedings of the Nineteenth Conference on Computational Natural Language Learning - Shared Task*, pages 42–49, Beijing, China, July. Association for Computational Linguistics.

John Duchi, Elad Hazan, and Yoram Singer. 2011. Adaptive subgradient methods for online learning and stochastic optimization. *The Journal of Machine Learning Research*, 12:2121–2159.

Nal Kalchbrenner, Edward Grefenstette, and Phil Blunsom. 2014. A convolutional neural network for modelling sentences. *arXiv preprint arXiv:1404.2188*.

Yoon Kim. 2014. Convolutional neural networks for sentence classification. *arXiv preprint arXiv:1408.5882*.

Majid Laali, Elnaz Davoodi, and Leila Kosseim. 2015. The clac discourse parser at CoNLL-2015. In *Proceedings of the Nineteenth Conference on Computational Natural Language Learning - Shared Task*, pages 56–60, Beijing, China, July. Association for Computational Linguistics.

Ziheng Lin, Min-Yen Kan, and Hwee Tou Ng. 2009. Recognizing implicit discourse relations in the penn discourse treebank. In *Proceedings of the 2009 Conference on Empirical Methods in Natural Language Processing: Volume 1-Volume 1*, pages 343–351. Association for Computational Linguistics.

Ziheng Lin, Hwee Tou Ng, and Min-Yen Kan. 2014. A pdtb-styled end-to-end discourse parser. *Natural Language Engineering*, 20(02):151–184.

Tomas Mikolov, Ilya Sutskever, Kai Chen, Greg S Corrado, and Jeff Dean. 2013. Distributed representations of words and phrases and their compositionality. In *Advances in neural information processing systems*, pages 3111–3119.

Son Nguyen, Quoc Ho, and Minh Nguyen. 2015. Jaist: A two-phase machine learning approach for identifying discourse relations in newswire texts. In *Proceedings of the Nineteenth Conference on Computational Natural Language Learning - Shared Task*, pages 66–70, Beijing, China, July. Association for Computational Linguistics.

Tsuyoshi Okita, Longyue Wang, and Qun Liu. 2015. The dcu discourse parser: A sense classification task. In *Proceedings of the Nineteenth Conference on Computational Natural Language Learning - Shared Task*, pages 71–77, Beijing, China, July. Association for Computational Linguistics.

Emily Pitler, Mridhula Raghupathy, Hena Mehta, Ani Nenkova, Alan Lee, and Aravind K Joshi. 2008. Easily identifiable discourse relations.

Martin Potthast, Tim Gollub, Francisco Rangel, Paolo Rosso, Efstathios Stamatatos, and Benno Stein. 2014. Improving the Reproducibility of PAN's Shared Tasks: Plagiarism Detection, Author Identification, and Author Profiling. In Evangelos Kanoulas, Mihai Lupu, Paul Clough, Mark Sanderson, Mark Hall, Allan Hanbury, and Elaine Toms, editors, *Information Access Evaluation meets Multilinguality, Multimodality, and Visualization. 5th International Conference of the CLEF Initiative (CLEF 14)*, pages 268–299, Berlin Heidelberg New York, September. Springer.

Rashmi Prasad, Nikhil Dinesh, Alan Lee, Eleni Miltsakaki, Livio Robaldo, Aravind K Joshi, and Bonnie L Webber. 2008. The penn discourse treebank 2.0. In *LREC*. Citeseer.

Yangqiu Song, Haoruo Peng, Parisa Kordjamshidi, Mark Sammons, and Dan Roth. 2015. Improving a pipeline architecture for shallow discourse parsing. In *Proceedings of the Nineteenth Conference on Computational Natural Language Learning - Shared Task*, pages 78–83, Beijing, China, July. Association for Computational Linguistics.

Evgeny Stepanov, Giuseppe Riccardi, and Ali Orkan Bayer. 2015. The unitn discourse parser in CoNLL 2015 shared task: Token-level sequence labeling with argument-specific models. In *Proceedings of the Nineteenth Conference on Computational Natural Language Learning - Shared Task*, pages 25–31, Beijing, China, July. Association for Computational Linguistics.

Jia Sun, Peijia Li, Weiqun Xu, and Yonghong Yan. 2015. A shallow discourse parsing system based on maximum entropy model. In *Proceedings of the Nineteenth Conference on Computational Natural Language Learning - Shared Task*, pages 84–88, Beijing, China, July. Association for Computational Linguistics.

Jianxiang Wang and Man Lan. 2015. A refined end-to-end discourse parser. In *Proceedings of the Nineteenth Conference on Computational Natural Language Learning - Shared Task*, pages 17–24, Beijing, China, July. Association for Computational Linguistics.

Rui Wang, Masao Utiyama, Isao Goto, Eiichro Sumita, Hai Zhao, and Bao-Liang Lu. 2013. Converting continuous-space language models into n-gram language models for statistical machine translation.

In *Proceedings of EMNLP*, pages 845–850, Seattle, Washington, USA, October.

Rui Wang, Hai Zhao, Bao-Liang Lu, Masao Utiyama, and Eiichiro Sumita. 2014. Neural network based bilingual language model growing for statistical machine translation. In *Proceedings of EMNLP*, pages 189–195, Doha, Qatar, October.

Peilu Wang, Yao Qian, Frank Soong, Lei He, and Hai Zhao. 2016. Learning distributed word representations for bidirectional lstm recurrent neural network. In *Proceedings of NAACL*, June.

Nianwen Xue, Hwee Tou Ng, Sameer Pradhan, Rashmi PrasadO Christopher Bryant, and Attapol T Rutherford. 2015. The CoNLL-2015 shared task on shallow discourse parsing. In *Proceedings of CoNLL*, page 2.

Nianwen Xue, Hwee Tou Ng, Sameer Pradhan, Bonnie Webber, Attapol Rutherford, Chuan Wang, and Hongmin Wang. 2016. The CoNLL-2016 shared task on multilingual shallow discourse parsing. In *Proceedings of the Twentieth Conference on Computational Natural Language Learning - Shared Task*, Berlin, Germany, August. Association for Computational Linguistics.

Yasuhisa Yoshida, Katsuhiko Hayashi, Tsutomu Hirao, and Masaaki Nagata. 2015. Hybrid approach to pdtb-styled discourse parsing for CoNLL-2015. In *Proceedings of the Nineteenth Conference on Computational Natural Language Learning - Shared Task*, pages 95–99, Beijing, China, July. Association for Computational Linguistics.

Ye Zhang and Byron Wallace. 2015. A sensitivity analysis of (and practitioners' guide to) convolutional neural networks for sentence classification. *arXiv preprint arXiv:1510.03820*.

Zhisong Zhang and Hai Zhao. 2016. Probabilistic graph-based dependency parsing with convolutional neural network. In *Proceedings of ACL*, Berlin, Germany, August.

Hai Zhao, Wenliang Chen, and Chunyu Kit. 2009a. Semantic dependency parsing of NomBank and PropBank: An efficient integrated approach via a large-scale feature selection. In *Proceedings of EMNLP*, pages 30–39, Singapore, August.

Hai Zhao, Wenliang Chen, Chunyu Kity, and Guodong Zhou. 2009b. Multilingual dependency learning: A huge feature engineering method to semantic dependency parsing. In *Proceedings of CoNLL*, pages 55–60, Boulder, Colorado, June.

Hai Zhao, Xiaotian Zhang, and Chunyu Kit. 2013. Integrative semantic dependency parsing via efficient large-scale feature selection. *Journal of Artificial Intelligence Research*, 46:203–233.

Zhi-Min Zhou, Yu Xu, Zheng-Yu Niu, Man Lan, Jian Su, and Chew Lim Tan. 2010. Predicting discourse connectives for implicit discourse relation recognition. In *Proceedings of the 23rd International Conference on Computational Linguistics: Posters*, pages 1507–1514. Association for Computational Linguistics.

SoNLP-DP System for ConLL-2016 Chinese Shallow Discourse Parsing

Junhui Li[1] **Fang Kong**[1] **Sheng Li**[2] **Muhua Zhu**[2] **Guodong Zhou**[1]

[1]Natural Language Processing Lab, Soochow University, China

{lijunhui, kongfang, gdzhou}@suda.edu.cn

[2] Alibaba Inc., Hangzhou, China

{lisheng.ls, muhua.zmh}@alibaba-inc.com

Abstract

This paper describes our submission to the CoNLL-2016 shared task (Xue et al., 2016) on end-to-end Chinese shallow discourse parsing. We decompose the end-to-end process into four steps. Firstly, we define a syntactically heuristic algorithm to identify elementary discourse units (EDUs) and further to recognize valid EDU pairs. Secondly, we recognize explicit discourse connectives. Thirdly, we link each explicit connective to valid EDU pairs to obtain explicit discourse relations. For those valid EDU pairs not linked to any explicit connective, they become non-explicit discourse relations.[1] Finally, we assign each discourse relation, either explicit or non-explicit with a discourse sense. Our system is evaluated on the closed track of the CoNLL-2016 shared task and achieves 35.54% and 23.46% in F1-measure on the official test set and blind test set, respectively.

1 Introduction

Shallow discourse parsing maps a piece of text into a set of discourse relations, each of which is composed of a discourse connective, two arguments, and the sense of the discourse connective. Shallow discourse parsing has been drawing more and more attention in recent years due to its importance in deep NLP applications, such as coherence modeling (Barzilay and Lapata, 2005; Lin et al., 2011), event extraction (Li et al., 2012), and statistical machine translation (Tu et al., 2014).

During the past few years, English shallow discourse parsing has dominated the research on dis-

course parsing, thanks to the availability of Penn Discourse TreeBank (PDTB) (Prasad et al., 2008). As a representative, Lin et al. (2014) decompose the end-to-end PDTB-styled discourse parser into a few components, including a connective classifier, an argument labeler, an explicit sense classifier, and a non-explicit sense classifier. The popularity of English shallow discourse parsing is further fueled by the CoNLL-2015 shared task (Xue et al., 2015). Meanwhile research on Chinese discourse parsing is also carried out smoothly (Zhou and Xue, 2012; Li et al., 2014). As a complement to PDTB annotated on English TreeBank, Chinese Discourse TreeBank (CDTB) (Zhou and Xue, 2012) annotates shallow discourse relations on Chinese TreeBank by using similar framework of PDTB. However, the two languages have many different properties. For example, the non-explicit discourse relations in the training data of CoNLL-2016 shared task dataset account for 54.75% in English while they account for 78.27% in Chinese, indicating the difficulties in Chinese shallow discourse parsing. Second, the two arguments of a Chinese non-explicit discourse relation are more apt to locate in the same sentence. This is verified by the statistics that 56.57% of Chinese non-explicit discourse relations are within one sentence while only 2.55% of English non-explicit discourse relations are. In particular, the English non-explicit discourse relations are usually composed of two consecutive sentences.

This paper describes our submission to the CoNLL-2016 shared task on end-to-end Chinese shallow discourse parsing. A participant system needs to (1) identify all explicit discourse connectives in the text (e.g., continuous connectives "尽管", "另一方面", discontinuous one "由于 ... 因此"), (2) identify the spans of text that function as the two arguments (i.e., Arg1 and Arg2) for each discourse connective, and (3) predict the

---

[1]In this paper, non-explicit discourse relations include discourse relations with type *implicit*, *entrel*, and *altlex*.

Proceedings of the 54th Annual Meeting of the Association for Computational Linguistics, pages 78–84,
Berlin, Germany, August 7-12, 2016. ©2016 Association for Computational Linguistics

sense of the discourse relations (e.g., *Cause, Condition, Contrast*). Due to the differences between Chinese and English, our approach to Chinese discourse parsing is very different from the one to English discourse parsing (Lin et al., 2014; Kong et al., 2014). For example, Lin et al. (2014) construct non-explicit discourse relations in English by looking for two consecutive sentences that are not connected to any explicit connective. However, it fails to discover non-explicit discourse relations in which the two arguments locate in one sentence. Alternatively, we decompose the whole process of our Chinese discourse parser into four steps. Firstly, we define a syntactically heuristic algorithm to identify elementary discourse units (EDUs) and further to recognize valid EDU pairs. Secondly, we recognize explicit discourse connectives. Thirdly, we link each explicit connective to valid EDU pairs to obtain explicit discourse relations. For those valid EDU pairs not linked to any explicit connective, they become non-explicit discourse relations. Finally, we assign each discourse relation, either explicit or non-explicit with a discourse sense. Our system is evaluated on the closed track of the CoNLL-2016 shared task and achieves 35.54% and 23.46% in F1-measure on the official test set and blind test set, respectively.

The rest of this paper is organized as follows. Section 2 describes the details of our Chinese shallow discourse parser. In Section 3, we present our experimental results, followed by the conclusion in Section 4.

2 System Architecture

In this section, we first present an overview of our system. Then we describe the details of our components in the end-to-end Chinese discourse parser.

2.1 System Overview

A typical text consists of sentences glued together in a systematic way to form a coherent discourse. In PDTB and CDTB, shallow discourse parsing focuses on shallow discourse relations either lexically grounded in explicit discourse connectives or associated with sentential adjacency. Different from deep discourse parsing, shallow discourse parsing transforms a piece of text into a set of discourse relations between two adjacent or non-adjacent discourse units, instead of connecting the relations hierarchically to one another to form a connected structure in the form of tree or graph.

Specifically, given a piece of text, the end-to-end shallow discourse parser returns a set of discourse relations in the form of a discourse connective (explicit or non-explicit) taking two arguments with a discourse sense. Figure 1 shows the framework of our end-to-end system which consists of six components (i.e., from A to F). Next, we decompose the process into four steps:

- Firstly, we define a heuristic algorithm to identify elementary discourse units (EDUs) and further to recognize valid EDU pairs. This step includes components of A and B in Figure 1.

- Secondly, we recognize explicit discourse connectives. This is task of component C in Figure 1.

- Thirdly, we link each explicit connective to valid EDU pairs to obtain explicit discourse relations. For those valid EDU pairs not linked to any explicit connective, they become non-explicit discourse relations. This is what component D does in Figure 1.

- Finally, we assign each discourse relation, either explicit or non-explicit with a discourse sense. Specifically, we use component E to assign sense for explicit discourse relations while using component F for non-explicit discourse relations.

2.2 EDU Identification

An EDU is a sequence of words that represents an event, which is usually driven by a VP (a.k.a. verbal phrase) node in parse tree. Given a parse tree, we collect all basic VPs in it. In contrast to a nested VP that is composed of either multiple sub-VPs or a VP and its modifiers, a basic VP is a VP that headed by a non-VP. For example, in Figure 2, VP_2 and VP_4 are basic VPs since VP_2 is headed by VE/无 while VP_4 is headed by VV/通过. In contrast, VP_1 and VP_3 are not basic VPs since they are both headed by basic VPs, i.e., VP_2 and VP_4. For each basic VP, we use the heuristic Algorithm 1 to find its left and right boundary nodes, and thus obtain the word sequence representing the corresponding EDU.

It is easy to find the right boundary node since we always set it as the basic VP node (*line1*). The algorithm initializes the left boundary node as the

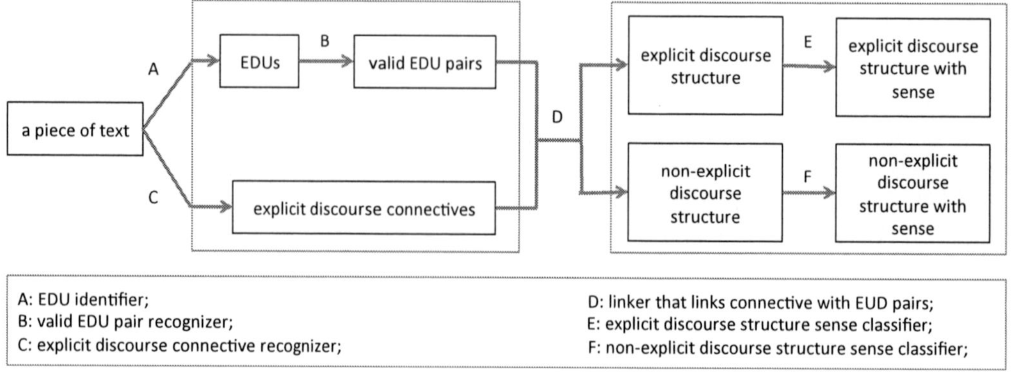

Figure 1: Framework of our end-to-end Chinese shallow discourse parser.

Algorithm 1: Obtaining EDU from a basic VP

Input: parse tree *tree*
       basic VP node vp
Output: its corresponding EDU
1. define right boundary node $rbn = vp$;
2. define left boundary node $lbn = vp$;
3. set current node c as vp;
4. **while** ($true$)
5.   set node p as c's parent;
6.   **if** ($p == null$) **break**;
7.   get p's production rule, say as $l_m \ .. \ l_1 \ c \ r_1 \ ..r_n$, indicating c has m left hand siblings and n right siblings;
8.   **for** i from 1 to m
9.   **if** l_i is dominated by c
10. $lbn = l_i$;
11.   **else**
12.   **break**;
13.   **if** $i <= m$ **break**;
14. $c = p$;
15. return word sequence from position leftmost of lbn to rightmost of rbn;

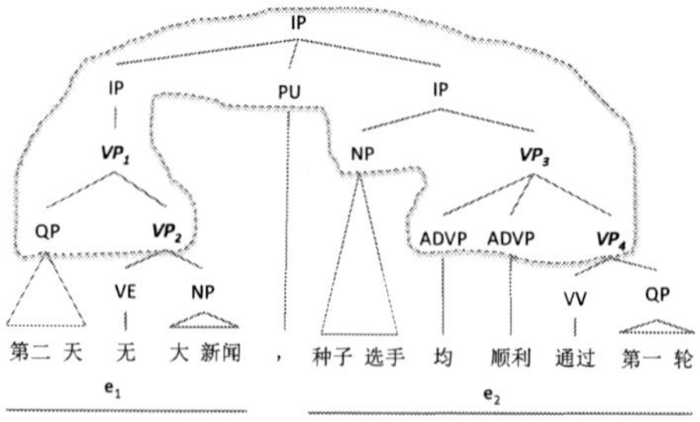

basic VP node as well (*line2*). Then it repeatedly update the left boundary node until it finds a proper one. To this end, the algorithm starts by setting the current node c as the basic VP node (*line 3*), and first examine the left siblings from right to left and see if they are dominated by c. It then iteratively moves one level up to the parent of c till it reaches the root of the tree (*line 14*). At each level, it repeatedly updates the left boundary node (*line 10*). Specifically, if there exists a left sibling which is *not* dominated by c, the algorithm stops (*line 12 & 13*). Once both the left and right boundary nodes are found. It uses the leftmost position of the left boundary node and the rightmost position of the right boundary node to obtain the word sequence of the corresponding EDU. For VP$_2$ and VP$_4$ in Figure 2, the algorithm will return "第二

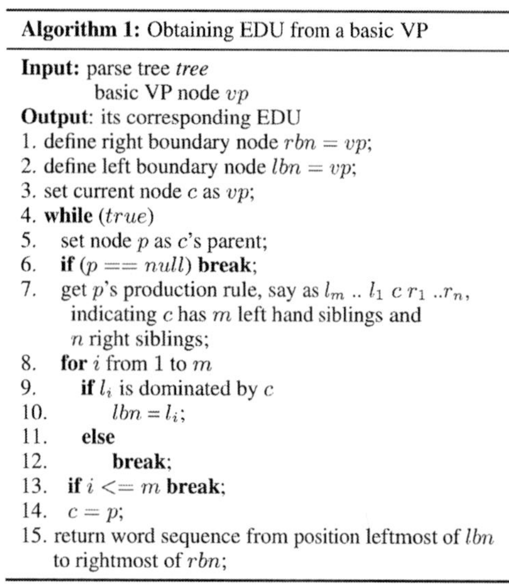

Figure 2: An example of recognizing EDUs.

天 无 大 新闻" and "种子 选手 均 顺利 通过 第 一 轮" as their EDUs, respectively.

Note that for two EDUs that occur in one sentence, they satisfy that either their spans have no overlapping at all (e.g., e_1 and e_2 in Figure 2), or one EDU fully covers the other.

2.3 Valid EDU Pair Recognition

A valid EDU pair is two EDUs that have discourse relation, either explicit or non-explicit. We first collect all potential EDU pairs as candidate, and then identify valid ones. In an EDU pair, we presume the first EDU locates on the left side of the second one.

Intra-EDU pair candidates. Intra-EDU pair candidates indicate that the two focusing EDUs locate in one sentence. If a sentence contains two or more EDUs, we enumerate all possible EDU pairs as candidates as long as the pair have no overlapping in position.

Inter-EDU pair candidates. The two EDUs in an inter-EDU pair candidate locate in two sentences. To make the task simple, we only consider such candidates if the two EDUs are in two consecutive sentences. For two consecutive sentences s_1 and s_2, we obtain their corresponding set (es_1 and es_2) of EDUs that are at top level (i.e., an EDU is at top level if it is not covered by another EDU). Then we enumerate all possible EDU pairs by selecting one from es_1 and the other from es_2.

To identify an EDU pair candidate is valid or not, we use tree kernel approach to explore implicitly structured features by directly computing the similarity between two subtrees. Given a parse tree and an EDU pair candidate in it,[2] we first find the lowest ancestor node that fully covers the two EDUs. Then we collect left and right siblings along the path from the lowest ancestor node to each basic VP node. For example, the dash circle in Figure 2 represents the subtree for the EDU pair of e_1 and e_2.

2.4 Explicit Discourse Connective Recognition

Connectives in Chinese are more obscure than those in English. For example, we extract 358 types of connective from the training data. Among them, 193 (or 54%) types of connective occur once while 197 (or 55%) types consist of two or more words. Being worse, 32 (or 9%) types of connective span two or more sentences. Our system keeps 326 (or 91%) types of connective that locate in one sentence as our connective set. That is to say, we ignore those connectives that locate in two or more sentences. The distribution of connective in training data suggests that the connective set is an open set. Given a piece of text, we first use the connective set to collect connective candidates. Then we identify each connective candidate is a functional connective or not. Different from previous work that defines diverse linguistic features, varying from lexical knowledge to syntactic parse trees, we use tree kernel approach to explore implicitly structured features by directly computing the similarity between two subtrees. Given a parse tree and a connective candidate in it, we first find the lowest *IP* node that fully covers the connective. Then we collect left and right siblings along the path from the *IP* node to each connective word. For instance, sentence "由于 新 组建 的 国家队 新 队员 将 占 一半 ， 而 她们 的 技术 水平 尚 待 提高 ， 因此 面临 的 任务 是 艰巨 的 " and

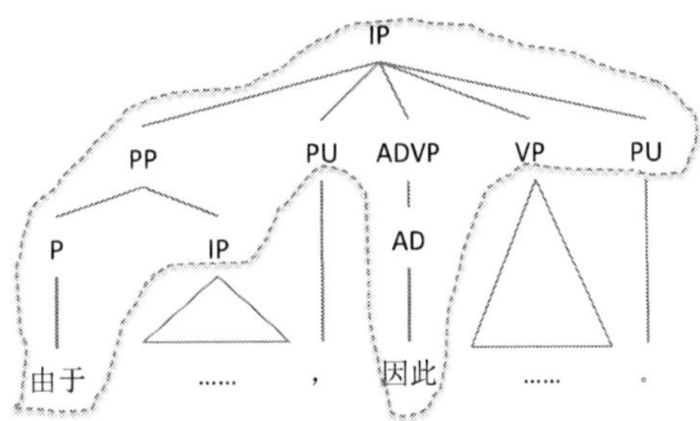

Figure 3: An example of subtree extraction for connective recognition.

a discontinuous connective candidate "由于 ... 因此" in it, we extract a subtree as shown in Figure 3.

2.5 Linking connective with EDU pairs

So far we have recognized both valid EDU pairs and explicit discourse connectives. Our next step is to link a connective to EDU pairs. Note that it is possible for a connective to link to one or more EDU pairs. To decide if a connective and an EDU pair is relevant, we continue to use tree kernel approach. The subtrees extraction algorithm is very similar to that of valid EDU pair recognition. The algorithm first finds the lowest ancestor node that covers the two EDUs and the connective. Then it collects left and right siblings along the path from the lowest ancestor node to connective word, and to the two basic VP nodes, respectively. For instance, in sentence "由于 新 组建 的 国家队 新 队员 将 占 一半 ， 而 她们 的 技术 水平 尚 待 提高 ， 因此 面临 的 任务 是 艰巨 的 ", we are about to predict if the connection exist between a discontinuous connective "由于 ... 因此" and an EDU pair colored in blue and green in Figure 4. To this end, the subtree extraction algorithm first looks for their lowest ancestor, i.e., the top *IP* in Figure 4, then the algorithm collect all siblings along the paths from the lowest ancestor node (i.e., *IP*) to each connective word (i.e., *P* and *ADVP*), and to the two basic VPs (i.e., the two colored VPs). Figure 4 also shows the extracted subtree.

Explicit discourse relations. If one or more valid EDU pairs are predicted to have connection to a connective,[3] we construct an explicit dis-

---

[2]for inter-EDU pair candidate, we manually create a top node and take the parse trees of the two consecutive sentences as children of top node.

[3]If none EDU pair is predicted to have connection to a connective, we take the pair with the highest probability as the one linking to the connective.

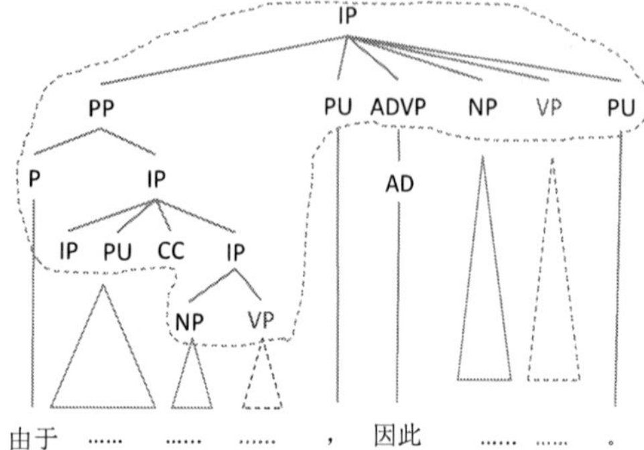

Figure 4: An example of subtree extraction for linking a connective with an EDU pair.

course relation by merging all the first EDUs of the EDU pairs as Arg1 of the connective, and merging all the second EDUs of the EDU pairs as Arg2.

Non-explicit discourse relations. If a valid EDU pair is not linked to any explicit connective, we construct a non-explicit discourse relation by regarding the first EDU as Arg1 and the second as Arg2.

2.6 Sense Classification for Explicit discourse relations

Once an explicit discourse relation is identified, the sense classifier is used to predict its sense. Due to the fact the connective themselves are strong hint for their sense, we follow (Lin et al., 2014) to define a few lexical features to train a sense classifier: the connective words themselves, their part-of-speeches and the previous words of each connective word.

2.7 Sense Classification for Non-explicit discourse relations

Due to the absence of discourse connectives, sense prediction for non-explicit discourse relations is more difficult. Following the work of Kong et al. (2015) on non-explicit sense classification in English, we define the following groups of features:

- **First three words of Arg1/Arg2:** This set of features include the first three words in Arg1 and Arg2.

- **Production rules:** According to Lin et al. (2009), the syntactic structure of one argument may constrain the relation type and the syntactic structure of the other argument. We extract production rules from training data with frequency larger than 5 times. Then for each production rule pr, we add features *pr-in-arg1=1*, *pr-in-arg2=1*, *pr-in-arg1arg2=1* if it occurs in Arg1, Arg2, and both, respectively.

- **Dependency rules:** Similar to the above features of production rules, three sets of features *dr-in-arg1=1*, *dr-in-arg2=1*, *dr-in-arg1arg2=1* if it occurs in Arg1, Arg2, and both, respectively.

- **Word pairs:** We include all word pairs by choosing one word from Arg1 and the other from Arg2.

- **Brown cluster pairs:** Similar to the above features of word pairs, we include all Brown cluster pairs by choosing one word cluster from Arg1 and the other from Arg2.

Besides the above features, the research on English sense classification for non-explicit discourse relations has explored other useful features about polarity, modality, and verb class (Karin et al., 2006). Unfortunately, the shared task on Chinese does not provide relevant resources to obtain those features.

3 Experimentation

We evaluate our system on the Chinese dataset provided in the close track of the CoNLL-2016 Shared Task. All our kernel-based classifiers (e.g., valid EDU pair recognizer, connective recognizer, and linker connecting connectives with EDU pairs) and flat feature-based classifiers (e.g., sense classifiers for either explicit discourse relations or non-explicit discourse relations) are trained using SVMLight toolkit for tree kernel.[4]

Table 1 shows our official performance on the development, test and blind test sets, respectively. From the table, we observe:

- For argument recognition, the performance of Arg2 is much better than that of Arg1 on the development and test datasets. This is similar to the performance trend in English. However, the performance gap between Arg1 and Arg2 recognition is very small on the blind test dataset.

---

[4]http://disi.unitn.it/moschitti/TK1.0-software/Tree-Kernel.htm

		Dev			Test			Blind test		
		P	R	F1	P	R	F1	P	R	F1
Explicit	Connective	79.22	83.56	81.33	75.00	80.00	77.42	63.07	65.99	64.50
	Arg1	45.45	47.95	46.67	40.62	43.33	41.94	36.57	38.26	37.40
	Arg2	58.44	61.64	60.00	53.12	56.67	54.84	39.05	40.85	39.93
	Arg1 & Arg2	33.77	35.62	34.67	28.12	30.00	29.03	22.79	23.84	23.31
	Overall	35.62	33.77	34.67	27.78	26.04	26.88	21.15	20.14	20.63
Non-Explicit	Connective	-	-	-	-	-	-	-	-	-
	Arg1	65.69	54.32	59.47	62.95	55.67	59.08	54.20	52.36	53.27
	Arg2	72.55	60.00	65.68	69.92	61.82	65.62	55.70	53.81	54.74
	Arg1 & Arg2	55.56	45.95	50.30	52.37	46.31	49.15	42.67	41.22	41.93
	Overall	32.97	39.87	36.09	34.24	38.72	36.34	23.35	24.17	23.75
All	Connective	79.22	83.56	81.33	75.00	80.00	77.42	63.07	65.99	64.50
	Arg1	65.01	56.21	60.29	61.10	56.05	58.46	54.64	53.90	54.27
	Arg2	71.54	61.85	66.34	68.79	63.10	65.83	53.64	52.91	53.27
	Arg1 & Arg2	52.74	45.60	48.91	48.79	44.76	46.69	38.55	38.03	38.29
	Overall	33.77	35.62	34.67	34.07	37.14	35.54	23.31	23.61	23.46

Table 1: Official results (%) of our parser on development, test and blind test sets. Group *Explicit* indicates the performance with respect to explicit discourse relations; group *Non-Explicit* indicates the performance with respect to non-explicit discourse relations, and group *all* indicates the performance with respect to all discourse relations, including both explicit and non-explicit ones.

- With respect to explicit discourse relations, the sense classification works almost perfectly on development data (e.g., almost no performance gap from *Arg1 & Arg2* to *Overall*. It also works well on the test and blind test sets.

- With respect to non-explicit discourse relations, the sense classification works much worse than that of explicit sense classification. The performance gap caused by non-explicit sense classification reaches 14% 18%.

- The overall performance on all discourse relations is dominated by non-explicit ones. This is because larger size of non-explicit discourse relations. For example, the size of non-explicit discourse relations is 3.6 times of that of explicit ones in training data.

- Our system achieves similar results on development set and test set. However, the performance on blind test decreases sharply, probably due to the differences in genres and the bad quality of parse trees.

4 Conclusion

In this paper we have described our submission to the CoNLL-2016 shared task on end-to-end Chinese shallow discourse parsing. Our system is evaluated on the closed track of the CoNLL-2016 shared task and achieves 35.54% and 23.46% in F1-measure on the official test set and blind test set, respectively.

Acknowledgments

The authors would like to thank the two anonymous reviewers for providing helpful suggestions. This research is supported by Project 61472264, 61401295, 61305088 and 61402314 under the National Natural Science Foundation of China.

References

Regina Barzilay and Mirella Lapata. 2005. Modeling local coherence: An entity-based approach. In *Proceedings of the 43rd Annual Meeting of the Association for Computational Linguistics*, pages 141–148.

Kipper Karin, Korhonen Anna, Ryant Neville, and Palmer Martha. 2006. Extending verbnet with novel verb classes. In *Proceedings of the 5th International Conference on Language Resources and Evaluation*.

Fang Kong, Hwee Tou Ng, and Guodong Zhou. 2014. A constituent-based approach to argument labeling with joint inference in discourse parsing. In *Proceedings of the 2014 Conference on Empirical Meth ods in Natural Language Processing*, pages 68–77.

Fang Kong, Sheng Li, and Guodong Zhou. 2015. The sonlp-dp system in the conll-2015 shared task. In *Proceedings of the Nineteenth Conference on Computational Natural Language Learning - Shared Task*, pages 32–36.

Peifeng Li, Guodong Zhou, Qiaoming Zhu, and Libin Hou. 2012. Employing compositional semantics and discourse consistency in Chinese event extraction. In *Proceedings of the 2012 Joint Conference on Empirical Methods in Natural Language*

Processing and Computational Natural Language Learning, pages 1006–1016.

Yancui Li, Wenhe Feng, Jing Sun, Fang Kong, and Guodong Zhou. 2014. Building Chinese discourse corpus with connective-driven dependency tree structure. In *Proceedings of the 2014 Conference on Empirical Methods in Natural Language Processing*, pages 2105–2114.

Ziheng Lin, Min-Yen Kan, and Hwee Tou Ng. 2009. Recognizing implicit discourse relations in the Penn Discourse Treebank. In *Proceedings of the 2009 Conference on Empirical Methods in Natural Language Processing*.

Ziheng Lin, Hwee Tou Ng, and Min-Yen Kan. 2011. Automatically evaluating text coherence using discourse relations. In *Proceedings of the 49th Annual Meeting of the Association for Computational Linguistics: Human Language Technologies*, pages 997–1006.

Ziheng Lin, Hwee Tou Ng, and Min-Yen Kan. 2014. A PDTB-styled end-to-end discourse parser. *Natural Language Engineering*, 20(2):151–184.

Rashmi Prasad, Nikhil Dinesh, Alan Lee, Eleni Miltsakaki, Livio Robaldo, Aravind Joshi, and Bonnie Webber. 2008. The Penn Discourse TreeBank 2.0. In *Proceedings of the 6th International Conference on Language Resources and Evaluation*.

Mei Tu, Yu Zhou, and Chengqing Zong. 2014. Enhancing grammatical cohesion: Generating transitional expressions for SMT. In *Proceedings of the 52nd Annual Meeting of the Association for Computational Linguistics (Volume 1: Long Papers)*, pages 850–860.

Nianwen Xue, Hwee Tou Ng, Sameer Pradhan, Rashmi Prasad, Christopher Bryant, and Attapol Rutherford. 2015. The CoNLL-2015 shared task on shallow discourse parsing. In *Proceedings of the Nineteenth Conference on Computational Natural Language Learning - Shared Task*, pages 1–16.

Nianwen Xue, Hwee Tou Ng, Sameer Pradhan, Attapol T. Rutherford, Bonnie Webber, Chuan Wang, and Hongmin Wang. 2016. The CoNLL-2016 shared task on multilingual shallow discourse parsing. In *Proceedings of the Twentieth Conference on Computational Natural Language Learning: Shared Task*.

Yuping Zhou and Nianwen Xue. 2012. PDTB-style discourse annotation of Chinese text. In *Proceedings of the 50th Annual Meeting of the Association for Computational Linguistics*, pages 69–77.

UniTN End-to-End Discourse Parser for CoNLL 2016 Shared Task

Evgeny A. Stepanov and **Giuseppe Riccardi**
Signals and Interactive Systems Lab
Department of Information Engineering and Computer Science
University of Trento, Trento, TN, Italy
{evgeny.stepanov,giuseppe.riccardi}@unitn.it

Abstract

Penn Discourse Treebank style discourse parsing is a composite task of detecting explicit and non-explicit discourse relations, their connective and argument spans, and assigning a sense to these relations. Due to the composite nature of the task, the end-to-end performance is greatly affected by the error propagation. This paper describes the end-to-end discourse parser for English submitted to the CoNLL 2016 Shared Task on Shallow Discourse Parsing with the main focus of the parser being on argument spans and the reduction of global error through model selection. In the end-to-end closed-track evaluation the parser achieves F-measure of 0.2510 outperforming the best system of the previous year.

1 Introduction

Discourse parsing is a Natural Language Processing (NLP) task with the potential utility for many other Natural Language Processing tasks (Webber et al., 2011). However, as was illustrated by the CoNLL 2015 Shared Task on Shallow Discourse Parsing (Xue et al., 2015), the task of Penn Discourse Treebank (PDTB) (Prasad et al., 2008) style discourse parsing is very challenging as the best system achieved the end-to-end parsing performance of $F_1 = 0.24$. The main reason for the low performance is the composite nature of the task and the error propagation through the long pipeline.

In PDTB discourse relations are binary: a discourse connective and its two arguments. The arguments are defined syntactically such that *Argument 2* is syntactically attached to the connective, and *Argument 1* is the other argument. A discourse relation is assigned a particular sense from the predefined sense hierarchy. Discourse connective, a member of the closed class, signals the presence of an *explicit* relation. Besides explicit discourse relations there are non-explicit relations: *implicit* relations where a connective is implied and can be inserted, *alternative lexicalizations* (AltLex) where a connective cannot be inserted and a relation is signaled by a phrase not in the list of discourse connectives, and *entity relations* (EntRel) where two arguments share the same entity.

Such definition of discourse relations naturally suggests at least two pipelines for the parsing: for explicit and non-explicit relations. Moreover, since in PDTB non-explicit relations are annotated only in the absence of explicit relations, explicit relation parsing pipeline precedes the non-explicit one. While detection of discourse connectives is only required for the explicit relations, for both relation types parsing requires identification of argument spans and relation senses. Consequently, PDTB-style discourse parsing is partitioned into several sub-tasks: (1) explicit discourse connective detection, (2) argument span extraction (with labeling for *Argument 1* and *2*), and (3) sense classification. The tasks are often conditioned on the type of a relation (explicit or non-explicit) and argument positions (intra- or inter-sentential).

In this paper we describe the end-to-end discourse parser submitted to CoNLL 2016 Shared Task on Shallow Discourse Parsing (Xue et al., 2016). The parser makes use of token-level sequence labeling with Conditional Random Fields (Lafferty et al., 2001) for the identification of connective and argument spans; and classification for the identification of relation senses and argument positions. The main focus of the parser is on argument spans. For the end-to-end parsing task the models are selected with respect to the global parsing score.

Proceedings of the 54th Annual Meeting of the Association for Computational Linguistics, pages 85–91,
Berlin, Germany, August 7-12, 2016. ©2016 Association for Computational Linguistics

The overall parser architecture is described in Section 1. The token-level features used for sequence labeling and argument and relation-level features used for sense classification are described in Section 3. The individual discourse parsing sub-tasks are described in Section 4. Section 5 describes the official CoNLL 2016 Shared Task evaluation results, and in Section 6 we compare the system to the best systems of the preceding shared task on discourse parsing (Xue et al., 2015). Section 7 provides concluding remarks.

2   System Architecture

The discourse parser submitted for the CoNLL 2016 Shared Task is the modified version of the parser developed by (Stepanov et al., 2015) for the shared task of 2015. The system is an extension of the explicit relation parser described in (Stepanov and Riccardi, 2013; Stepanov and Riccardi, 2014). The overall architecture of the parser is depicted in Figure 1. The approach implements discourse parsing as a pipeline of several tasks such that connective and argument span decisions are cast as sequence labeling and sense decisions as classification.

The discourse parsing pipelines starts with the identification of discourse connectives and their spans (*Discourse Connective Detection* (DCD)), and is followed by *Connective Sense Classification* (CSC) and *Argument Position Classification* (APC) steps. While CSC assigns sense to explicit discourse relations, APC classifies them as intra- and inter-sentential (*Same Sentence* (SS) and *Previous Sentence* (PS) *Argument 1*). Both tasks operate using the connective span tokens only.

With respect to the decision of the *Argument Position Classification* the pipeline is split into explicit and non-explicit tasks. For the explicit relations, specific *Argument Span Extraction* (ASE) models are applied for each of the arguments with respect to their begin intra- or inter-sentential. Since *Argument 2* is syntactically attached to the discourse connective, its identification is easier. Thus, for the intra-sentential (SS) relations, models are applied in a cascade such that the output of *Argument 2* span extraction in the input for *Argument 1* span extraction. For the inter-sentential (PS) relations, on the other hand, a sentence containing the connective is selected as *Argument 2*, and the sentence immediately preceding it as a candidate for *Argument 1*.

For non-explicit discourse relations, a set of candidate argument pairs is constructed using adjacent sentence pairs within a paragraph and removing all the sentence pair already identified as inter-sentential explicit relations. Each of these argument pairs is assigned a sense using *Non-Explicit Relation Sense Classification* (NE-RSC) models and their argument spans are extracted using *Non-Explicit Argument Span Extraction* step.

In the discourse parser, the *Non-Explicit Relation Sense Classification*, *Connective Sense Classification*, and *Argument Position Classification* tasks are cast as supervised classification using AdaBoost algorithm (Freund and Schapire, 1997) implemented in *icsiboost* (Favre et al., 2007). The span extraction tasks (*Discourse Connective Detection* and explicit and non-explicit *Argument Span Extraction*), on the other hand, are cast as token-level sequence labeling with CRFs (Lafferty et al., 2001) using CRF++ (Kudo, 2013). Besides training the CRF models for ASE, for inter-sentential *Argument 1* span and both non-explicit argument spans, we also make use of the 'heuristics': taking an argument sentence as a whole and removing leading and trailing punctuation (Lin et al., 2014; Stepanov et al., 2015). In the next section we describe the features used for the tasks.

3   Features

The PDTB corpus distributed to the shared task participants contains raw text and syntactic constituency and dependency parses. Besides the token and part-of-speech tags, these resources are used to extract and generate both token-level and argument/relation-level features. Additionally, for argument/relation-level features for *Non-Explicit Relation Sense Classification* we make use of Brown Clusters (Turian et al., 2010), MPQA subjectivity lexicon (Wilson et al., 2005) and VerbNet (Kipper et al., 2008). The feature sets for each task are selected using greedy hill climbing approach, also considering the amount of contribution of each individual feature.

3.1   Token-level Features

All the discourse parsing sub-tasks (both classification and sequence labeling) except *Non-Explicit Relation Sense Classification* make use of token-level features. However, the feature sets for each task are different. Table 1 gives an overview of feature sets per task. Besides tokens and POS-

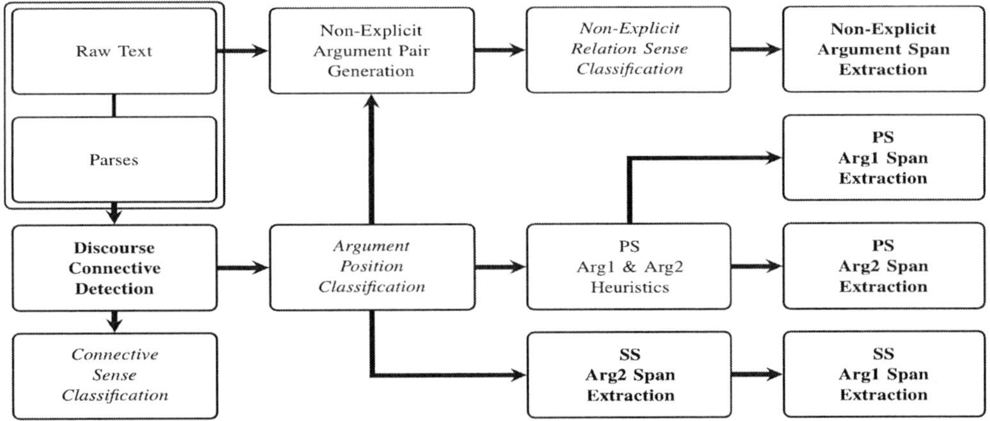

Figure 1: Discourse parsing architecture: the sequence labeling modules are in **bold** and the classification modules are in *italics*.

tags, the rest of the features are described below.

Chunk-tag is the syntactic chunk prefixed with the information whether a token is at the beginning (B-), inside (I-) or outside (O) of the constituent (i.e. IOB format) (e.g. 'B-NP' indicates that a token is at the beginning of Noun Phrase chunk). The information is extracted from constituency parse trees using chunklink script (Buchholz, 2000).

IOB-chain is the path string of the syntactic tree nodes from the root node to the token, similar to Chunk-tag, it is prefixed with the IOB information. For example, the IOB-chain 'I-S/B-VP' indicates that a token is the first word of the verb phrase (B-VP) of the main clause (I-S).The feature is also extracted using the chunklink script (Buchholz, 2000).

Dependency chain (Stepanov et al., 2015) is a feature inspired by *IOB-chain* and is the path string of the functions of the parents of a token, starting from the root of a dependency parse.

VerbNet Class (Kipper et al., 2008) is a feature intended to capture attributions. The feature requires lemmas, which were extracted using TreeTagger (Schmid, 1995).

Connective Label and *Argument 2 Label* are the output labels of the *Discourse Connective Detection* and *Argument 2 Span Extraction* models respectively.

Using templates of CRF++ the token-level features are enriched with ngrams (2 & 3-grams) in the window of ±2 tokens, such that for each token there are 12 features per feature type: 5 unigrams, 4 bigrams and 3 trigrams. All features are conditioned on the output label independently of each other. Additionally, CRFs consider the previous token's output label as a feature.

3.2 Argument and Relation-level Features

In this section we describe the features used for *Non-Explicit Relation Sense Classification*. Previous work on the task makes use of a wide range of features; however, due to the low state-of-the-art on the task, we focused on the features obtainable from the provided resources: sentiment polarities from MPQA lexicon (Wilson et al., 2005), Brown Clusters (Turian et al., 2010), and VerbNet (Kipper et al., 2008). Similar to VerbNet Class feature, described above, lemmas from TreeTagger (Schmid, 1995) are used to compute the polarity features.

There are four features generated for *Polarity*: (1-2) Individual argument polarities computed from token-level polarities as a difference of counts of positive and negative polarity words. The feature is assigned either 'negative' or 'positive' value with respect to the difference. (3) The concatenation of the argument polarity values (e.g. *negative-positive*). (4) The boolean feature indicating whether the argument polarities match.

The Brown Cluster and VerbNet features are extracted only for specific tokens. Starting from the dependency parse trees of the arguments we extract the main verb (root), subject (including passive), direct and indirect objects for each of them. Since for extracting VerbNet features we make use of lemmas, the lemmas themselves are considered for classification as well. Similar to polarity, the *VerbNet* features (4) are main-verbs' classes of the

Feature	DCD	CSC	APC	ASE: SS		ASE: PS		NE-ASE	
				A1	*A2*	*A1*	*A2*	*A1*	*A2*
Token	Y	Y	Y	Y	Y	Y	Y	Y	Y
POS-tag	Y		Y		Y	Y	Y	Y	Y
Chunk-tag	Y								
IOB-chain	Y		Y	Y	Y	Y	Y	Y	Y
Dependency chain					Y				
VerbNet class					Y				
Connective Label				Y	Y		Y		
Argument 2 Label				Y					

Table 1: Token-level features for classification and sequence labeling tasks: Discourse Connective Detection (DCD), Connective Sense Classification (CSC), Argument Position Classification (APC), and Argument Span Extraction (ASE) of intra- (SS) and inter-sentential (PS) explicit and non-explicit (NE) relations.

arguments, their concatenation, and a boolean feature indicating their match.

The *Brown Cluster* and *Lemma* features are main-verbs' brown clusters and lemmas, their concatenation and boolean features for matches (4). Unlike VerbNet, these features are also generated for a Cartesian product for the arguments' subject, direct and indirect objects. Consequently, there are 4 features for verbs and 24 for other dependency roles (3 + 3 + 9 + 9) per feature type.

4 Individual Modules

In this section we provide implementation details for the individual components of the discourse parser. We first address explicit and then non-explicit relations.

4.1 Explicit Discourse Relations

The explicit relation pipeline consists of *Discourse Connective Detection, Connective Sense Classification, Argument Position Classification* and *Argument Span Extraction* tasks.

4.1.1 Discourse Connective Detection

Since *Discourse Connective Detection* is the first step in discourse parsing, the performance of the task is critical. The task is cast as sequence labeling with CRFs. The performance of the models is tuned by feature ablation to yield a model that achieves F_1 of 0.9332 on the development set. The best model is trained on cased tokens, POS-tags, Chunk-tag and IOB-chain features.

4.1.2 Connective Sense Classification

Following (Stepanov et al., 2015) the *Connective Sense Classification* step assigns a sense to a connective considering only cased tokens. The classification is performed directly into 14 explicit relation senses.

4.1.3 Argument Position Classification

Due to the fact that explicit discourse connectives have a strong preference on the positions of their arguments, depending on whether they appear at the beginning or in the middle of a sentence (Stepanov and Riccardi, 2013), the task is easy. The features used for the task are cased tokens, POS-tags and IOB-chains. Case of the tokens carries position information. The accuracy on the development set without error propagation is 0.9868.

4.1.4 Argument Span Extraction

Argument Span Extraction is the main focus of the development for the submission. We train CRF model for each of the arguments of the intra- and inter-sentential relations considering a single sentence as a candidate (i.e. all multi-sentence relations are missed). As a candidate for the inter-sentential *Argument 1* we consider only immediately preceding sentence (effectively missing all non-adjacent *Argument 1* relations).

Since *Argument 2* models make use of connective span labels as a feature, and intra-sentential *Argument 1* model makes use of both connective and *Argument 2* labels; these models are trained using reference annotation spans. For the *Argument Span Extraction* of inter-sentential *Argument 1*, additional to the training of the CRF models we also make use of the heuristic, that takes the sentence as a whole and removes leading and trailing punctuation.

There are 4 CRF models for the task with the additional heuristic for the inter-sentential *Argument 1*. The feature sets for each of the models are selected such that they maximize the F-measure of both arguments together.

The CRF model for the inter-sentential *Argument 1* yields higher performance than the heuristic. However, the submitted system exploits the heuristic, since the difference between the two for the both argument spans is not large (0.4981 vs. 0.4936 for the heuristic).

4.2 Non-Explicit Discourse Relations

The non-explicit relation parsing pipeline consists of *Relation Sense Classification* (NE-RSC) and *Argument Span Extraction* (NE-ASE) tasks. Even though, NE-ASE is applied after NE-RSC with the idea of exploiting classification confidences for filtering out the candidate relations, the two tasks are fairly independent.

4.2.1 Non-Explicit Relation Sense Classification

The set of features for the task is described in Section 3. It is the only task that makes use of the argument and relation level features. Due to the low state-of-the-art on the task, the focus is on the development of the models that maximize the performance of the majority senses – *EntRel* and *Expansion.Conjunction*. The flat classification mode is considered as it yields higher performance for these senses (e.g. for EntRel the classification into 4 top-level senses + EntRel yields F_1 of ≈ 0.30, while flat classification into 14 full senses + EntRel F_1 of 0.44).

4.2.2 Non-Explicit Argument Span Extraction

The task is implemented similar to the *Argument Span Extraction* of the inter-sentential *Argument 1*, and considers the same feature set (cased token, POS-tag, and IOB-chain). Similarly, we experiment with the span extraction heuristic by only removing leading and trailing punctuation.

Unlike explicit relations, the CRF models for the non-explicit argument span extraction perform significantly better than the heuristics. However, due to the error propagation from the Relation Sense Classification task, the heuristics yield the higher F_1-measure for the end-to-end parsing of non-explicit relations. Thus, the submitted system contains purely heuristic *Non-Explicit Argument Span Extraction*.

5 Official Evaluation Results

The official end-to-end parsing evaluation of the CoNLL 2016 Shared Task on Shallow Discourse Parsing carried on TIRA platform (Potthast et al., 2014) is on a per-discourse relation basis. A relation is considered to be predicted correctly only in case the parser correctly predicts (1) discourse connective head, (2) exact spans and labels of both arguments, and (3) sense of a relation. The official evaluation is reported for the PDTB development and test sets (sections 22 and 23, respectively) and a blind test set.

The reported evaluation metrics are (1) explicit discourse connective, (2-4) *Argument 1* and *Argument 2* spans individually and together, and the sense of a relation. The reported micro-F_1 measure of the sense classification is equivalent to the end-to-end parsing performance as it considers the error propagation from the upstream tasks. The metrics are reported for explicit and non-explicit relations individually and jointly. The performance of the submitted system on all the metrics is reported in Table 2. On the closed-track evaluation, the system achieves end-to-end parsing F_1 of 0.3246, 0.2789 and 0.2510 on the development, test and blind test sets respectively.

6 Comparison to CoNLL 2015 Systems

The current shared task is the second edition of the CoNLL Shared Task on Shallow Discourse Parsing. Thus, it makes sense to compare the performances of the submission to the systems of the first edition (i.e. the winner (Wang and Lan, 2015) and (Stepanov et al., 2015), which is taken as the baseline). Since the submitted system is an extension of (Stepanov et al., 2015), the main focus of the comparison is on the changes and their effects on the performance.

We first compare the system performance to the last year's systems on the end-to-end parsing score on the blind test set (see Table 3). The current submission outperforms the baseline (Stepanov et al., 2015) as well as the best system (ECNU) (Wang and Lan, 2015). The recall of the 2015 winner is slightly higher (0.2407 vs. 0.2432 for ECNU); however, the difference is well compensated by the higher precision (0.2622 vs. 0.2369 for ECNU).

Task	All Relations			Explicit			Non-Explicit		
	Dev	Test	Blind	Dev	Test	Blind	Dev	Test	Blind
Connective	0.9332	0.9243	0.8856	0.9332	0.9243	0.8856	–	–	–
Arg 1	0.6417	0.5890	0.5991	0.5566	0.4964	0.5028	0.6951	0.6558	0.6683
Arg 2	0.7664	0.7188	0.7586	0.7907	0.7651	0.7205	0.7451	0.6778	0.7911
Arg 1+2	0.5471	0.4844	0.5060	0.4936	0.4456	0.4184	0.5940	0.5180	0.5805
Parser	0.3246	0.2780	0.2510	0.4589	0.3960	0.3174	0.2089	0.1756	0.1946

Table 2: Task-level and end-to-end F_1-measures of the discourse parser on the development, test, and blind test sets for explicit and non-explicit relations individually and jointly for all relations. The task-level performances are reported with the error propagation. Thus, the *sense classification* performances are equivalent to the end-to-end parser performances.

System	P	R	F
our system	**0.2622**	0.2407	**0.2510**
ECNU	0.2369	**0.2432**	0.2400
(Stepanov et al., 2015)	0.2094	0.2283	0.2184

Table 3: Precision (**P**), recall (**R**) and F_1 (**F**) of the end-to-end discourse parsing on the blind test set for the best CoNLL 2015 Shared Task systems and the current submission.

System	Dev	Test	Blind
Arg 1+2 Span Extraction			
our system	**0.5940**	**0.5180**	**0.5805**
(Stepanov et al., 2015)	0.4000	0.3730	0.3831
Non-Explicit Parsing			
our system	**0.2089**	**0.1756**	**0.1946**
(Stepanov et al., 2015)	0.1577	0.1330	0.1577

Table 4: F_1 for the non-explicit argument extraction and parsing.

System	Dev	Test	Blind
Discourse Connective Detection			
our system	**0.9332**	0.9243	0.8856
(Stepanov et al., 2015)	0.9219	**0.9271**	**0.8992**
Explicit SS Arg 2			
our system	**0.7907**	**0.7651**	**0.7205**
(Stepanov et al., 2015)	0.7748	0.7616	0.7068

Table 5: F_1 for the *Discourse Connective Detection* and explicit intra-sentential *Argument 2* span extraction.

The major change from (Stepanov et al., 2015) is the elimination of the *Non-Explicit Relation Detection* step. The step classified non-explicit relation candidates into relations and non-relations. However, the ratio of non-related adjacent sentence pairs in the PDTB is very low (circa 1%). Consequently, the step was penalizing the performance on non-explicit relations. As it can be observed from Table 4, there is a major improvement in performance for non-explicit argument spans.

The other changes are in the feature sets of *Connective Detection* and the *Argument Span Extraction* of the explicit intra-sentential *Argument 2*. For the former we improved the performance on the development set, but the performance on the test and blind test sets dropped (see Table 5). For the latter, we introduced a new feature – VerbNet (Kipper et al., 2008) classes – intended to capture the attribution spans. From the results it appears that the feature is useful, as they are better than the results of (Stepanov et al., 2015) despite the lower connective detection performance.

7 Conclusions

In this paper we have presented the parser submitted to CoNLL 2016 Shared Task on Shallow Discourse Parsing. The parser is a modified version of the system of (Stepanov et al., 2015). We have described the discourse parsing architecture and models for each of the sub-tasks. The distinct feature of the approach is casting the span extraction tasks are token-level sequence labeling with Conditional Random Fields. The focus of the development for the shared task was on *Argument Span Extraction* and its optimization for the end-to-end parsing score on the development set. The main change made to the baseline version of the system is the elimination of non-explicit relation detection step, which boosted the overall performance of the system to outperform the CoNLL 2015 Shared Task winner.

Acknowledgments

The research leading to these results has received funding from the European Union – Seventh Framework Programme (FP7/2007-2013) under grant agreement No. 610916 – SENSEI.

References

Sabine Buchholz. 2000. chunklink.pl. `http://ilk.uvt.nl/software/`.

Benoit Favre, Dilek Hakkani-Tür, and Sebastien Cuendet. 2007. Icsiboost. `https://github.com/benob/icsiboost/`.

Yoav Freund and Robert E. Schapire. 1997. A decision-theoretic generalization of on-line learning and an application to boosting. *Journal of Computer and System Sciences*, 55(1):119–139, August.

Karin Kipper, Anna Korhonen, Neville Ryant, and Martha Palmer. 2008. A large-scale classification of english verbs. *Language Resources and Evaluation Journal*, 42(1):21–40.

Taku Kudo. 2013. CRF++. `http://taku910.github.io/crfpp/`.

John Lafferty, Andrew McCallum, and Fernando C. N. Pereira. 2001. Conditional random fields: Probabilistic models for segmenting and labeling sequence data. In *Proceedings of 18th International Conference on Machine Learning*, pages 282–289.

Ziheng Lin, Hwee Tou Ng, and Min-Yen Kan. 2014. A PDTB-styled end-to-end discourse parser. *Natural Language Engineering*, 20:151 – 184.

Martin Potthast, Tim Gollub, Francisco Rangel, Paolo Rosso, Efstathios Stamatatos, and Benno Stein. 2014. Improving the Reproducibility of PAN's Shared Tasks: Plagiarism Detection, Author Identification, and Author Profiling. In *Information Access Evaluation meets Multilinguality, Multimodality, and Visualization. 5th International Conference of the CLEF Initiative (CLEF 14)*, pages 268–299, Berlin Heidelberg New York.

Rashmi Prasad, Nikhil Dinesh, Alan Lee, Eleni Miltsakaki, Livio Robaldo, Aravind Joshi, and Bonnie Webber. 2008. The Penn Discourse Treebank 2.0. In *Proceedings of the 6th International Conference on Language Resources and Evaluation (LREC 2008)*.

Helmut Schmid. 1995. Improvements in part-of-speech tagging with an application to german. In *Proceedings of the ACL SIGDAT-Workshop*, Dublin, Ireland.

Evgeny A. Stepanov and Giuseppe Riccardi. 2013. Comparative evaluation of argument extraction algorithms in discourse relation parsing. In *The 13th International Conference on Parsing Technologies (IWPT 2013)*, pages 36–44, Nara, Japan, November. ACL.

Evgeny A. Stepanov and Giuseppe Riccardi. 2014. Towards cross-domain PDTB-style discourse parsing. In *EACL Workshops - The Fifth International Workshop on Health Text Mining and Information Analysis (Louhi 2014)*, pages 30–37, Gothenburg, Sweden, April. ACL.

Evgeny A. Stepanov, Giuseppe Riccardi, and Ali Orkan Bayer. 2015. The UniTN discourse parser in CoNLL 2015 shared task: Token-level sequence labeling with argument-specific models. In *Proceedings of the SIGNLL Conference on Computational Natural Language Learning (CoNLL) - Shared Task*, pages 25–31, Beijing, China, July. ACL.

Joseph Turian, Lev Ratinov, and Yoshua Bengio. 2010. Word representations: A simple and general method for semisupervised learning. In *In ACL*, pages 384–394.

Jianxiang Wang and Man Lan. 2015. A refined end-to-end discourse parser. In *Proceedings of the Nineteenth Conference on Computational Natural Language Learning: Shared Task*.

Bonnie L. Webber, Markus Egg, and Valia Kordoni. 2011. Discourse structure and language technology. *Natural Language Engineering*, pages 1–54.

Theresa Wilson, Janyce Wiebe, and Paul Hoffmann. 2005. Recognizing contextual polarity in phrase-level sentiment analysis. In *Proceedings of Human Language Technology Conference and Conference on Empirical Methods in Natural Language Processing (HLT-EMNLP)*, Vancouver, B.C., Canada, October.

Nianwen Xue, Hwee Tou Ng, Sameer Pradhan, Rashmi Prasad, Christopher Bryant, and Attapol Rutherford. 2015. The CoNLL-2015 Shared Task on Shallow Discourse Parsing. In *Proceedings of the Nineteenth Conference on Computational Natural Language Learning: Shared Task*.

Nianwen Xue, Hwee Tou Ng, Sameer Pradhan, Bonnie Webber, Attapol Rutherford, Chuan Wang, and Hongmin Wang. 2016. The CoNLL-2016 Shared Task on Multilingual Shallow Discourse Parsing. In *Proceedings of the Twentieth Conference on Computational Natural Language Learning - Shared Task*, Berlin, Germany, August. Association for Computational Linguistics.

The CLaC Discourse Parser at CoNLL-2016

Majid Laali[*] **Andre Cianflone**[*] **Leila Kosseim**

Department of Computer Science and Software Engineering
Concordia University, Montreal, Quebec, Canada
`{Laali, Cianflone, Kosseim}@encs.concordia.ca`

Abstract

This paper describes our submission (*CLaC*) to the CoNLL-2016 shared task on shallow discourse parsing. We used two complementary approaches for the task. A standard machine learning approach for the parsing of explicit relations, and a deep learning approach for non-explicit relations. Overall, our parser achieves an F_1-score of 0.2106 on the identification of discourse relations (0.3110 for explicit relations and 0.1219 for non-explicit relations) on the blind CoNLL-2016 test set.

1 Introduction

Shallow discourse parsing is defined as the identification of two discourse units, or discourse arguments, and labeling their relation. Although the topic of shallow discourse parsing has received much interest in the past few years (e.g. (Zhang et al., 2015; Weiss, 2015; Ji et al., 2015; Rutherford and Xue, 2014; Kong et al., 2014; Feng et al., 2014)), the performance of the state-of-the-art discourse parsers is not yet adequate to be used in other downstream Natural Language Processing applications. For example, the best parser submitted at CoNLL-2015 (Wang and Lan, 2015) achieved an F_1 score of 0.2400 on the blind test dataset.

For the CoNLL 2016 task of shallow discourse parsing, four types of discourse relations have to be annotated in texts (more details of the task can be found in (Xue et al., 2016)):

1. *Explicit Discourse Relations*: explicit discourse relations are explicitly signalled within the text through *discourse connectives* such as *because, however, since,* etc.

2. *Implicit Discourse Relations*: implicit discourse relations are inferred by the reader and no discourse connective is used within the text to convey the relation. As a reader, implicit discourse relations can be inferred by inserting a discourse connective (called an *implicit discourse connective*) in the text that best expresses the inferred relation.

3. *AltLex Discourse Relations*: Similarly to implicit discourse relations, AltLex are not signalled through the presence of discourse connectives in the text. However, the relation is alternatively lexicalized by some non-connective expression, hence inserting an *implicit discourse connective* to express the inferred relation would lead to a redundancy.

4. *EntRel Discourse Relations*: EntRel discourse relations are defined between two discourse arguments where only an entity-based coherence relation could be perceived.

In this paper, we report on the development and results of our discourse parser for the CoNLL 2016 shared task. As shown in Figure 1, our parser, named *CLaC Discourse Parser*, consists of two main components: the Explicit Discourse Relation Annotator and the Non-Explicit Discourse Relation Annotator .

The Explicit Discourse Relation Annotator is based on the parser that we submitted last year to CoNLL 2015 (Laali et al., 2015). For this year's submission, we improved its components by (1) adding new features (see Section 2 for more details), (2) using a sequence classifier instead of a multiclass classifier in the Discourse Argument Segmenter, and (3) defining a new component, the Discourse Argument Trimmer, to identify attributes and prune discourse arguments.

---

[*]Both authors contributed equally

Proceedings of the 54th Annual Meeting of the Association for Computational Linguistics, pages 92–99,
Berlin, Germany, August 7-12, 2016. ©2016 Association for Computational Linguistics

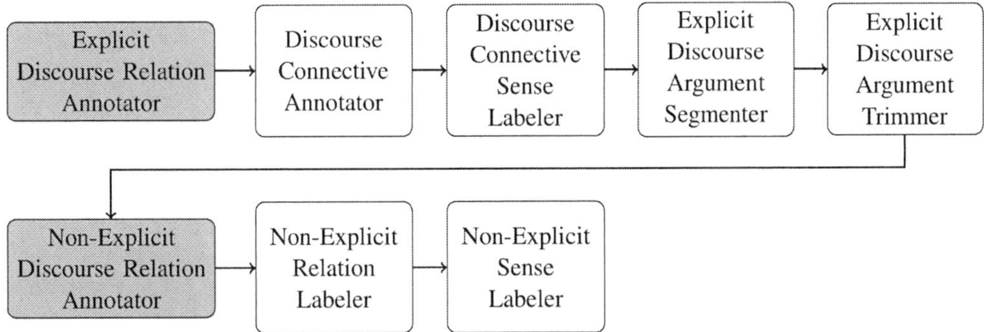

Figure 1: Pipeline of the CLaC Discourse Parser

Last year's system did not address the annotation of non-explicit discourse relations (i.e. implicit, AltLex and EntRel discourse relations). For this year, we therefore built this module from scratch. The Non-Explicit Discourse Relation Annotator first uses a binary Convolutional Neural Network (ConvNet) to detect whether a relation exists in a text devoid of a discourse connective, then uses a multiclass ConvNet to label the relation.

2 Explicit Discourse Relation Annotator

Figure 1 shows the pipeline of the CLaC parser. The top row in Figure 1 focuses on the Explicit Discourse Relation Annotator. This pipeline consists of four main components: (1) *Discourse Connective Annotator*, (2) *Discourse Connective Sense Labeler*, (3) *Explicit Relation Argument Segmenter* and (4) *Discourse Argument Trimmer*.

Modules 1, 2 and 3 are based on last year's system (Laali et al., 2015) while module 4 has been newly developed to address a weak issue from last year.

2.1 Discourse Connective Annotator

The *Discourse Connective Annotator* annotates discourse connectives within a text. To label discourse connectives, the annotator first searches the input texts for terms that match any of the 100 discourse connectives listed in the Penn Discourse Treebank (Prasad et al., 2008a). Inspired by (Pitler et al., 2009), a C4.5 decision tree binary classifier (Quinlan, 1993) is used to detect if each discourse connective is used in a discourse usage or not. In addition to the six features proposed by (Pitler et al., 2009), this year we also used four of the features proposed by (Lin et al., 2014). In total 10

features were used:

1. The discourse connective text in lowercase.

2. The categorization of the case of the connective: *all lowercase* or *initial uppercase*.

3. The highest node (called the *SelfCat* node) in the parse tree that covers the connective words but nothing more.

4–6. The parent, the left sibling and the right sibling of the *SelfCat*.

7–10. The left and the right word of discourse connective and their parts of speech.

2.2 Discourse Connective Sense Labeler

Once discourse connectives have been classified as discourse usage or not, the *Discourse Connective Sense Labeler* labels the discourse relation signalled by the annotated discourse connectives with one of the 14 labels specified by the task. This component also uses a C4.5 decision tree classifier (Quinlan, 1993) with the same 10 features used by the *Discourse Connective Annotator* (see Section 2.1).

2.3 Discourse Argument Segmenter

The goal of the *Discourse Argument Segmenter* is to detect the discourse argument boundaries. This module first assumes that both discourse arguments (i.e. ARG1 and ARG2) are located in the same sentence that contains the discourse connective. If ARG1 is not found in the sentence, then the Discourse Argument Segmenter selects the immediately preceding sentence as ARG1.

We used a similar approach proposed by (Kong et al., 2014) to identify discourse arguments that appear in the same sentence. That is to say, we first select all the constituents in the parse tree that are directly connected to one of the nodes in the path from the discourse connective to the root of the sentence and classify them into to one of three categories: *part-of*-ARG1, *part-of*-ARG2 or NON (i.e. not part of any discourse argument). Then, all constituents which are tagged as part of ARG1 or as part of ARG2 are merged to obtain the actual boundaries of ARG1 and ARG2.

Instead of using integer programming as proposed by Kong et al. (2014), we used a Conditional Random Field (CRF) in order to leverage global information (i.e. information across all constituent candidates). CRFs have been previously used for discourse argument identification (Ghosh et al., 2011) but at the token level. Kong et al. (2014)'s approach generates a sequence of constituents and therefore, CRFs can be applied at the constituent level.

We used the following categories of features for the CRF:

1. *Discourse connective features:* This category includes all 10 features used in the Discourse Connective Annotator (see Section 2.1).

2. *Constituent features:* Motivated by Kong et al. (2014)'features, we defined the following five features:

   (a) The constituents in the path from the current constituent to the *SelfCat* node in the parse tree.
   (b) The length of the path between the current constituent and the *SelfCat* node.
   (c) The context of the current constituent in the parse tree. The context of a constituent is defined by its label, the label of its parent and the label of its left and right siblings in the parse tree.
   (d) The position of the current constituent relative to the *SelfCat* node (i.e. left or right).
   (e) The syntactic production rule of the current constituent.

3. *Lexical features:* This year, we also used lexical features including the head of the current constituent and four tokens that appear in the constituent boundary (the first token of the constituent and its previous token and the last token of the constituent and its following token).

2.4 Discourse Argument Trimmer

According to the PDTB manual (Prasad et al., 2008b), annotators should keep the span of two discourse arguments as small as possible and should remove any extra information that is not necessary for the discourse relation. Following this idea, the *Discourse Argument Trimmer* is a classifier that excludes any constituent from the discourse argument span that is not related to the discourse relations.

To do so, we developed a binary classifier that labels all the constituents and tokens in the annotated discourse arguments with either *part-of-Argument* or *Not-part-of-Argument* to exclude tokens that are not part of the discourse argument. Once the classifier has labeled all the tokens and constituents, we remove from the discourse arguments all tokens that are labeled as *Not-Part-of-Argument* or part of a constituent with the *Not-Part-of-Argument* label.

A C4.5 decision tree binary classifier was developed using the following features:

1. The head of the constituent or the text of the token.

2. The label of the constituent in the syntax tree or the POS of token.

3. The position of the constituent/token (i.e whether it appears at the beginning, inside or at the end of the discourse argument).

4. The syntactic production rule of the constituent's parent and grand parent or "null" for tokens.

5. The type of the argument (i.e. ARG1 or ARG2)

6. The node label/POS of the left and right siblings of the constituent/token in the syntactic tree.

3 Non-Explicit Discourse Relation Annotator

As mentioned in Section 1, last year, the CLaC Discourse Parser did not address non-explicit relations. Therefore, for this year's participation we developped this module from scratch. Because Convolutional Neural Networks (ConvNets) have been successful at several sentence classification tasks (e.g. (Zhang and Wallace, 2016; Kim,

2014)), we wanted to investigate if similar networks could be used to address the task of non-explicit discourse relation recognition.

The Non-Explicit Discourse Relation Annotator begins where the Explicit Discourse Relation Annotator ends. The Explicit Discourse Relation Annotator only analyzes texts which contain a discourse connective; all other segments are sent to the Non-Explicit Discourse Relation Annotator.

Because these text segments may or may not contain a discourse relation, the Non-Explicit Discourse Relation Annotator first sends each text segment to a binary ConvNet to identify which segments contain a discourse relations and which do not. The Non-Explicit Discourse Relation Annotator trims trailing discourse punctuation as per the shared task requirement. Only discourses with two consecutive arguments are considered as possible non-explicit discourses. Non-discourse segments are removed from the pipeline. Sense labelling is then performed on the remaining segments using a multiclass ConvNet.

3.1 Input

The two ConvNets have an identical setup. The input to the models are pretrained word embeddings from the Google News set, as trained with Word2Vec[1]. Words not in the Google News set are randomly initialized. Word embeddings are non-static, meaning that they are allowed to change during training.

Each input to the networks is composed of the two padded discourse arguments. ARG1 is padded to the length of the longest ARG1, and ARG2 is similarly padded to the length of the longest ARG2. Since the training set contains a few unusually long arguments, we limited the argument size to the size of the 99.5[th] percentile. This reduced the length of ARG1 from 1000 to 60 words, and that of ARG2 from 400 to 61 words. This dramatically decreased the model complexity with insignificant impact on performance. The two arguments are then concatenated to form a single input. Each word is then replaced with their embedded vector representation.

Let l be the length of a single input (the number of words in the discourse plus padding, 121). Let d be the dimensionality of a word vector (300 for our pretrained embedding). Then the input to the networks, the matrix of discourse embedding, can

---

[1]https://code.google.com/archive/p/word2vec/

be denoted $Q \in \mathbb{R}^{l \times d}$.

3.2 Network

The network configuration is largely based on (Kim, 2014). We applied a narrow convolution over Q with height w (i.e. w words) and width d (the entire word vector) defined as region $h \in \mathbb{R}^{d \times w}$. We added a bias b and applied a nonlinear function f on the convolution to give us features c_i, where i is the ith word in the discourse input. This is shown in Formula 1.

$$c_i = f(h \cdot Q_{i:i+w-1} + b) \qquad (1)$$

The nonlinear function f in our case was the exponential linear unit (ELU) (Clevert et al., 2016), indicated in Formula 2.

$$f(x) = \begin{cases} x & \text{if } x > 0 \\ \alpha(exp(x) - 1) & \text{if } x \leq 0 \end{cases} \qquad (2)$$

Since the convolution is narrow, there are $l - w + 1$ such features, giving us a *feature map* $c \in \mathbb{R}^{l-w+1}$. We applied max-over-time pooling on c to extract the most "important" feature as in Formula 3.

$$y = max(c) \qquad (3)$$

We applied 128 feature maps and pooled each one of these. We repeated the entire process 3 times for $w = 3, 4$ and 5, and concatenated them together. This gave us a final matrix $M \in \mathbb{R}^{3 \times 128}$. We reshaped M to a flat vector and applied dropout as our regularization (Srivastava et al., 2014), giving us vector $u \in \mathbb{R}^{384}$. u is fully connected to a softmax output layer where loss is measured with cross-entropy. The network was trained in mini-batches and optimized with the *Adam* algorithm (Kingma and Ba, 2015).

4 Results and Analysis

Table 1 shows the F_1 scores of the CLaC Discourse Parser and the best parser at CoNLL 2015 (Wang and Lan, 2015) for different datasets. The overall F_1 score of the CLaC parser is 0.2106 with the blind test dataset which is lower than the F_1 score of the best parser at CoNLL 2015 (i.e. 0.2400). For explicit relations, the performance of our parser (F_1=0.3110) is higher than the performance of last year's best parser (F_1=0.3038); however, for non-explicit relations there is gap between the performance of our parser (F_1=0.1219) and the performance of last year's best parser (F_1=0.1887).

	Development Dataset (PDTB)		Test Dataset (PDTB)		Blind Test Dataset (Wikinews)	
	CLaC	Best (2015)	CLaC	Best (2015)	CLaC	Best (2015)
Full Parsing						
Overall	**0.3260**	0.3851	**0.2442**	0.2499	**0.2106**	0.2400
Explicit	0.4457	0.4977	0.3572	0.3447	0.3110	0.3038
Non-Explicit	0.2167	0.2876	0.1395	0.1511	0.1219	0.1887
Identification of Explicit Discourse Connective						
Explicit	0.9203	0.9514	0.9100	0.9421	**0.9020**	0.9186
Argument Identification						
Overall	0.4929	0.5704	0.4173	0.4377	0.3912	0.4637
Explicit	0.4867	0.5352	0.4023	0.3882	**0.3989**	0.4135
Non-Explicit	0.4987	0.6014	0.4311	0.4881	**0.3844**	0.5041
Sense Labeling (Supplementary task)						
Overall	0.6222	-	0.5736	0.6802	0.5000	0.6327
Explicit	0.9074	-	0.8948	0.9079	**0.7622**	0.7685
Non-Explicit	0.3712	-	0.2813	0.4734	**0.2772**	0.5176

Table 1: F_1-score of the CLaC Discourse Parser and the best parser of 2015 with Different Datasets.

4.1 Explicit Discourse Relation Annotator

Table 1 shows that the argument segmentation component is the bottleneck of the Explicit Discourse Relation Annotator. While the CLaC Discourse parser achieves competitive results in the identification of explicit discourse connectives (F_1=0.9020) and labeling the sense signalled by the discourse connectives (F_1=0.7622) with the blind test dataset, its performance is rather low (F_1=0.3989) for the identification of the discourse argument boundaries.

Our results show that the CLaC Discourse Parser has difficulty in detecting ARG1. As Table 2 shows, the precision and recall for the identification of ARG1 (i.e. P=0.4928 and R=0.4749) are significantly lower than for ARG2 (i.e. P=0.7194 and R=0.6932). ARG2 is syntactically bound to discourse connectives and therefore, it is easier to detect its boundaries. Moreover, as mentioned in Section 2.3, our approach does not account for arguments that appear in non-adjacent sentences. However, according to Prasad et al. (2008a), 9.02% of ARG1 in the PDTB do not appear in the sentence adjacent to the discourse connective.

The exact match of CoNLL is a strict evaluation measure for the argument identification. For example, in Sentence (1), our parser did not detect the word '*it*' (boxed) and therefore, accordingly to the exact match scoring schema, the boundaries of the discourse arguments are incorrect.

	P	R	F_1
Arg1	0.4928	0.4749	0.4837
Arg2	0.7194	0.6932	0.7061
Arg1 & Arg2	0.4065	0.3917	0.3989

Table 2: Results of the CLaC Discourse parser for the identification of discourse arguments with the blind test dataset (exact match).

(1) *The law does allow the RTC to borrow from the Treasury up to $5 billion at any time.* <u>Moreover,</u> it **says the RTC's total obligations may not exceed $50 billion, but that figure is derived after including notes and other debt, and subtracting from it the market value of the assets the RTC holds.**[2]

Such cases where the CLaC parser misses the argument boundaries by only a few words (added or deleted) are frequent. For example, as Table 3 shows, if we evaluate the argument boundaries with the partial match metric defined in the CoNLL evaluator, the performance increases significantly. The partial match metric accepts the argument boundaries if 70% of the tokens of the identified discourse arguments are correct. Using this metric, the F_1 score of the identification of ARG1 and ARG2 increases by 0.1917 and 0.0777 respectively.

---

[2]This example is taken from the CoNLL development dataset.

	P	**R**	**F$_1$**
Arg1	0.6740	0.6768	0.6754
Arg2	0.7695	0.7986	0.7838
Arg1 & Arg2	0.6386	0.6667	0.6523

Table 3: Results of the CLaC Discourse parser for the identification of discourse argument with the blind test dataset (partial match).

We also observed that the Explicit Discourse Argument Trimmer has a difficulty detecting what parts of the texts are related to discourse relations especially if multiple events appear in the text with a TEMPORAL discourse relation. For example, in Sentence (2) the parser identified the boxed words as ARG1 and missed required information. On the other hand in Sentence (3) the parser included extra information in ARG1. This type of error appears more frequently for ARG1 which explains why the partial match metric improves the identification of ARG1 more than the identification of ARG2.

(2)   *We would have to wait* $\boxed{\textit{until we have}}$ $\boxed{\textit{collected on those assets}}$ <u>before</u> **we can move forward**.

(3) $\boxed{\text{But the RTC also requires "working"}}$ $\boxed{\text{capital \textit{to maintain the bad assets of}}}$ $\boxed{\textit{thrifts that are sold}}$, <u>until</u> **the assets can be sold separately**.

4.2 Non-Explicit Discourse Relation Annotator

Table 1 shows that for the task of non-explicit sense labelling the Non-Explicit Discourse Relation Annotator achieves an F_1-score of 0.2813 on the test dataset and 0.2772 on the blind dataset, versus 0.3712 on the developement dataset. The similar performance on the test and blind datasets and the 10% difference with the development dataset suggest overfitting of our neural network.

For argument segmentation, just removing tailing punctuations from consecutive sentences achieves an F_1-score of 0.3884. According to Prasad et al. (2008a), non-explicit relations are present between successive pairs of sentences within paragraphs, but also intra-sententially between complete clauses separated by a semicolon or a colon. Our simple argument segmentation heuristic ignores intra-sentential arguments. We

believe that this accounts for its poor performance on the identification of discourse arguments.

When looking more closely at the sense labelling performance (data not shown), it seems that our network tends to overweight a few high prior probability senses, notably *EntRel* and *Expansion.Conjunction*. *EntRel* is predicted for 46% of samples, whereas it only represents 29% of the development dataset. *Expansion.Conjunction* is predicted for 24% of samples, whereas it represents only 17% of the development dataset.

We believe that one of the key issues for the Non-Explicit Discourse Relation Annotator is the size of the training set for non-explicit discourse. 17,813 samples is limited for a ConvNet, hence reducing the possible complexity of our model. The Non-Explicit Discourse Relation Annotator underperformed the best parser from CoNLL-2015 on sense labeling by 24.04% for the blind dataset, showing the advantage of non-neural network machine learning techniques when training data is scarce.

5   Conclusion and Future Work

A major area of concern in our system is the argument identification, both for explicit and non-explicit discourse relations. If we compare the results of the Supplementary task and Full Parsing task in Table 1, we can see that the Full Parsing F_1-scores are about half of the Supplementary task F_1-scores due to mis-identification of arguments.

It is necessary to consider cases where ARG1 appears in non-adjacent sentences to improve the identification of discourse arguments for explicit relations. We believe that by considering co-references in texts, we can expand our approach to address non-adjacent discourse arguments. Furthermore, it would be interesting to define new features by using ARG2 to detect what information can be added to or removed from ARG1. Finally, we believe that new ways to identify discourse arguments, such as Recurrent Neural Networks (Long Short Term Memory), could enhance the performance of the argument identification. To improve the identification of discourse arguments for non-explicit relations, we plan to expand the Explicit Discourse Argument Trimmer for non-explicit relations.

For non-explicit sense labeling, we would like to experiment with a larger training set possibly by automatically expanding it.

Acknowledgments

The authors would like to thank Sohail Hooda for his programming help and the anonymous reviewers for their comments on the paper. This work was financially supported by an NSERC Discovery Grant.

References

Djork-Arné Clevert, Thomas Unterthiner, and Sepp Hochreiter. 2016. Fast and accurate deep network learning by exponential linear units (elus). In *Proceeding of the 2016 International Conference on Learning Representation (ICLR 2016)*, San Juan, Puerto Rico, May.

Vanessa Wei Feng, Ziheng Lin, and Graeme Hirst. 2014. The Impact of Deep Hierarchical Discourse Structures in the Evaluation of Text Coherence. In *Proceedings of the 25th International Conference on Computational Linguistics (COLING-2014)*, Dublin, Ireland.

Sucheta Ghosh, Richard Johansson, and Sara Tonelli. 2011. Shallow discourse parsing with conditional random fields. In *Proceedings of the 5th International Joint Conference on Natural Language Processing*, pages 1071–1079, Chiang Mai, Thailand, November.

Yangfeng Ji, Gongbo Zhang, and Jacob Eisenstein. 2015. Closing the Gap: Domain Adaptation from Explicit to Implicit Discourse Relations. In *Proceedings of the 2015 Conference on Empirical Methods in Natural Language Processing (EMNLP 2015)*, pages 2219–2224, Lisbon, Portugal, September.

Yoon Kim. 2014. Convolutional neural networks for sentence classification. In *Proceedings of the 2014 Conference on Empirical Methods in Natural Language Processing (EMNLP 2014)*, pages 1746–1751, Doha, Qatar, October.

Diederik Kingma and Jimmy Ba. 2015. Adam: A method for stochastic optimization. In *Proceeding of the 2015 International Conference on Learning Representation (ICLR 2015)*, San Diego, California.

Fang Kong, Hwee Tou Ng, and Guodong Zhou. 2014. A Constituent-Based Approach to Argument Labeling with Joint Inference in Discourse Parsing. In *Proceedings of the 2014 Conference on Empirical Methods in Natural Language Processing (EMNLP 2014)*, pages 68–77, Doha, Qatar, October.

Majid Laali, Elnaz Davoodi, and Leila Kosseim. 2015. The CLaC Discourse Parser at CoNLL-2015. In *Proceedings of the Nineteenth Conference on Computational Natural Language Learning - Shared Task (CoNLL 2015)*, pages 56–60, Beijing, China, July.

Ziheng Lin, Hwee Tou Ng, and Min-Yen Kan. 2014. A PDTB-styled end-to-end discourse parser. *Natural Language Engineering*, 20(2):151–184.

Emily Pitler, Annie Louis, and Ani Nenkova. 2009. Automatic sense prediction for implicit discourse relations in text. In *Proceedings of 47th Annual Meeting of the Association for Computational Linguistics and the 4th International Joint Conference on Natural Language Processing of the AFNLP (ACL-IJCNLP 2009)*, page 683–691, Suntec, Singapore, August.

Rashmi Prasad, Nikhil Dinesh, Alan Lee, Eleni Miltsakaki, Livio Robaldo, Aravind K. Joshi, and Bonnie L. Webber. 2008a. The Penn Discourse Tree-Bank 2.0. In *Proceedings of the Sixth International Conference on Language Resources and Evaluation (LREC'08)*, pages 28–30, Marrakech, Morocco, May.

Rashmi Prasad, Eleni Miltsakaki, Nikhil Dinesh, Alan Lee, Aravind Joshi, Livio Robaldo, and Bonnie L. Webber. 2008b. The Penn Discourse Treebank 2.0 annotation manual. Technical Report IRCS-08-01, Institute for Research in Cognitive Science, University of Pennsylvania.

J. Ross Quinlan. 1993. *C4.5: Programs for Machine Learning*. Morgan Kaufmann Publishers Inc., San Francisco, CA, USA.

Attapol T. Rutherford and Nianwen Xue. 2014. Discovering Implicit Discourse Relations Through Brown Cluster Pair Representation and Coreference Patterns. In *Proceedings of the 14th Conference of the European Chapter of the Association for Computational Linguistics (EACL 2014)*, pages 645–654, Gothenburg, Sweden, April.

Nitish Srivastava, Geoffrey Hinton, Alex Krizhevsky, Ilya Sutskever, and Ruslan Salakhutdinov. 2014. Dropout: A simple way to prevent neural networks from overfitting. *The Journal of Machine Learning Research*, 15(1):1929–1958.

Jianxiang Wang and Man Lan. 2015. A refined end-to-end discourse parser. In *Proceedings of the Nineteenth Conference on Computational Natural Language Learning: Shared Task (CoNLL 2015)*, pages 17–24, Beijing, China, July.

Gregor Weiss. 2015. Learning representations for text-level discourse parsing. In *Proceedings of the ACL-IJCNLP 2015 Student Research Workshop*, pages 16–21, Beijing, China, July.

Nianwen Xue, Hwee Tou Ng, Sameer Pradhan, Bonnie Webber, Attapol Rutherford, Chuan Wang, and Hongmin Wang. 2016. The CoNLL-2016 shared task on multilingual shallow discourse parsing. In *Proceedings of the Twentieth Conference on Computational Natural Language Learning - Shared Task*, Berlin, Germany, August. Association for Computational Linguistics.

Ye Zhang and Byron Wallace. 2016. A sensitivity analysis of (and practitioners' guide to) convolutional neural networks for sentence classification. *Computing Research Repository, abs/1510.03820.*

Biao Zhang, Jinsong Su, Deyi Xiong, Yaojie Lu, Hong Duan, and Junfeng Yao. 2015. Shallow Convolutional Neural Network for Implicit Discourse Relation Recognition. In *Proceedings of the 2015 Conference on Empirical Methods in Natural Language Processing (EMNLP 2015)*, pages 2230–2235, Lisbon, Portugal, September.

Discourse Relation Sense Classification Using Cross-argument Semantic Similarity Based on Word Embeddings

Todor Mihaylov and Anette Frank
Research Training Group AIPHES
Department of Computational Linguistics
Heidelberg University, 69120 Heidelberg, Germany
{mihaylov,frank}@cl.uni-heidelberg.de

Abstract

This paper describes our system for the CoNLL 2016 Shared Task's supplementary task on Discourse Relation Sense Classification. Our official submission employs a Logistic Regression classifier with several cross-argument similarity features based on word embeddings and performs with overall F-scores of 64.13 for the *Dev* set, 63.31 for the *Test* set and 54.69 for the *Blind* set, ranking first in the *Overall* ranking for the task. We compare the feature-based Logistic Regression classifier to different Convolutional Neural Network architectures. After the official submission we enriched our model for Non-Explicit relations by including similarities of explicit connectives with the relation arguments, and part of speech similarities based on modal verbs. This improved our *Non-Explicit* result by 1.46 points on the *Dev* set and by 0.36 points on the *Blind* set.

1 Introduction

The CoNLL 2016 Shared Task on Shallow Discourse Parsing (Xue et al., 2016) focuses on identifying individual discourse relations presented in text. This year the shared task has a main track that requires end-to-end discourse relation parsing and a supplementary task that is restricted to discourse relation sense classification. For the main task, systems are required to build a system that given a raw text as input can identify arguments *Arg1* and *Arg2* that are related in the discourse, and also classify the type of the relation, which can be *Explicit*, *Implicit*, *AltLex* or *EntRel*. A further attribute to be detected is the relation *Sense*, which can be one of 15 classes organized hierarchically

in 4 parent classes. With this work we participate in the Supplementary Task on Discourse Relation Sense Classification in English. The task is to predict the discourse relation sense when the arguments *Arg1*, *Arg2* are given, as well as the *Discourse Connective* in case of explicit marking.

In our contribution we compare different approaches including a Logistic Regression classifier using similarity features based on word embeddings, and two Convolutional Neural Network architectures. We show that an approach using only word embeddings retrieved from *word2vec* (Mikolov et al., 2013) and cross-argument similarity features is simple and fast, and yields results that rank first in the *Overall*, second in the *Explicit* and forth in the *Non-Explicit* sense classification task. Our system's code is publicly accessible[1].

2 Related Work

This year's CoNLL 2016 Shared Task on Shallow Discourse Parsing (Xue et al., 2016) is the second edition of the shared task after the CoNLL 2015 Shared task on Shallow Discourse Parsing (Xue et al., 2015). The difference to last year's task is that there is a new Supplementary Task on Discourse Relation Sense classification, where participants are not required to build an end-to-end discourse relation parser but can participate with a sense classification system only.

Discourse relations in the task are divided in two major types: Explicit and Non-Explicit (*Implicit*, *EntRel* and *AltLex*). Detecting the sense of Explicit relations is an easy task: given the discourse connective, the relation sense can be determined with very high accuracy (Pitler et al., 2008). A challenging task is to detect the sense of Non-Explicit discourse relations, as they usually don't

---

[1] https://github.com/tbmihailov/
conll16st-hd-sdp - Source code for our Discourse
Relation Sense Classification system

Proceedings of the 54th Annual Meeting of the Association for Computational Linguistics, pages 100–107,
Berlin, Germany, August 7-12, 2016. ©2016 Association for Computational Linguistics

have a connective that can help to determine their sense. In last year's task *Non-Explicit* relations have been tackled with features based on Brown clusters (Chiarcos and Schenk, 2015; Wang and Lan, 2015; Stepanov et al., 2015), VerbNet classes (Kong et al., 2015; Lalitha Devi et al., 2015) and MPQA polarity lexicon (Wang and Lan, 2015; Lalitha Devi et al., 2015). Earlier work (Rutherford and Xue, 2014) employed Brown cluster and coreference patterns to identify senses of implicit discourse relations in naturally occurring text. More recently Rutherford and Xue (2015) improved inference of implicit discourse relations via classifying explicit discourse connectives, extending prior research (Marcu and Echihabi, 2002; Sporleder and Lascarides, 2008). Several neural network approaches have been proposed, e.g., Multi-task Neural Networks (Liu et al., 2016) and Shallow-Convolutional Neural Networks (Zhang et al., 2015). Braud and Denis (2015) compare word representations for implicit discourse relation classification and find that denser representations systematically outperform sparser ones.

3 Method

We divide the task into two subtasks, and develop separate classifiers for Explicit and Non-Explicit discourse relation sense classification, as shown in Figure 1. We do that because the official evaluation is divided into Explicit and Non-Explicit (Implicit, AltLex, EntRel) relations and we want to be able to tune our system accordingly. During training, the relation type is provided in the data, and samples are processed by the respective classifier models in *Process 1 (Non-Explicit)* and *Process 2 (Explicit)*. During testing the gold *Type* attribute is not provided, so we use a simple heuristic: we assume that *Explicit* relations have connectives and that *Non-Explicit*[2] relations do not.

As the task requires that the actual evaluation is executed on the provided server, we save the models so we can load them later during evaluation.

For classifying *Explicit* connectives we follow a feature-based approach, developing features based on word embeddings and semantic similarity measured between parts of the arguments *Arg1* and *Arg2* of the discourse relations. Classification is

---

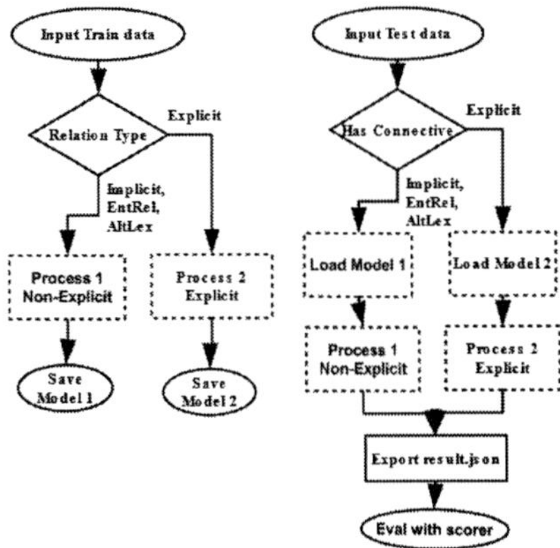

Figure 1: System architecture: Training and evaluating models for Explicit and Non-Explicit discourse relation sense classification

into one of the given fifteen classes of relation senses. For detecting *Non-Explicit* discourse relations we also make use of a feature-based approach, but in addition we experiment with two models based on Convolutional Neural Networks.

3.1 Feature-based approach

For each relation, we extract features from *Arg1*, *Arg2* and the *Connective*, in case the type of the relation is considered *Explicit*.

Semantic Features using Word Embeddings. In our models we only develop features based on word embedding vectors. We use *word2vec* (Mikolov et al., 2013) word embeddings with vector size 300 pre-trained on Google News texts.[3] For computing similarity between embedding representations, we employ cosine similarity:

$$1 - \frac{u.v}{\|u\| . \|v\|} \tag{1}$$

Embedding representations for Arguments and Connectives. For each argument *Arg1*, *Arg2* and *Connective* (for Explicit relations) we construct a centroid vector (2) from the embedding vectors $\vec{w}_i$ of all words w_i in their respective surface yield.

$$centroid(\vec{w}_1 ... \vec{w}_n) = \frac{\sum\limits_{i=1}^{n} \vec{w}_i}{n} \tag{2}$$

---

[2] In fact, some *AltLex* discourse relations do have connectives, but they are considered *Non-Explicit*. More detailed analysis will be required to improve on this simple heuristic. Given that their distribution across the data sets is very small, they do not have much influence on the overall performance.

[3] https://code.google.com/archive/p/word2vec/ - Pre-trained vectors trained on part of Google News dataset (about 100 billion words).

Cross-argument Semantic Vector Similarities.
We calculate various similarity features on the basis of the centroid word vectors for the arguments and the connective, as well as on parts of the arguments:

Arg1 to Arg2 similarity. We assume that for given arguments *Arg1* and *Arg2* that stand in a specific discourse relation sense, their centroid vectors should stand in a specific similarity relation to each other. We thus use their cosine similarity as a feature.

Maximized similarity. Here we rank each word in *Arg2*'s text according to its similarity with the centroid vector of *Arg1*, and we compute the average similarity for the top-ranked N words. We chose the similarity scores of the top 1,2,3 and 5 words as features. The assumption is that the average similarity between the first argument (*Arg1*) and the top N most similar words in the second argument (*Arg2*) might imply a specific sense.

Aligned similarity. For each word in *Arg1*, we choose the most similar word from the yield of *Arg2* and we take the average of all best word pair similarities, as suggested in Tran et al. (2015).

Part of speech (POS) based word vector similarities. We used part of speech tags from the parsed input data provided by the organizers, and computed similarities between centroid vectors of words with a specific tag from *Arg1* and the centroid vector of *Arg2*. Extracted features for POS similarities are symmetric: for example we calculate the similarity between *Nouns* from *Arg1* with *Pronouns* from *Arg2* and the opposite. The assumption is that some parts of speech between *Arg1* and *Arg2* might be closer than other parts of speech depending on the relation sense.

Explicit discourse connectives similarity. We collected 103 explicit discourse connectives from the Penn Discourse Treebank (Prasad et al., 2008) annotation manual[4] and for all of them construct vector representations according to (2), where for multi-token connectives we calculate a centroid vector from all tokens in the connective. For every discourse connective vector representation we calculate the similarity with the centroid vector representations from all *Arg1* and *Arg2* tokens. This

results in adding 103 similarity features for every relation. We use these features for implicit discourse relations sense classification only.

We assume that knowledge about the relation sense can be inferred by calculating the similarity between the semantic information of the relation arguments and specific discourse connectives.

Our feature-based approach yields very good results on Explicit relations sense classification with an F-score of 0.912 on the *Dev* set. Combining features based on word embeddings and similarity between arguments in Mihaylov and Nakov (2016) yielded state-of-the art performance in a similar task setup in Community Question Answering (Nakov et al., 2016), where two text arguments (question and answer) are to be ranked.

3.2 CNNs for sentence classification

We also experiment with Convolutional Neural Network architectures to detect Implicit relation senses. We have implemented the CNN model proposed in Kim (2014) as it proved successful in tasks like sentence classification and modal sense classification (Marasović and Frank, 2016). This model (Figure 2) defines one convolutional layer that uses pre-trained *Word2Vec* vectors trained on the Google News dataset. As shown in Kim (2014), this architecture yields very good results for various single sentence classification tasks. For our relation classification task we input the concatenated tokens of *Arg1* and *Arg2*.

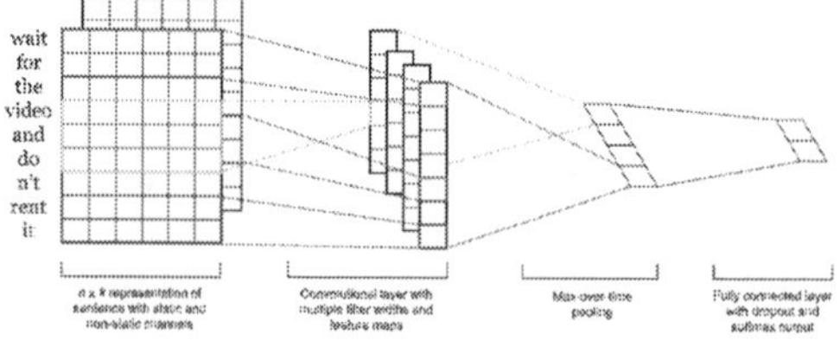

Figure 2: CNN architecture by Kim (2014).

3.3 Modified ARC-1 CNN for sentence matching

An alternative model we try for Implicit discourse relation sense classification is a modification of the *ARC-1* architecture proposed for sentence matching by Hu et al. (2015). We will refer to this model as *ARC-1M*. The modified architecture is depicted in Figure 3. The input of the model are two sentences S_x and S_y represented as sequence of

---

[4] https://www.seas.upenn.edu/~pdtb/PDTBAPI/
pdtb-annotation-manual.pdf - The Penn Discourse Treebank 2.0 Annotation Manual

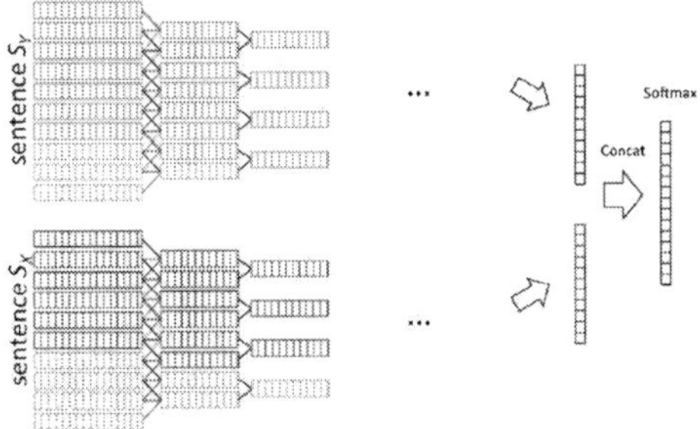

Figure 3: Modified ARC-I CNN architecture for sentence matching.

tokens' vector representations of *Arg1* and *Arg2*. Here, separate convolution and max-pooling layers are constructed for the two input sentences, and the results of the max-pooling layers are concatenated and fed to a single final *SoftMax* layer. The original ARC-1 architecture uses a *Multilayer Perceptron* layer instead of *SoftMax*. For our implementation we use TensorFlow (Abadi et al., 2015).

4 Experiments and Results

4.1 Data

In our experiments we use the official data (English) provided from the task organizers: *Train* (15500 Explicit + 18115 Non-Explicit), *Dev* (740 Explicit + 782 Non-Explicit), *Test* (990 Explicit + 1026 Non-Explicit), *Blind* (608 Explicit + 661 Non-Explicit). All models are trained on *Train* set.

4.2 Classifier settings

For our feature-based approach we concatenate the extracted features in a feature vector, scale their values to the 0 to 1 range, and feed the vectors to a classifier. We train and evaluate a L2-regularized Logistic Regression classifier with the LIBLINEAR (Fan et al., 2008) solver as implemented in *scikit-learn* (Pedregosa et al., 2011). For most of our experiments, we tuned the classifier with different values of the C (cost) parameter, and chose C=0.1 as it yielded the best accuracy on 5-fold cross-validation on the training set. We use these settings for all experiments that use the logistic regression classifier.

4.3 Official submission (LR with E+Sim)

Our official submission uses the feature-based approach described in Section 3.1 for both *Explicit* and *Non-Explicit* relations with all features de-

scribed above, except for the *Explicit connective similarities (Conn)* and *Modal verbs similarities (POS MD)* which have been added after the submission deadline. Table 1 presents the results divided by senses from our official submission performed on the TIRA evaluation platform (Potthast et al., 2014) server. We also compare our official and improved system results to the best performing system in the CoNLL 2015 Shared Task (Wang and Lan, 2015) and the best performing systems in the CoNLL 2016 Discourse Relation Sense Classification task. With our official system we rank first in the *Overall*[5] ranking. We rank second in the *Explicit* ranking with a small difference of 0.07 behind the best system and fourth in the *Non-Explicit* ranking with more significant difference of 2.75 behind the best system. We can see that similar to (Wang and Lan, 2015) our system performs well in classifying both types, while this year's winning systems perform well in their winning relation type and much worse in the others[6].

4.4 Further experiments on Non-Explicit relations

In Table 2 we compare different models for *Non-Explicit* relation sense classification trained on the *Train* and evaluated on the *Dev* set.

Embeddings only experiments. The first three columns show the results obtained with three approaches that use only features based on word embeddings. We use *word2vec* word embeddings. We also experimented with pre-trained *dependency-based* word embeddings (Levy and Goldberg, 2014), but this yielded slightly worse results on the *Dev* set.

Logistic Regression (LR). The *LR* column shows the results from a Logistic Regression classifier that uses only the concatenated features from the centroid representations built from the words of *Arg1* and *Arg2*.

CNN experiments. The *CNN* column shows results obtained from the Convolutional Neural Network for sentence classification (Section 3.2) fed with the concatenated *Arg1* and *Arg2* word tokens' vector representations from *Word2Vec* word embeddings. For our experiments we used default

---

[5]*Overall* score is the F-score on All (both *Explicit* and *Non-Explicit*) relations.

[6]The winner team in *Non-Explicit* (Rutherford and Xue, 2016) does not participate in *Explicit*.

Sense	WSJ Dev Set			WSJ Test Set			Blind Set (Official task ranking)		
	Overall	Exp	Non-E	Overall	Exp	Non-E	Overall	Exp	Non-E
Comparison.Concession	33.33	40.00	0.00	36.36	44.44	0.00	91.67	100.00	0.00
Comparison.Contrast	74.31	94.44	16.07	65.99	92.19	9.60	21.24	25.81	0.00
Contingency.Cause.Reason	51.48	78.95	38.51	64.36	94.03	47.93	35.71	82.61	18.03
Contingency.Cause.Result	38.94	91.43	15.38	40.74	100.00	17.53	53.33	91.67	27.78
Contingency.Condition	95.56	95.56	-	87.50	87.50	-	89.66	89.66	-
EntRel	58.73	-	58.73	70.97	-	70.97	47.06	-	47.06
Expansion.Alt	92.31	92.31	-	100.00	100.00	-	100.00	100.00	-
Expansion.Alt.Chosen alt	71.43	90.91	0.00	22.22	100.00	6.67	0.00	-	100.00
Expansion.Conjunction	70.45	97.00	40.00	75.88	98.36	40.26	63.48	94.52	27.51
Expansion.Instantiation	47.73	100.00	34.29	57.14	100.00	44.29	55.56	100.00	50.00
Expansion.Restatement	31.13	66.67	29.56	31.31	14.29	31.94	32.39	66.67	30.88
Temporal.Async.Precedence	78.46	98.00	13.33	82.22	100.00	11.11	84.44	97.44	0.00
Temporal.Async.Succession	82.83	87.23	0.00	58.82	63.49	0.00	96.08	96.08	-
Temporal.Synchrony	77.30	80.77	0.00	80.25	83.33	0.00	59.70	59.70	100.00
System	**All senses - comparison**								
Our system (Official)	64.13	91.20	40.32	**63.31**	89.80	**39.19**	54.69	78.34	34.56
Our improved system	64.77	91.05	41.66	62.69	90.02	37.81	**54.88**	78.38	34.92
Wang and Lan, 2015	**65.11**	90.00	**42.72**	61.27	**90.79**	34.45	54.76	76.44	36.29
Rutherford and Xue, 2016	-	-	40.32	-	-	36.13	-	-	**37.67**
Jain, 2016	62.43	**91.50**	36.85	50.90	89.70	15.60	41.47	**78.56**	9.95

Table 1: Evaluation of our official submission system, trained on Train 2016 and evaluated on Dev, Test and Blind sets. Comparison with our official system and our improved system with the official results of CoNLL 2015 Shared task's best system (Wang and Lan, 2015) and CoNLL 2016 Shared Task best systems in *Explicit* (Jain, 2016) and Non-Explicit (Rutherford and Xue, 2016). F-Score is presented.

system parameters as proposed in Kim (2014): filter windows with size 3,4,5 with 100 feature maps each, dropout probability 0.5 and mini-batch of size 50. We train the model with 50 epochs.

CNN ARC-1M experiments The *CNN ARC-1M* column shows results from our modification of ARC-1 CNN for sentence matching (see Section 3.3) fed with *Arg1* and *Arg2* word tokens' vector representations from the *Word2Vec* word embeddings. We use filter windows with size 3,4,5 with 100 feature maps each, shared between the two argument convolutions, dropout probability 0.5 and mini-batch of size 50 as proposed in Kim (2014). We train the model with 50 epochs.

Comparing *LR*, *CNN* and *CNN ARC-1M* according to their ability to classify different classes we observe that *CNN ARC-1M* performs best in detecting *Contingency.Cause.Reason* and *Contingency.Cause.Result* with a substantial margin over the other two models. The *CNN* model outperforms the *LR* and *CNN-ARC1M* for *Comparison.Contrast, EntRel, Expansion.Conjunction* and *Expansion.Instantiation* but cannot capture any *Expansion.Restatement* which leads to worse overall results compared to the others. These insights show that the Neural Network models are able to capture some dependencies between the relation arguments. For *Contingency.Cause.Results*, *CNN ARC-1M* even clearly outperforms the LR models enhanced with similarity features (discussed below). We also implemented a modified version of the *CNN ARC-2* architecture of Hu et al. (2015), which uses a cross-argument convolution layer, but it yielded much worse results.[7]

LR with Embeddings + Features The last three columns in Table 2 show the results of our feature-based Logistic Regression approach with different feature groups on top of the embedding representations of the arguments. Column *E+Sim* shows the results from our official submission and the other two columns show results for additional features that we added after the submission deadline.

Adding the cross-argument similarity features (without the POS modal verbs similarities) improves the overall result of the embeddings-only Logistic Regression (*LR*) baseline significantly from F-score 35.54 to 40.32. It also improves the result on almost all senses individually. Adding *Explicit connective similarities* features improves the *All* result by 0.67 points (E+Sim+Conn). It also improves the performance on *Tem-*

---

[7]We are currently checking our implementation.

| | | Embeddings only | | Logistic Regression with Embeddings + Features | | |
Sense	LR	CNN	CNN ARC-1M	E+Sim	E+Sim+Conn	E+Sim+Conn+POS MD
Comparison.Concession	0.00	0.00	0.00	0.00	0.00	0.00
Comparison.Contrast	2.33	13.68	8.51	16.07	**18.80**	17.86
Contingency.Cause.Reason	25.00	29.30	35.90	38.51	40.24	**42.17**
Contingency.Cause.Result	3.57	9.20	**19.28**	15.38	15.38	13.70
EntRel	53.13	59.53	56.87	58.73	60.80	**61.26**
Expansion.Alt.Chosen alt	0.00	0.00	0.00	0.00	0.00	0.00
Expansion.Conjunction	35.90	38.29	14.67	40.00	40.91	**41.27**
Expansion.Instantiation	0.00	21.98	4.08	**34.29**	31.43	33.80
Expansion.Restatement	12.74	0.00	21.56	**29.56**	26.87	27.45
Temporal.Async.Precedence	0.00	0.00	0.00	13.33	**17.65**	12.90
Temporal.Async.Succession	0.00	0.00	0.00	0.00	0.00	0.00
Temporal.Synchrony	0.00	0.00	0.00	0.00	0.00	0.00
All	35.54	34.34	36.21	40.32	40.99	**41.66**

Table 2: Evaluation of different systems and feature configurations for Non-Explicit relation sense classification, trained on Train 2016 and evaluated on Dev. F-score is presented.

poral.Async.Precedence, Expansion.Conjunction, EntRel, Contingency.Cause.Reason and *Comparison.Contrast* individually. We further added *POS similarity features* between *MD (modal verbs)* and other part of speech tags between *Arg1* and *Arg2*. The obtained improvement of 0.67 points shows that the occurrence of modal verbs within arguments can be exploited for implicit discourse relation sense classification. Adding the modal verbs similarities also improved the individual results for the *Contingency.Cause.Reason*, *EntRel* and *Expansion.Conjunction* senses.

Some relations are hard to predict, probably due to the low distribution in the train and evaluation data sets: *Comparison.Concession*[8], *Expansion.Alt.Chosen alt*[9], *Temporal.Async. Succession*[10], *Temporal. Synchrony*[11].

5 Conclusion and Future work

In this paper we describe our system for the participation in the CoNLL Shared Task on Discourse Relation Sense Classification. We compare different approaches including Logistic Regression classifiers using features based on word embeddings and cross-argument similarity and two Convolutional Neural Network architectures. Our official submission uses a logistic regression classifier with several similarity features and performs with overall F-scores of 64.13 for the *Dev* set, 63.31 for the *Test* set and 54.69 for the *Blind* set. After the official submission we improved our system

by adding more features for detecting senses for Non-Explicit relations and we improved our *Non-Explicit* result by 1.46 points to 41.66 on the *Dev* set and by 0.36 points to 34.92 on the *Blind* set.

We could show that dense representations of arguments and connectives jointly with cross-argument similarity features calculated over word embeddings yield competitive results, both for Explicit and Non-Explicit relations. First results in adapting CNN models to the task show that further gains can be obtained, beyond LR models.

In future work we want to explore further deep learning approaches and adapt them for discourse relation sense classification, using among others Recurrent Neural Networks and CNNs for matching sentences, as well as other neural network models that incorporate correlation between the input arguments, such as the MTE-NN system (Guzmán et al., 2016a; Guzmán et al., 2016b). Since we observe that the neural network approaches improve on the *LR* Embeddings-only models for most of the senses, in future work we could combine these models with our well-performing similarity features. Combining the output of a deep learning system with additional features has been shown to achieve state of the art performance in other tasks (Kreutzer et al., 2015).

Acknowledgments. This work is supported by the German Research Foundation as part of the Research Training Group "Adaptive Preparation of Information from Heterogeneous Sources" (AIPHES) under grant No. GRK 1994/1.

We thank Ana Marasović for her advice in the implementation of CNN models.

---

[8] Comparison.Concession, Non-Explicit: Train:1.10 %, Dev:0.66 %: Test:0.59 %.

[9] Expansion.Alt.Chosen-alt, Non-Explicit: Train:0.79 %, Dev:0.26 %: Test:1.49 %.

[10] Temporal.Async.Succ, Non-Explicit: Train:0.80 %, Dev:0.39 %: Test:0.49 %.

[11] Temporal.Synchrony, Non-Explicit: Train:0.94 %, Dev:1.19 %: Test:0.49 %.

References

Martín Abadi, Ashish Agarwal, Paul Barham, Eugene Brevdo, Zhifeng Chen, Craig Citro, Greg S. Corrado, Andy Davis, Jeffrey Dean, Matthieu Devin, Sanjay Ghemawat, Ian Goodfellow, Andrew Harp, Geoffrey Irving, Michael Isard, Yangqing Jia, Rafal Jozefowicz, Lukasz Kaiser, Manjunath Kudlur, Josh Levenberg, Dan Mané, Rajat Monga, Sherry Moore, Derek Murray, Chris Olah, Mike Schuster, Jonathon Shlens, Benoit Steiner, Ilya Sutskever, Kunal Talwar, Paul Tucker, Vincent Vanhoucke, Vijay Vasudevan, Fernanda Viégas, Oriol Vinyals, Pete Warden, Martin Wattenberg, Martin Wicke, Yuan Yu, and Xiaoqiang Zheng. 2015. TensorFlow: Large-scale machine learning on heterogeneous systems. Software available from tensorflow.org.

Chloé Braud and Pascal Denis. 2015. Comparing word representations for implicit discourse relation classification. In *Proceedings of the 2015 Conference on Empirical Methods in Natural Language Processing*, pages 2201–2211, Lisbon, Portugal, September. Association for Computational Linguistics.

Christian Chiarcos and Niko Schenk. 2015. A minimalist approach to shallow discourse parsing and implicit relation recognition. In *Proceedings of the Nineteenth Conference on Computational Natural Language Learning - Shared Task*, pages 42–49, Beijing, China, July. Association for Computational Linguistics.

Rong-En Fan, Kai-Wei Chang, Cho-Jui Hsieh, Xiang-Rui Wang, and Chih-Jen Lin. 2008. Liblinear: A library for large linear classification. *J. Mach. Learn. Res.*, 9:1871–1874, June.

Francisco Guzmán, Lluís Màrquez, and Preslav Nakov. 2016a. Machine translation evaluation meets community question answering. In *Proceedings of the 54th Annual Meeting of the Association for Computational Linguistics*, ACL '16, Berlin, Germany.

Francisco Guzmán, Lluís Màrquez, and Preslav Nakov. 2016b. MTE-NN at SemEval-2016 Task 3: Can machine translation evaluation help community question answering? In *Proceedings of the 10th International Workshop on Semantic Evaluation*, SemEval '16, San Diego, California, USA.

Baotian Hu, Zhengdong Lu, Hang Li, and Qingcai Chen. 2015. Convolutional neural network architectures for matching natural language sentences. *CoRR*, abs/1503.03244.

Yoon Kim. 2014. Convolutional neural networks for sentence classification. In *Proceedings of the 2014 Conference on Empirical Methods in Natural Language Processing (EMNLP)*, pages 1746–1751, Doha, Qatar, October. Association for Computational Linguistics.

Fang Kong, Sheng Li, and Guodong Zhou. 2015. The sonlp-dp system in the conll-2015 shared task. In *Proceedings of the Nineteenth Conference on Computational Natural Language Learning - Shared Task*, pages 32–36, Beijing, China, July. Association for Computational Linguistics.

Julia Kreutzer, Shigehiko Schamoni, and Stefan Riezler. 2015. Quality estimation from scratch (quetch): Deep learning for word-level translation quality estimation. In *Proceedings of the Tenth Workshop on Statistical Machine Translation*, pages 316–322, Lisbon, Portugal, September. Association for Computational Linguistics.

Sobha Lalitha Devi, Sindhuja Gopalan, Lakshmi S, Pattabhi RK Rao, Vijay Sundar Ram, and Malarkodi C.S. 2015. A hybrid discourse relation parser in conll 2015. In *Proceedings of the Nineteenth Conference on Computational Natural Language Learning - Shared Task*, pages 50–55, Beijing, China, July. Association for Computational Linguistics.

Omer Levy and Yoav Goldberg. 2014. Dependency-based word embeddings. In *Proceedings of the 52nd Annual Meeting of the Association for Computational Linguistics (Volume 2: Short Papers)*, pages 302–308, Baltimore, Maryland, June. Association for Computational Linguistics.

Yang Liu, Sujian Li, Xiaodong Zhang, and Zhifang Sui. 2016. Implicit discourse relation classification via multi-task neural networks. *CoRR*, abs/1603.02776.

Ana Marasović and Anette Frank. 2016. Multilingual Modal Sense Classification using a Convolutional Neural Network. In *Proceedings of the 1st Workshop on Representation Learning for NLP*, Berlin, Germany, August.

Daniel Marcu and Abdessamad Echihabi. 2002. An unsupervised approach to recognizing discourse relations. In *Proceedings of 40th Annual Meeting of the Association for Computational Linguistics*, pages 368–375, Philadelphia, Pennsylvania, USA, July. Association for Computational Linguistics.

Todor Mihaylov and Preslav Nakov. 2016. SemanticZ at SemEval-2016 Task 3: Ranking relevant answers in community question answering using semantic similarity based on fine-tuned word embeddings. In *Proceedings of the 10th International Workshop on Semantic Evaluation*, SemEval '16, San Diego, California, USA.

Tomas Mikolov, Wen-tau Yih, and Geoffrey Zweig. 2013. Linguistic regularities in continuous space word representations. In *Proceedings of the 2013 Conference of the North American Chapter of the Association for Computational Linguistics: Human Language Technologies*, NAACL-HLT '13, pages 746–751, Atlanta, Georgia, USA.

Preslav Nakov, Lluís Màrquez, Alessandro Moschitti, Walid Magdy, Hamdy Mubarak, Abed Alha Freihat, Jim Glass, and Bilal Randeree. 2016. SemEval-2016 task 3: Community question answering. In

Proceedings of the 10th International Workshop on Semantic Evaluation, SemEval '16, San Diego, California, USA.

F. Pedregosa, G. Varoquaux, A. Gramfort, V. Michel, B. Thirion, O. Grisel, M. Blondel, P. Prettenhofer, R. Weiss, V. Dubourg, J. Vanderplas, A. Passos, D. Cournapeau, M. Brucher, M. Perrot, and E. Duchesnay. 2011. Scikit-learn: Machine learning in Python. *Journal of Machine Learning Research*, 12:2825–2830.

Emily Pitler, Mridhula Raghupathy, Hena Mehta, Ani Nenkova, Alan Lee, and Aravind Joshi. 2008. Easily identifiable discourse relations. In *Coling 2008: Companion volume: Posters*, pages 87–90, Manchester, UK, August. Coling 2008 Organizing Committee.

Martin Potthast, Tim Gollub, Francisco Rangel, Paolo Rosso, Efstathios Stamatatos, and Benno Stein. 2014. Improving the Reproducibility of PAN's Shared Tasks: Plagiarism Detection, Author Identification, and Author Profiling. In Evangelos Kanoulas, Mihai Lupu, Paul Clough, Mark Sanderson, Mark Hall, Allan Hanbury, and Elaine Toms, editors, *Information Access Evaluation meets Multilinguality, Multimodality, and Visualization. 5th International Conference of the CLEF Initiative (CLEF 14)*, pages 268–299, Berlin Heidelberg New York, September. Springer.

Rashmi Prasad, Nikhil Dinesh, Alan Lee, Eleni Miltsakaki, Livio Robaldo, Aravind Joshi, and Bonnie Webber. 2008. The penn discourse treebank 2.0. In *In Proceedings of LREC*.

Attapol Rutherford and Nianwen Xue. 2014. Discovering implicit discourse relations through brown cluster pair representation and coreference patterns. In *Proceedings of the 14th Conference of the European Chapter of the Association for Computational Linguistics*, pages 645–654, Gothenburg, Sweden, April. Association for Computational Linguistics.

Attapol Rutherford and Nianwen Xue. 2015. Improving the inference of implicit discourse relations via classifying explicit discourse connectives. In *Proceedings of the 2015 Conference of the North American Chapter of the Association for Computational Linguistics: Human Language Technologies*, pages 799–808, Denver, Colorado, May–June. Association for Computational Linguistics.

Caroline Sporleder and Alex Lascarides. 2008. Using automatically labelled examples to classify rhetorical relations: An assessment. *Nat. Lang. Eng.*, 14(3):369–416, July.

Evgeny Stepanov, Giuseppe Riccardi, and Ali Orkan Bayer. 2015. The unitn discourse parser in conll 2015 shared task: Token-level sequence labeling with argument-specific models. In *Proceedings of the Nineteenth Conference on Computational Natural Language Learning - Shared Task*, pages 25–31,
Beijing, China, July. Association for Computational Linguistics.

Quan Hung Tran, Vu Tran, Tu Vu, Minh Nguyen, and Son Bao Pham. 2015. JAIST: Combining multiple features for answer selection in community question answering. In *Proceedings of the 9th International Workshop on Semantic Evaluation*, SemEval '15, pages 215–219, Denver, Colorado, USA.

Jianxiang Wang and Man Lan. 2015. A refined end-to-end discourse parser. In *Proceedings of the Nineteenth Conference on Computational Natural Language Learning - Shared Task*, pages 17–24, Beijing, China, July. Association for Computational Linguistics.

Nianwen Xue, Hwee Tou Ng, Sameer Pradhan, Rashmi Prasad, Christopher Bryant, and Attapol Rutherford. 2015. The conll-2015 shared task on shallow discourse parsing. In *Proceedings of the Nineteenth Conference on Computational Natural Language Learning - Shared Task*, pages 1–16, Beijing, China, July. Association for Computational Linguistics.

Nianwen Xue, Hwee Tou Ng, Sameer Pradhan, Bonnie Webber, Attapol Rutherford, Chuan Wang, and Hongmin Wang. 2016. The conll-2016 shared task on multilingual shallow discourse parsing. In *Proceedings of the Twentieth Conference on Computational Natural Language Learning - Shared Task*, Berlin, Germany, August. Association for Computational Linguistics.

Biao Zhang, Jinsong Su, Deyi Xiong, Yaojie Lu, Hong Duan, and Junfeng Yao. 2015. Shallow convolutional neural network for implicit discourse relation recognition. In *Proceedings of the 2015 Conference on Empirical Methods in Natural Language Processing*, pages 2230–2235, Lisbon, Portugal, September. Association for Computational Linguistics.

IIT (BHU) Submission for the CoNLL-2016 Shared Task: Shallow Discourse Parsing using Semantic Lexicon

Manpreet Kaur, Nishu Kumari, Anil Kumar Singh, Rajeev Sangal
Department of Computer Science, IIT-BHU,
Varanasi, Uttar Pradesh, India - 221005
`f2012687@goa.bits-pilani.ac.in, {kumari.nishu.apm11,`
`aksingh.cse}@iitbhu.ac.in, sangal@iiit.ac.in`

Abstract

This paper describes the Shallow Discourse Parser (SDP) submitted as a part of the Shared Task of CoNLL, 2016. The discourse parser takes newswire text as input and outputs relations between various components of the text. Our system is a pipeline of various sub-tasks which have been elaborated in the paper. We choose a data driven approach for each task and put a special focus on utilizing the resources allowed by the organizers for creating novel features. We also give details of various experiments with the dataset and the lexicon provided for the task.

1 Introduction

Shallow Discourse Parsing (SDP) is a linguistic task that identifies semantic relations between a pair of lexical units in a piece of discourse. Discourse relation is defined by three entities: a connective, a pair of lexical units between which the relation exists and the type or sense of relation between them (Xue et al., 2016). The discourse relations can be explicit, in which relations are expressed by certain words or phrases, or implicit, where words are not directly used to convey the relation, but instead, the meaning is implied. These words or phrases which convey the existence of a discourse relation directly are called connectives. The lexical units between which relation exists, could be a pair of clauses, a pair of sentences or even multiple sentences which can be adjacent or non-adjacent. These are called arguments.

A discourse treebank called the Penn Discourse TreeBank or PDTB (Prasad et al., 2008) serves as the gold standard for this task and is used as training data. The output of our system follows the same format as PDTB. Development data is also provided to perform experiments on the system. Phrase structure and dependency parses of both the training and development data have also been provided to assist in the task. Further details of the Shared Task can be found in the overview paper (Xue et al., 2016). Final evaluation of the parser is on test and blind data sets through TIRA platform set up by (Potthast et al., 2014). Besides automating the submission and evaluation system, TIRA also has provision for plagiarism detection, author identification and author profiling.

The SDP task can be broadly classified into two categories of explicit and non-explicit relation detection. We discuss the pipeline for explicit parser in section 2 and non-explicit parser in Section 3. Various results and experiments carried out are reported in the relevant sub-sections. These results are based on individual stages without error propagation from previous stages, unless specified otherwise. We report results on test and blind datasets and conclude our work in Section 4 and 5 respectively.

2 Explicit SDP

Identification of explicit discourse relations consists of several stages. First stage is the detection of discourse connectives in the text. This connective binds the arguments syntactically and semantically (Prasad et al., 2008) which is helpful in feature creation for the following tasks of argument position detection and argument span extraction. Once the arguments of the relation are extracted, we perform sense classification of the relation.

2.1 Connective Detection

This is the first stage of the parser which detects the existence of discourse connectives in the text. The input to this stage is raw text and we analyze the entire text for the presence of connectives which could form a discourse relation. Around 100 connective spans have been identified upon extensive research by the team that annotated PDTB (Prasad et al., 2008). However, the occur-

Proceedings of the 54th Annual Meeting of the Association for Computational Linguistics, pages 108–114,
Berlin, Germany, August 7-12, 2016. ©2016 Association for Computational Linguistics

rence of these words does not guarantee that it will form a discourse connective as can be seen in the following example:

My Father once worked on that project.

- 'once' is a non-discourse connective

You cannot change your statement once it comes out of your mouth.

-'once' is a discourse connective

Here the connective 'once' acts as a discourse connective based on the context. A string matching script is not sufficient for this task and we therefore use Maximum Entropy Classifier to identify whether a potential connective keyword actually forms a discourse relation or not. This task has been sufficiently mastered and high F1 scores have been reported by previous teams. Mostly syntactic features have been used for this classification task such as Connective, connectivePOS, PrevWord, PrevPOSTag, PrevPOS + connectivePOS, nextWord, nextPOSTag, nextPOS + connectivePOS, root2Leaf, root2LeafCompressed, leftSibling, rightSibling, parentCategory. These features have been borrowed from previous work of (Wang and Lan, 2015).

2.2 Argument Labeler

After identifying the discourse connective span present in the input text, we need to locate the relative position of the arguments w.r.t. the sentence containing the connective. Arg2 is taken as the argument which occurs in the same sentence as the connective and is therefore syntactically associated with it (Prasad et al., 2008). Hence, we identify the position of Arg1 relative to Arg2 and the connective. The Argument Labeling task can be divided into the following sub-tasks:

- Identifying the relative position of Arg1 w.r.t. Arg2 (and the connective)

- Extracting clauses which are potential argument spans

- Classifying the candidate clauses into Arg1, Arg2 or Null

2.2.1 Argument Position Classifier

We need to identify whether arguments are located in the same sentence (the SS case) or in a sentence before the connective (the PS case). We ignore the following sentence (FS) case and the non-adjacent PS case since these types have a small percentage of instances.

Features used for Argument Position Classifier are connectiveString, connecivePOS, connecivePosition, prevWord, prevWord+connecive, prevPOS, prevPOS+connecivePOS, prev2Word, prev2Word+connecive, prev2POStag, prev2POS+connecivePOS. The feature names are self-explanatory. Connective string itself is a very good feature for this stage. For instance, when the connective token is 'And' (with first letter capitalized), there is a continuation of an idea from previous sentence and thus Arg1 is likely to be in PS. Whereas, when the first letter of connective is in lowercase such as 'and', Arg1 is very likely to be the clause on the left-hand side of 'and', making Arg1 in SS as connective. Connective position, which takes the values 'start', 'middle' and 'end' is also a very useful feature. This argument position classifier is trained using Maximum Entropy Classifier.

2.2.2 Argument Span Extractor

This stage of the pipeline extracts the span of the arguments from the sentence or sentences containing the discourse relation. To extract arguments, we first break the sentence into clauses. Two methods have been proposed in literature to carry out this task: Lin's tree subtract method (Lin et al., 2014) and Kong's constituency based method (Kong et al., 2014). According to (Kong et al., 2014), Kong's constituency based approach outperforms Lin's tree subtraction algorithm. However, since Kong's method is based on using the connective node in the parse tree as the base node for recursion, we can only use this method for those sentences which contain the connective. Hence, we use Kong's extraction method for Same Sentence Argument Extraction.

SS Argument Extractor: Kong's constituency-based approach is a recursion in which the connective's lowest tree node is chosen as the target node, and its left and right siblings are chosen as candidates for arguments. The target node is updated to the current target node's parent and the process is repeated. There is a slight modification in the algorithm for multi-word connectives. Similar to Kong et al's approach for multi-word connectives, we choose the immediate left siblings of the first word in the connective and immediate right siblings of the last word of the connective as candidate arguments

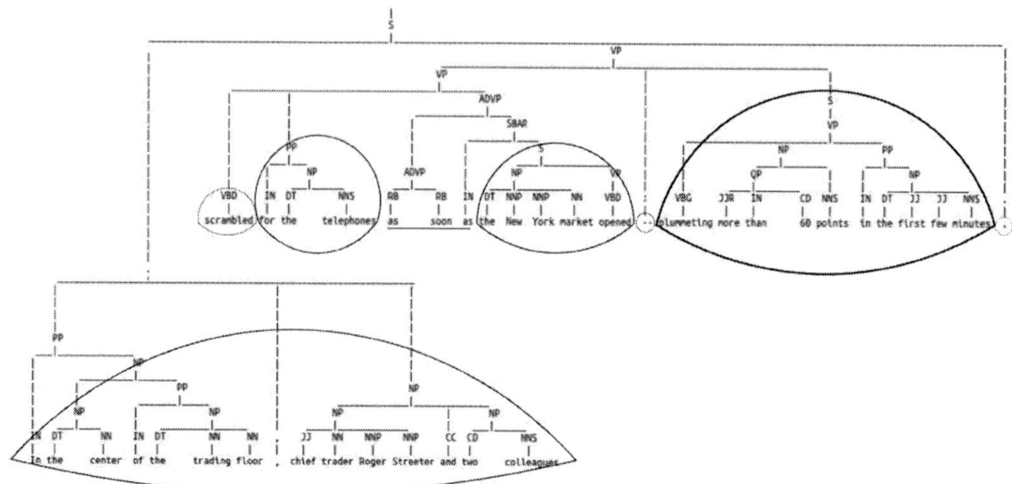

Figure 1: Parse tree showing candidate argument nodes using Kong's Extraction algorithm for a multi-word connective

in addition to taking left and right siblings of the lowest node that covers the entire connective. This modification of algorithm for multi-word cases is important as the modified algorithm extracts more refined constituents from the sentence. In the following example, the updated algorithm extracts *'the New York market opened'* as a constituent, whereas the algorithm without multi-word case would not have extracted it at all.

Consider the following example with its gold-standard parse tree as shown in Figure 1:

(1) *In the center of the trading floor, chief trader Roger Streeter and two colleagues scrambled for the telephones* **as soon as** *the new York market opened – plummeting more than 60 points in the first few minutes.*

Argument candidates detected are: *'In the center of the trading floor'* , *','* , *'chief trader Roger Streeter and two colleagues'* , *'scrambled'* , *'for the telephones'* , *'the New York market opened'* , *'–'* , *'plummeting more than 60 points in the first few minutes'* , *'.'*

The final extracted arguments are:

Arg1 - 'In the center of the trading floor, chief trader Roger Streeter and two colleagues scrambled for the telephones'

Arg2 - 'the New York market opened'

Table 1 compares the results of Kong's Extractor with and without incorporating multi-word scenario. As expected, the F1 score of Arg2 with multi-word case is better by about 2.7%.

	Arg1 F1 score	Arg2 F1 score
Kong's pruning algo (w/o multi-word case)	50.11	70.02
Kong's pruning algo (w/ multi-word case)	50.11	72.71

Table 1: Argument Extraction experiments on development data

PS Argument Extractor: In this case, we take the entire previous sentence as Arg1. Arg2 is taken as the sentence containing the connective after subtracting connective tokens from the sentence. For this task, we can also use Lin's clause tree subtraction method (2014) to extract Arg1 and Kong's constituency based approach (2014) to extract Arg2 for better performance.

2.2.3 Argument Classification

Features used for classification of extracted phrases into arguments have been borrowed from previous works of Kong (Kong et al., 2014) and Wang (Wang and Lan, 2015). These features are used to classify each candidate into one of the three categories: 'Arg1', 'Arg2' or 'Null'. Both connective and constituent-candidate based features are used: `Connective String`, `POS tag` of the connective, `leftSiblingNo` is

			Connective	Arg1	Arg2	Arg1+Arg2	Sense	Overall
Explicit	**Our Parser**	**Dev**	93.39	51.35	65.02	39.79	34.94	34.94
		Test	93.01	43.93	58.47	34.10	29.74	29.74
		Blind	89.03	40.37	60.09	29.49	23.43	23.43
	Wang's Parser	**Test**	94.16	50.68	77.33	45.22	34.93	-
		Blind	91.86	48.31	74.29	41.35	25.91	-
Implicit	**Our Parser**	**Dev**	-	41.22	40.96	32.25	4.59	4.59
		Test	-	38.59	36.44	27.42	3.44	3.44
		Blind	-	37.03	41.49	26.24	8.78	8.78
	Wang's parser	**Test**	-	67.08	68.32	52.98	9.06	-
		Blind	-	60.87	74.58	50.41	7.69	-
Overall	**Our parser**	**Dev**	93.39	45.52	49.63	34.97	15.41	15.41
		Test	93.01	41.34	44.36	29.82	12.82	12.82
		Blind	89.03	38.77	48.19	27.41	12.41	12.41
	Wang's parser	**Test**	94.16	60.10	72.52	49.36	29.83	29.72
		Blind	91.86	55.84	74.45	46.37	21.82	24.00

Table 2: System performance and comparison on development, test and blind datasets

	F1 score	**Accuracy**
Naive Bayes	82.27	88.2
Maxent	75.6	86.9

Table 3: Explicit sense classification: feature experimentation with NB and MaxEnt on development data

the number of left siblings of the connective, `rightSiblingNo` is the number of right siblings of the connective, `ConnCat` is the syntactic category of the connective which takes the values 'subordinating', 'coordinating' or 'discourse adverbial', `clauseRelPos` is position of the constituent candidate relative to the connective which takes the values 'left' , 'right' or 'previous', `clausePOS` is the POS tag of the constituent candidate, `clauseContext` is the context of the constituent, i.e., POS combination of the constituent, its parent, left sibling and right sibling (when there is no parent or sibling, it is marked as NULL), `conn2clausePath` is the path from connective node to the node of the constituent.

Once, the classifier tags the clauses with its labels, Arg1 and Arg2 are obtained by stitching the strings of ordered arg1 clauses and arg2 clauses respectively.

2.3 Explicit Sense Classification

After determining the spans of Arg1 and Arg2, we feed these arguments into the next stage of the pipeline which detects the sense of the explicit discourse relation. The connective string itself is a good indicator of the sense of the relation due to lexical mapping between them. However, there are cases of ambiguity, in which a connective word is used to describe multiple senses. For this reason, the task requires machine learning in which the classifier uses other syntactic features to determine the sense of the relation.

The features we used for training are connectiveString, connectiveHead, connectivePOS, connectivePrev, connectivePosition, connectiveCategory, subjectivityStrengthArg1, subjectivityStrengthArg2, verbNetClassArg2 and verbNetClassArg2. Subjectivity Strength and VerbNet class features are created from the semantic lexicons provided for the shared task and are described in the next section.

From the results in Table 3, we note that Naive Bayes performs better than MaxEnt classifier. We conjecture the cause for this is that MaxEnt classifier tends to overfit the data. Hence, Naive Bayes is chosen to perform sense classification.

3 Non-Explicit SDP

There are three types of Non-Explicit relations: Implicit, EntRel and AltLex. The remaining pair of sentences which did not contain explicit connectives are fed into this stage of the pipeline. Our system now treats all the remaining adjacent sentences as Implicit relations. This hard coding cost us a high performance dip as EntRel relations constitute about a third of the non-explicit data (215 EntRel relations and 522 Implicit relations in development data) and not all remaining sentences contain an implicit relation.

In our implicit argument span detector, we treat the first sentence in adjacent sentence pair as Arg1 and the second sentence as Arg2. Next, we focus on the Implicit Sense Classification task.

3.1 Implicit Sense Classification

This task is considered as the bottleneck of SDP systems and is especially challenging due to lack to connective based features. We create a different set of baseline features as borrowed from (Lin et al., 2014). We describe semantic features used for this task in detail in this section.

3.1.1 Baseline features

Baseline features chosen for this task are syntactic features created from the dependency and constituency parses of the two arguments. First, both dependency and constituency parses from the entire training corpus were extracted. This created around 12,489 constituency parses and 89 dependency parses. However, the number of parse features was too high and unnecessary to work with. Hence, we put a frequency cap of 5 on the feature set which brought the features down to 2,515. We also used NLTK's stop-words to filter out dependency parses created by common words as these parse rules are highly recurring over the distribution of the entire corpus.

3.1.2 Semantic Features

Sense detection is essentially a semantic task since we are trying to determine the "meaning" of the relation. For this reason, we have experimented with semantic tools like MPQA Subjectivity, VerbNet classes and Word2Vec. Each of these tools and lexicons have been provided for the closed track of Shallow Discourse Parsing.

MPQA Subjectivity: The semantic feature created using MPQA subjectivity lexicon measures the negativity and positivity strength of the arguments. For calculating the subjectivity strength of the arguments, subjectivity annotation for each word of the argument is taken. If the word has negative and strong polarity, it is assigned -2, for negative and weak polarity it is assigned -1, for strong positive polarity +2 and for weak positive polarity +1 respectively. The subjectivity strength of all words in the argument is summed up. If the sum is 0 then it is neutral, otherwise it is positive or negative.

VerbNet Classes: VerbNet is a verb lexicon with mappings to WordNet and FrameNet. VerbNet is organized into classes (with subclasses) on the basis of syntactic and semantic similarity (Kipper et al., 2006). We have created `verbNetClassArg1` and `verbNetClassArg2` features, which contain the VerbNet class of the lemmatized forms of the main verbs of the respective arguments (Zhou, 2015). VerbNet classes are important features and this was verified by analyzing the most informative features of this classification task. We find that many VerbNet classes are more informative than even baseline features.

Word2Vec: Subjectivity strength and VerbNet classes only capture information about specific albeit important words of a sentence. To capture the context of the entire argument and interaction between the arguments, we use the Word2Vec tool. Word2Vec is a deep learning tool that outputs vector representation of an input word in a large-dimensional vector space. We have used Google's Word2Vec model trained on a part of Google News dataset of 100 billion words. This Word2Vec model contains 300 dimensional vectors for 3 million words and phrases.

Words with similar meaning are expected to have vectors in close proximity in the vector space (Mikolov et al., 2013). Inspired from (Yih et al., 2013), a work on Question-Answering system, we represent the entire Arg1 and Arg2 as vectors. We take each argument, drop the stopwords and then take a weighted sum over the vector representations of remaining words of the argument. Even after removing stop words, there is a difference in importance and relevance of the remaining words. This is why we choose to take a weighted sum of the word vectors. We chose `TF-IDF` (Term Frequency-Inverse Document Frequency) scores as weights. The TF-IDF value increases proportionally with the number of times a word appears in the document and decreases with the frequency of the word in the corpus. This balances the weights of words which occur more frequently in literature.

We created three features using Word2Vec tool: `Arg1Cluster`, `Arg2Cluster` and `cosineDistance`. We perform PCA (Principle-Component Analysis) over the Arg vectors to reduce the vector dimensions from 300 to 3 as the depth of sense classes is also three or less. By intuition, we only require three dimensions to represent the three levels of sense classes. We perform K-Means clustering over Arg vectors of the training data and assign clusters to Arg1 and Arg2 of development, test and blind data as `Arg1Cluster` and `Arg2Cluster`. We used sklearn's TfIdfVectorizer to compute the `TF-IDF` scores and sklearn's PCA and K-Means to perform clustering over the vectors.

The `cosineDistance` feature is a dot product of Arg1 and Arg2 vectors. We hope to capture the similarity or closeness of the two arguments using this numerical value. Following is the formula used for calculating cosine distance:

$$d = \sum_{k=1}^{n} \left(\left(\sum_{w_i \in Arg1} tfidf(w_i) * word2vec(w_i) \right)_k * \left(\sum_{w_j \in Arg2} tfidf(w_j) * word2vec(w_j) \right)_k \right) \tag{1}$$

Here, d is the cosineDistance and n is 300, the dimension of the vector space of GoogleNews-vectors-negative300.bin, the word2vec model trained on Google News dataset.

3.1.3 Experimentation

We used a combination of the features described above to gauge their performance on sense classification task. VerbNet and Subjectivity features are known to perform well according to previous literature. Hence, we test the novel Word2Vec features on top of baseline features, Subjectivity strength and VerbNet classes. For this reason, we call the combination of baseline features, Subjectivity strength and VerbNet classes as baseline in Table 4.

The results reported the Table 4 are on development dataset. As expected, Word2Vec features improve the F1 score by about 2.3%. Thus, we use a combination of all the baseline features, Subjectivity features, VerbNet features and Word2Vec features in the Implicit Sense classification task. Also, the number of parse features is very high (2515), making total number of features equal to 2522. Therefore, we use NLTK's Naive Bayes Classifier over Maximum Entropy as NLTK's implementation of Maximum Entropy is not able to handle the vast number of features.

	F1 score	Accuracy
baseline	11.17	25.47
baseline+cosineDist	12.00	24.52
baseline+cosineDist +argclusters	13.44	24.52

Table 4: Implicit sense feature experimentation on development dataset

4 Results

Table 2 contains the results of our updated system on development, test and blind datasets. In the updated system, we fixed a small bug in argument index alignment code which doubled our overall parser F1 score on the development data. Hence, we report the updated results in the paper. We also used Word2Vec features in our updated system. The Word2Vec features did not improve the F1 score of Implicit Sense Classification on development and test datasets. This is probably because of error propagation from previous stages. Surprisingly, the updated Implicit Classifier performs better on blind dataset as compared to development and test dataset.

There are several weak links in our pipeline. For instance, the PS-Explicit and Implicit argument extractors are naive and hard-coded. This is one major cause of low F1 scores as compared to Wang et al. We feel that by fixing these links, we can improve the result by a significant margin.

5 Conclusion

In this work, we have implemented a discourse parser trained on PDTB corpus with a special focus on using semantic lexicons. We have described the system architecture and various experimentation results in the paper. Our contribution to the SDP system is the introduction of novel features to the bottleneck of SDP systems, i.e., the Implicit Sense Classification task. Specifically, we have created `Arg1Cluster`, `Arg2Cluster` and `cosineDistance` features using Word2Vec tool for Implicit Sense Classification task, which improved F1 score of the task by about 2.3%. The task of Shallow Discourse Parsing will give more promising results by making use of other lexical and semantic tools, thus encouraging further research to obtain better results.

References

Karin Kipper, Anna Korhonen, Neville Ryant, and Martha Palmer. 2006. Extending verbnet with novel verb classes. In *Proceedings of LREC*. Citeseer.

Fang Kong, Hwee Tou Ng, and Guodong Zhou. 2014. A constituent-based approach to argument labeling with joint inference in discourse parsing. In *EMNLP*, pages 68–77.

Ziheng Lin, Hwee Tou Ng, and Min-Yen Kan. 2014. A pdtb-styled end-to-end discourse parser. volume 20, pages 151–184. Cambridge Univ Press.

Tomas Mikolov, Ilya Sutskever, Kai Chen, Greg S Corrado, and Jeff Dean. 2013. Distributed representations of words and phrases and their compositionality. In *Advances in neural information processing systems*, pages 3111–3119.

Martin Potthast, Tim Gollub, Francisco Rangel, Paolo Rosso, Efstathios Stamatatos, and Benno Stein. 2014. Improving the Reproducibility of PAN's Shared Tasks: Plagiarism Detection, Author Identification, and Author Profiling. In Evangelos Kanoulas, Mihai Lupu, Paul Clough, Mark Sanderson, Mark Hall, Allan Hanbury, and Elaine Toms, editors, *Information Access Evaluation meets Multilinguality, Multimodality, and Visualization. 5th International Conference of the CLEF Initiative (CLEF 14)*, pages 268–299, Berlin Heidelberg New York, September. Springer.

Rashmi Prasad, Nikhil Dinesh, Alan Lee, Eleni Miltsakaki, Livio Robaldo, Aravind K Joshi, and Bonnie L Webber. 2008. The penn discourse treebank 2.0. In *LREC*. Citeseer.

Jianxiang Wang and Man Lan. 2015. A refined end-to-end discourse parser. In *The Nineteenth Conference on Computational Natural Language Learning*, pages 17–24, Beijing, China, July.

Nianwen Xue, Hwee Tou Ng, Sameer Pradhan, Bonnie Webber, Attapol Rutherford, Chuan Wang, and Hongmin Wang. 2016. The conll-2016 shared task on multilingual shallow discourse parsing. In *Proceedings of the Twentieth Conference on Computational Natural Language Learning - Shared Task*, Berlin, Germany, August. Association for Computational Linguistics.

Wen-tau Yih, Ming-Wei Chang, Christopher Meek, and Andrzej Pastusiak. 2013. Question answering using enhanced lexical semantic models. Citeseer.

Fang Kong Sheng Li Guodong Zhou. 2015. The sonlp-dp system in the conll-2015 shared task. In *The Nineteenth Conference on Computational Natural Language Learning*, pages 32–36, Beijing, China, July. Association for Computational Linguistics.

The Virginia Tech System at CoNLL-2016 Shared Task on Shallow Discourse Parsing

Prashant Chandrasekar[1]   Xuan Zhang[1]   Saurabh Chakravarty[1]
Arijit Ray[2]   John Krulick[1]   Alla Rozovskaya[1]
[1]Department of Computer Science
[2]Department of Electrical and Computer Engineering
Virginia Polytechnic Institute and State University
Blacksburg, VA 24060
{peecee,xuancs,saurabc,ray93,jtk0,alla}@vt.edu

Abstract

This paper presents the Virginia Tech system that participated in the CoNLL-2016 shared task on shallow discourse parsing. We describe our end-to-end discourse parser that builds on the methods shown to be successful in previous work. The system consists of several components, such that each module performs a specific subtask, and the components are organized in a pipeline fashion. We also present our efforts to improve several components – explicit sense classification and argument boundary identification for explicit and implicit arguments – and present evaluation results. In the closed evaluation, our system obtained an F1 score of 20.27% on the blind test.

1   Introduction

The CoNLL-2016 shared task on shallow discourse parsing is an extension of last year's competition where participants built end-to-end discourse parsers. In this paper, we present the Virginia Tech system that participated in the CoNLL-2016 shared task. Our system is based on the methods and approaches introduced in earlier work that focused on developing individual components of an end-to-end shallow discourse parsing system, as well as the overall architecture ideas that were introduced and proved to be successful in the competition last year.

Our discourse parser consists of multiple components that are organized using a pipeline architecture. We also present novel features – for the explicit sense classifier and argument extractors – that show improvement over the respective components of state-of-the-art systems submitted last year. In the closed evaluation track, our system

achieved an F1 score of 20.27% on the official blind test set.

The remainder of the paper is organized as follows. Section 2 describes the shared task. In Section 3, we present our system architecture. In Section 4, each component is described in detail. The official evaluation results are presented in Section 5. Section 6 concludes.

2   Task Description

The CoNLL-2016 shared task (Xue et al., 2016) focuses on shallow discourse parsing and is a second edition of the task. The task is to identify discourse relations that are present in natural language text. A discourse relation can be expressed explicitly or implicitly. Explicit discourse relations are those that contain an overt discourse connective in text, e.g. *because, but, and*. Implicit discourse relations, in contrast, are not expressed via an overt discourse connective. Each discourse relation is also associated with two arguments – Argument 1 (Arg1) and Argument 2 (Arg2) – that can be realized as clauses, sentences, or phrases; each relation is labeled with a sense. The overall task consists of identifying all components of a discourse relation – explicit connective (for an explicit relation), arguments with exact boundaries, as well as the sense of a relation. In addition to explicit and implicit relations that are related by an overt or a non-overt discourse connective, two other relation types (*AltLex* and *EntRel*) are marked and need to be identified. The arguments of these two relation types always correspond to entire sentences. Examples below illustrate an explicit relation (1), an implicit relation (2); *AltLex* (3) and *EntRel* (4). The connective is underlined; Arg1 is italicized, and Arg2 is in bold in each example. The relation sense is shown in parentheses.

1. *He believes in what he plays,* <u>and</u> **he plays superbly**. (Expansion.Conjunction) [wsj_0207]

115

Proceedings of the 54th Annual Meeting of the Association for Computational Linguistics, pages 115–121,
Berlin, Germany, August 7-12, 2016. ©2016 Association for Computational Linguistics

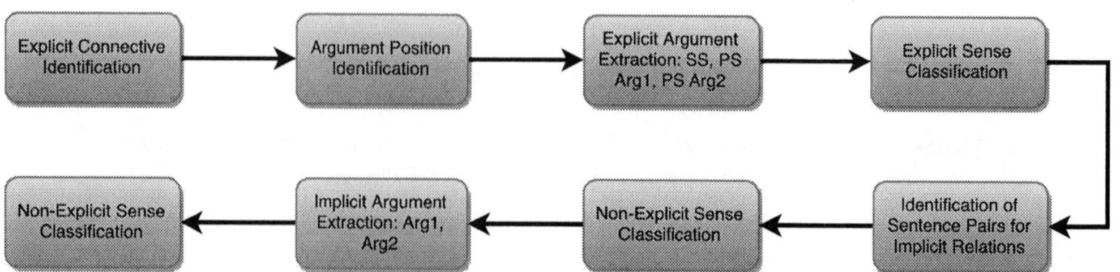

Figure 1: Overview of the system architecture.

2. *In China, a great number of workers are engaged in pulling out the male organs of rice plants using tweezers, and one-third of rice produced in that country is grown from hybrid seeds.* Implicit=on the other hand **At Plant Genetic Systems, researchers have isolated a pollen-inhibiting gene that can be inserted in a plant to confer male sterility**. (Comparison.Contrast) [wsj_0209]

3. *On a commercial scale, the sterilization of the pollen-producing male part has only been achieved in corn and sorghum feed grains.* That's because **the male part, the tassel, and the female, the ear, are some distance apart on the corn plant**. (Contingency.Cause.Reason) [wsj_0209]

4. *In a labor-intensive process, the seed companies cut off the tassels of each plant, making it male sterile.They sow a row of male-fertile plants nearby, which then pollinate the male-sterile plants.* EntRel **The first hybrid corn seeds produced using this mechanical approach were introduced in the 1930s and they yielded as much as** 20% **more corn than naturally pollinated plants**. [wsj_0209]

The training and the development data for the shared task was adapted from the Penn Discourse Treebank 2.0 (PDTB-2.0) (Prasad et al., 2008). Our system was trained on the training partition and tuned using the development data. Results in the paper are reported for the development and the test sets from PDTB, as well as for the blind test.

3   System Description

The system consists of multiple modules that are applied in a pipeline fashion. This architecture is a standard approach that was originally proposed in Lin et al. (2014) and was followed with slight variations by systems in the last year competition (Xue et al., 2015). Our design most closely resembles the pipeline proposed by the top system last year (Wang and Lan, 2015), in that argument extraction for explicit relations is performed separately for Arg1 and Arg2, the non-explicit sense classifier is run twice. The overall architecture of the system is shown in Figure 1.

Given the input text, the connective classifier identifies explicit discourse connectives. Next, the position classifier is invoked that determines for each explicit relation whether Arg1 is located in the same sentence as Arg2 (SS) or in a previous sentence (PS). The following three modules – SS Arg1/Arg2 Extractor, PS Arg1 Extractor, and PS Arg2 Extractor – extract text spans of the respective arguments. Finally, the explicit sense classifier is applied.

Next, candidate sentence pairs for non-explicit relations are identified. The non-explicit sense classifier is applied to these sentence pairs. At this stage, it is run with the goal of separating *EntRel* relations from implicit relations, as *EntRel* relations have arguments corresponding to entire sentences, while the latter also require argument boundary identification. Two argument extractors are then used to determine the argument boundaries boundaries of implicit relations. After the argument boundaries of the implicit relations are identified, the non-explicit sense classifier is run again (the assumption is that with better boundary identification sense prediction can be improved).

4   System Components

This section describes each component of the pipeline and introduces novel features.

4.1   Identifying Explicit Connectives

The purpose of the explicit connective classifier is to identify discourse connectives in text. This is a binary classifier that, given a connective word or phrase (e.g. *but* or *if . . . then*) determines whether the connective functions as a discourse connective in the specific context. We use the training data to generate a list of 145 connective words and phrases that may function as discourse connectives. Only consecutive connectives that contain up to three tokens are addressed. The features are based on previous work (Pitler et al., 2009; Lin et al., 2014; Wang and Lan, 2015). Our classifier is a Maximum Entropy classifier implemented with the NLTK toolkit (Bird, 2006).

4.2 Identifying Arg1 Position

For explicit relations, position of Arg2 is fixed to be the sentence where the connective itself occurs. Arg1, on the other hand, can be located in the same sentence as the connective or in a previous sentence. Given a connective and the sentence in which it occurs, the goal of the position classifier is to determine the location of Arg1. This is a binary classifier with two classes: SS and PS.

We employ the features proposed in Lin et al. (2014) and additional features described in last year's top system (Wang and Lan, 2015). The position classifier is trained using the Maximum Entropy algorithm and achieves an F1 score of 99.186% on the development data.

In line with prior work (Wang and Lan, 2015), we consider PS to be the sentence that immediately precedes the connective. About 10% of explicit discourse relations have Arg1 occurring in a sentence that does not immediately precede the connective. These are missed at this point.

4.3 Explicit Relations: Argument Extraction

SS Argument Extractor: SS argument extractor identifies spans of Arg1 and Arg2 of explicit relations where Arg1 occurs in the same sentence, as the connective and Arg2. We follow the constituent-based approach proposed in Kong et al. (2014), without the joint inference and enhance it using features in Wang and Lan (2015). This component is also trained with the Maximum Entropy algorithm.

PS Arg1 Extractor: We implement features described in Wang and Lan (2015) and add novel features. To identify candidate constituents, we follow Kong et al. (2014), where constituents are defined loosely based on punctuation occurring in the sentence and clause boundaries as defined by *SBAR* tags. We used the constituent split implemented in Wang and Lan (2015). Based on earlier work (Wang and Lan, 2015; Lin et al., 2014), we implement the following features: surface form of the verbs in the sentence (three features), last word of the current constituent (*curr*), last word

of the previous constituent (*prev*), the first word of *curr*, and the lowercased form of the connective. The novel features that we add are shown in Table 1. These features use POS information of tokens in the constituents, punctuation between the constituents, and feature conjunctions.

PS Arg2 Extractor: Similar to PS Arg1 extractor, for this component we implement features described in Wang and Lan (2015) and add novel features. The novel features are the same as those introduced for PS Arg1 but also include the following additional features:

- *nextFirstW&puncBefore* – the first word token of *next* and the punctuation before *next*.

- *prevLastW&puncAfter* – the last word token of *prev* and the punctuation after *prev*.

- *POS of the connective string*.

- The *distance* between the connective and the position of *curr* in the sentence.

The argument extractors are trained with the Averaged Perceptron algorithm, implemented within Learning Based Java (LBJ) (Rizzolo and Roth, 2010).

4.4 Explicit Sense Classifier

The goal of the explicit sense classifier is to determine what sense (e.g. *Comparison.Contrast*, *Expansion.Conjunction*, etc.) an explicit relation conveys. A 3-level sense hierarchy has been defined in PDTB, which has four top-level senses: *Comparison*, *Contingency*, *Expansion*, and *Temporal*. We use lexical and syntactic features based on previous work and also introduce new features:

- *C* (Connective) string, *C* POS, *prev* + *C*, proposed in Lin et al. (2014).

- C self-category, parent-category of C, left-sibling-category of C, right-sibling-category of C, 4 *C-Syn* interactions, and 6 *Syn-Syn* interactions, introduced in Pitler et al. (2009).

- C parent-category linked context, previous connective and its POS of "as"(the connective and its POS of previous relation, if the connective of current relation is "as"), previous connective and its POS of "when", adopted from Wang and Lan (2015).

- Our new features: first token of *C*, second token of *C* (if exists), next word (*next*), *C* + *next*, *prev* + *next*, *prev* + *C* + *next*.

	Feature name	Description
(1)	isFirst, isLast, sameAs	is the *curr* first (last, same as) one in the sentence
(2)	currFirstWAndCurrSecondW, currLastWAndNextFirstW, prevLastW, nextFirstW	word tokens and conjunctions of *curr*, *prev*, and *next*
(3)	puncBefore, puncAfter	1 if there is a punctuation mark before (after) *curr*
(4)	currFirstPOS, currLastPOS, currFirstPOSAndCurrSecondPOS, prevLastPOS, nextFirstPOS	POS and their conjunctions in *curr*, *prev*, and *next*
(5)	conjunctions	(2)&(3)

Table 1: **Novel features used in the PS Arg1 and PS Arg2 extractors.** *Curr*, *prev*, and *next* refer to the current, previous, and next constituent in the same sentence, respectively. *W* denotes word token, and *POS* denotes the part-of-speech tag of a word. For example, *currFirstWAndCurrSecondW* refers to the first two word tokens in *curr*, while *prevLastPOS* refers to the POS of the last token of *prev*, and *nextFirstPOS* refers to the POS of the first token of *next*.

For this task, we trained two classifiers – using Maximum Entropy and Averaged Perceptron algorithms – and chose Averaged Perceptron, as its performance was found to be superior.

4.5 Identifying Non-Explicit Relations

The first step in identifying non-explicit relations is the generation of sentence pairs that are candidate arguments for a non-explicit relation. Following Wang and Lan (2015), we extract sentence pairs that satisfy the following three criteria:

- Sentences are adjacent
- Sentences occur within the same paragraph
- Neither sentence participates in an explicit relation

For all pairs of sentences that meet those criteria, we take the first sentence to be the location of Arg1, and the second sentence – the location of Arg2. This approach is quite noisy since about 24% of all consecutive sentence pairs in the training data do not participate in a discourse relation. We leave this for future work.

4.6 Non-Explicit Sense Classifier

Following previous work on non-explicit sense classification (Lin et al., 2009; Pitler et al., 2009; Rutherford and Xue, 2014), we define four sets of binary feature groups: Brown clustering pairs, Brown clustering arguments, first-last words, and production rules. Dependency rules and polarity features were also extracted, but did not improve the results and were removed from the final model.

A cutoff of 5 was used to prune all of the features. Additionally, Mutual Information (MI) was used to determine the most important features. The MI calculation took the 50 most important rules in each feature group, for each of the sixteen *level 1* and *level 2* hierarchies and *EntRel*. This provided a total of 4 groups of 800 rules.

Recall that the non-explicit sense classifier has two passes. On the first iteration, its primary goal is to separate *EntRel* from implicit relations. On the second iteration, which is performed after the argument boundaries of implicit relations are identified, the sense classifier is run again on implicit relations with the predicted argument boundaries. Note that the classifier in both cases is trained in the same way, as a multiclass classifier, even though the first time it is run with the purpose of distinguishing between *AltLex* relations and all other (implicit) relations. This component is trained with the Naïve Bayes algorithm.

4.7 Implicit Relations: Argument Extraction

The argument extractors for implicit relations are implemented in a way similar to explicit relation argument extraction. Candidate sentences are split into constituents based on punctuation symbols and clause boundaries using the *SBAR* tag. We use features in Lin et al. (2009) and Wang and Lan (2015) and augment these with novel features.

Implicit Arg1 Extractor: The Implicit Arg1 extractor employs a rich set of features. Most of these are similar to those presented for PS Arg1 and PS Arg2 extractors in that we take into account POS information, punctuation symbols that occur on the boundaries of the constituents, as well as dependency relations in the constituent itself.

One key distinction of how we define the depen-

118

dency relation features is that, in contrast to prior work that treats each dependency relation as a separate binary feature, we only consider the first two relations (r1 and r2, respectively) in *curr*, *prev*, and *next*, and take their conjunctions. Our intuition is that the relations in the beginning of a constituent are most important, while the other relations are not that relevant. This approach to feature generation also avoids sparseness, which was found to be a problem in earlier work. Overall, we generate seven features that use dependency relations.

Implicit Arg2 Extractor: We use most of the features in Lin et al. (2014) and Wang and Lan (2015) to train the Arg2 extractor (for more details and explanation about the features, we refer the reader to the respective papers):

- Lowercased and lemmatized verbs in *curr*

- The first and last terms of *curr*

- The last term of *prev*

- The first term of *next*

- The last term of *prev* + the first term of *curr*

- The last term of *curr* + the first term of *next*

- The position of *curr* in the sentence: start, middle, end, or whole sentence

- Product of the *curr* and *next* production rules

5   Evaluation and Results

Evaluation in the shared task is conducted using a new web service called TIRA (Potthast et al., 2014). We first evaluate the contribution of new features in individual components in 5.1. In 5.2, we report performance of all components of the final system on the development set using gold. Finally, in 5.3, we show official results on the development, test, and blind test sets. Since the system is implemented as a pipeline, each component contributes errors. We refer to the results as no error propagation (EP) when gold predictions are used, or with EP when automatic predictions generated from previous steps are employed.

The components of our final system are trained as follows: connective, position classifier, SS Arg1/Arg2 extractor and implicit Arg2 extractor (Maximum Entropy); explicit sense, PS Arg1, PS Arg2 extractors, Implicit Arg1 extractor (Averaged Perceptron); non-explicit sense (Naïve Bayes). The choice of the learning algorithms was primarily motivated by prior work. Additional experiments on argument extractors and explicit

Features	P	R	F1
Base features	90.96	90.14	90.55
+ new features	91.88	91.05	**91.46**

Table 2: **Explicit sense classifier.** *Base* refers to features described in Wang and Lan (2015). The new set of features is presented in Section 3. Evaluation using gold connectives and argument boundaries (no EP).

Model	P	R	F1
Baseline	64.79	64.79	64.79
Base features	66.67	66.67	66.67
All features	69.48	69.48	**69.48**

Table 3: **PS Arg1 extractor, no EP.** *Baseline* denotes taking the entire sentence as argument span. *Base* features refer to features used in Wang and Lan (2015).

sense classification indicated that Averaged Perceptron should be preferred for these sub-tasks. Due to time constraints, we did not compare all three algorithms on all sub-tasks.

5.1   Improving Individual Components

We first evaluate the components for which we introduce new features. We use gold annotations for evaluating the individual components below.

Explicit Sense Classifier: Table 2 evaluates the explicit sense classifier. We compare our baseline model that implements the features proposed in Wang and Lan (2015) with the model that employs additional features introduced in 4.4. Our baseline model performs slightly better than the one reported in Wang and Lan (2015): we obtain 90.55 vs. 90.14, as reported in Wang and Lan (2015). Adding the new features provides an additional improvement of almost 1 F1 point.

Extraction of Explicit Arguments: We now evaluate explicit argument extractors PS Arg1 and PS Arg2, for which novel features have been intro-

Model	P	R	F1
Baseline	64.32	64.32	64.32
Base features	72.30	72.30	72.30
All features	75.59	75.59	**75.59**

Table 4: **PS Arg2 extractor, no EP.** *Baseline* denotes taking the entire sentence, without the connective words, as argument span. *Base* features refer to features used in Wang and Lan (2015).

Model	P	R	F1
Baseline	58.62	58.62	58.62
All features	70.50	70.50	**70.50**

Table 5: **Implicit Arg1 extractor, no EP.** *Baseline* denotes taking the entire sentence as argument span.

Component	P	R	F1
Explicit connectives	92.80	95.10	93.97
SS Arg1	68.46	71.33	69.86
SS Arg2	83.45	86.95	85.16
SS Arg1/Arg2	63.31	65.97	64.61
PS Arg1	69.48	69.48	69.48
PS Arg2	75.59	75.59	75.59
Explicit sense	91.88	91.05	91.46
Implicit Arg1	70.50	70.50	70.50
Implicit Arg2	70.11	70.11	70.11
Implicit sense	35.25	35.25	35.25

Table 6: **Evaluation of each component on the development set (no EP).**

duced. We implement the features in Wang and Lan (2015) and add our novel features shown in Table 1. Results for PS Arg1 extractor are shown in Table 3. The baseline refers to taking the entire sentence as argument span. Overall, we obtain a 5 point improvement over the baseline method. Similarly, Table 4 shows results for PS Arg2 extractor. For PS Arg2 extractor, the classifiers are able to obtain a larger improvement compared to the baseline method. Adding new features improves the results by three points. We note that in Wang and Lan (2015) the numbers that correspond to the entire sentence baselines are not the same as those that we obtain, so we do not report a direct comparison with their models. However, our base models implement the features they use.

Implicit Arg1 Extractor: In Table 5, we evaluate the Implicit Arg1 extractor. It achieves an improvement of 12 F1 points over the baseline method that considers the entire sentence to be the argument span.

5.2 Results on the Development Set (no EP)

Performance of each component on the development set, as implemented in the submitted system, without EP, is shown in Table 6.

Component	P	R	F1
Explicit connectives	93.09	92.95	93.02
Arg1 extractor	62.60	54.03	58.00
Arg2 extractor	68.38	59.01	63.35
Arg1/Arg2	50.21	43.33	46.52
Overall performance	28.58	33.59	**30.88**

Table 7: **Official results on the development set.**

Component	P	R	F1
Explicit connectives	89.92	91.51	90.71
Arg1 extractor	56.83	45.80	50.72
Arg2 extractor	63.54	51.21	56.71
Arg1/Arg2	42.24	34.04	37.70
Overall performance	20.80	25.84	**23.05**

Table 8: **Official results on the test set.**

5.3 Official Evaluation Results

The overall system results on the three data sets – development, test, and blind test – are shown in Tables 7, 8, and 9, respectively.

Component	P	R	F1
Explicit connectives	88.13	90.41	89.25
Arg1 extractor	50.87	47.02	48.87
Arg2 extractor	65.51	60.55	62.93
Arg1/Arg2	39.45	36.47	37.90
Overall performance	19.51	21.09	**20.27**

Table 9: **Official results on the blind test set.**

6 Conclusion

This paper introduces an end-to-end discourse parser for English developed for the CoNLL-2016 shared task. The entire system includes multiple components, which are organized in a pipeline fashion. We also present novel features and improve performance of several system components by incorporating these new features.

Acknowledgments

The authors thank the anonymous reviewers for the insightful comments on the paper.

References

Steven Bird. 2006. Nltk: the natural language toolkit. In *Proceedings of the COLING/ACL on Interactive presentation sessions*, pages 69–72. Association for Computational Linguistics.

Fang Kong, Hwee Tou Ng, and Guodong Zhou. 2014. A constituent-based approach to argument labeling with joint inference in discourse parsing. In *EMNLP*, pages 68–77.

Ziheng Lin, Min-Yen Kan, and Hwee Tou Ng. 2009. Recognizing implicit discourse relations in the penn discourse treebank. In *Proceedings of the 2009 Conference on Empirical Methods in Natural Language Processing: Volume 1-Volume 1*, pages 343–351. Association for Computational Linguistics.

Ziheng Lin, Hwee Tou Ng, and Min-Yen Kan. 2014. A pdtb-styled end-to-end discourse parser. *Natural Language Engineering*, 20(02):151–184.

Emily Pitler, Annie Louis, and Ani Nenkova. 2009. Automatic sense prediction for implicit discourse relations in text. In *Proceedings of the Joint Conference of the 47th Annual Meeting of the ACL and the 4th International Joint Conference on Natural Language Processing of the AFNLP: Volume 2-Volume 2*, pages 683–691. Association for Computational Linguistics.

Martin Potthast, Tim Gollub, Francisco Rangel, Paolo Rosso, Efstathios Stamatatos, and Benno Stein. 2014. Improving the reproducibility of PAN's shared tasks: Plagiarism detection, author identification, and author profiling. In Evangelos Kanoulas, Mihai Lupu, Paul Clough, Mark Sanderson, Mark Hall, Allan Hanbury, and Elaine Toms, editors, *Information Access Evaluation meets Multilinguality, Multimodality, and Visualization. 5th International Conference of the CLEF Initiative (CLEF 14)*.

Rashmi Prasad, Nikhil Dinesh, Alan Lee, Eleni Miltsakaki, Livio Robaldo, Aravind K Joshi, and Bonnie L Webber. 2008. The penn discourse treebank 2.0. In *LREC*. Citeseer.

N. Rizzolo and D. Roth. 2010. Learning based java for rapid development of nlp systems. In *Proceedings of the International Conference on Language Resources and Evaluation (LREC)*, Valletta, Malta, 5.

Attapol Rutherford and Nianwen Xue. 2014. Discovering implicit discourse relations through brown cluster pair representation and coreference patterns. In *EACL*, volume 645, page 2014.

Jianxiang Wang and Man Lan. 2015. A refined end-to-end discourse parser. In *Proceedings of the Nineteenth Conference on Computational Natural Language Learning - Shared Task*, pages 17–24, Beijing, China, July. Association for Computational Linguistics.

Nianwen Xue, Hwee Tou Ng, Sameer Pradhan, Rashmi Prasad, Christopher Bryant, and Attapol T Rutherford. 2015. The CoNLL-2015 shared task on shallow discourse parsing. In *Proceedings of the Nineteenth Conference on Computational Natural Language Learning - Shared Task*, pages 1–16.

Nianwen Xue, Hwee Tou Ng, Sameer Pradhan, Bonnie Webber, Attapol Rutherford, Chuan Wang, and Hongmin Wang. 2016. The CoNLL-2016 shared task on multilungual shallow discourse parsing. In *Proceedings of the Twentieth Conference on Computational Natural Language Learning - Shared Task*.

DA-IICT Submission for PDTB-styled Discourse Parser

Devanshu Jain
DA-IICT
Gandhinagar, Gujarat
India
devanshu.jain919@gmail.com

Prasenjit Majumder
DA-IICT
Gandhinagar, Gujarat
India
prasenjit.majumder@gmail.com

Abstract

The CONLL 2016 Shared task focusses on building a Shallow Discourse Parsing system, which is given a piece of newswire text as input and it returns all discourse relations in that text in the form of discourse connectives, its two arguments and the relation sense. We have built a parser for the same. We follow a pipeline architecture to build the system. We employ machine learning methods to train our classifiers for each component in the pipeline. The system achieves an overall F1 score of 0.1065 when tested on blind dataset provided by the task organisers. On the same dataset, for explicit relations, F1 score of 0.2067 is achieved, while for non explicit relations, an F1 score of 0.0112 is achieved.

1 INTRODUCTION

Discourse Parsing is the process of assigning a discourse structure to the input provided in the form of natural language. The term "Shallow" signifies that the annotation of one discourse relation is independent of all other discourse relations, thus leaving room for a high level analysis that may attempt to connect them.

For the purpose of training and testing the system, we used PDTB (Penn Discourse Tree Bank), which is a discourse-level annotation on top of PTB (Penn Tree Bank). The corpus provides annotation for all discourse relations present in the documents. A discourse relation is composed of discourse connectives, its two arguments and the relation sense. PDTB provides a list of 100 discourse connectives, which may indicate the presence of a relation. A discourse connective can fall in any of 3 categories: Coordinating Conjunctions (e.g.: and, but, etc.), Subordinating Conjunctions (e.g.: if, because, etc.) or Discourse Adverbial (e.g.: however, also, etc.).

There are four kinds of relations, namely

1. Explicit

2. Implicit

3. AltLex (Alternative Lexicalisation)

4. EntRel (Entity Based Coherence)

Explicit Relations are marked by the presence of 100 connectives pre-defined by PDTB. Implicit Relations are realised by the reader. There are no words explicitly indicating the relationship. Sometimes, words not pre-defined like connectives by PDTB indicate a relationship. Such relations are called AltLex relations. EntRel relations exist between two sentences in which same entity is being realised. EntRel relations do not have a sense. Some examples are specified in figure 1. Here, the underlined word represents the discourse connective. Italicised text represents argument 1 and bold text represents argument 2. The right indented text following each relation represents the relation sense. The text in the bracket represents the relation type.

There are many challenges associated with this task. Firstly, we need to identify when a word works as a discourse connective and when it does not. In figure 1, consider examples 1 and 3. Both relations contain the word *and* which is present in the list of explicit connectives. But it acts as a discourse connective in example 1 and not in 3. In 3, it just links *political* and *currency* in a noun phrase. Secondly, we need to extract the arguments from sentences. And finally, we need to identify the relation sense.

Study of discourse parsing has a variety of applications in the field of Natural Language Processing. For instance, in summarisation systems,

Proceedings of the 54th Annual Meeting of the Association for Computational Linguistics, pages 122–128,
Berlin, Germany, August 7-12, 2016. ©2016 Association for Computational Linguistics

1. *The agency has already spent roughly $19 billion selling 34 insolvent SLs,* <u>and</u> **it is likely to sell or merge 600 by the time the bailout concludes**.

Expansion.Conjunction (Explicit)

2. *But it doesn't take much to get burned.* Implicit = FOR EXAMPLE **Political and currency gyrations can whipsaw the funds.**

Expansion.Restatement.Specification (Implicit)

3. *Political and currency gyrations can whipsaw the funds.* <u>AltLex</u> [Another concern]: **The funds' share prices tend to swing more than the broader declared San Francisco batting coach Dusty Baker after game two market.**

Expansion.Conjunction (AltLex)

4. *Pierre Vinken, 61 years old, will join the board as a non-executive director Nov. 29.* **Mr. Vinken is chairman of Elsevier N.V., the Dutch publishing group.**

(EntRel)

Figure 1: Examples of various types of discourse relations

redundancy is an important aspect. We can analyse discourse relations with *Expansion* sense to weed out the redundant material. Also, in Question Answering systems, we can make use of relations with *Cause* senses to answer the *why* questions.

The report is organised as follows. Section 2 gives a brief overview of the system. Section 3 describes each component in detail and features deployed to build our parser. Section 4 reports the evaluation strategy and results achieved by our parser.

2 System Overview

There are five major components involved in the process of discourse parsing as shown in figure 2.

1. Explicit Connective Classifier

2. Explicit Argument Labeller

3. Explicit Sense Classifier

4. Non Explicit Classifier

5. Non Explicit Argument Extractor

Explicit Connective Classifier identifies the cases when explicit connectives are being used as discourse connectives as opposed to when they are not.

Explicit Argument Labeller extracts arguments of the relation. This component itself consists of two sub-components:

- Argument Position Identifier

- Argument Extractor

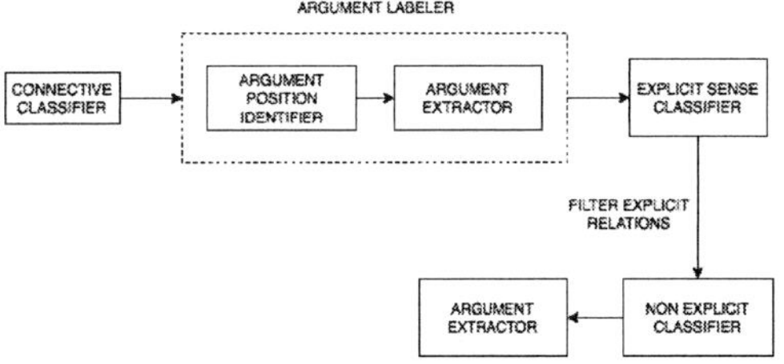

Figure 2: System Pipeline

In PDTB corpus for explicit relations, argument 2 is always syntactically bound to the connective (i.e. it is in the same sentence as connective). As far as argument 1 is concerned, it can either be in one of the previous sentences (PS case), in the same sentence (SS case) or after that sentence (FS case). Since, FS cases' occurance was too low (only 4 instances out of total 32000 relations), therefore, such cases are ignored by our system. Argument Position Identifier tries to identify this relative position of argument 1 with respect to argument 2.

If the PS case appears, then the immediately previous sentence is considered as the sentence containing argument 1. This is true for 92% of the cases in training data. Argument Extractor extracts the argument span from the sentence.

Explicit Sense Classifier identifies the relation sense. It is important to identify this as same connective may convey different meanings in different contexts. For example the word *since* can either be used in different senses as shown in figure 3. In 1, it is used in temporal sense while in 2, it is being used in causal sense.

1. There have been more than 100 mergers and acquisitions within the European paper industry since the most recent wave of friendly takeovers was completed in the U.S. in 1986.

2. It was a far safer deal for lenders since NWA had a healthier cash flow and more collateral on hand.

Figure 3: *Since* being used in different senses

Non Explicit Classifier tries to identify one of the non-explicit relations (Implicit, AltLex, EntRel) and otherwise NoRel (no relation) between adjecent sentences within the same paragraph.

Non Explicit Argument Extractor tries to extract the argument spans for non-explicit relations.

For the purpose of classification, our system uses MaxEnt Classification Algorithm without smoothing.

3 COMPONENTS AND FEATURES

3.1 Connective Classifier

The input to this component is free text from the documents. We sift through all the words in all the documents and identify the occurences of pre-defined explicit connectives. Then, we identify whether these connectives actually work as discourse connectives or not. For this task, we used Pitler and Nenkova 's (2009) syntactic features. Lin et al. (2014) approached this problem by using POS tags and context based features . They used used features from syntax tree, namely path from connective word to the root and compressed path (i.e. same subsequent nodes in the path are clubbed). We too, have used the similar features, as shown in table 1. Here, C-syn features refer to the combination of Connective string with each of syntactic feature and syn-syn features mean the pairing of a syntactic feature with another different syntactic feature.

3.2 Argument Labeller

Here, we first identify the relative position of argument 1 with respect to argument 2. Given this position, we extract the arguments from sentences.

3.2.1 Argument Position Identifier

To identify the position of argument 1, we extract the features mentioned in table 2:

3.2.2 Argument Extractor

After predicting the position of argument 1, we employed different tactics for different positions:

- If the position is SS (that is, both arguments are in same sentence), then we use constituency based approach by Kong et.al. without Joint Inference to extract arguments. This consists of two steps:

  - Pruning: In the parse tree of sentence, identify the node dominating all the connective words. From that node move towards the root and collect all the siblings. If this node does not exactly contain the connective words, collect all its children too. These nodes are termed as constituents.
  - Classification: For all these constituents, we extract the features mentioned in table 3.

- If the position is PS, then we consider the immediately previous sentence as a candidate for containing argument 1 and the sentence containing connective string as a candidate for containing argument 2. Extracting the arguments from sentence is a two step process:

  - Cause Splitter: We split the sentence into clauses using punctuation symbols. For the resulting clauses, we again separate SBAR (Subordinating clauses) components from them.
  - Now we classify each of these clauses. For immediately previous sentence, a clause can belong to either Arg1 or none and for the sentence containing connetive string, a clause may belong to Arg2 or none. To classify each clause, for both Arg1 and Arg2 , we employ the features mentioned in table 4.

Feature Type	Feature ID	Feature
Lexical	1	Connective String
	2	Lowercased Connective String
	3	POS tag of Connective String
	4	Word previous to first word of connective String
	5	Word previous to first word of connective + Connective String
	6	POS tag of the word previous to first word of Connective String
	7	POS tag of the word previous to first word of Connective String + POS tag of Connective String
	8	Word next to last word of Connective String
	9	Connective String + Word next to last word of Connective String
	10	POS tag of the word next to last word of Connective String
	11	POS tag of Connective String + POS tag of the word next to last word of Connective String
	12	1st Previous Word + Connective String + 1st Next Word
	13	1st Previous Word's POS + Connective POS + 1st Next Word's POS
Syntactic	14	Path of connective to root in syntax tree
	15	Compressed path of connective to root in syntax tree
	16	Self Category : Parent of the connective in syntax tree
	17	Parent Category : Parent of self category in syntax tree
	18	Left Sibling Category : Left sibling of self category in syntax tree
	19	Right Sibling Category : Right sibling of self category in syntax tree
	20	C-syn features
	21	syn-syn features

Table 1: Features for Connective Classifier

Feature ID	Feature
1	Connective String
2	Position of Connective String in sentence
3	POS tag of Connective String
4	1st previous word to Connective String
5	POS tag of 1st previous word to Connective String
6	2nd previous word to Connective String
7	POS tag of 2nd previous word to Connective String
8	1st previous word + Connective String
9	POS of 1st previous word + POS of Connective String
10	2nd previous word + Connective String
11	POS of 2nd previous word + POS of Connective String

Table 2: Features for Argument Position Classifier

Feature ID	Feature
1	Connective String
2	Lowercased Connective String
3	Category of Connective String : Subordinating, Coordinating or Discourse Adverbials
4	Constituent Context: Value of Constituent Node + its parent + its left sibling + its right sibling
5	Path of Connective String to the constituent node in syntax tree
6	Relative Position of constituent node with respect to Connective String
7	Path of Connective String to the constituent node in syntax tree + whether number of left siblings of Connective String ¿ 1

Table 3: Features for Kong's approach in SS case

Feature ID	Feature
1	Production Rules in the clause
2	Lowercased Verbs in the clause
3	Lemmatised Verbs in the clause
4	Connective String
5	Lowercased Connective String
6	Category of Connective String : Subordinating, Coordinating or Discourse Adverbials
7	First word in this clause
8	Last word in this clause
9	Last word in previous clause
10	First word in next clause
11	Last word in previous clause + First word in this clause
12	Last word in this clause + First word in next clause
13	Position of this clause in sentence: start, middle or end

Table 4: Features for Classifying clauses in PS case

Feature Type	Feature ID	Feature
Lexical Features	1	Connective String
	2	Lowercased Connective String
	3	POS tag of Connective String
	4	Previous word to Connective String + Connective String
Syntactic Features	5	Self Category : Parent of the connective in syntax tree
	6	Parent Category : Parent of self category in syntax tree
	7	Left Sibling Category : Left sibling of self category in syntax tree
	8	Right Sibling Category : Right sibling of self category in syntax tree
	9	C-syn features
	10	syn-syn features

Table 5: Features for Explicit Sense Classifier

Feature ID	Feature
1	Production Rules in syntax tree
2	Dependency Rules in dependency tree
3	Word Pair features
4	First 3 terms of argument 2 sentence

Table 6: Features for Non Explicit Classifier

Feature ID	Feature
1	Production Rules in syntax tree
2	Lower cased verbs in this clause
3	Lemmatised Verbs in this clause
4	First Word in this clause
5	Last Word in this clause
6	Last Word in previous clause
7	Fist word in next clause
8	Last Word in previous clause + First word in this clause
9	Last Word in this clause + First Word in next clause
10	Position of this clause in the sentence

Table 7: Features for Non Explicit Argument Extraction

3.3 Explicit Sense Classifier

To determine the relation sense, we use Lin's as well as Pitler's features, as shown in table 5.

3.4 Non Explicit Classifier

Non Explicit Relations occur between adjacent sentences within same paragraph. We consider the first sentence as the one containing argument 1 and second containing argument 2. Then, we extract the features mentioned in table 6.

3.4.1 Argument Extractor

To extract argument spans for Non Explicit and Non EntRel Relations, we first use clause splitter as mentioned before and then extract the features for each clause as mentioned in table 7. For EntRel relations, we simply mention the first sentence as argument 1 and second sentence as argument 2.

4 EXPERIMENTS AND RESULTS

4.1 System Setup

We used the training datasets provided by CONLL 2016 organisers (LDC2016E50). In addition we also used the brown clusters (3200 classes). For Stemming purposes, we used snowball stemmer and for lemmatising, we used stanford core nlp library.

For the purpose of classification, we used Apache OpenNLP implementation of MaxEnt classifier. We used Java programming language to implement the parser.

4.2 Evaluation Strategy

A relation is seen correct iff:

- The discourse connective is correctly detected (for explicit relations)

- Sense of relation is correctly predicted.

- Text spans of two arguments as well as their labels (Arg1 and Arg2) are correctly predicted. Partial matches are not identified as correct.

4.3 Results

Results are mentioned in tables 8. As we can see, explicit connective classifier achieves only a precision score of around 0.77 while the best team previous year (Wang) achieved a precision of 0.93. This is not good enough and perhaps is the major reason for error being propagated towards subsequent components. The results of non explicit relations were also discouraging with an F1 score of only 0.012.

5 Conclusion and Further Work

This paper describes the PDTB-styled discourse parser system we implemented for CONLL '16 shared task. We divided the system into different components and arrange in a pipeline. We apply Maximum Entropy for each of these components.

It is an ongoing work. We plan to incorporate deep learning mehods in each component to try to improve the system. We also plan to do feature selection to optimise the components of our system.

References

DINES, N., LEE, A., MILTSAKAKI, E., PRASAD, R., JOSHI, A., AND WEBBER, B. Attribution and the (non-)alignment of syntactic and discourse arguments of connectives. In *Proceedings of the Workshop on Frontiers in Corpus Annotations II: Pie

Components	Dev Set			Test Set			Blind Test		
	Precision	Recall	F1	Precision	Recall	F1	Precision	Recall	F1
Connectives	0.6971	0.9405	0.8007	0.6706	0.9436	0.7840	0.7770	0.9371	0.8496
Arg1	0.2820	0.3662	0.3186	0.2517	0.3249	0.2836	0.2349	0.3242	0.2724
Arg2	0.3384	0.4394	0.3824	0.3074	0.3968	0.3464	0.3259	0.4498	0.3779
Arg1 & Arg2	0.1818	0.2360	0.2054	0.1496	0.1931	0.1686	0.1489	0.2055	0.1727
Sense	0.1774	0.1385	0.1556	0.1319	0.1023	0.1153	0.1269	0.0918	0.1065
Overall	0.1774	0.1385	0.1556	0.1319	0.1023	0.1153	0.1269	0.0918	0.1065

Table 8: Overall Results

in the Sky (Stroudsburg, PA, USA, 2005), CorpusAnno '05, Association for Computational Linguistics, pp. 29–36.

KNOTT, A. *A Data-Driven Methodology for Motivating a Set of Coherence Relations.* PhD thesis, Department of Artificial Intelligence, University of Edinburgh, 1996.

KONG, F., NG, H. T., AND ZHOU, G. A constituent-based approach to argument labeling with joint inference in discourse parsing. In *Proceedings of the 2014 Conference on Empirical Methods in Natural Language Processing, EMNLP 2014, October 25-29, 2014, Doha, Qatar, A meeting of SIGDAT, a Special Interest Group of the ACL* (2014), pp. 68–77.

LIN, Z., NG, H. T., AND KAN, M. A pdtb-styled end-to-end discourse parser. *Natural Language Engineering 20*, 2 (2014), 151–184.

PITLER, E., AND NENKOVA, A. Using syntax to disambiguate explicit discourse connectives in text. In *ACL 2009, Proceedings of the 47th Annual Meeting of the Association for Computational Linguistics and the 4th International Joint Conference on Natural Language Processing of the AFNLP, 2-7 August 2009, Singapore, Short Papers* (2009), pp. 13–16.

POTTHAST, M., GOLLUB, T., RANGEL, F., ROSSO, P., STAMATATOS, E., AND STEIN, B. Improving the Reproducibility of PAN's Shared Tasks: Plagiarism Detection, Author Identification, and Author Profiling. In *Information Access Evaluation meets Multilinguality, Multimodality, and Visualization. 5th International Conference of the CLEF Initiative (CLEF 14)* (Berlin Heidelberg New York, Sept. 2014), E. Kanoulas, M. Lupu, P. Clough, M. Sanderson, M. Hall, A. Hanbury, and E. Toms, Eds., Springer, pp. 268–299.

RUTHERFORD, A., AND XUE, N. Discovering implicit discourse relations through brown cluster pair representation and coreference patterns. In *Proceedings of the 14th Conference of the European Chapter of the Association for Computational Linguistics, EACL 2014, April 26-30, 2014, Gothenburg, Sweden* (2014), pp. 645–654.

WANG, J., AND LAN, M. A refined end-to-end discourse parser. In *Proceedings of the Nineteenth Conference on Computational Natural Language Learning - Shared Task* (Beijing, China, July 2015), Association for Computational Linguistics, pp. 17–24.

XUE, N., NG, H. T., PRADHAN, S., WEBBER, B., RUTHERFORD, A., WANG, C., AND WANG, H. The conll-2016 shared task on shallow discourse parsing. In *Proceedings of the Twentieth Conference on Computational Natural Language Learning - Shared Task* (Berlin, Germany, August 2016), Association for Computational Linguistics.

Discourse Relation Sense Classification with Two-Step Classifiers

Yusuke Kido
The University of Tokyo
7-3-1 Hongo, Bunkyo-ku
Tokyo, Japan
`y.k@is.s.u-tokyo.ac.jp`

Akiko Aizawa
National Institute of Informatics
2-1-2 Hitotsubashi, Chiyoda-ku
Tokyo, Japan
`aizawa@nii.ac.jp`

Abstract

Discourse Relation Sense Classification is the classification task of assigning a sense to discourse relations, and is a part of the series of tasks in discourse parsing. This paper analyzes the characteristics of the data we work with and describes the system we submitted to the CoNLL-2016 Shared Task. Our system uses two sets of two-step classifiers for Explicit and AltLex relations and Implicit and EntRel relations, respectively. Regardless of the simplicity of the implementation, it achieves competitive performance using minimalistic features.

The submitted version of our system ranked 8th with an overall F_1 score of 0.5188. The evaluation on the test dataset achieved the best performance for Explicit relations with an F_1 score of 0.9022.

1 Introduction

In the CoNLL-2015 Shared Task on Shallow Discourse Parsing (Xue et al., 2015), all the participants adopted some variation of the pipeline architecture proposed by Lin et al. (2014). Among the components of the architecture, the main challenges are the exact argument extraction and Non-Explicit sense classification (Lin et al., 2014).

Argument extraction is a task to identify two argument spans for a given discourse relation. Although the reported scores were relatively low for these components this is partially because of the "quite harsh" evaluation[1]. This led to the

introduction of a new evaluation criterion based on partial argument matching in the CoNLL-2016 Shared Task. On the other hand, the sense classification components, which assign a sense to each discourse relation, continue to perform poorly. In particular, Non-Explicit sense classification is a difficult task, and even the best system achieved an F_1 score of only 0.42 given the gold standard argument pairs without error propagation (Wang and Lan, 2015).

In response to this situation, Discourse Relation Sense Classification has become a separate task in the CoNLL-2016 Shared Task (Xue et al., 2016). In this task, participants implement a system that takes gold standard argument pairs and assigns a sense to each of them. To tackle this task, we first analyzed the characteristics of the discourse relation data. We then implemented a classification system based on the analysis. One of the distinctive points of our system is that, compared to existing systems, it uses smaller number of features, which enables the source code to be quite short and clear, and the training time to be fast. The performance is nonetheless competitive, and its potential for improvement is also promising owing to the short program.

This paper aims to reorganize the ideas about what this task actually involves, and to show the future direction for improvement. It is organized as follows: Section 2 presents the data analysis. Then the implementation of the system we submitted is described in Section 3. The experimental results and the conclusion are provided in Section 4 and 5.

2 Data Analysis

There are four types of discourse relations, i.e., Explicit, Implicit, AltLex, and EntRel. In the official scorer, these discourse relations are

---

[1]CoNLL 2016 Shared Task Official Blog
`http://conll16st.blogspot.com/2016/04/partial-scoring-and-other-evaluation.html`

Proceedings of the 54th Annual Meeting of the Association for Computational Linguistics, pages 129–135,
Berlin, Germany, August 7-12, 2016. ©2016 Association for Computational Linguistics

divided into two groups, namely, Explicit and Non-Explicit relations, and they are evaluated separately. AltLex relations are classified into Non-Explicit relations, but they share some characteristics with Explicit relations in that they have words that explicitly serve as connective words in the text. These connective words are one of the most important features in sense classification, as explained later; therefore, we divide the types of relations into (i) Explicit and AltLex and (ii) Implicit and EntRel types in this analysis. Throughout this paper, we do not distinguish between Explicit connective and words that work as connective in AltLex relations, and they are simply referred to as connective.

2.1 Explicit and AltLex Discourse Relations

In the sense classification of Explicit and AltLex relations, connective words serve as important features.

Figure 1 shows the distribution of sense per connective word over the Explicit relations. For example, 91.8% of relations with connective word *and* are labeled as Expansion.Conjunction, and 5.8% as Contingency.Cause.Result. As can be seen, each kind of connective word is mostly covered by only a few senses. Some words such as *also* and *if* have more than 98.8% coverage by a single sense.

According to this observation, it is easy to build a reasonably accurate sense classifier simply by taking connective words as a feature. For example, one obvious method is a majority classifier that assigns the most frequent sense for the relations with the same connective words in the training dataset. Figure 2 shows the accuracy per sense of such a classifier in the training dataset. The method is rather simple, but it achieves more than 80% accuracy for most of the senses.

One exception is Comparison.Concession, which had only a 17.4% accuracy. This is a sense derived from Comparison.Concession and Comparison.Pragmatic concession in the original PDTB, and applies "when the connective indicates that one of the arguments describes a situation A which causes C, while the other asserts (or implies) $\neg C$" (Prasad et al., 2007). Discourse relations with connective words such as *although*, *but*, and *however* are assigned this sense. In the evaluation using the development data, the system assigned Comparison.Contrast to most discourse

Table 1: System output for discourse relations that are labeled as Comparison.Concession in the golden data. The left and right columns show the connective words and the sense assigned by the system, respectively.

Connective	Assigned Sense
while	Comparison.Contrast
even though	Comparison.Concession
still	Comparison.Contrast
nevertheless	Comparison.Contrast
but	Comparison.Contrast
yet	Comparison.Contrast
though	Comparison.Contrast
nonetheless	Comparison.Concession
even if	Contingency.Condition
although	Comparison.Contrast

relations labeled as Comparison.Concession in the golden data. Table 1 shows the senses the system assigned. For example, some of the discourse relations that have a connective word *while* are labeled as Comparison.Concession in the golden data, but the system assigned them as Comparison.Contrast.

According to the annotation manual, Contrast and Concession are different in that only Concession has directionality in the interpretation of the arguments. Distinguishing these two senses is, however, ambiguous and difficult, even for human annotators.

2.2 Implicit and EntRel Discourse Relations

By definition, Implicit and EntRel relations have no connective words in the text, which complicates the sense classification task considerably. Other researchers overcame this problem by applying machine-learning techniques such as a Naive Bayes classifier (Wang and Lan, 2015) or AdaBoost (Stepanov et al., 2015). They use various features including those obtained from parses of the argument texts.

As a baseline, we first implemented a support vector machine (SVM) classifier taking a bag-of-words of tokens in the argument texts as features. The evaluation was found to assign EntRel to a large part of the input data. This trend is particularly noticeable for relatively infrequent senses. This problem is partially attributable to the unbalanced data. In fact, there are more EntRel instances included in the training data than

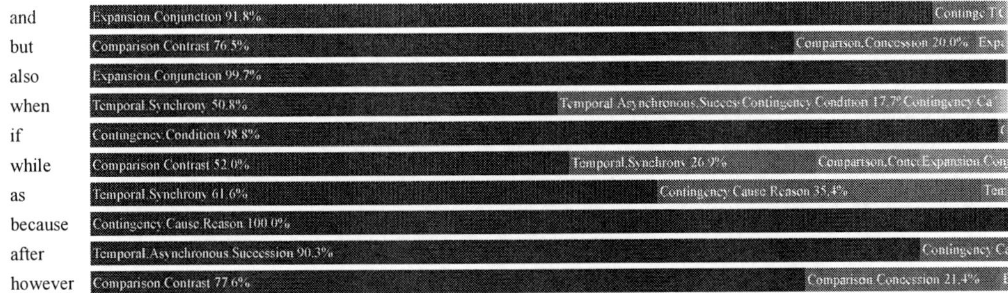

Figure 1: Distribution of the sense assigned to each connective word. All explicit relations with the ten most frequent connective words are extracted from the official training data for the CoNLL-2016 Shared Task.

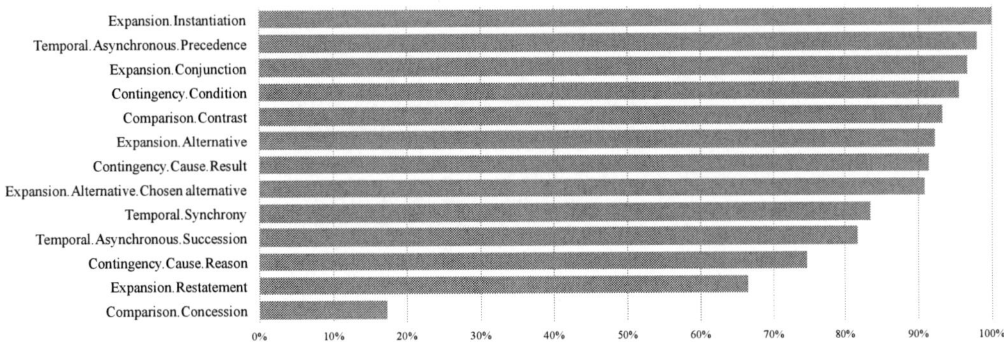

Figure 2: Accuracy of a simple majority classifier that assigns the most popular sense of the discourse relations in the training data with the same connective. Training was conducted on the official training data, and the evaluation used the development data.

the most frequent Implicit sense. We also tried automated weight balancing of the SVM classifier, but the accuracy gain was small.

3 Proposed System

We describe the implementation of our system based on the analysis above. First, the system classifies a discourse relation into two categories, namely (i) Explicit and AltLex or (ii) Implicit and EntRel. This classification is determined simply by checking whether the relation has connective words annotated in the text. The input is then passed to the next two-step classifier components. The following sections detail the three components, i.e., (i) Unknown Connective Substitution (*CS*), (ii) Explicit and AltLex Sense Classifier including Concession vs. Contrast Classifier (*CC*), and (iii) Implicit and EntRel Sense Classifier (*IE*). Figure 3 shows the system overview.

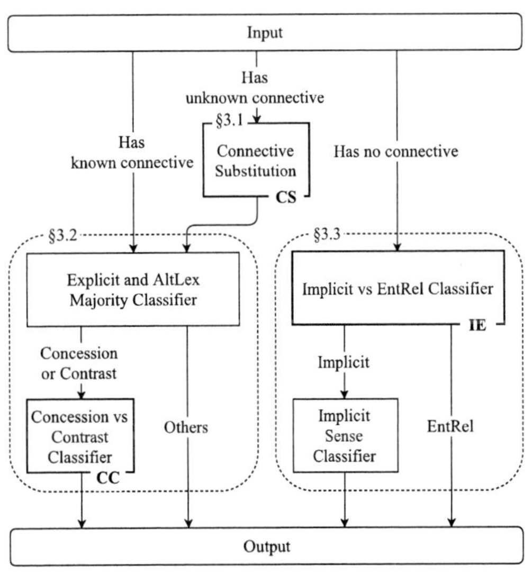

Figure 3: Pipeline of our system.

3.1 Unknown Connective Substitution

If a discourse relation is classified into an Explicit and AltLex category, it will then be passed to a simple majority classifier, i.e., the most frequent sense in the training dataset with the same connective word is assigned. If connective words are alternatively lexicalized, then instances with the same connective words are not necessarily found in the training data. In that case, the majority classifier does not know which sense to assign, whereupon we apply a preprocess, named *unknown connective substitution*, to find a clue for the classifier.

First, the connective words are mapped to a real vector using skip-gram neural word embeddings (Mikolov et al., 2013). For connective words with more than one word, the average vector of every word weighted by term frequency is used. Using this vector, the known connective words in training data that are the closest to the unknown connective words are looked up. Then the connective words are substituted with the closest one, and passed to the next process. Thus, we can use this substitution to reduce the difference between Explicit and AltLex such that it can be ignored, which contributes to the reusability of the components.

3.2 Explicit and AltLex Sense Classifier

As already mentioned, the Explicit and AltLex sense classifier is a majority classifier. It assigns the most popular sense in the training examples that have the same connective words (or those substituted in the pre-process) with the input. Although this classifier already had reasonably good accuracy at this point, we improved it by analyzing which pair of senses are confusing and difficult to distinguish.

In the previous section, we saw that distinguishing between Comparison.Concession and Comparison.Contrast is difficult. The system attempts to solve this problem by repeating the classification using another classifier in cases in which the output of the classifier was Comparison.Concession or Comparison.Contrast. For the second classifier, we use the following features:

1. the connective words,

2. the Arg1 and Arg2 texts: the frequency count of the tokens in the argument texts converted into integer vectors (bag-of-words),

3. the nodes of the parse trees Arg1 and Arg2: similarly to 2, the frequency count of the nodes of the parse trees of argument texts, and

4. the MPQA subjectivity lexicon: each token in the argument texts is classified into nine groups according to the MPQA lexicon, and the number of tokens was counted, ignoring words not in the lexicon.

These are chiefly general-purpose features and widely used in various NLP tasks, and actually a subset of the features used in several previous studies including (Lin et al., 2014) and (Pitler and Nenkova, 2009).

3.3 Implicit and EntRel Sense Classifier

Similar to the Explicit and AltLex sense classification, the Implicit and EntRel sense classification is also a two-step process: first it is determined whether the type is Implicit or EntRel, and then a sense is assigned if classified as Implicit.

Connective words themselves cannot be used as features in Implicit and EntRel sense classification; therefore, other features need to be prepared. There are many candidates for the features. Here, to simplify the implementation, and also because we cannot afford the time for task-specific feature engineering, we merely reuse the same features of the Concession vs. Contrast classifier described in the last section.

4 Experiments

4.1 Experimental Settings

We trained our system on the official training dataset of the CoNLL-2016 Shared Task, and evaluated it on several test datasets. We implemented SVM classifiers, which are popular among various NLP tasks, and MaxEnt classifiers, which have been used in the previous studies. Both are implemented using scikit-learn (Pedregosa et al., 2011), with the default parameters except for the automated weight balancing between classes (`class_weight='balanced'`) in order to overcome the imbalance of the data distribution[2]. In the balanced mode, the weights of samples are automatically adjusted inversely proportional to class frequencies in the input data. We

---

[2]It should be noted, however, that we also conducted an evaluation on the test and blind test dataset without weight balancing, and found that its effect is small.

Table 2: Experimental results using the two datasets. F_1 scores are shown. "Maj" = majority classifier for Explicit and AltLex relations. "CS" = substitution of unknown AltLex connectives. "IE" = Implicit vs. EntRel classification before Implicit sense classification. "CC" = Concession vs. Contrast classification after Explicit and AltLex sense classification.

	test			blind-test		
	All	**Explicit**	**NonExp**	**All**	**Explicit**	**NonExp**
Maj+SVM (Baseline)	0.5116	0.8991	0.1589	0.4404	0.7495	0.1776
Maj+SVM (TIRA Official)	0.5473	0.9022	0.2261	0.5188	0.7543	0.3231
Maj+MaxEnt	0.6093	0.9002	0.3445	0.5215	0.7532	0.3247
Maj+MaxEnt+CS	**0.6145**	**0.9046**	**0.3504**	0.5257	0.7622	0.3241
Maj+MaxEnt+CS+IE	0.5540	**0.9046**	0.2340	0.5290	0.7622	**0.3308**
Maj+MaxEnt+CS +CC	0.5866	0.8460	**0.3504**	0.5357	**0.7838**	0.3241
Maj+MaxEnt+CS+IE+CC	0.5261	0.8460	0.2340	**0.5389**	**0.7838**	**0.3308**

also attempted hyperparameter tuning using the development dataset, but the performance was almost the same.

As a baseline, the majority classifier described in Section 2.1 is used for Explicit and AltLex relations, and an SVM classifier is used for Implicit and EntRel relations. The features for the SVM classifier were bag-of-words of Arg1 and Arg2 texts. The system used in the official evaluation on TIRA was an old version because of deployment problems. This means it is almost the same as the baseline system, except that the MPQA subjectivity lexicon is added as features.

The systems are evaluated using the script provided by the CoNLL-2016 Shared Task organizers. The official evaluation is carried out on TIRA (Potthast et al., 2014).

4.2 Results

Table 2 lists the F_1 scores our systems achieved in the evaluation using the test and blind-test datasets. In the first column, "CS" indicates the substitution of unknown AltLex connectives. "IE" indicates that the Implicit vs EntRel classifier was used, and "CC" indicates the Concession vs. Contrast classifier. A comparison of the two classification algorithms revealed that MaxEnt classifiers were more effective than SVM. This is because SVM is unsuitable for this text classification problem, because text data is high dimensional and sparse. The training of MaxEnt classifiers took only 40 minutes in the longest case, but SVM classifiers required more than 10 hours. In the evaluation using the blind-test dataset, the performance of our system was optimal with the full functions. The blind-test dataset is taken from Wikinews materials; thus, these results imply a good generalization of our system.

4.2.1 AltLex Connective Substitution

As can be seen from the third and fourth columns in Table 2, the substitution of unknown connectives using skip-gram described in Section 3.1 contributed to an improvement on average. Table 4 presents examples of substituted unknown AltLex connectives. The words in the first column are found in AltLex relations, but they are not included in the training data. By applying the substitution preprocess, the known connectives shown in the second column are found to be the closest. As a result, the senses in the third column were chosen by the majority classifier. The fourth column shows the golden sense. This process worked well in the cases of the first three rows. The last two rows are examples of failure. The connective *one reason is that* introduces the following clause as the reason for the preceding phrases, but the word *reason* was omitted from the substituted connective, causing misclassification into Contingency.Cause.Result. In order to distinguish Result and Reason, the system has to consider the word order, but now its information is omitted during the mapping from words to real vectors. In addition, the word2vec model used in this system is a pre-trained model, and it does not include functional words such as *and* or *a*. These words play an important role for our purpose; therefore, an unprocessed model should be used.

4.2.2 Features

We also conducted experiments using different sets of the features. The results are provided in

Table 3: Experimental results using different sets of the features. F_1 scores are shown. Feature 1 = tokens in argument texts. Feature 2 = parse tree nodes of argument texts. Feature 3 = MPQA subjectivity lexicon. All classifiers share these features, and they also use connective words as a feature.

	test			blind-test		
	All	**Explicit**	**NonExp**	**All**	**Explicit**	**NonExp**
Features 2+3	0.5717	**0.9067**	0.2661	0.4883	0.7604	0.2571
Features 1 +3	0.6036	0.9056	0.3287	0.4950	0.7617	0.2674
Features 1+2	**0.6160**	0.9035	**0.3544**	0.5228	0.7617	0.3195
Features 1+2+3	0.6145	0.9046	0.3504	**0.5257**	**0.7622**	**0.3241**

Table 4: Preprocessing results on AltLex relations with unknown connective words.

Unknown Connective	Closest Connective	Output	Golden Sense
the delay resulted from	the rise resulted from	**Contingency.Cause.Reason**	Contingency.Cause.Reason
that change will obviously impact	that will cinch	**Contingency.Cause.Result**	Contingency.Cause.Result
that rise came on top of	on top of that	**Expansion.Conjunction**	Expansion.Conjunction
one reason is that	that is why	Contingency.Cause.Result	Contingency.Cause.Reason
one reason is	one is	Expansion.Instantiation	Contingency.Cause.Reason

Table 3. The score is lowest when the token feature is omitted, except for the Explicit relations in the test dataset. The impact of the MPQA feature is small but not expectable, which led to the unstable results.

5 Conclusion

We analyzed the characteristics of the data used in the CoNLL-2016 Shared Task and described the implementation details of our system. The performance on the Implicit and EntRel sense classification task is still low and has room for improvement. These results imply that these tasks are essentially difficult and require a deeper understanding of semantics, pragmatics, and background knowledge behind the text. A more detailed analysis of the materials is essential to effectively improve the performance on these tasks.

6 Acknowledgments

This work was supported by the Japan Society for the Promotion of Science KAKENHI Grant Number 15H02754 and 16K12546.

References

Ziheng Lin, Hwee Tou Ng, and Min-Yen Kan. 2014. A PDTB-styled end-to-end discourse parser. *Natural Language Engineering*, 20:151–184, 4.

Tomas Mikolov, Kai Chen, Greg Corrado, and Jeffrey Dean. 2013. Efficient estimation of word representations in vector space. *arXiv preprint arXiv:1301.3781*.

Fabian Pedregosa, Gael Varoquaux, Alexandre Gramfort, Vincent Michel, Bertrand Thirion, Olivier Grisel, Mathieu Blondel, Peter Prettenhofer, Ron Weiss, Vincent Dubourg, Jake VanderPlas, Alexandre Passos, David Cournapeau, Matthieu Brucher, Matthieu Perrot, and Edouard Duchesnay. 2011. Scikit-learn: Machine learning in Python. *Journal of Machine Learning Research*, 12:2825–2830.

Emily Pitler and Ani Nenkova. 2009. Using syntax to disambiguate explicit discourse connectives in text. In *Proceedings of the ACL-IJCNLP 2009 Conference Short Papers*, ACLShort '09, pages 13–16, Stroudsburg, PA, USA. Association for Computational Linguistics.

Martin Potthast, Tim Gollub, Francisco Rangel, Paolo Rosso, Efstathios Stamatatos, and Benno Stein. 2014. Improving the reproducibility of PAN's shared tasks: Plagiarism detection, author identification, and author profiling. In Evangelos Kanoulas, Mihai Lupu, Paul Clough, Mark Sanderson, Mark Hall, Allan Hanbury, and Elaine Toms, editors, *Information Access Evaluation meets Multilinguality, Multimodality, and Visualization. 5th International Conference of the CLEF Initiative (CLEF 14)*, pages 268–299, Berlin Heidelberg New York, September. Springer.

Rashmi Prasad, Eleni Miltsakaki, Nikhil Dinesh, Alan Lee, Aravind Joshi, Livio Robaldo, and Bonnie L Webber. 2007. The Penn Discourse Treebank 2.0 annotation manual.

Evgeny A. Stepanov, Giuseppe Riccardi, and Ali Orkan Bayer. 2015. The UniTN discourse parser in CoNLL 2015 Shared Task: Token-level sequence labeling with argument-specific models. In *Proceed-

ings of the 19th Conference on Computational Natural Language Learning: Shared Task, pages 25–31.

Jianxiang Wang and Man Lan. 2015. A refined end-to-end discourse parser. In *Proceedings of the 19th Conference on Computational Natural Language Learning: Shared Task*, pages 17–24.

Nianwen Xue, Hwee Tou Ng, Sameer Pradhan, Rashmi Prasad, Christopher Bryant, and Attapol Rutherford. 2015. The CoNLL-2015 shared task on shallow discourse parsing. In *Proceedings of the 19th Conference on Computational Natural Language Learning: Shared Task*, pages 1–16.

Nianwen Xue, Hwee Tou Ng, Sameer Pradhan, Bonnie Webber, Attapol Rutherford, Chuan Wang, and Hongmin Wang. 2016. The CoNLL-2016 shared task on multilingual shallow discourse parsing. In *Proceedings of the Twentieth Conference on Computational Natural Language Learning - Shared Task*, Berlin, Germany, August. Association for Computational Linguistics.

Adapting Event Embedding for Implicit Discourse Relation Recognition

Maria Leonor Pacheco, I-Ta Lee, Xiao Zhang, Abdullah Khan Zehady
Pranjal Daga, Di Jin, Ayush Parolia, Dan Goldwasser
Department of Computer Science, Purdue University
West Lafayette, IN 47907
{pachecog, lee2226, zhang923, azehady
daga, jind, aparolia, dgoldwas}@purdue.edu

Abstract

Predicting the sense of a discourse relation is particularly challenging when connective markers are missing. To address this challenge, we propose a simple deep neural network approach that replaces manual feature extraction by introducing event vectors as an alternative representation, which can be pre-trained using a very large corpus, without explicit annotation. We model discourse arguments as a combination of word and event vectors. Event information is aggregated with word vectors and a Multi-Layer Neural Network is used to classify discourse senses. This work was submitted as part of the CoNLL 2016 shared task on Discourse Parsing. We obtain competitive results, reaching an accuracy of 38%, 34% and 34% for the development, test and blind test datasets, competitive with the best performing system on CoNLL 2015.

1 Introduction

The CoNLL 2016 shared task focuses on Discourse Parsing. Building on the CoNLL 2015 task, this year teams were able to focus on a supplementary task, limited to sense classification of discourse relations, given their (gold) arguments (Xue et al., 2016). Identifying the sense is particularly challenging in the case of implicit relations, where explicit connective words (e.g., *however, but, because*) are not present. Last year, most submitted systems used algorithms traditionally applied for this task, such as Support Vector Machine (SVM) and Maximum Entropy classifiers learned over binary features as input representation. This included the best performing system, which reached an accuracy of 34.45 in the test data

and an accuracy of 36.29 in the blind test data for implicit relations (Xue et al., 2015; Wang and Lan, 2015).

We followed the intuition that obtaining a significant increase in performance using traditional classifiers and feature engineering would be difficult given the effort that was previously spent on such systems. Neural-network-based classifiers present a different and less explored approach to the discourse sense problem, which can potentially lead to considerable improvement. Our system, described in this paper, takes a step in this direction.

We explore different input representation types and introduce event vectors for this task. Following the work of (Chambers and Jurafsky, 2009), we look into event chains as a way to represent structure in the discourse arguments. Then, we adapt the skip-gram approach originally used to learn word vectors from sentences (Mikolov et al., 2013b) to learn event vector representations from event sequences. To do so, we draw a clear analogy between words and events, as well as between sentences and event chains. Finally, each input relation is represented with the pre-trained event and word vectors of its arguments and a multi-layer neural network is used to classify senses.

2 System Description

The dataset used in the CoNLL shared task corresponds to the Penn Discourse Treebank (Prasad et al., 2008), in which pairs of sentences are annotated with an optional discourse connective and a sense that best explains the discourse relation between them. The annotation was done over a set of Wall Street Journal articles.

Each relation, either explicit or implicit, consists of two arguments, typically composed of short phrases and an associated sense. In the case of explicit relations, a connective is present in the

Proceedings of the 54th Annual Meeting of the Association for Computational Linguistics, pages 136–142,
Berlin, Germany, August 7-12, 2016. ©2016 Association for Computational Linguistics

text. This problem can be stated as a standard multi-class classification problem, where the inputs correspond to the argument pairs and there is a direct mapping to a finite and known set of labels.

We use two different classifiers for sense identification: a SVM classifier with linear kernel for explicit relations that uses state-of-the-art features and a multi-layer neural network for the implicit relations, which is the main focus of our submission. The following sections describe each of the systems in detail.

2.1 Explicit Discourse Relations

Explicit discourse relation detection depends on identifying explicit discourse connectives. In the sense classification task, the connective and the two corresponding arguments are supplied, therefore, we trained a linear SVM multi-class classifier to choose from 14 different senses.

We used the syntactic features described in (Lin et al., 2009; Pitler and Nenkova, 2009). We also used the connective string, PoS tags, the connective's previous word and PoS tag from Lin's features in our classifier. The features described in (Pitler and Nenkova, 2009) are extracted using constituency parse trees and consist of self-category, parent-category, left-sibling-category and right-sibling category.

(Pitler and Nenkova, 2009) has shown that using only the syntactic features, ignoring the identity of the connective gives better result. As the discourse usage of a connective may strongly rely on the syntactic context it appeared, we have added Pitler's pairwise interaction (C-Syn interaction) features between the connective C and each category feature (i.e., self-category, parent-category, left-sibling-category, right-sibling- category). The interaction features (Syn-Syn interaction) between pairs of category features are also used.

2.2 Implicit Discourse Relations

Sense classification for implicit discourse relations is notoriously hard. For this reason, we focus our efforts on this task, and explore several types of input representation and neural net architectures to deal with the challenges.

We move from the simple lexical representation of word pairs used in (Lin et al., 2009; Pitler et al., 2009), and explore the benefits of using pre-trained word vectors (Mikolov et al., 2013b) to capture combinations and similarities. Finally,

we introduce the notion of an event to discourse parsing, inspired by the work of (Chambers and Jurafsky, 2009) as a way to represent structured knowledge and long range dependencies. Similar to (Modi and Titov, 2014; Pichotta and Mooney, 2016) we embed the event representation in a low dimension continuous space. More details on the definition of events and the derivation of the event vectors are given in section 2.2.1.

The sense classification task is defined over two arguments. Each argument is represented as two single vectors: a series of concatenated event vectors and a series of concatenated word vectors. A multi-layer neural network architecture receives these inputs to predict senses. The specifications of the architecture used are outlined in section 2.3.

2.2.1 Word and Event Embeddings

A word embedding is a function $W \rightarrow R^n$, mapping words to a dense low-dimensional vector space. Word embedding, recently popularized by (Mikolov et al., 2013b), can be trained to capture semantic and syntactic relationships between words, by mapping related words to vectors that lie close in the embedding vector space.

This property is often used to construct feature representations that can identify similarities and relationships between words. For example, discourse parsers often use lexical features, consisting of the product between words appearing in each of the two arguments. While such features can capture relationships between the two arguments, this representation is extremely brittle, as small variations in word usage are likely to result in lower performance. Using word embedding, instead of the arguments' words directly, can help overcome such issues.

Despite these advantages, using word embedding can potentially have several drawbacks. For example, the relationships captured between words sometimes reflect syntactic dependencies (e.g., determiners tend to be followed by nouns) rather than semantic ones, and word senses are typically ignored when word embedding are constructed. In addition, word vectors, despite their robustness, still do not capture the input argument structure.

To alleviate some of these problems, we looked for a representation that can capture a higher level of abstraction of the input arguments. We propose to represent arguments as a set of events and use pre-trained event embeddings to facilitate this

| | Implicit | | |
Class	Words	Words + Events	Number of Occurrences
Comparison.Concession	0.000	0.000	5
Comparison.Contrast	0.022	0.067	90
Contingency.Cause.Reason	0.256	0.487	78
Contingency.Cause.Result	0.036	0.143	56
Contingency.Condition	-	-	-
EntRel	0.637	0.609	215
Expansion.Alternative	-	-	-
Expansion.Alternative.Chosen alternative	0.000	0.000	2
Expansion.Conjunction	0.520	0.544	125
Expansion.Instantiation	0.000	0.163	49
Expansion.Restatement	0.173	0.260	104
Temporal.Asynchronous.Precedence	0.000	0.000	28
Temporal.Asynchronous.Succession	0.000	0.000	3
Temporal.Synchrony	0.000	0.000	20
Total	0.315	0.369	775

Table 1: Accuracy in the development data (Unofficial) by sense classes using different input representations: words, events and words + events

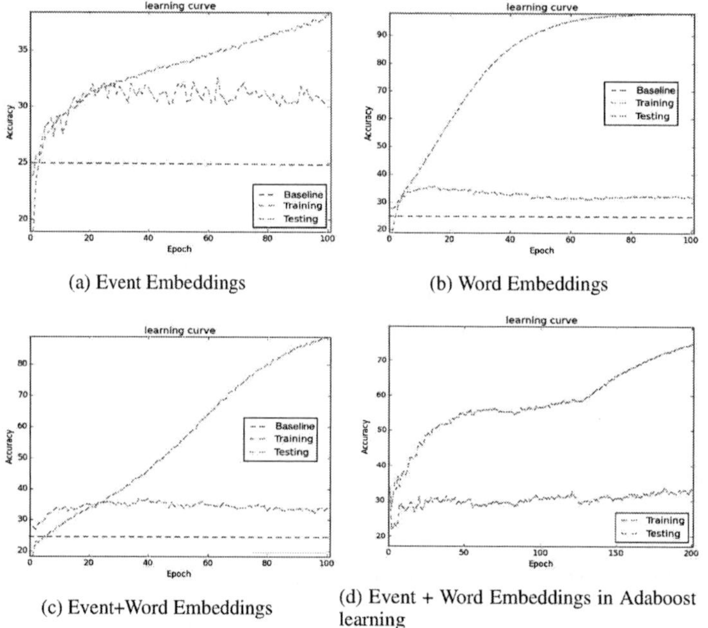

(a) Event Embeddings

(b) Word Embeddings

(c) Event+Word Embeddings

(d) Event + Word Embeddings in Adaboost learning

Figure 1: Training and testing accuracy for 100 epochs with three different implicit classifier models in Fig (a), (b), (c). Fig (d) shows the cumulative training and testing accuracy as the number of hypothesis increases from 0 to 200 in adaboost.

task. Simply put, an event can be defined as a verb and *subject* or *object* dependency relationship. An event *chain* is formed by connecting the events whose argument nodes are coreferent. We adapt the skip-gram model (Mikolov et al., 2013b) to generate event embedding by treating event chains as sentences, in which each event is a word. Note, that unlike word embedding that relies on word proximity and as a result captures syntactic infor-

mation, event proximity is likely to capture temporal and causal relationships which align better with discourse relationships. Since event embedding omits much of the information contained in the input arguments, we take advantage of both word and event embeddings, and build a neural network model over both representations of the discourse arguments.

	Implicit			Explicit		
Class	Dev	Test	Blind	Dev	Test	Blind
Comparison.Concession	0.0000	0.0000	0.0000	0.5000	0.4667	0.0000
Comparison.Contrast	0.1263	0.0576	0.0000	0.9544	0.9088	0.1633
Contingency.Cause.Reason	0.3673	0.3740	0.2794	0.7568	0.8710	0.0784
Contingency.Cause.Result	0.1892	0.0896	0.0400	0.8889	0.9474	0.8571
Contingency.Condition	-	-	-	0.9318	0.8718	0.9804
EntRel	0.5647	0.5475	0.5195	-	-	-
Expansion.Alternative	-	-	-	0.9231	0.7692	0.0000
Expansion.Alternative.Chosen alternative	0.0000	0.0000	0.0000	0.9091	1.0000	-
Expansion.Conjunction	0.4069	0.3123	0.2269	0.9537	0.9495	0.6194
Expansion.Instantiation	0.2286	0.3604	0.1852	1.0000	1.0000	0.0000
Expansion.Restatement	0.2647	0.2671	0.3282	0.0000	0.4444	0.0000
Temporal.Asynchronous.Precedence	0.0000	0.3636	0.0000	0.9375	0.9459	0.0000
Temporal.Asynchronous.Succession	0.0000	0.0000	-	0.8352	0.7429	0.1562
Temporal.Synchrony	0.0000	0.0000	0.0000	0.8000	0.7742	0.4500
Total	0.3818	0.3435	0.3365	0.8968	0.8796	0.4860

Table 2: F1 score (Unofficial) by sense classes for both implicit and explicit classifier.

Pre-Training of Event Embedding The creation of event embeddings follows the Skip-gram model proposed by (Mikolov et al., 2013a). Instead of using word sequences as input to train the embeddings, we use event chains extracted by connecting events with co-referencing entities. Each entity has a chain of events and each event is represented in a form of verb and dependency pairs.

Specifically, we represent an event e as a pair $e = (v, d)$ where v denotes a verb and d denotes a grammatical dependency relation between the verb and its entity. Vector representations for events are learned from chains of events extracted from a large corpus (we used the Wikipedia dump). To start, we use Stanford CoreNLP toolkit (Manning et al., 2014) to extract dependency trees and resolve co-referent entities from the corpus. For each entity in the co-reference chain, events are extracted by looking at the adjacent verb v in the dependency tree and its correspondent grammatical dependency relation d, creating tuples (v, d) as described above. This way, chains of the form $e_i, ..., e_k$ are extracted and are used as inputs to the embedding training model.

Similar to the Word2Vec skip-gram model (Mikolov et al., 2013a), we use the following objective function.

$$J = \frac{1}{T} \sum_{t=1}^{T} \sum_{-c \leq j \leq c, j \neq 0} \log \frac{exp(V'_{e_O} V_{e_I})}{\sum_{e=1}^{E} exp(V'_e V_{e_I})}$$

Where V_e is the vector representation of event e and e_I, e_O specify whether the event is an input or output (Rong, 2014). Note, that in our model, unlike the Word2Vec model that uses sentences as inputs, event chains are used as input for generating the event embedding (i.e., c refers to current event and j refers to context events in the equation above), thus capturing a higher level abstraction of the sentence semantics.

To make training feasible, we apply negative sampling following the techniques used in the word2vec model, including rare event pruning, high frequency event subsampling and a dynamic window size (Goldberg and Levy, 2014). Five negative samples are sampled for each event.

2.3 Discourse Relation Classifier

We used a Multi-layer perceptron with three hidden layers to combine the arguments' representation in our system. This layout is depicted in figure 2.

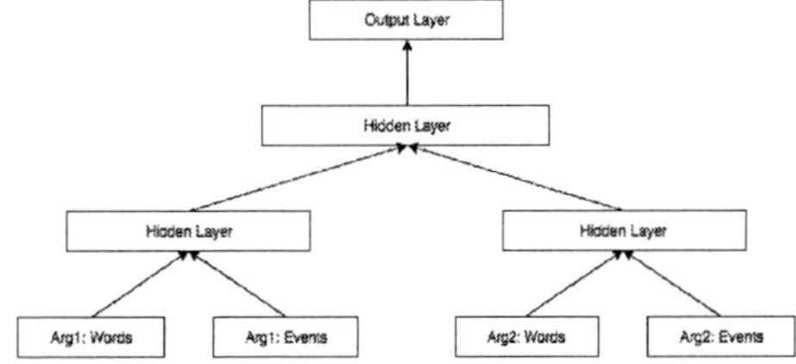

Figure 2: Three hidden layer Perceptron taking events and word vectors as input.

Two parallel hidden layers at the same level are used to combine event and word representations for every argument, this way, each hidden layer works as an abstraction of one argument. Another hidden layer is stacked on top of them to combine both arguments into a single representation. Finally an output layer with a softmax function is built on top to classify the sense. A 50% drop-out rate is applied over all the hidden layers for the purpose of regularization. The activation function for all the hidden layers is the rectified linear function, which sets up a threshold such that all the values less than zero will be clipped to zero. In addition to this setting, we applied a drop-out rate of 20% over all the input layers. We argue that due to the high dimensionality of a combined representation of event and word embeddings, using drop-out even on the input layer can boost the model performance by avoiding overfitting.

The number of hidden units is tuned using a separate validation set. Events and word vectors are concatenated in the input layer, where the maximum number of events and words in an argument is taken from the entire date set in order to fix the size of the input and padding is performed on both sides if the number of words and/or events are less than the maximum value. In this study, we used the word embedding pre-trained on Google news corpus, which is widely used in NLP community (Mikolov et al., 2013a). For each word in this discourse parsing task, if it is in the embedding corpus, we used its mapped vector; if it is not in the embedding corpus, it is initialized to random values very close to zero. As we trained our own event embedding, we dealt with all the extracted events in a similar fashion as word embedding.

In the final model, the number of hidden nodes is 175 for agument one, 350 for agument two, and the number of units in the hidden layer stacked on them is 700.

During training, we used stochastic gradient descent with mini-batches to minimize our loss function, which we defined as the negative log-likelihood of the data. The standard back-propagation algorithm is used to compute the gradient. The whole training process is performed on an Nvidia GTX 980 GPU.

3   Experiments

Since our main focus is implicit relations, we carried out a series of experiments to test the three different input representations in the implicit sense identification task. In all these experiments, we used a neural network architecture, and used as a baseline a simple lexical classifier based on word pairs. Since during the development of the system we only had direct access to the train and development folds, most of our experiments were performed on the development data set alone.

Word pairs have been widely used for implicit sense classification (Lin et al., 2009; Pitler et al., 2009), and most systems submitted to CoNLL 2015 shared task incorporated word pairs as a fundamental part of their feature set. In table 3 we can see the aggregated results for this simple approach using Support Vector Machines on the development dataset. For this test, the top 500 word pairs ranked by information gain were used.

Input	Precision	Recall	F1
Word Pairs	0.24	0.26	0.25
Word Vectors	0.29	0.31	0.30
Event + Word Vectors	0.37	0.37	0.37

Table 3: Performance metrics on the development data for the implicit classifier

The best performing systems, however, had to go beyond simple word pairs to reach scores near 0.35. To prove the effectiveness of looking at words in a richer space, we tested a very simple neural network architecture on word vectors. This architecture incorporated only one hidden layer to combine both arguments into a single representation and an output layer with a softmax function was built on top to classify the sense. The layout for this simple architecture can be observed in figure 3. The input word vectors are concatenated in the input layer with padding and unknown words are initialized to random values very close to zero (see section 2.3).

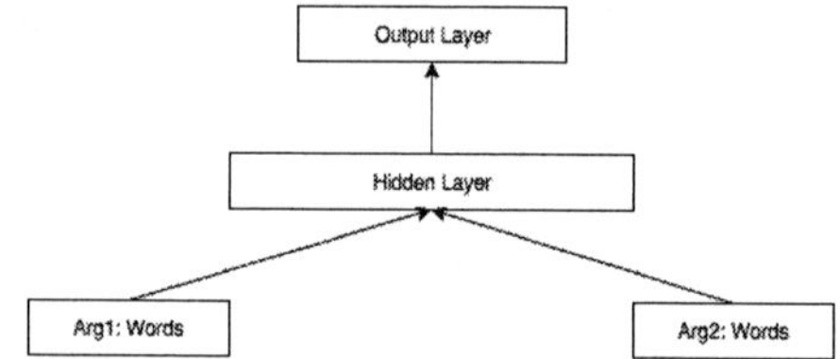

Figure 3: Single hidden layer perceptron taking word vectors as input.

Results using word vectors can be observed in table 1. We can see that there is a significant improvement in the general case, reaching to an accuracy of 0.315 in the development data. We attribute this improvement to the word vectors ability to capture similarities implicitly between words as well as providing a distributed continuous representation allowing words to be combined in the hidden layer.

Following the improvement obtained by using word vectors, we introduce event vectors into the

Class	Implicit			Explicit		
	Dev	Test	Blind	Dev	Test	Blind
Total	0.3805	0.3445	0.291	0.8968	0.8796	-

Table 4: Official TIRA F1 score for both implicit and explicit classifier.

input using the architecture described in section 2.3. After some experimentation, we decided to keep word vectors as a way to expand the information encoded in events, where the reference to the entities and other helpful lexical information is lost. Table 1 shows the improvement attained when throwing event vectors into the picture. We can observe a stable boost in performance among all classes, except EntRel, where there is a slight drop in accuracy. Total accuracy improves from 0.315 to 0.369 using event vectors, a result that is competitive with the best performing system in CoNLL 2015.

Figure 1 (a)-(c) shows the learning curve of the implicit classifier for all input types and architectures. The baseline corresponds to the word pair classifier with an accuracy of 0.25. We can observe that using word embedding overfits quickly, as the neural network starts to memorize the the training set vocabulary. Using event embedding helps combat overfitting, and the best behavior is obtained when combining the two embedding types. In this case, the learning curve in the development set reaches a higher peak. We can see the combined model overfits as the number of training epochs increases, albeit slower compared to word embedding alone. We tried to slow overfitting even further by experimenting with random sampling from training data set and combining multiple hypothesis using Adaboost, Figure 1 (d) shows the learning curve resulting from these attempts. While overfitting is indeed slower, performance suffers. We speculate that increasing the number of epochs until training accuracy reaches the optimum, may give even more competitive performance.

Tables 2 and 4 include our final results. On table 2 we can observe the performance by class on the three evaluation datasets: development, test and blind test for both the implicit and the explicit classifier. In our preliminary experiments for the implicit case, we obtained a very low score for infrequent classes. For this reason, we opted for removing infrequent classes from the training set and improved overall results, increasing F1 score from 0.36 to 0.38 for the development data.

Table 4 includes the official results obtained through TIRA (Potthast et al., 2014). Due to technical difficulties, we had to use an older model for the blind test set, that was trained over all labels (including the infrequent ones). The improvement from 0.291 to 0.3365 corresponds to the elimination of infrequent labels from the training procedure. Similarly, the system used for the blind data did not include the explicit classifier. For this reason, the result is omitted in table 4.

We looked at the class distribution in the dataset in table 1, and identified common senses that our classifier fails to distinguish. Analyzing the confusion matrix we identified the following: It is hard to differentiate Expansion.Instantiation from Expansion.Restatement and Contingency.Cause.Result from Contingency.Cause.Reason, and finally, the rest of the classes get confused with Expansion.Conjunction, which is the biggest class after EntRel.

4 Conclusion

We presented our submission for the CoNLL 2016 shared task, focusing on implict discourse sense identification[1]. We looked into deep learning approaches, as it seems that approaches that manually craft features have reached their peak. We explored different input representations for the problem and reached competitive results with CoNLL 2015 best performing system without engineering features directly.

Two types of embedding were combined: Google News pre-trained word vectors (Mikolov et al., 2013b) and our main contribution, event vectors inspired by the work of (Chambers and Jurafsky, 2009) and (Modi and Titov, 2014). We showed that event embedding for argument pairs can provide rich semantic information for the implicit discourse parsing task, significantly improving the performance of word pairs alone, even when using a very simple neural network model.

Our experiments suggest several possible future directions. First, improving event representations to include more structure seems promising. We also intend to explore using more complex learning architectures.

---

[1]To submit a complete system we developed a different model for explicit relations

References

Nathanael Chambers and Dan Jurafsky. 2009. Unsupervised learning of narrative schemas and their participants. In *Proceedings of the Joint Conference of the 47th Annual Meeting of the ACL and the 4th International Joint Conference on Natural Language Processing of the AFNLP: Volume 2 - Volume 2*, ACL '09, pages 602–610, Stroudsburg, PA, USA. Association for Computational Linguistics.

Yoav Goldberg and Omer Levy. 2014. word2vec explained: deriving mikolov et al.'s negative-sampling word-embedding method. *arXiv preprint arXiv:1402.3722*.

Ziheng Lin, Min-Yen Kan, and Hwee Tou Ng. 2009. Recognizing implicit discourse relations in the penn discourse treebank. In *Proceedings of the 2009 Conference on Empirical Methods in Natural Language Processing: Volume 1 - Volume 1*, EMNLP '09, pages 343–351, Stroudsburg, PA, USA. Association for Computational Linguistics.

Christopher D. Manning, Mihai Surdeanu, John Bauer, Jenny Finkel, Steven J. Bethard, and David McClosky. 2014. The Stanford CoreNLP natural language processing toolkit. In *Association for Computational Linguistics (ACL) System Demonstrations*, pages 55–60.

Tomas Mikolov, Kai Chen, Greg Corrado, and Jeffrey Dean. 2013a. Efficient estimation of word representations in vector space. *CoRR*, abs/1301.3781.

Tomas Mikolov, Wen-tau Yih, and Geoffrey Zweig. 2013b. Linguistic regularities in continuous space word representations. In *Proc. of NAACL*.

Ashutosh Modi and Ivan Titov. 2014. Inducing neural models of script knowledge. In *Proceedings of the Eighteenth Conference on Computational Natural Language Learning*, pages 49–57, Ann Arbor, Michigan, June. Association for Computational Linguistics.

Karl Pichotta and Raymond J. Mooney. 2016. Learning statistical scripts with LSTM recurrent neural networks. In *Proceedings of the 30th AAAI Conference on Artificial Intelligence (AAAI-16)*, Phoenix, Arizona.

Emily Pitler and Ani Nenkova. 2009. Using syntax to disambiguate explicit discourse connectives in text. In *Proceedings of the ACL-IJCNLP 2009 Conference Short Papers*, pages 13–16. Association for Computational Linguistics.

Emily Pitler, Annie Louis, and Ani Nenkova. 2009. Automatic sense prediction for implicit discourse relations in text. In *Proceedings of the Joint Conference of the 47th Annual Meeting of the ACL and the 4th International Joint Conference on Natural Language Processing of the AFNLP: Volume 2 - Volume 2*, ACL '09, pages 683–691, Stroudsburg, PA, USA. Association for Computational Linguistics.

Martin Potthast, Tim Gollub, Francisco Rangel, Paolo Rosso, Efstathios Stamatatos, and Benno Stein. 2014. Improving the Reproducibility of PAN's Shared Tasks: Plagiarism Detection, Author Identification, and Author Profiling. In Evangelos Kanoulas, Mihai Lupu, Paul Clough, Mark Sanderson, Mark Hall, Allan Hanbury, and Elaine Toms, editors, *Information Access Evaluation meets Multilinguality, Multimodality, and Visualization. 5th International Conference of the CLEF Initiative (CLEF 14)*, pages 268–299, Berlin Heidelberg New York, September. Springer.

Rashmi Prasad, Nikhil Dinesh, Alan Lee, Eleni Miltsakaki, Livio Robaldo, Aravind Joshi, and Bonnie Webber. 2008. The penn discourse treebank 2.0. In *In Proceedings of LREC*.

Xin Rong. 2014. word2vec parameter learning explained. *arXiv preprint arXiv:1411.2738*.

Jianxiang Wang and Man Lan. 2015. A refined end-to-end discourse parser. In *Proceedings of the Nineteenth Conference on Computational Natural Language Learning - Shared Task*, pages 17–24, Beijing, China, July. Association for Computational Linguistics.

Nianwen Xue, Hwee Tou Ng, Sameer Pradhan, Rashmi Prasad, Christopher Bryant, and Attapol Rutherford. 2015. The conll-2015 shared task on shallow discourse parsing. In *Proceedings of the Nineteenth Conference on Computational Natural Language Learning - Shared Task*, pages 1–16, Beijing, China, July. Association for Computational Linguistics.

Nianwen Xue, Hwee Tou Ng, Sameer Pradhan, Bonnie Webber, Attapol Rutherford, Chuan Wang, and Hongmin Wang. 2016. The conll-2016 shared task on multilingual shallow discourse parsing. In *Proceedings of the Twentieth Conference on Computational Natural Language Learning - Shared Task*, Berlin, Germany, August. Association for Computational Linguistics.

SDP-JAIST: A Shallow Discourse Parsing system @ CoNLL 2016 Shared Task

Nguyen Truong Son
University Of Sience, VNU
Ho Chi Minh City
Viet Nam
`ntson@fit.hcmus.edu.vn`
`nguyen.son@jaist.ac.jp`

Nguyen Le Minh
Japan Advanced Institute of
Science and Technology
Ishikawa, 923-1292
Japan
`nguyenml@jaist.ac.jp`

Abstract

In this paper, we present an improvement of the last year architecture for identifying shallow discourse relations in texts. In the first phase, the system will detect the connective words and both of arguments by performing the Conditional Random Fields (CRFs) learning algorithm with models that are trained based on a set of features such as words, part-of-speech (POS) and pattern based features extracted from parsing trees of sentences. The second phase will classify arguments and explicit connectives into one of thirteen types of senses by using the Sequential Minimal Optimization (SMO) and Random Forest classifiers with a set of features extracted from arguments and connective along with a set of given resources. The evaluation results of the whole system on the development, test and blind data set are 29.65%, 24.67% and 20.37% in terms of F1 scores. The results are competitive with other top baseline systems in recognition of explicit discourse relations.

1 Introduction

The shared task of Shallow Discourse Parsing proposed by Xue et al. (2015) Xue et al. (2016) brings many opportunities for different teams in the world to solve the same task. Moreover, all built systems are evaluated objectively on the blind data sets and the TIRA evaluation platform (Potthast et al., 2014) helps us can compare and analyze the performance of different approaches . The result last year was impressive with many approaches had been implemented to solve this task (Xue et al., 2015). However, this task is still challenging task in the Natural Language Processing field because it has some difficult sub-tasks such as recognizing implicit discourse relations.

Our participating system of this year is an improvement of the last year system. It also has two main phases including recognizing arguments and connective words in the first phase then predicting the sense of discourse relations in the second phase. However, there are some changes in this year implementation. In the first phase, instead of tagging connective words and arguments at the same time as the last year one, we split this step into some sub steps. That means connective words will be identified at the first step then they are used as features for arguments tagging steps. Besides, we exploit more kinds of pattern based features based on syntactic parse trees to recognize arguments. In the phase of sense prediction, this year we also focus for both explicit and non-explicit sense classification with the exploiting of many kind of features based on resources such as MPQA Subjective lexicon, word embedding representation. These changes make a significant improvement for recognizing connective words, arguments and sense classification. The results are very competitive with top baseline systems in recognizing of explicit discourse relations.

This paper is organized as follows. Section 2 describes the details of our implemented system. Section 3 presents experimental results and some result analysis. Finally, Section 4 presents some conclusions and future works.

2 System Description

Our system focuses on recognizing discourse relations whose arguments are located in the same sentences (SS-type) and discourse relations whose arguments in two consecutive sentences (2CS-type) because they account for over 92% of total relations. Our system consists of two main phases in-

Proceedings of the 54th Annual Meeting of the Association for Computational Linguistics, pages 143–149,
Berlin, Germany, August 7-12, 2016. ©2016 Association for Computational Linguistics

cluding *Connective and Argument detection phase* and *Sense classification phase* . In the first phase, the system will take parsed documents to identify explicit connective words and then identify arguments for both SS-type and 2CS-type discourse relations. After connective words and arguments are identified, they will be passed through the sense classification phase to identify the sense of discourse relations. The work-flow of our discourse parsing system is displayed in Figure1. We

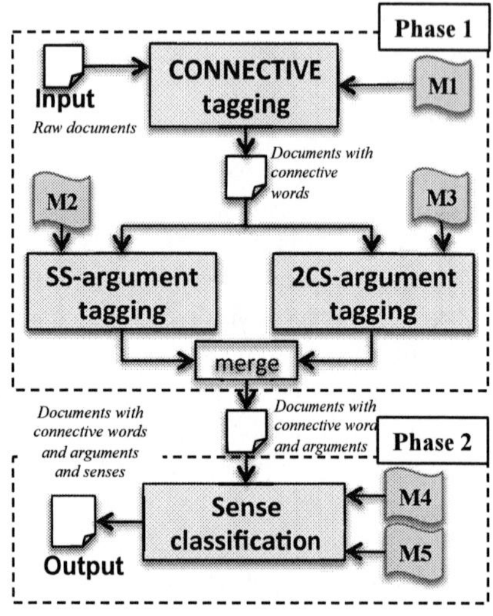

Figure 1: System work flows

have trained 5 models to recognize components of discourse relations. Models M1, M2 and M3, which are trained using CRF++ toolkit of Kudo (2005), an implementation of Conditional Random Fields proposed by Lafferty et al. (2001), are used for identifying connective words and SS-type and 2CS-type arguments. Besides, models M4 and M5, which are trained by SMO (Platt, 1998) and Random Forest (Breiman, 2001), are used for identifying the sense of explicit and non-explicit discourse relations. The details of these two phases are described in Section 2.1 and Section 2.2.

2.1 Phase 1: Identify connective words and arguments

We use the same approach for identifying connective words and arguments. We cast the task of recognizing these elements as a sequence labeling task. We train CRFs models to assign a specific IOB label for each token (e.g. B-C and I-C for tokens which are begin or inside of a connective

word). In order to train these models, we have extracted many kind features of token. For each token, we capture features in a window size of 5 tokens including two previous tokens, the current one and two next tokens.

2.1.1 Features for identifying connective words

Table 1 contains a list of features (Group A) which was used to train the model for identifying explicit connective words. Beside words and their POSs (A1), we use a feature that indicates whether or not the token belongs to the list of predefined candidates extracted from the training corpus (A2). Moreover, we use two features based on syntactic parse trees of sentences including the *path-to-root* from token's POS node to the ROOT node (A3) and the *sibling-nodes-sequence* of token's POS node (A4). These features can help the machine learning algorithms to avoid some borderline cases. An example of these features are showed in Figure 2. In the case (a) of this example, *path-to-root* and *sibling-nodes-sequence* of token *"and"* are *CC-NP-...-ROOT* and *NNS-CC-NNS*. In the case (b), *path-to-root* and *sibling-nodes-sequence* of token *"and"* are *CC-S-ROOT* and *S-,-CC-S*. In this example, based on the values of these two features, it is easy to see that the token *"and"* in case (b) is likely a correct connective word more than the one in case (a). Furthermore, which parts of a verb phrase, noun phrase or a preposition phrase that the token belongs to (A5) are also a helpful information to help identifying connective words.

#	Feature description
A1	Word; Part of Speech
A2	Does the token belong to candidate list?
A3	Path to root node of the token
A4	Sibling paths of POS node
A5	Which parts of NP, VP, PP does the token belongs?
A6	Position of token in sentence

Table 1: Features for the connective tagging step

2.1.2 Features for identifying SS-type and 2CS-type arguments

All features for identifying arguments are listed in Table 2. There are three groups of features. While group B contains features that help to identify both of two argument types, group C and D contain

Figure 2: Example of path-to-root and sibling sequence feature for connective tagging

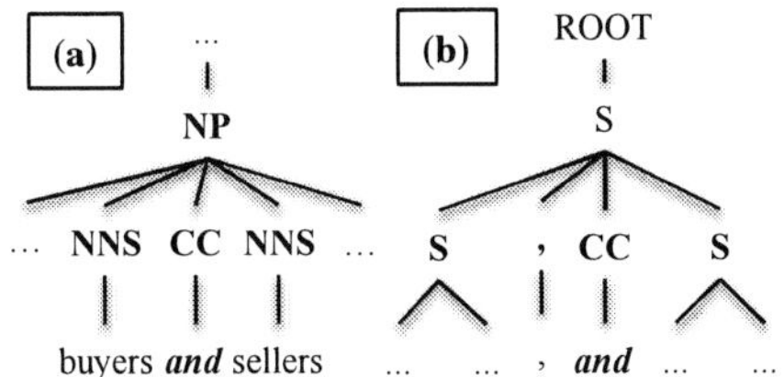

specialized features for recognizing SS-type and 2CS-type arguments. We categorize these features into two types including non-pattern-based features and pattern-based features.

The non-pattern-based features of a token consists of the token and its POS (B1), the labels received from the connective tagging step (B2), the category of Brown cluster that the token belongs to (B3), and the sentence order (1 or 2) of the token in a pair of two consecutive sentences.

Moreover, by analyzing the training corpus and linguistic features of discourse relations, we realize that there is a strong relationship between the syntactic parse trees of sentences and the boundaries of arguments and connective words. Therefore, we exploit a set of *pattern-based features* built from syntactic parse trees to capture arguments and connective of discourse relations as well as to capture some syntactic units such as phrases or clauses. If a text span matches with a pattern, their tokens will receive special values for this pattern-based feature. Below is the list of pattern-based features:

- Patterns that capture syntactic units such as subordinate clauses and phrases (B4, D6)

- Patterns that capture some useful language expressions including report statements (B5) and relative clauses (C1). For example, pattern B5 can capture some span texts such as *"he said that ..."* or *"Mr. X said ... "* or pattern C1 can capture relative clause such as *"which ..."* and *"who ..."* . If a text span matches with these patterns, their tokens rarely belong to discourse relations.

- Patterns that capture SS-type arguments: We use 4 types of pattern based features (C1, C2, C3, C4) in order to capture some popular of SS-type discourse expressions in natural language. Figure 3 shows an example of

a text span with two clauses connected by a conjunction that matches the pattern S-CC-C (feature C2). In this case, it is no doubt that these two clauses and the conjunction are two arguments and the connective of a discourse relation. Another example is illustrated in Figure 4.

- Patterns that capture 2CS-type arguments: we used pattern based features D2, D3, D4 and D5 to capture text spans that are usually use in the second arguments of discourse relations. Figure 5 shows a sentence that matches with the pattern D5.

Table 2: List of features for the arguments tagging task

#	Feature description
Group B: common features	
B1	Word; Part of Speech
B2	Connective label
B3	Brown cluster
B4	*Pattern* NP, VP, PP
B5	*Pattern* Report statements
Group C: Features for identifying SS-type Args	
C1	*Pattern* SBAR relative clause pattern
C2	*Pattern* S-CC-S, SBAR-CC-SBAR
C3	*Pattern* SBAR-NP-VP
C4	*Pattern* SBAR begins with preposition
Group D: Features for identifying 2CS-type Args	
D1	Which order of sentence does the token belong ?
D2	*Pattern* SBAR begins with a conjunctive
D3	*Pattern* SBAR begins with a NP follows by an adverb (e.g. also) and VP
D4	*Pattern* Adverb is followed by a clause
D5	*Pattern* Sentences with preposition phrases such as "for example", "by comparison", ...
D6	*Pattern* SBAR subordinate clause

2.2 Phase 2: Sense classification

We use SMO and Random Forest classifier for training the models for sense classification of explicit and non-explicit discourse relations. From arguments and connectives of all discourse discourses we extract a set of features that help classifiers to build the models and classify new instances. Below are features used for non-explicit sense classification task in our system, features of

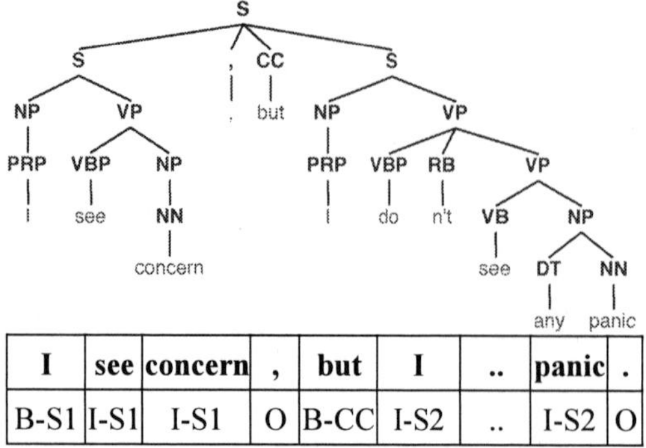

I	see	concern	,	but	I	..	panic	.
B-S1	I-S1	I-S1	O	B-CC	I-S2	..	I-S2	O

Figure 3: Example of pattern S-CC-S. If a text span matches with this pattern, their tokens will receive values in{B-S1, I-S1, B-S2, I-S2, B-CC} for this feature

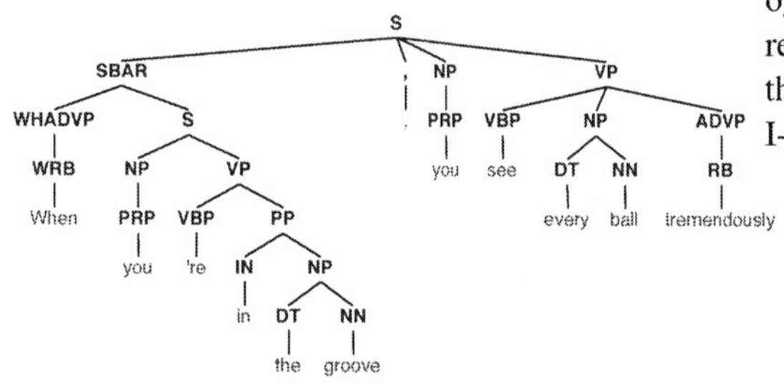

When	you	...	groove	,	you	...	tremendously
B-A	B-S1	...	I-S1	O	B-S2	..	I-S2

Figure 4: Example of pattern SBAR-NP-VP. If a text span matches with this pattern, their tokens will receive values in {B-S1, I-S1, B-S2, I-S2, B-A} for this feature

explicit sense classification are described in the end of this section:

- **Similarity features**: instead of using the cosine similarity between whole text span of two arguments, we compute 5 cosine similarity scores of nouns, noun phrases, verbs, verb phrase, adjectives between two arguments to obtain similarity features.

- **MPQA Subjectivity Lexicon** (Wilson et al., 2009)- feature): We realize that the polarity (positive, negative, neural) of words may be a good indicator for machine learning algorithms to identify the sense of discourse rela-

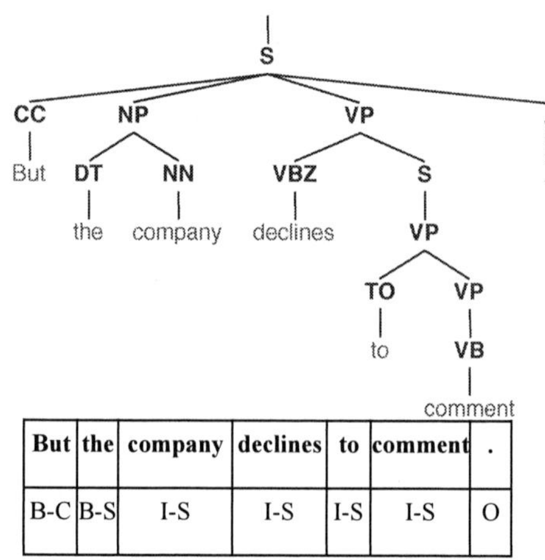

But	the	company	declines	to	comment	.
B-C	B-S	I-S	I-S	I-S	I-S	O

Figure 5: Example of pattern D2, which help recognizing second arguments of 2CS-type discourse relations. If a text span matches with this pattern, their tokens will receive values in {B-S, I-S, B-P, I-P} for this feature

tions, especially some kinds of discourse relations such as *Comparison.Contrast* of *Contingency.Condition*. We create these features based on the presence of words of arguments in the lexicon.

- **Word pair features**: From the training corpus, we extract frequent word pairs of arguments (frequency $>= 100$) as a feature set for sense classification. Moreover, we have used Information Gain (Sebastiani, 2002) method to reduce the size of this feature set and keep important pairs. We check the present of word pair in two arguments in these lists to obtain these features.

- **POS Pattern features**: POS patterns of sentences may indicate some sentence patterns that useful for sense classification such as patterns with modal verbs, patterns indicate the passive voice expression or patterns begin with a prepositions which express the purpose. Base on pre-defined regular expressions, we extract a list of POS patterns that have high frequency ($>= 100$) in training corpus. Table 3 shows top patterns extracted from the training corpus.

- **Word2Vec pair features**: Some pair of words have the same context relationship that may reveal the meaning of discourse relation. Such as, *"find"* and *"know"* may reveal a *Contingency.Cause.Result* discourse relations. First, for each sense, we create a word pair list from word pairs of arguments of discourse relation of that sense in the training corpus that have the cosine similarity score using word2vec higher than a given threshold (we use threshold = 0.2). Then, for feature extraction step, we check whether or not a pair of word from argument exists in these lists.

- **Regular expressions**: We use patterns that catch the appearance of some useful expressions for sense classification such as "could", "would", "should", etc.

- **Other features**: Beside above features, we use some extra information such as the proportion of length of argument texts over the length of sentence, number of sentences that arguments of a discourse relations covers.

Table 3: Top frequent POS patterns in arguments of discourse relations training corpus

Pattern in ARG1	count	Pattern in ARG2	count
MD VB	4094	MD VB	4014
VBZ VBN	1982	VBZ VBN	2074
MD VB VBN	926	MD VB VBN	969
MD RB VB	912	MD RB VB	932
VBZ RB VBN	413	VBZ RB VBN	417
IN DT NN TO	307	IN DT NN TO	273
MD VB TO VB	294	MD VB TO VB	256
IN NN TO	272	IN NN TO	247
IN NNS TO	173	MD RB VB VBN	179
MD RB VB VBN	162	IN NNS TO	168

Although all above feature types have a somehow contribute for identifying senses of non-explicit discourse relations, sometimes it does not help algorithms to predict sense of explicit discourse relations. Therefore, beside connective words, a very strong features, we just use 3 more features including POS of connective words, POS-patterns, Regular expressions for sense classification of explicit discourse relations.

3 Experimental results

Table 4 shows the official results of our system on three given data sets. Due to the changes in the system architecture and more kinds of features, our system this year has a significant improvement in identifying discourse relations, especially explicit discourse relations. The results of recognizing explicit discourse relations are very competitive with top-rated systems last year. That means our discovery feature sets played an important role for the task of Shallow Discourse Parsing. Moreover, the result on the development data set are higher than blind and test data sets. With the support from connective words, the results of explicit discourse relations are better than non-explicit discourse relations. The results of recognizing non-explicit discourse relations are still low because we do not have effective features for this kind of discourse relations. Table 5 and Table 6 show the

Table 4: Official result of main task on development, test and blind data sets

	DEV dataset			TEST dataset			BLIND dataset		
	ALL	Exp.	Non Exp.	ALL	Exp.	Non Exp.	ALL	Exp.	Non Exp.
Arg1 extraction									
P	53.9	58.5	47.5	49.5	51.3	45.7	48.5	48.7	45.6
R	57.9	63.1	50.9	53.0	56.7	47.5	48.2	56.1	40.6
F1	55.8	60.7	49.1	51.2	53.8	46.6	48.3	52.2	43.0
Arg2 extraction									
P	61.7	69.7	54.5	58.7	68.4	49.9	61.7	65.5	58.5
R	66.3	75.1	58.4	62.9	75.6	52.0	61.3	75.4	52.0
F1	63.9	72.3	56.4	60.8	71.8	50.9	61.5	70.1	55.1
Arg 1 Arg2 extraction									
P	45.8	50.4	41.7	40.6	43.1	38.3	39.0	38.7	39.4
R	49.3	54.4	44.7	43.5	47.7	39.9	38.8	44.5	35.0
F1	47.5	52.3	43.1	42.0	45.3	39.1	38.9	41.4	37.1
Explicit connective									
P	85.0	85.0	-	83.4	83.4	-	79.5	79.5	-
R	91.6	91.6	-	92.2	92.2	-	91.5	91.5	-
F1	88.2	88.2	-	87.6	87.6	-	85.1	85.1	-
Parser									
P	30.6	48.1	15.1	25.5	41.4	11.9	20.3	33.2	11.9
R	28.8	45.4	14.2	23.9	37.5	11.5	20.4	28.8	13.3
F1	29.7	46.7	14.6	24.7	39.4	11.7	20.4	30.8	12.6

comparison of our system and 4-top-rated last year systems. On both of two these data sets, our results are not good at recognizing non-explicit discourse relations.

Moreover, there may have more than one explicit discourse relations in a pair of consecutive sentence but our current implementation just keeps only one and remove the others. Therefore, this may affects the performance of recognizing explicit connective words.

The result of supplement task are showed in Table 7. We have chosen Random Forest classifier for non-explicit discourse relations and SMO for explicit discourse relations because they achieved best results in the development data set. Table 8 shows the contribution of exploited feature sets. In non-explicit sense classification the result would improve significantly if we use these features.

Table 5: Result on test data set of our system and top-4 last year systems including **lan**: (Wang and Lan, 2015), **ste.** (Stepanov et al., 2015), **yo.** (Yoshida et al., 2015)

	System	lan	step.	yo.	xue	**Our system**
ALL	Arg 1 Arg2	49.4	40.7	43.8	30.2	42.0
	Arg1	60.1	47.8	52.5	37.8	51.2
	Arg2	72.5	60.7	64.4	46.5	60.8
	Connective	94.2	92.7	89.1	89.4	87.6
	Parser	29.7	25.4	25.0	21.8	24.7
Exp.	Arg 1 Arg2	45.2	44.6	38.8	41.6	45.3
	Arg1	50.7	50.1	46.1	49.8	53.8
	Arg2	77.3	76.2	68.3	68.6	71.8
	Connective	94.2	92.7	89.1	89.4	87.6
	Parser	40.0	39.6	34.5	37.6	39.4
Non-Expl	Arg 1 Arg2	53.0	37.3	48.8	19.4	39.1
	Arg1	67.1	44.4	57.9	24.7	46.6
	Arg2	68.3	47.4	60.1	25.3	50.9
	Parser	20.8	13.3	15.1	6.6	11.7

Table 6: Result on blind data set of our system and top-4 last year systems including **lan** , **ste.** (Stepanov et al., 2015), **li** (Kong et al., 2015), **minh** (Nguyen et al., 2015)

	System	lan	ste.	li	minh	**Our system**
ALL	Arg 1 Arg2	46.4	38.9	33.2	32.1	38.9
	Arg1	55.8	46.5	46.3	41.0	48.3
	Arg2	74.5	62.6	61.7	48.5	61.5
	Connective	91.9	89.9	91.6	61.7	85.1
	Parser	24.0	21.8	18.5	18.3	20.4
Exp.	Arg 1 Arg2	41.4	39.6	30.4	34.2	41.4
	Arg1	48.3	49.0	36.4	44.1	52.2
	Arg2	74.3	70.7	73.0	51.4	70.1
	Connective	91.9	89.9	91.6	61.7	85.1
	Parser	30.4	30.0	23.0	27.2	30.8
Non-Expl	Arg 1 Arg2	50.4	38.3	35.9	30.4	37.1
	Arg1	60.9	43.3	49.9	36.9	43.0
	Arg2	74.6	56.6	51.1	46.1	55.1
	Parser	18.9	15.8	14.4	11.3	12.6

Table 7: Result of sense classification task

	DEV dataset			**TEST dataset**			**BLIND dataset**		
	ALL	Exp.	Non-Exp.	ALL	Exp.	Non Ex.	ALL	Exp.	Non-Exp.
P	60.5	90.3	34.3	57.4	88.7	28.8	51.4	74.9	31.4
R	60.5	90.3	34.3	57.4	88.7	28.8	51.3	74.6	31.4
F1	60.5	90.3	34.3	57.4	88.7	28.8	51.3	74.8	31.4

Table 8: Comparison between feature sets in sense classification task

	Features	Random Forest	SMO
Non-Exp.	Similarity features	28.0	29.9
	All features mentioned above	36.5	30.3
Exp.	Connective words	89.4	89.4
	Connective words and their POS POS pattern of arguments, Regular expression and Others	87.1	90.3

4 Conclusion

Our approach has some positive points. It achieved a better result in comparison with our system last year. Moreover, compare to top-rated systems, the result of explicit discourse parsing is very competitive. This year we concentrated on solving both of explicit and non-explicit sense classification tasks. In non-explicit sense classification, it achieved some initial results.

There are a few things that can be improved in our system such as solving the problem that there may be more than one explicit discourse relations in pairs of consecutive sentences or finding effective features for implicit sense classifications.

Recognizing non-explicit discourse relations and explicit discourse relations whose arguments are not located in two adjacent sentences is still difficult for both identification of arguments and sense classification task. They are still a challenge for us at the moment. In the future, deep learning techniques may be promising approaches to achieve the better results.

Acknowledgment

This research is supported by JAIST Student Research Grants program.

References

Leo Breiman. 2001. Random forests. *Machine learning*, 45(1):5–32.

Fang Kong, Sheng Li, and Guodong Zhou. 2015. The sonlp-dp system in the conll-2015 shared task. In *Proceedings of the Nineteenth Conference on Computational Natural Language Learning - Shared Task*, pages 32–36, Beijing, China, July. Association for Computational Linguistics.

Taku Kudo. 2005. Crf++: Yet another crf toolkit. *Software available at http://crfpp. sourceforge. net*.

John Lafferty, Andrew McCallum, and Fernando CN Pereira. 2001. Conditional random fields: Probabilistic models for segmenting and labeling sequence data.

Son Nguyen, Quoc Ho, and Minh Nguyen. 2015. Jaist: A two-phase machine learning approach for identifying discourse relations in newswire texts. In *Proceedings of the Nineteenth Conference on Computational Natural Language Learning - Shared Task*, pages 66–70, Beijing, China, July. Association for Computational Linguistics.

John Platt. 1998. Sequential minimal optimization: A fast algorithm for training support vector machines. Technical Report MSR-TR-98-14, Microsoft Research, April.

Martin Potthast, Tim Gollub, Francisco Rangel, Paolo Rosso, Efstathios Stamatatos, and Benno Stein. 2014. Improving the Reproducibility of PAN's Shared Tasks: Plagiarism Detection, Author Identification, and Author Profiling. In Evangelos Kanoulas, Mihai Lupu, Paul Clough, Mark Sanderson, Mark Hall, Allan Hanbury, and Elaine Toms, editors, *Information Access Evaluation meets Multilinguality, Multimodality, and Visualization. 5th International Conference of the CLEF Initiative (CLEF 14)*, pages 268–299, Berlin Heidelberg New York, September. Springer.

Fabrizio Sebastiani. 2002. Machine learning in automated text categorization. *ACM computing surveys (CSUR)*, 34(1):1–47.

Evgeny Stepanov, Giuseppe Riccardi, and Ali Orkan Bayer. 2015. The unitn discourse parser in conll 2015 shared task: Token-level sequence labeling with argument-specific models. In *Proceedings of the Nineteenth Conference on Computational Natural Language Learning - Shared Task*, pages 25–31, Beijing, China, July. Association for Computational Linguistics.

Jianxiang Wang and Man Lan. 2015. A refined end-to-end discourse parser. In *Proceedings of the Nineteenth Conference on Computational Natural Language Learning - Shared Task*, pages 17–24, Beijing, China, July. Association for Computational Linguistics.

Theresa Wilson, Janyce Wiebe, and Paul Hoffmann. 2009. Recognizing contextual polarity: An exploration of features for phrase-level sentiment analysis. *Computational linguistics*, 35(3):399–433.

Nianwen Xue, Hwee Tou Ng, Sameer Pradhan, Rashmi Prasad, Christopher Bryant, and Attapol Rutherford. 2015. The conll-2015 shared task on shallow discourse parsing. In *Proceedings of the Nineteenth Conference on Computational Natural Language Learning - Shared Task*, pages 1–16, Beijing, China, July. Association for Computational Linguistics.

Nianwen Xue, Hwee Tou Ng, Sameer Pradhan, Bonnie Webber, Attapol Rutherford, Chuan Wang, and Hongmin Wang. 2016. The conll-2016 shared task on multilingual shallow discourse parsing. In *Proceedings of the Twentieth Conference on Computational Natural Language Learning - Shared Task*, Berlin, Germany, August. Association for Computational Linguistics.

Yasuhisa Yoshida, Katsuhiko Hayashi, Tsutomu Hirao, and Masaaki Nagata. 2015. Hybrid approach to pdtb-styled discourse parsing for conll-2015. In *Proceedings of the Nineteenth Conference on Computational Natural Language Learning - Shared Task*, pages 95–99, Beijing, China, July. Association for Computational Linguistics.

Finding Arguments as Sequence Labeling in Discourse Parsing

Ziwei Fan, Zhenghua Li,* Min Zhang
Soochow University, Suzhou, China
`fanniufen@gmail.com, {zhli13,minzhang}@suda.edu.cn`

Abstract

This paper describes our system for the CoNLL-2016 Shared Task on Shallow Discourse Parsing on English. We adopt a cascaded framework consisting of nine components, among which six are casted as sequence labeling tasks and the remaining three are treated as classification problems. All our sequence labeling and classification models are implemented based on linear models with averaged perceptron training. Our feature sets are mostly borrowed from previous works. The main focus of our effort is to recall cases when Arg1 locates at sentences far before the connective phrase, with some yet limited success.

1 General Description

This paper descirbes our participating system for CoNLL-2016 discourse parsing shared task (Xue et al., 2016). We participate in the closed track, and due to the time limitation, we focus on English. Given an document, which contains several paragraphs and each paragraph is composed of a few sentences, discourse parsing aims to identify explicit and non-explict discourse relations, including explicit connnective phrases (CP), explicit/non-explicit arguments and senses. Figure 1 presents a graphical illustration of the task.

Following the official requirement, we use Section 2-21 of the PDTB 2.0 (Prasad et al., 2008; Prasad et al., 2014) as the training data, Section 22 as the development data, and Section 23 as the test data. A blind test is also used for evaluation. Table 1 presents the data statistics.

Due to the complexity of the task, our system follows previous practice and employs a cas-

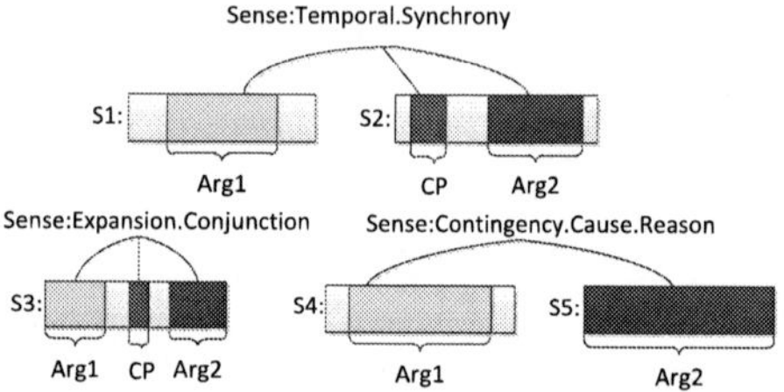

Figure 1: Illustration of discourse parsing.

	Train	Dev
Document	2000	100
Paragraph	17619	783
Sentence	38967	1675
Explicit relations	14722	680
Non-explicit relations	17813	756

Table 1: Data statistics of English.

caded framework and comprises 9 components, as shown in Figure 2. In the following, we will introduce each component in detail. The codes are released at `http://hlt.suda.edu.cn/~zhli` for future research study.

2 Classification and Sequence Labeling Based on Linear Model

In this work, we implement our classification and sequence labeling models based on linear model due to its simplicity and good performance on variety of natural language processing tasks (Collins, 2002). Given an input instance x and a label y, a linear model defines the score of labeling x as y:

$$Score(x, y) = \mathbf{w} \cdot \mathbf{f}(x, y)$$

*Correspondence author.

Proceedings of the 54th Annual Meeting of the Association for Computational Linguistics, pages 150–157,
Berlin, Germany, August 7-12, 2016. ©2016 Association for Computational Linguistics

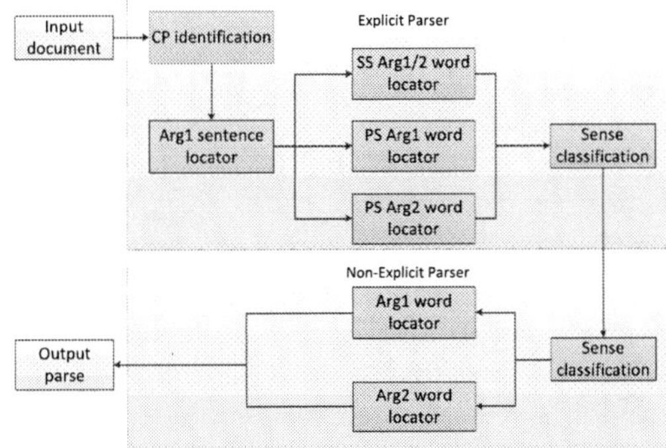

Figure 2: Framework of our system.

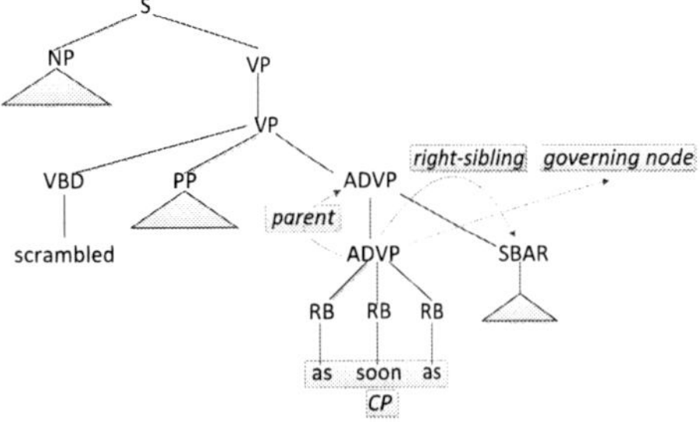

Figure 3: Example of a parse tree from which we extract features.

where $\mathbf{f}(.)$ is a feature vector constructed according to a hand-crafted feature template list and $\mathbf{w}$ is the corresponding feature weight vector.

The decoding task in the linear model is to find the maximum-scoring label:

$$\hat{y} = \arg\max_{y} Score(x, y)$$

To learn $\mathbf{w}$, we use the standard online training procedure, which use one instance for feature weight update at a time:

$$\mathbf{w}^{(t+1)} = \mathbf{w}^{(t)} + \mathbf{f}(x, y^*) - \mathbf{f}(x, \hat{y})$$

where t is the global time of feature weight updates (i.e., the number of instances used for feature weight updates so far); $\hat{y}$ is the best label according to the current feature weights $\mathbf{w}^{(t)}$; y^* is the gold-standard label. In this sense, online training is also known as decoding-based training, meaning that decoding is invoked during training.

Following Collins (2002), after training, we use the averaged feature weights $\sum_{t=1}^{T} \mathbf{w}^{(t)}/T$ for final evaluation, which is known as *averaged perceptron*.

For sequence labeling tasks, y is a sequence of labels instead of a single label. Besides many unigram features which only consider the label in the current position, as used in multi-class classification tasks, we also use label-transition bigram features in our sequence labeling models. The training procedure is nearly the same with the case of classification problems, except that a dynamic programming based decoding algorithm is need for exact search for the optimal label sequence $\hat{y}$.

3   CP Identification

Given an input document, the first task is to extract all connective phrases (CPs) (e.g., "so that") in the document,[1] which we refer to as *CP identification*. We directly adopt the method described in previous works (Wang and Lan, 2015; Kong et al., 2015), and take two steps for this task.

1. **Candidate CP extraction.** We extract all candidate CPs in the input document by exact matching with a phrase dictionary. If a string in a sentence exactly matchs a phrase in the dictionary, it then is considered as a candidate CP and will be verified in the second step. The dictionary is provided by the official organizer and contains 100 phrases.

2. **CP classification.** In this step, we use a statistical classifier based on the linear model to check whether each candidate CP functions as a CP or not.

We directly borrow and merge the features proposed in Lin et al. (2014) and Pitler and Nenkova (2009), as listed in Table 2. We spent little time on feature engineering, since we found our model achieved similar accuracy to last year's best system (Wang and Lan, 2015) using these features. On the dev data, our proposed CP identification method achieves 95.23% precison, 93.96% recall, and 94.59% F score. Figure 3 gives an example of the parse tree to better illustrate the features.

---

[1] Since a discourse connective may contain more than one words, we use "connective phrase" as a more accurate terminology in this paper.

| **Lexical:** $word(CP)$, $POS(CP)$, $POS(prev_1(CP))$, $POS(next_1(CP))$, |
| $word(prev_1(CP)) + word(CP)$, $POS(prev_1(CP)) + POS(CP)$, $POS(prev_1(CP)) + POS(first_1(CP))$, |
| $word(CP) + word(next_1(CP))$, $POS(CP) + POS(next_1(CP))$, $POS(last_1(CP)) + POS(next_1(CP))$ |
| **Syntactic:** $label(govern\_node(CP))$, $label(parent(govern\_node(CP)))$, |
| $label(l\_sib(govern\_node(CP)))$, $label(r\_sib(govern\_node(CP)))$, $path\_to\_root(govern\_node(CP))$, |

Table 2: Features for CP classification. $word(p)$: word sequence of the given phrase p; $POS(p)$: POS tag sequence of p; $prev_1(p)$: the first previous position of p; $next_1(p)$: the first next position of p; $first(p)$: the first position of p; $last(p)$: the last position of p; $govern\_node(p)$: the highest node in the parse tree that covers p; $parent(o)$: the parent node of the node o in the parse tree; $l\_sib(o)$: the left sibling node of o in the parse tree; $r\_sib(o)$: the right sibling node of o in the parse tree; $path\_to\_root(o)$: the label sequence along the path from the node o to the root node in the parse tree.

Distance	Train	Dev
0	8880	447
1	4047	162
2	560	18
3	244	11
4	131	6
5	79	9
≥ 6	202	7

Table 3: Distribution of instances in terms of distance between the sentence containing Arg1 and the sentence containing CP, where "0" means that Arg1 locates at the same sentence containing CP, "1" means that Arg1 is in the previous sentence of the sentence containing CP, and so on. We throw instances in which Arg1 or Arg2 locates at multiple sentences.

#Sentence	Train	Dev
1	14231 (0)	661 (0)
2	364 (44)	14 (1)
3	70 (18)	4 (2)
≥ 4	57(22)	1(1)

Table 4: Distribution of instances in terms of the number of sentences that one Arg1 locates at, where the numbers in parenthesis mean the case when the sentences are discontinuous.

4 Explicit-Arg1 Sentence Locator: Sequence Labeling

As far as we know, most previous participating systems last year assume that Arg1 lies in the same sentence or the previous sentence of CP. However, we find that there exist many cases that Arg1 locates at longer-distance sentences from the CP. Table 3 shows data statistics regarding the sentence-level distance of Arg1 and CP.

We also find that there are cases that Arg1 locates at more than one sentences, and the sentences may be discontinuous, as shown in Table 4. However, for simplicity, in this work we throw away training instances when Arg1 locates at more than one sentence.

For the Explicit-Arg1 sentence locator, we adopt a sequence labeling model and try to recall cases of long-distance Arg1. The model starts from the sentence containing CP (with an index 0),

and perform dynamic programming based search from right to left. For simplicity, we set the window size to 6, meaning that the model considers at most six sentences, from the 0th sentence containing CP, to the 5th sentence in front. For the features, we directly adopt those described in Lin et al. (2014), Pitler et al. (2009), Pitler and Nenkova (2009), and Knott (1996).

Especially, we design a three-tag label set in order to enforce the model to return exactly one sentence with Arg1.

1. *Arg1_yes*: the current sentence contains Arg1.

2. *None_yes*: the current sentence does not contain Arg1, but some sentence in its right does contain Arg1.

3. *None_no*: the current sentence and all sentences in its right do not contain Arg1.

Using such label set, we can conveniently constrain the model not to return a sequence where Arg1 occurs more than once by *constrained decoding*. The idea is that during decoding we do not allow a set of illegal transitions: {*Arg1_yes* $\rightarrow$ *Arg1_yes*, *Arg1_yes* $\rightarrow$ *None_no*, *None_yes* $\rightarrow$ *None_no*, *None_yes* $\rightarrow$ *Arg1_yes*}.

Label Set	Constrained	w/o Error Propagation Accuracy	Explicit, w/ Error Propagation			
			Arg1	Arg2	Arg1/2	Sense
3 tags	none	86.18	50.85	73.39	42.25	38.70
	test	**88.09**	**51.00**	**73.98**	**42.70**	**39.30**
	train & test	81.03	48.78	70.42	40.03	36.53
2 tags	none	85.74	51.15	73.68	42.70	39.15
PS/SS classification	none	**89.12**	**51.89**	**74.13**	**43.14**	**39.61**

Table 5: Results of different Explicit-Arg1 sentence locators on dev data.

Label Set	Constrained	Distance					
		0	1	2	3	4	5
3 tags	none	424 (424)	256 (**162**)	0	0	0	0
	test	458 (**445**)	222 (154)	0	0	0	0
	train & test	415 (409)	197 (131)	34 (**5**)	12 (**3**)	6 (0)	16 (**3**)
2 tags	none	497 (**444**)	182 (139)	1 (0)	0	0	0
PS/SS classification	none	445 (**444**)	235 (**162**)	–	–	–	–

Table 6: Result analysis of different Explicit-Arg1 sentence locators on dev data. We report the distribution of the outputs of each model in terms of distance between the predicted sentence containing Arg1 and the sentence with CP, where numbers in parenthesis count correct prediction according to gold-standard answers.

As discussed in Section 2, our model is based on a linear model and uses online training to learn the feature weights. Moreover, online training is a decoding-based training procedure, meaning that a best result is found by the decoding procedure based on the current feature weights, and the result is then used for weight update. Therefore, we have three options for applying constrained decoding.

1. **None**: We do not use any constraints and apply post-processing to handle inconsistent outputs. When the model classifies multiple sentence into *Arg1*, we only keep the nearest sentence tagged as *Arg1*. If no sentence is tagged as *Arg1*, we use the sentence containing CP as *Arg1*.

2. **Test**: We add constraints during the test phase. In the train phase, the optimal $\hat{y}$ is directly used for feature weight update without post-processing. However, we may also post-process $\hat{y}$ so that it contains exactly one Arg1 label before feature update weight during training, which we leave for future work.

3. **Train & test**: We add constraints during both train and test phases.

For comparison, we also implement a model based on a two-tag label set of {*Arg1*, *None*}, in which we cannot guarantee the output label sequence always contains only one *Arg1* through constrained decoding. Therefore, we post-process the results in the similar way to the case of the three-tag model with no constraint.

Table 5 reports the results both with and without error propagation. The "PS/SS classification" model is our re-implementation of the method described in Wang and Lan (2015) under our linear model framework with only unigram features, which only considers the current and previous sentences of CP with a binary classifier. The three-tag model performs best with "test" constraints, and surprisingly worse with "train & test" constraints. Even though the "PS/SS classification" model is very simple, it is very competitive and achieves better results on the dev data than our proposed three-tag sequence labeling model. We will look into this issue in future.

Table 6 further investigates the ability of different models on recalling cases when the sentence containing Arg1 locates far before the sentence containing CP. Although using "train & test" constraints leads to bad performance, we actually find that the model can actually recall cases when Arg1 locates at long-distance sentences, whereas the model with "test" constraints and the model with "none" constraints almost always return results that Arg1 locates at the sentence with CP or the previous sentence. We will look into this problem in future.

	True Positive	False Positive
Train	16940	4850
Dev	718	200

Table 7: Distribution of adjacent sentences having non-explicit relation.

5 Explicit-Arg1/2 Word Locator: Sequence Labeling

Data statistics show that for explicit relations, nearly all Arg2 locates at the the same sentence with CP. Therefore, based on the results of Arg1 sentence locator, we have two cases to handle: Arg1 and Arg2 locate at the same sentence with CP (SS), or Arg1 locates at a previous sentence of CP (PS). Then, we use three sequence labeling models to locate the exact words of Arg1/2. All three models perform at the level of words, and each time assign a *"Arg1/Arg2/None"* tag to a word.

Many systems in CoNLL-2015 (Xue et al., 2015) evaluation also treat Arg1/2 word location as a sequence labeling problem, and uses conditional random filed (CRF) based models (Stepanov et al., 2015; Nguyen et al., 2015; Lalitha Devi et al., 2015) or recurrent neural networks (RNN) (Wang et al., 2015).

5.1 Explicit: SS Arg1/2 Word Locator

For the SS case, the sequence labeling model performs decoding from left to right on the CP sentence, and classifies each word into four categories: *"Arg1/Arg2/None/CP"*. The words inside the CP (given as input) are fixed to be *"CP"* before decoding, and all other words are not allowed to be tagged as *"CP"* during decoding. For the features, we directly adopt those described in Lin et al. (2014), Pitler et al. (2009), Pitler and Nenkova (2009), Knott (1996), Kong et al. (2015). On the dev data, the model achieves an word-level accuracy of 53.45% without error propagation.

5.2 Explicit: PS Arg1 Word locator

For the PS case, we first use a sequence labeling model to locate the words of Arg1. The model perform decoding from left to right on the sentence returned by the Explicit-Arg1 sentence locator, and classifies each word into two categories: *"Arg1/None"*. For the features, we directly adopt those described in Lin et al. (2014), Pitler et al. (2009), Knott (1996). On the dev data, the model achieves an word-level accuracy of 67.14% without error propagation.

5.3 Explicit: PS Arg2 Word Locator

To locate the Arg2 words in the PS case, we use a sequence labeling model to perform decoding from left to right on the CP sentence, and classifies each word into two categories: *"Arg2/None"*. Please note that the words in CP always have a special tag "CP" when decoding. For the features, we directly adopt those described in Lin et al. (2014), Pitler et al. (2009), Wang and Lan (2015), Kong et al. (2015), Knott (1996). On the dev data, the model achieves an word-level accuracy of 67.14% without error propagation.

6 Explicit Sense Classification

After obtaining the CP and the Arg1/2 words, we then use a linear model based classifier to classify the sense of each explicit relation. We directly adopt the features described in Lin et al. (2014). On the dev data, the model achieves an accuracy of 87.65% without error propagation.

7 Non-explicit Sense Classification

After processing the explicit relations, we then turn to the problem of non-explicit relation parsing. As suggested by the official organizer, if two adjacent sentences do not have explicit relation after previous processing, we consider them as a candidate sentence pair having non-explicit relation. Please note that we only consider sentence pairs that are in the same paragraph.

As far as we know, most previous work directly considers all adjacent sentences without explicit relation as having non-explicit relation, and use a classifier to predict their non-explicit senses. However, our data statistics in Table 7 show that there exist many false non-explicit cases, which we call negative instances. We add a special tag *"None"* into the non-explicit sense set and use such false non-explicit cases as negative training instances , so that the trained classifier can make not-a-non-explicit-relation decision. However, our preliminary results show that adding negative instances does not improve parser performance on

Component	Dev			Test			Blind test		
	P	R	F	P	R	F	P	R	F
All Arg1 extractor	57.31	62.40	59.75	53.43	56.86	55.09	41.85	53.89	47.11
All Arg2 extractor	70.06	76.27	73.03	67.30	71.62	69.40	57.73	74.33	64.99
All Arg1&Arg2 extractor	47.84	52.08	49.87	42.75	45.50	44.08	33.66	43.34	37.90
All Sense	32.72	30.47	**31.56**	27.47	25.84	**26.63**	24.49	18.94	**21.36**
Explicit Connectives	93.53	95.07	94.29	94.69	94.79	94.74	89.57	92.57	91.04
Explicit Arg1 extractor	50.59	51.42	51.00	44.96	45.01	44.99	41.19	42.57	41.86
Explicit Arg2 extractor	73.38	74.59	73.98	72.05	72.13	72.09	68.71	71.00	69.84
Explicit Arg1&Arg2 extractor	42.35	43.05	42.70	37.38	37.42	37.40	32.91	34.01	33.46
Explicit Sense	39.16	39.45	39.30	32.97	32.97	32.97	27.99	26.98	27.47
Non-Explicit Arg1 extractor	62.17	72.31	66.86	59.74	67.44	63.36	41.81	68.08	51.80
Non-Explicit Arg2 extractor	67.06	78.00	72.12	62.99	71.11	66.81	48.39	78.80	59.96
Non-Explicit Arg1&Arg2 extractor	52.78	61.38	56.76	47.64	53.78	50.52	34.30	55.86	42.50
Non-Explicit Sense	26.12	22.56	24.21	21.83	19.35	20.51	19.95	12.10	15.06

Table 8: Official results of our system on the dev, test, and blind test datasets. "All" means both explicit and non-explicit relations.

the dev data. We will look into this problem in future.

For the features, we directly adopt those described in Lin et al. (2014), Pitler et al. (2009), Rutherford and Xue (2014), Kong et al. (2015). On the dev data, the model achieves an accuracy of 34.04% without error propagation.

8 Non-explicit Arg1/2 Word Locator: Sequence Labeling

According to data statistics, if two adjacent sentences have non-explicit relation, Arg1 locates at the first sentence while Arg2 locates at the second sentence. Therefore, we use two separate sequence labeling models to locate Arg1/2 words in the two sentences respectively. If the non-explicit sense is "*EntRel*", we directly label the whole first sentence as Arg1 and the whole second sentence as Arg2, according to data statistics. For the features, we directly adopt those described in Lin et al. (2014), Pitler et al. (2009), Wang and Lan (2015), Kong et al. (2015). On the dev data, the two models achieve word-level accuracy of 68.14% on Arg1 and 75.82% on Arg2 without error propagation.

9 Final Results

Table 8 shows the official results of our system on the dev, test and blind test datasets from the organizers through the TIRA platform (Potthast et al., 2014). Our system ranks the 7th place among 14

	Linear	Maximum Entropy
Explicit Sense	39.30	44.60 (+5.30)
All Sense	31.56	32.81 (+1.25)

Table 9: Comparison of the linear model and the maximum entropy model on Explicit relations with error propagation on dev data.

systems in both test and blind test datasets in the closed track of CoNLL-2016 shared task on shallow discourse parsing of English.

10 Explicit Sense Classification with a Maximum Entropy Model

After obtaining the evaluation results of all systems, we find that our system achieves clearly lower performances on sense classifications than other systems. Therefore, we replace the linear classification model with a log-linear maximum entropy model in the Explicit sense classification task. We use AdaGrad for deciding the feature update step (Duchi et al., 2011). Table 9 shows the results. We can see that using maximum entropy leads to large improvement.

We then try to replace the linear model with the maximum entropy model in the CP classification task, but obtain very little gain, possibly because the accuracy is already very high with the linear model. We plan to use the maximum entropy model for non-explicit sense classification.

11 Conclusions and Future Work

So far, our approach is composed of too many components without any interaction. In the future, we would like to pursue two directions. First, we will try to design a more principled and unified framework so that tasks at different levels can influence each other. Second, we plan to try other machine learning techniques such as neural networks for better representing and modeling discourse-level information.

Acknowledgments

The authors would like to thank the anonymous reviewers for the helpful comments. In building our system, we use a lot of codes of two participating teams last year, and we are very grateful for their kind sharing (Kong et al., 2015; Wang and Lan, 2015). We also would like to thank the organizer of this shared task for their hard work, especially in data annotation and preparation. This work was supported by National Natural Science Foundation of China (Grant No. 61502325, 61525205), and the Natural Science Foundation of the Jiangsu Higher Education Institutions of China (No. 15KJB520031).

References

Michael Collins. 2002. Discriminative training methods for hidden markov models: Theory and experiments with perceptron algorithms. In *Proceedings of EMNLP 2002*, pages 1–8.

John Duchi, Elad Hazan, and Yoram Singer. 2011. Adaptive subgradient methods for online learning and stochastic optimization. *Journal of Machine Learning Research*, 12(Jul):2121–2159.

Alistair Knott. 1996. A data-driven methodology for motivating a set of coherence relations.

Fang Kong, Sheng Li, and Guodong Zhou. 2015. The sonlp-dp system in the conll-2015 shared task. In *Proceedings of the Nineteenth Conference on Computational Natural Language Learning - Shared Task*, pages 32–36, Beijing, China, July. Association for Computational Linguistics.

Sobha Lalitha Devi, Sindhuja Gopalan, Lakshmi S, Pattabhi RK Rao, Vijay Sundar Ram, and Malarkodi C.S. 2015. A hybrid discourse relation parser in conll 2015. In *Proceedings of the Nineteenth Conference on Computational Natural Language Learning - Shared Task*, pages 50–55, Beijing, China, July. Association for Computational Linguistics.

Ziheng Lin, Hwee Tou Ng, and Min-Yen Kan. 2014. A pdtb-styled end-to-end discourse parser. *Natural Language Engineering*, 20(02):151–184.

Son Nguyen, Quoc Ho, and Minh Nguyen. 2015. Jaist: A two-phase machine learning approach for identifying discourse relations in newswire texts. In *Proceedings of the Nineteenth Conference on Computational Natural Language Learning - Shared Task*, pages 66–70, Beijing, China, July. Association for Computational Linguistics.

Emily Pitler and Ani Nenkova. 2009. Using syntax to disambiguate explicit discourse connectives in text. In *Proceedings of the ACL-IJCNLP 2009 Conference Short Papers*, pages 13–16. Association for Computational Linguistics.

Emily Pitler, Annie Louis, and Ani Nenkova. 2009. Automatic sense prediction for implicit discourse relations in text. In *Proceedings of the Joint Conference of the 47th Annual Meeting of the ACL and the 4th International Joint Conference on Natural Language Processing of the AFNLP: Volume 2-Volume 2*, pages 683–691. Association for Computational Linguistics.

Martin Potthast, Tim Gollub, Francisco Rangel, Paolo Rosso, Efstathios Stamatatos, and Benno Stein. 2014. Improving the Reproducibility of PAN's Shared Tasks: Plagiarism Detection, Author Identification, and Author Profiling. In Evangelos Kanoulas, Mihai Lupu, Paul Clough, Mark Sanderson, Mark Hall, Allan Hanbury, and Elaine Toms, editors, *Information Access Evaluation meets Multilinguality, Multimodality, and Visualization. 5th International Conference of the CLEF Initiative (CLEF 14)*, pages 268–299.

Rashmi Prasad, Nikhil Dinesh, Alan Lee, Eleni Miltsakaki, Livio Robaldo, Aravind K Joshi, and Bonnie L Webber. 2008. The penn discourse treebank 2.0. In *LREC*. Citeseer.

Rashmi Prasad, Bonnie Webber, and Aravind Joshi. 2014. Reflections on the penn discourse treebank, comparable corpora, and complementary annotation. *Computational Linguistics*.

Attapol Rutherford and Nianwen Xue. 2014. Discovering implicit discourse relations through brown cluster pair representation and coreference patterns. In *EACL*, volume 645, page 2014.

Evgeny Stepanov, Giuseppe Riccardi, and Ali Orkan Bayer. 2015. The UniTN discourse parser in conll 2015 shared task: Token-level sequence labeling with argument-specific models. In *Proceedings of the Nineteenth Conference on Computational Natural Language Learning - Shared Task*, pages 25–31, Beijing, China, July. Association for Computational Linguistics.

Jianxiang Wang and Man Lan. 2015. A refined end-to-end discourse parser. In *Proceedings of the Nine-*

teenth Conference on Computational Natural Language Learning - Shared Task, pages 17–24, Beijing, China, July. Association for Computational Linguistics.

Longyue Wang, Chris Hokamp, Tsuyoshi Okita, Xiaojun Zhang, and Qun Liu. 2015. The dcu discourse parser for connective, argument identification and explicit sense classification. In *Proceedings of the Nineteenth Conference on Computational Natural Language Learning - Shared Task*, pages 89–94, Beijing, China, July. Association for Computational Linguistics.

Nianwen Xue, Hwee Tou Ng, Sameer Pradhan, Rashmi Prasad, Christopher Bryant, and Attapol Rutherford. 2015. The conll-2015 shared task on shallow discourse parsing. In *Proceedings of the Nineteenth Conference on Computational Natural Language Learning - Shared Task*, pages 1–16, Beijing, China, July. Association for Computational Linguistics.

Nianwen Xue, Hwee Tou Ng, Sameer Pradhan, Bonnie Webber, Attapol Rutherford, Chuan Wang, and Hongmin Wang. 2016. The conll-2016 shared task on multilingual shallow discourse parsing. In *Proceedings of the Twentieth Conference on Computational Natural Language Learning - Shared Task*, Berlin, Germany, August. Association for Computational Linguistics.

Discourse Relation Sense Classification Systems for CoNLL-2016 Shared Task

Ping Jian, Xiaohan She, Chenwei Zhang, Pengcheng Zhang, Jian Feng
School of Computer Science and Technology, Beijing Institute of Technology
`pjian,xhshe,zcwhzy,pengchengzhang,zzhy@bit.edu.cn`

Abstract

This paper reports the submitted discourse relation classification systems of the language information processing group of Beijing Institute of Technology (BIT) to the CoNLL-2016 shared task. In this work, discriminative methods were employed according to the different characteristics of English and Chinese discourse structures. Additionally, distributed representations were introduced to catch the deep semantic relations. Experiments shows their effectiveness on both English and Chinese tasks.

1. Introduction

In natural language processing (NLP), discourse parsing is the process of understanding the internal structure of a text and identifying the discourse relations in between its text unites (Lin et al., 2014). It is a recognized challenging task since deep semantic understanding and discourse wide global information even world knowledge are essential to achieve well acceptable solutions. According to alternative discourse structure theoretical frameworks, RST-DT Corpus (Carlson et al., 2003) provides the possibility of data-driven modeling for complete tree structure while PDTB (Prasad et al., 2008) offers a framework to predicting shallow discourse structures statistically in a "predicate-argument" style. Compared with RST-DT, PDTB is larger, so it draws more attentions in these years to support discourse parsing model verification.

In this situation, CoNLL launched Shallow Discourse Parsing Shared Task in the year 2015[1] and called for PDTB-styled individual discourse relations that are presented in a free text under an end-to-end paradigm (Xue et al., 2015). According to the annotation framework of PDTB, relations held between arguments can be either explicit or non-explicit. Non-explicit relations are further divided into implicit, EntRel and AltLex ones (Prasad et al., 2008). In CoNLL-2015 Shared Task, the PDTB senses were regularized into more reasonable 15 categories to facilitate machine learning (Xue et al., 2015). Participants were required to run their systems on a web-based evaluation platform and the systems should (1) locate the explicit discourse connectives (e.g., "because", "however") in the text, (2) identify the spans of text that serve as the two arguments for each discourse connective, and (3) predict the sense of the discourse relations (e.g., "Cause", "Condition", "Contrast").

This is the 2nd edition of the CoNLL Shared Task on Shallow Discourse Parsing this year. Besides the English PDTB-styled end-to-end paradigm, PDTB-styled Chinese end-to-end parsing is also involved (Xue et al., 2016). It is attributed to the annotation of discourse structures in Chinese texts, a PDTB-styled Chinese discourse Treebank (CDTB) (Zhou and Xue, 2012). Based on the adapted PDTB annotation scheme, discourse structures in CDTB own the same "predicate-argument" pattern and similar sense hierarchy.

The same as English discourse parsing, the CDTB sense in CoNLL-2016 Shared Task is also transferred. 8 categories for explicit and non-explicit relations are refactored: "Causation", "Conditional", "Conjunction", "Contrast", "Expansion", "Purpose", "Temporal" and "Progression".

In addition to the Chinese discourse parsing, CoNLL-2016 Shared Task also allows participants to do the supplementary task which is sense classification using gold standard argument pairs both in English and Chinese. It is proved that implicit sense discrimination is the most difficult subtask in discourse parsing, not only as an individual task but also as a key component in pipeline end-to-end system (Hong et al., 2012; Lin et al., 2014). Implicit discourse relation is also the most attended issue at the

---

[1] http://www.cs.brandeis.edu/~clp/conll15st/

Proceedings of the 54th Annual Meeting of the Association for Computational Linguistics, pages 158–163,
Berlin, Germany, August 7-12, 2016. ©2016 Association for Computational Linguistics

beginning of the release of PDTB (Pitler et al., 2008; Lin et al., 2009; Zhou et al., 2010; Prasad et al., 2010).

Due to the lack of effective structural semantic representation model, discourse relation sense disambiguation, which is a deep semantic analysis problem, is always conducted by modeling large scale shallow linguistic features. We can see that the named efficient features such as lexical and syntactic features (word co-occurrences, function words, phrase or dependency parses), partial shallow semantic features (co-reference patterns, semantic attribute of words, e.g., polarity) and a few dynamic features are adopted in existing works (Marcu and Echihabi, 2002; Pitler et al., 2008; Lin et al., 2009; Zhou et al., 2010; Prasad et al., 2010; Feng and Hirst, 2012; Rutherford and Xue, 2014). In response to the data scarcity problem, semi-supervised and unsupervised methods are explored for implicit relations inference in recent years (Hernault et al., 2011; Hong et al., 2012; Lan et al., 2013; Fisher and Simmons, 2015). Experiments demonstrate that these kinds of methods can acquire more stable statistical distribution via large scale unlabeled corpus hence achieve higher classification accuracy.

In this Shared Task, we focus on the supplementary task and submit both the English and Chinese discourse relation sense classification systems. According to the different characteristics of English and Chinese discourse structures, we examine rule-based and statistical discriminative classification approaches, conventional and distributed semantic representation models, as well as the expressiveness of extra resources.

The organization of this work is as follows. Section 2 presents our explicit relation classifiers. Section 3 gives the description of the non-explicit relation classification models in our system. Section 4 reports the preliminary experimental results on the training and development dataset, and the final results on two test datasets. Conclusions are provided in Section 5.

2. Explicit Discourse Relation Sense Classification

The explicit discourse relation refers to the relationship between two elementary discourse units which are connected by a discourse connective. As pointed in (Dinesh et al., 2005), the connective itself is a very good feature for sense discrimination, because only a few connectives are

Num. of different senses	Ratio of connectives	Frequency	Ratio of frequency
1	30%	623	3.4%
2	17%	1214	6.6%
3	14%	1025	5.6%
4	5%	1799	9.6%
more than 4	34%	13783	74.8%

Table 1: Distributions of the connectives and relation senses in the training set from PDTB

Num. of different senses	Ratio of connectives	Frequency	Ratio of frequency
1	64.9%	5525	66.6%
2	18.6%	1997	25.4%
3	12.4%	594	7.6%
4	4.1%	32	0.4%
more than 4	0%	0	0%

Table 2: Distributions of the connectives and relation senses in the training set from CDTB

ambiguous. In CDTB, this phenomenon is more common.

Table 1 and Table 2 show the distributions of the connectives and the relation senses they acting in the PDTB training set and CDTB training set respectively. In training set extracted from PDTB, 30% connectives act as unique sense and these connectives appear 623 times totally in the set, which occupy only 3.4% in all of the tokens. Whereas, there are 64.9% connectives express unique sense in Chinese texts and their frequency achieves 2/3. On the whole, we can see that more than 92% connective tokens correspond to less than 3 relation senses in CDTB. On the contrary, nearly 85% connective tokens correspond to more than 3 relation senses in PDTB.

We further check the different senses' distribution of ambiguous connectives. There are 85% ambiguous connectives in Chinese texts tend to express one sense, and the reliability of this tendency is 90%. For example, the connective "不过" acts as two senses in the training set: "Contrast" and "Expansion". But the number of "Contrast" samples is 430 while "Expansion" appears only 10 times.

In a word, compared with English, Chinese connectives present less sense perplexity when forming the discourse structures.

2.1 Explicit Relation Classification for English

We employ a SVM classifier to predict the sense of connectives in English task. Following the work of Lin et al. (2014), three features are introduced to train the classifier: the connective itself, its POS tag and the previous word.

Connective	Sense
不过	Contrast
并	Conjunction
但是	Contrast
…	…
通过	Causation

Table 3: Part of the connective-sense table used in Chinese connective sense classification

2.2 Explicit Relation Classification for Chinese

According to the analyses on the sense distribution of Chinese connectives, we prefer rule-based method to conduct explicit relation classification on CDTB.

We calculate the probability distribution of the discourse relation for each connective:

$$p(s_j|c_i) = \frac{\text{num}(s_j, c_i)}{\sum_{s \in S} \text{num}(s, c_i)}$$

where $\text{num}(s_j, c_i)$ is the number of connective c_i acting as sense s_j. Connectives are classified to the sense who has the maximum probability $p(s_j|c_i)$ in the test set. It is safe in most cases because the majority of Chinese connectives tend to express unique relations sense. Table 3 shows a part of our connective-sense table.

As no extra resources were employed in above models, our explicit classification systems were conducted in the closed track.

3. Non-explicit Discourse Relation Sense Classification

The non-explicit discourse relation refers to the relationship expressed implicitly, lexicalized or entity-based inferred between abstract object units[2]. As a typical classification problem, we build a SVM classifier to predict the senses and put attentions on more efficient feature representations.

We employ three primary features which perform well in our preliminary study:

Polarity Tags: Polarity is always a useful feature when processing semantic problems. We count the number of positive, negative and neutral words in the given abstract units (which are called Arg1 and Arg2 in the following) as an intuitional feature for non-explicit relation disambiguation. All of content words' polarity is

derived from Multi-perspective Question Answering Opinion Corpus (Wilson et al., 2005) in English, and HowNet[3] in Chinese.

Inquirer Tags: Verb is one of the most important components bearing the semantic information of a sentence. The General Inquirer lexicon (Stone et al., 1966) provides semantic categories of verbs and we sum the Inquirer tags of verbs appeared in Arg1 and Arg2 of English sentences. We prefer the General Inquirer lexicon rather than the provided VerbNet because the former has much more information when dealing with synsets.

Word Pairs: Extracting words respectively from Arg1 and Arg2 has been proved to be helpful for implicit discourse relation prediction (Pitler et al., 2009). But there is still disagreement on the use of the function words. Due to probable data sparseness, we ignore all of function words in both arguments and focus on only content words in our systems. Also as a way to release the sparseness, we use information gain to reduce the dimension of word pairs and keep more discriminative ones.

3.1 Distributed Representation in Implicit Relation Classification

To enhance the semantically expressing power of lexical features, distributed representation is introduced into our implicit relation prediction in different ways.

Simple Embedding: We generate embedding for each word pair by catenating the embedding of its member words one by one. The average of those word-pairs' embedding is brought to replace the one-hot representation of the word pair in the classification.

Huffman Tree-based Prediction: As one of the significant optimization methods in word embedding, hierarchical softmax (Mikolov et al., 2013) predicts the most probable word to co-occur with the corresponding context. All words appeared in the training set are stored in a Huffman tree, organized by word frequency. The Huffman tree which is demonstrated to take efficiency and overfitting issue into account is expected to be a more advanced structure to incorporate distributed representations. Furthermore, the Huffman tree takes the prior probabilities of the connective candidates into account via locating them at the different positions (depths) in the tree. It is expected to achieve better performance than simple embedding and SVM

---

[2] Because the EntRel and AltLex relations are incorporated into the implicit ones to induce an integrated disambiguation, we call all of them "implicit relations" in the following sections for simplicity.

[3] http://www.keenage.com/

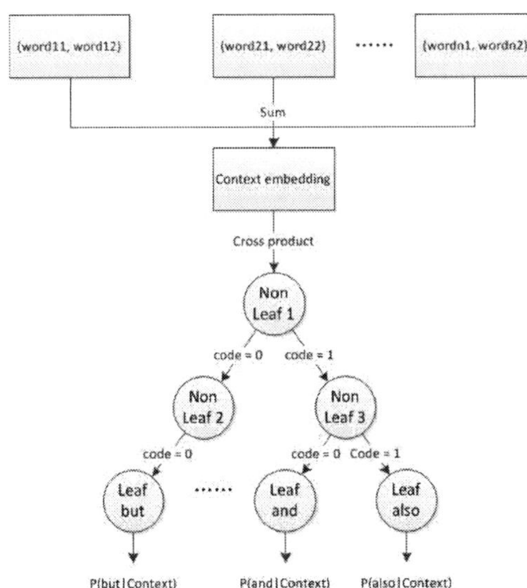

Figure 1: Huffman Tree-based prediction for implicit connectives

classifiers.

The original objective function in Huffman tree prediction is to calculate words' probability when the corresponding context is given. We set the context as content word pairs extracted from the arguments, and all of implicit discourse connectives are going to be predicted. The prediction process is illustrated in Figure 1.

In the Huffman Tree-based prediction, word pair vectors are summed to make context embedding. The posterior probability of each connective[4] predicted is put together to build a new feature for the SVM classifier.

We utilize a larger scale corpus "Central News Agency of Taiwan, English Service"[5] (CNA) to train the Huffman tree. All the explicit discourse relations are extracted from the corpus by pattern matching (Marcu and Echihabi, 2002) and the explicit connectives are dropped to make "pseudo-implicit" training samples.

3.2 Implicit Relation Classification models for English and Chinese

Including the conditional classification with one-hot representation, we build up three comparative models for English implicit relation task (Table 4) and two for Chinese task (Table 5). Since the inconsistency between the distributions of the "pseudo-implicit" and real implicit

Learning method	Resources	Extra resources
SVM with One-Hot features	MPQA	General Inquirer lexicon
SVM with Simple Embedding	MPQA, word embeddings	General Inquirer lexicon
SVM with Simple Embedding+Huff. Tree Prediction	*MPQA, word embeddings*	*General Inquirer lexicon, CNA*

Table 4: Comparative models for English implicit relation prediction. The submitted model is in italic.

Learning method	Resources	Extra resources
SVM with One-Hot features	No	HowNet
SVM with Simple Embedding	*Word embeddings*	*HowHet*

Table 5: Comparative models for Chinese implicit relation prediction. The submitted model is in italic.

instances is more serious in Chinese, Huffman Tree-based Prediction is not conducted for Chinese task.

As the sparseness of word pairs is more severe in Chinese situation, a strategy of **Word Pairs Fuzzy Matching** is proposed: Based on the word embedding library, some word similarity groups are formed to ensure that the majority of arguments to be disambiguated contain discriminative word pairs.

4. Experiments

The same as the CoNLL-2015's task, participants are required to deploy their systems on the provided platform instead of submitting the output. The organizer also offers potentially useful linguistic resources for the closed track. In this section, the experimental results are presented and the experimental analyses are induced. All the systems are evaluated on TIRA evaluation platform (Potthast et al., 2014).

4.1 Explicit Relation Classification Experiments

Table 6 presents the English connective sense classification results conducted by SVM classifier. All the SVM classifiers utilized in our experiments were implemented by the LibSVM[6].

Unfortunately, we submitted a wrong edition of our system during the competition for technical reasons and the official outputs produced by this edition are also listed in Table 6 (*System submitted*).

Sense classification results for Chinese connectives are displayed in Table 7. For compari-

---

[4] For the sparseness issue, implicit connectives which appear more than 1% of all the implicit relation instances are considered and the dimension of the feature vector is 19 in our model.

[5] https://catalog.ldc.upenn.edu/LDC2011T07

[6] http://www.csie.ntu.edu.tw/~cjlin/libsvm/index.html

Method	Dev			Test			Blind test		
	P	**R**	**F1**	**P**	**R**	**F1**	**P**	**R**	**F1**
SVM classification	**89.89**	**62.06**	**73.43**	**87.10**	**53.47**	**66.26**	**75.44**	**61.87**	**67.98**
System submitted	*23.22*	*23.22*	*23.22*	*24.62*	*24.62*	*24.62*	*17.99*	*17.99*	*17.99*

Table 6: Explicit connective sense classification results for English. The system submitted is in italic.

Method	Dev			Test			Blind test		
	P	**R**	**F1**	**P**	**R**	**F1**	**P**	**R**	**F1**
Rule-based	*92.21*	*92.21*	*92.21*	*94.74*	*93.75*	*94.24*	*75.27*	*75.27*	*75.27*
SVM classification	71.43	71.43	71.43	79.17	79.17	79.17	45.94	45.94	45.94

Table 7: Explicit connective sense classification results for Chinese. The system submitted is in italic.

Method	Dev			Test			Blind test		
	P	**R**	**F1**	**P**	**R**	**F1**	**P**	**R**	**F1**
SVM with One-Hot features	16.56	16.56	16.56	15.89	15.89	15.89	18.22	18.22	18.22
SVM with Simple Embedding	17.09	17.09	17.09	16.39	16.39	16.39	18.99	18.99	18.99
SVM with Simple Embedding +Huff. Tree Prediction	*17.36*	*17.36*	*17.36*	*16.58*	*16.58*	*16.58*	*19.30*	*19.30*	*19.30*

Table 8: Implicit relation sense classification results for English. The system submitted is in italic.

Method	Dev			Test			Blind test		
	P	**R**	**F1**	**P**	**R**	**F1**	**P**	**R**	**F1**
SVM with One-Hot features	15.69	15.69	15.69	11.42	11.42	11.42	16.29	16.29	16.29
SVM with Simple Embedding	*21.90*	*21.90*	*21.90*	*21.73*	*21.73*	*21.73*	*18.11*	*18.11*	*18.11*

Table 9 Implicit relation sense classification results for Chinese. The system submitted is in italic.

son, we also conducted a typical SVM classifier in which two features are applied: the connective itself and its POS tag. Since the Chinese training data is much smaller and there are too many low-frequency connectives involved, only the connectives which appear more than 10 times are considered in the experiment. Because of the serious imbalance and small quantity of training samples, the SVM classifier gets a poor classification precisions. Whereas, the rule-based approach performs soundly and achieves acceptable results. It is simple, crude but practically effective in Chinese explicit relation classification.

4.2 Implicit Relation Classification Experiments

The implicit relation sense classification results for English and Chinese are listed in Table 8 and Table 9 respectively.

As we can see, although the overall performance of English system is not good enough, the results of Simple Embedding and Huffman Tree-based Prediction are always better than the One-Hot paradigm. The Huffman Tree Prediction outperforms the Simple Embedding slightly mainly because the training samples from CNA are seriously imbalance. A finer sifted corpus will be introduced in the future work to improve this work.

In Chinese experiments, the Simple Embedding with Word Pairs Fuzzy Matching gains significant improvement compared with the One-Hot paradigm, which means that the sparseness of word pairs is alleviated effectively.

5. Conclusion

In this paper we report our English and Chinese discourse relation classification systems which handle explicit and non-explicit relations separately. It is showed that the discourse devices usages and the patterns of the discourse organization are quite different from Chinese to English. Adaptations are required to access better performance when transfer typical methods designed for English to Chinese texts.

Implicit relation disambiguation is still the most challenge task in discourse analysis. Distributed representation is an effective manner to release the data sparseness and explores relatively deep semantics. However, delicate semantic models such as structural semantic models are still remain to be explored to capture the real deep semantics of the texts for more meaningful conclusions.

Acknowledgement

The authors would like to thank the organizers of CoNLL-2016 and the reviewers for their helpful suggestions. This research is supported by the National Natural Science Foundation of China (61202244, 61502259) and the National Basic Re-search Program of China (973 Program, 2013CB329303).

References

Lynn Carlson, Daniel Marcu, and Mary E. Okurowski. 2003. Building a discourse-tagged corpus in the framework of Rhetorical Structure Theory. In *Current Directions in Discourse and Dialogue*, pages 85-112.

Nikhil Dinesh, Alan Lee, Eleni Miltsakaki, Rashmi Prasad, Aravind Joshi, and Bonnie Webber. 2005. Attribution and the (non)-alignment of syntactic and discourse arguments of connectives. In *Proceedings of the ACL Workshop in Frontiers in Corpus Annotation*, pages 29-36.

Vanessa W. Feng and Graeme Hirst. 2012. Textlevel discourse parsing with rich linguistic features. In *Proceedings of ACL*, pages 60-68.

Robert Fisher and Reid Simmons. 2015. Spectral semi-supervised discourse relation classification. In *Proceedings of ACL-IJCNLP (Short Papers)*, pages 89-93.

Hugo Hernault, Danushka Bollegala, and Mitsuru Ishizuka. 2011. Semi-supervised discourse relation classification with structural learning. In *Proceedings of Computational Linguistics and Intelligent Text (CICLing)*, pages 340-352.

Yu Hong, Xiaopei Zhou, Tingting Che, Jianmin Yao, Guodong Zhou, and Qiaoming Zhu. 2012. Cross-Argument Inference for Implicit Discourse Relation Recognition. In *Proceedings of CIKM*, pages 295-304.

Man Lan, Yu Xu, and Zheng-Yu Niu. 2013. Leveraging synthetic discourse data via multi-task learning for implicit discourse relation recognition. In *Proceedings of ACL*, pages 476-485.

Ziheng Lin, Min-Yen Kan, and Hwee T. Ng. 2009. Recognizing implicit discourse relations in the penn discourse treebank. In *Proceedings of EMNLP*, pages 343-351.

Ziheng Lin, Hwee T. Ng and Min-Yen Kan. 2014. A PDTB-Styled End-to-End Discourse Parser. *Natural Language Engineering*, 20(2): 151-184.

Daniel Marcu and Abdessamad Echihabi. 2002. An unsupervised approach to recognizing discourse relations. In *Proceedings of ACL*, pages 368-375.

Tomas Mikolov, Ilya Sutskever, Kai Chen, Greg S Corrado, and Jeff Dean. 2013. Distributed representations of words and phrases and their compositionality. *Advances in neural information processing systems*, page 3111--3119.

Joonsuk Park and Claire Cardie. 2012. Improving implicit discourse relation recognition through feature set optimization. In *Proceedings of the 13th Annual Meeting of the Special Interest Group on Discourse and Dialogue*, pages 108-112.

Emily Pitler, Annie Louis, and Ani Nenkova. 2009. Automatic sense prediction for implicit discourse relations in text. In *Proceedings of ACL-IJCNLP*, pages 683-691.

Emily Pitler, Mridhula Raghupathy, Hena Mehta, Ani Nenkova, Alan Lee, and Aravind Joshi. 2008. Easily identifiable discourse relations. In *Proceedings of Coling, Companion volume - Posters and Demonstrations*, pages 87-90.

Martin Potthast, Tim Gollub, Francisco Rangel, Paolo Rosso, Efstathios Stamatatos, and Benno Stein. 2014. Improving the Reproducibility of PAN's Shared Tasks: Plagiarism Detection, Author Identification, and Author Profiling. *The 5th International Conference of the CLEF Initiative*, pages 268–299.

Rashmi Prasad, Nikhil Dinesh, Alan Lee, Eleni Miltsakaki, Livio Robaldo, Aravind K. Joshi, and Bonnie L. Webber. 2008. The Penn discourse Treebank 2.0. In *Proceedings of LREC*, pages 2961-2968.

Rashmi Prasad, Aravind K. Joshi, and Bonnie L. Webber. 2010. Realization of discourse relations by other means: Alternative lexicalizations. In *Proceedings of Coling*, pages 1023-1031.

Attapol T Rutherford and Nianwen Xue. 2014. Discovering implicit discourse relations through brown cluster pair representation and coreference patterns. In *Proceedings of EACL*, pages 645-654.

Philip J. Stone, and Cambridge Computer Associates. 1966. The General Inquirer: A Computer Approach to Content Analysis, MIT Press.

Theresa Wilson, Janyce Wiebe, and Paul Hoffmann. 2005. Recognizing contextual polarity in phrase-level sentiment analysis. In *Proceedings of HLT-EMNLP*, pages 347-354.

Nianwen Xue, Hwee T. Ng, Sameer Pradhan, Rashmi Prasad, Christopher Bryant, and Attapol Rutherford. 2015. The conll-2015 shared task on shallow discourse parsing. In *Proceedings of CoNLL Shared Task*, pages 1-15.

Nianwen Xue, Hwee T. Ng, Sameer Pradhan, Attapol T. Rutherford, Bonnie Webber, Chuan Wang, and Hongmin Wang. 2016. The CoNLL-2016 shared task on multilingual shallow discourse parsing. In *Proceedings of CoNLL Shared Task*.

Yuping Zhou and Nianwen Xue. 2012. PDTB-style discourse annotation of Chinese text. In *Proceedings of ACL*, pages 69-77.

Zhi-Min Zhou, Yu Xu, Zheng-Yu Niu, Man Lan, Jian Su, and Chew-Lim Tan. 2010. Predicting discourse connectives for implicit discourse relation recognition. In *Proceedings of Coling*, pages 1507-1514.

Author Index

Association for Computational Linguistics
209 N. Eighth Street
Stroudsburg, Pennsylvania 18360

ISBN 978-1-5108-8136-5